MW00442702

International Issues in Early Intervention
Series Editor: Michael J. Guralnick

ISEI

Early Intervention Practices Around the World

A book series from the
International Society on Early Intervention

Other books in this series:

Interdisciplinary Clinical Assessment
of Young Children with Developmental Disabilities
edited by Michael J. Guralnick, Ph.D.

ISEI

Early Intervention Practices Around the World

edited by

Samuel L. Odom, Ph.D.
Indiana University, Bloomington

Marci J. Hanson, Ph.D.
San Francisco State University

James A. Blackman, M.D., M.P.H.
Kluge Children's Rehabilitation Center
University of Virginia, Charlottesville

and

Sudha Kaul, Ph.D.
Indian Institute of Cerebral Palsy, Calcutta

·P·A·U·L·H·
BROOKES
PUBLISHING CO. ®

Baltimore • London • Sydney

Paul H. Brookes Publishing Co.
Post Office Box 10624
Baltimore, Maryland 21285-0624

www.brookespublishing.com

Copyright © 2003 by Paul H. Brookes Publishing Co., Inc.
All rights reserved.

"Paul H. Brookes Publishing Co." is a registered
trademark of Paul H. Brookes Publishing Co., Inc.

Typeset by International Graphic Services, Inc.,
Newtown, Pennsylvania.
Manufactured in the United States of America by
Sheridan Books, Fredericksburg, Virginia.

The photograph on the left side of the cover and on page 173 is reprinted with
permission from Anders Fredrickson.

The stories in this book are based on the authors' experiences. Some of the
vignettes represent actual people and circumstances. Individuals' names and
identifying details have been changed to protect their identities. Other vignettes
are composite accounts that do not represent the lives or experiences of specific
individuals, and no implications should be inferred.

Library of Congress Cataloging-in-Publication Data

Early intervention practices around the world / edited by Samuel L.
Odom . . . [et al.].
    p.   cm. — (International issues in early intervention)
  Includes bibliographical references and index.
  ISBN 1-55766-645-8
  1. Developmentally disabled children—Services for—Cross-cultural studies.
2. Family services—Cross-cultural studies. I. Odom, Samuel L.   1. Series.
HV891.E323 2003
362.1'98928—dc21

2003041773

British Library Cataloguing in Publication data are available from the British
Library.

Contents

Series Preface

The *International Issues in Early Intervention* book series was created in recognition of the fact that problems and advances relevant to early intervention transcend national boundaries. Indeed, providing effective early intervention programs for vulnerable children and their families constitutes one of the most important challenges for all contemporary societies. The rapidly expanding knowledge base of early intervention is the product of contributions from researchers, clinicians, program developers, and policy makers from numerous countries. The diverse and creative approaches taken to address early intervention within the historical and cultural contexts of one's own country provide the international community with unique and valuable insights.

Yet, international early intervention collaborations and sharing of knowledge are far from adequate. Accordingly, the *International Issues in Early Intervention* series is designed to enhance awareness and knowledge of international efforts in early intervention and serve as well as a catalyst for collaborations at many levels. Of importance, this book series is one component of the International Society on Early Intervention (ISEI), whose primary purpose is to provide a framework and forum for professionals from around the world to communicate about advances in the field of early intervention (see http://depts. washington.edu/isei for additional information). The membership of ISEI is composed of basic and clinical researchers relevant to the field of early intervention representing a diverse array of biomedical and behavioral disciplines, as well as clinicians and policy makers in leadership positions. Every effort has been made to ensure that this book series will be of interest to all involved and that the information will advance the field of early intervention and improve the development and well-being of vulnerable children and their families.

Michael J. Guralnick, Ph.D.
Chair, International Society
on Early Intervention
Seattle, Washington

About the Editors

Samuel L. Odom, Ph.D., Otting Professor of Special Education, Department of Curriculum and Instruction, School of Education, Indiana University, 3234 W.W. Wright Education Building, 201 North Rose Avenue, Bloomington, Indiana 47405

Formerly the William C. Friday Distinguished Professor of Child Development and Family Studies at The University of North Carolina at Chapel Hill, Dr. Odom joined the faculty of Indiana University in January 1999. Throughout his career, Dr. Odom has held positions as a preschool teacher, student teaching supervisor, program coordinator, teacher educator, and researcher. He has authored many articles and chapters about programs for young children and their families and has served as co-editor of four books on early childhood special education. Dr. Odom's research addresses issues related to the inclusion of young children with disabilities in early childhood education environments with typically developing children. He received a doctoral degree in education and human development from the University of Washington.

Marci J. Hanson, Ph.D., Professor, Department of Special Education, San Francisco State University, 1600 Holloway Avenue, San Francisco, California 94132

Dr. Hanson has extensive experience in developing and implementing early intervention programs for infants, toddlers, and preschoolers with disabilities and their families. She directed two Handicapped Children's Early Education Program (HCEEP) model demonstration projects and has worked actively in all areas of early intervention. Dr. Hanson has contributed actively to the peer-reviewed professional literature and authored, co-authored, or edited six books on early intervention. Her work focuses on cross-cultural competence in early intervention. She received a doctoral degree in special education from the University of Oregon.

James A. Blackman, M.D., M.P.H., Professor of Pediatrics, Director of Research, Kluge Children's Rehabilitation Center, Children's Medical Center, University of Virginia, 2270 Ivy Road, Charlottesville, Virginia 22908

Dr. Blackman has been very involved in the study, implementation, and educational aspects of early intervention services through interdisciplinary collaborations at the local, state, and national levels, In 1988, he founded *Infants and Young Children,* an interdisciplinary journal on special care practices. Dr. Blackman has authored or edited numerous books on early intervention, including *Medical Aspects of Developmental Disabilities in Children Birth to Three* (Aspen Publishers, 1997). He received a doctoral degree in medicine from The Ohio State University and received fellowship training in developmental pediatrics at Harvard University. As a 1998–1999 recipient of the Mary E. Switzer Fellowship, sponsored by the U.S. Department of Education's National Institute on Disability and Rehabilitation Research, Dr. Blackman studied early intervention practices in Europe.

Sudha Kaul, Ph.D., Executive Director, Indian Institute of Cerebral Palsy, P-35/1 Taratalla Road, Calcutta, West Bengal, 700 088 India

Dr. Kaul received a doctoral degree in augmentative and alternative communication (AAC) from Manchester Metropolitan University in the United Kingdom. She has worked as a classroom teacher and teacher trainer. In addition to serving as Executive Director of the Indian Institute of Cerebral Palsy, Dr. Kaul is the Institute's Founder Vice Chairperson. She also serves as Director of the Post Graduate Diploma Course in Special Education at Jadavpur University in Calcutta. Dr. Kaul developed a test in receptive language of Hindi-speaking children, co-authored a book on AAC, and has developed various video teaching programs on early intervention. In 1990, she received the President's Award from the International Society for Augmentative and Alternative Communication (ISAAC) and is the Indian representative on ISAAC's board of directors. Her research focuses on child language and the communication interaction patterns of typically developing children and children who do not speak.

Contributors

Maria Salete Fábio Aranha, Ph.D.
Psychologist
State University of São Paulo
"Julio de Mesquita Filho"
(UNESP–Bauru)
Avenida Luis Edmundo C. Coube s/n
Bauru, São Paulo, Brazil 17033-360

Eva Björck-Åkesson, Ph.D.
Professor of Education
Department of Social Sciences
Mälardalen University
Box 883
Västerås, Sweden SE-721 23

José Boavida, M.D.
Chairman
National Early Intervention
    Association (ANIP)
Developmental Pediatrician
Child Development Center
Hospital Pediátrico de Coimbra
Av. Dr. Bissaya Barreto
    (HPC–Pavilhão 4)
3000-075 Coimbra, Portugal

Leonor Carvalho, M.A.
Management Board Member
National Early Intervention
    Association (ANIP)
Developmental Psychologist
Child Development Center
Hospital Pediátrico de Coimbra
Av. Dr. Bissaya Barreto
    (HPC-Pavilhão 4)
3000-075 Coimbra, Portugal

Madhabi Chattopadhyay, B.S., Diploma in Teaching Children with Multiple Handicaps
Special Educator
Coordinator, Early Intervention
    Clinic
Indian Institute of Cerebral Palsy
P-35/1 Taratalla Road
Calcutta, West Bengal
700 088 India

Eglal Chenouda, Diploma in Logopedics
Head of the Family Rehabilitation
    Department, Cario Office
Seti Center, Caritas-Egypt
El-Sabaa Street
c/o Collège de la Salle (Frères)
Post Office Box 31
El Daher 11563
Cairo, Egypt

Asis Kumar Ghosh, B.S., Diploma in Physiotherapy, Certificate in Neuro Developmental Treatment for Children with Cerebral Palsy
Physiotherapist
Head, Out Patients Division
Indian Institute of Cerebral Palsy
P-35/1 Taratalla Road
Calcutta, West Bengal
700 088 India

Mats Granlund, Ph.D.
Professor of Psychology
Department of Social Sciences
Mälardalen University
Box 883
Västerås, Sweden SE-721 23

Summer Tsai-Hsing Hsia, Ph.D.
Assistant Professor
Department of Special Education
San Francisco State University
1600 Holloway
San Francisco, California 94132

Christine F. Johnston, Ph.D.
Associate Professor in
  Education–Special Education
School of Education and Early
  Childhood Studies
University of Western Sydney
Locked Bag 1797
Penrith South DC
New South Wales 1797, Australia

Naguib Khouzam, Ph.D.
Professor of Educational Psychology
Ain Shams University
General Supervisor
Seti Center, Caritas–Egypt
El-Sabaa Street
c/o Collège de la Salle (Frères)
Post Office Box 31
El Daher 11563
Cairo, Egypt

Pnina S. Klein, Ph.D.
Director, Baker Center for the Study
  of Developmental Disorders of
  Infants and Young Children
Head, Graduate Program for Early
  Childhood Education
Bar-Ilan University
Ramat Gan, Israel 52900

SoHyun Lee, Ph.D.
Associate Professor
Department of Special Education
Ewha Woman's University
11-1 Daehyundong Seodaemunku
Seoul, Korea 120-750

Bao-Jen Li, B.A.
Director
Xiang Yang Children's Development
  Center
Xiang Yang Street
Jiang Jin, Chongqing
People's Republic of China 402260

H. Garren Lumpkin, M.A.
UNICEF Regional Adviser,
  Education
UNICEF Regional Office for Latin
  America and the Caribbean
Morse Avenue, Building 131
Ciudad del Saber
Republic of Panama

Helen McCabe, M.A.
Doctoral Candidate
School of Education
Indiana University
3211 W.W. Wright Education
  Building
201 North Rose Avenue
Bloomington, Indiana 47405

**Swapna Mukherjee, M.A.,
  Post-Graduate Certificate in
  Special Education**
Special Educator
Deputy Head, Out Patients Division
Indian Institute of Cerebral Palsy
P-35/1 Taratalla Road
Calcutta, West Bengal
700 088 India

Georgette Naguib, M.D.
Head, Family Rehabilitation
  Department, Alexandria Office
Seti Center, Caritas–Egypt
El-Sabaa Street
c/o Collège de la Salle (Frères)
Post Office Box 31
El Daher 11563
Cairo, Egypt

Franz Peterander, Ph.D.
Ludwig-Maximilians University
Department of Psychology
Early Childhood Intervention
Leopoldstrasse 13
D-80802 Munich, Germany

Utsab Sil, M.S.W.
Supervisor, Out Patients Division
Social Service Division
Indian Institute of Cerebral Palsy
P-35/1 Taratalla Road
Calcutta, West Bengal
700 088 India

Tirussew Teferra, Ph.D.
Professor of Special Needs
  Education
Addis Ababa University
Post Office Box 30891
Addis Ababa, Ethiopia

Marigold J. Thorburn, M.D.
Part-Time Lecturer
Faculty of Medical Sciences
University of the West Indies
Consultant
3D Projects
6 Courtney Drive
Kingston 10, Jamaica

Preface

In preparing this book, a curious event occurred. Authors and co-editors had sent their chapters to me, and I was assembling the chapter manuscripts to send to the publisher. Several of the manuscripts had arrived in airtight mailing envelopes. As I opened an envelope, the trapped air escaped the package, spreading a pleasing aroma throughout my office. As I read the draft of the particular chapter, I realized that I was also breathing a little of that country's air. On a Sunday afternoon in Bloomington, Indiana, having atmospheric particles of India, South Korea, Portugal, and other countries swirling around my office was a unique and pleasant experience.

In early intervention practices, we do metaphorically breathe the air of other countries in the work that we do with infants and young children with disabilities and their families. We borrow, replicate, rearrange, and modify the work of others, as well as develop practices that fit the particular cultures within which we live. A goal of *Early Intervention Practices Around the World* is to share early intervention practices followed in different countries. The purpose is not only to illustrate the commonality and diversity that exists across countries but also to serve as a venue for learning from each other.

This volume was initially inspired by an important book written by Robert Myers (1995), *The Twelve Who Survive: Strengthening Programmes of Early Childhood Development in the Third World.* Myers's book describes early childhood programs that exist in a number of developing countries in the world and how these countries have uniquely addressed, within their sociopolitical and cultural milieu, the needs of young children. Over the course of approximately a year, the editorial partnership for *Early Intervention Practices Around the World* emerged—first, with Marci J. Hanson, whose important work on cultural issues in the United States has informed early intervention practice; then, with James A. Blackman, whose editorship of the journal *Infants and Young Children* supported the sharing of international perspectives on early intervention; and, finally, with Sudha Kaul, whose worldview on early intervention practice has been an important influence on this book. The compatibility of these scholars was a welcome and essential feature of this book's production.

Samuel L. Odom, Ph.D.

REFERENCE

Myers, R. (1995). *The twelve who survive: Strengthening programmes of early child-hood development in the third world.* Ypsilanti, MI: High/Scope Press.

Acknowledgments

For including this book in the *International Issues in Early Intervention* series, published by Paul H. Brookes Publishing Co., we are indebted to Michael J. Guralnick, Series Editor, and Heather Shrestha, Acquisitions Editor at Paul H. Brookes Publishing Co. In addition, the expertise of the production editors at Paul H. Brookes Publishing Co. has been invaluable in shaping chapters into a common language, style, and format. Finally, we thank the authors of each chapter. English is not the first language of many chapter authors but all submitted chapters that poignantly and richly describe the ways in which early intervention has been carried out in their countries. We hope that this book helps early intervention professionals learn from each other, and to the extent that such learning occurs, it will be due in large part to the scholarly and very practical work of each chapter author.

Early Intervention
Practices Around the World

CHAPTER 1

Early Intervention

James A. Blackman

AN OVERVIEW

A stitch in time saves nine.

The world has focused increasingly on the importance of early intervention to enhance the development of infants, toddlers, and young children. Even in countries where infant survival is a high priority, governments and international relief agencies recognize that living fully is as important as not dying (Young, 1996). The period from conception through early childhood is the most important in human development for maximizing the potential for living fully. The more that is learned about brain development, the more poignant this point becomes.

The goal of early intervention is to prevent or minimize the physical, cognitive, emotional, and resource limitations of young children with biological or environmental risk factors. Whereas interventions for older children and adults with similar limitations focus on the individual, an important premise of early intervention for young children is the family's key role. Without family involvement, interventions are unlikely to succeed. The intervention often must target the family even though the primary concern is an infant's growth, behavior, or development. A child is unlikely to thrive in any of these domains if his or her family is stressed by parental unemployment, unsanitary living conditions, or neighborhood violence.

Community also plays a large role. An African proverb claims, "It takes a village to raise a child" (Clinton, 1996). Children thrive only if society cares enough and has the resources to support families. Alone, a family, a health worker, a therapist, or even a social worker is unlikely to achieve the same success that the involvement and coordination of the community could.

These two elements—family and community—are key to the success of early intervention. This introductory chapter reviews concepts about the sensible and scientific bases for specific components of early intervention. Yet, without family support and coordinated community involvement, any single activity will not achieve the goal of optimal development for a given child.

PREVENTION AS EARLY INTERVENTION

Early intervention can be viewed as prevention. The World Health Organization (WHO) defined three levels of prevention: primary, secondary, and tertiary. *Primary prevention* includes measures to preclude disorders or circumstances that lead to disability. For example, administering the rubella (German measles) vaccine to prepubertal girls diminishes the risk of their contracting the disease as adults and causing serious damage to the fetal brain during pregnancy. Supplemental nutrition programs eliminate chronic anemia that leads to cognitive impairments. Sometimes science points to the right direction but political, economic, and cultural realities impede implementation of effective preventive measures. For instance, it has taken many years to overcome forces that blocked fortification of all cereal grain products with folic acid to reduce the incidence of spina bifida.

Once an impairment has occurred, *secondary prevention* efforts are aimed at avoiding additional impairments that might arise. For example, hearing impairment, if unrecognized and untreated, can lead to permanent communication impairments, and hypertonia in children with cerebral palsy reduces joint range of motion. Without a number of secondary preventive treatment modalities—such as physical therapy, orthotic devices, or orthopedic surgery—permanent joint contractures are likely to develop, reducing the child's functional mobility. For an infant who is blind, secondary prevention activities would teach parents how to encourage mobility, play, and environmental exploration for typical cognitive development.

Tertiary prevention is designed to minimize the impact of a particular disability. A worldwide trend toward integration into community life has markedly diminished the institutionalization of children with disabilities, supported families to care for these children at home, and led to their inclusion in general education schools and community activities. Outcomes for children with Down syndrome exemplify the wisdom of this change. Many children with Down syndrome were once placed in institutions or special schools, often at very early ages and far from their homes. In these environments, children failed to learn adequate social and communication skills for success in family and community environments, resulting in dependency on segregated placements. With family and community support, children with Down syndrome grow up to be productive, employable adults—even television stars.

EXPANDING DISABILITY CONCEPTS

The lexicon of disability has changed over the years. This evolution of the language is as important for infants and toddlers as it is for adults. In one of its earliest documents on disability, WHO expanded the conceptualization of disability by distinguishing among *impairment, disability,* and *handicap* (1980). *Impairment* referred to the loss or abnormality of body structure or function, such as spasticity due to injury of the motor tracts in the brain. The resulting inability to perform a certain function (e.g., walking) was termed a *disability.* The limitation that society places on the individual because of the disability (e.g., high curbs at street corners) was termed a *handicap*. This classification system was designed to aid the measurement, management, and investigation of disabling conditions and their impact on individuals and society.

In 2001, WHO revised its classification system to be more inclusive, to emphasize positive rather than negative aspects of disability, and to remove the distinctions between medical and social models of rehabilitation service delivery. Figure 1.1 illustrates the concepts that interact to form the *International Classification of Functioning, Disability and Health (ICF)*.

Certain treatments are aimed at reducing impairment at the Body Structures and Functions level, such as inhibiting primitive reflexes or reducing increased muscle tone. Various interventions are directed toward functional skill improvement and expanding activities. However, increased skills and activity mean little if they do not enable the child to participate in family and community activities. Intervention should always consider skills that enhance participation, such as independent feeding and effective communication. Even with the most successful interventions, external barriers—such as poor health, substandard housing, lack of preschool special education services, or regional unemployment—may ultimately limit a child and family's participation.

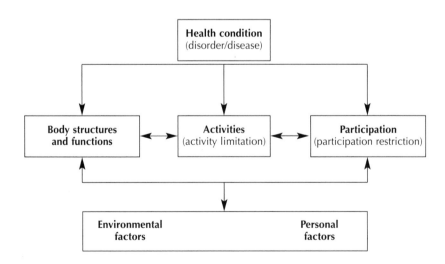

Figure 1.1. Concepts that interact to form the *International Classification of Functioning, Disability and Health.* (From R.J. Simeonsson, personal communication, October 2001.)

INTEGRATING NATURE AND NURTURE

For centuries, philosophers, artists, theologians, and psychologists have debated whether humans are born with innate behavioral and moral tendencies or are completely shaped by the environment. The terminology of this debate has varied: nature versus nurture, nativism versus culturism, genetics versus environment, maturation versus learning.

John Locke, a 17th-century English philosopher, argued against the doctrine of "innate ideas"—that is, that ideas are part of the mind of birth and not learned or acquired later. He claimed that the mind at birth is a "tabula rasa" (blank slate) on which experiences of life sketch the contents of the mind. At the other extreme in the 1700s was Swiss/French philosopher Jean Jacques Rousseau, who considered the child's inherited nature to be the most influential force in determining development.

The debate in western societies continued through subsequent centuries. In the early 20th century, Viennese psychiatrist Sigmund Freud said that an infant seeks only to satisfy his or her needs for food, drink, warmth, elimination, and affection. Id was Freud's term for all that was inherited, particularly instincts that give force and direction to all psychological activities throughout life. According to Freud, the ego develops out of the growing infant's efforts to satisfy his or her needs through transactions with the environment. The superego develops later as the internal representative of the rules and values of society.

B.F. Skinner, a 20th-century American psychologist, believed that behavioral development completely depends on the consequences that followed behaviors in the past. It was his contention that all or nearly all behavior results from conditioning. Nevertheless, Skinner acknowledged that genetic endowment does account for a significant amount of variation among children (Thomas, 2000).

Formal child development theory appeared predominantly in the European and American scientific literature, particularly during the 20th century. However, important insights into non-Western child development theory can be gained indirectly. East Asian cultures have been highly influenced by religious doctrines and philosophies (Chan, 1998). Confucianism, Taoism, and Buddhism, for example, dictate many facets of life including ethics, social mores, values, and even child-rearing practices. In most Asian cultures, the family is the basic unit of society, overriding autonomy and individualism. Parental authority is paramount, with hierarchy determined by generation, age, and gender. The child's duty is to listen and obey. Viewed as extensions of parents, children are considered relatively helpless and not responsible for their actions. Needs are gratified immediately, and close physical contact is emphasized over vocal stimulation. Infants rarely sleep alone and need not adhere to rigid schedules. The environment for the child is typically nurturing, indulgent, secure, and predictable.

Similarly, in Middle Eastern countries, Islam has had a major influence on society and, therefore, on child-rearing practices (Sharifzadeh, 1998). In its extended form, the family is the most important institution. Whereas Anglo-European culture emphasizes early individuation and independence, Islamic culture emphasizes parent–child bonding and interdependence of the child and his or her family and society. Identification with the family's achievements is generally as important as—sometimes even more important than—one's personal achievements.

There have been many theories of child development over the years attributing increased or decreased importance of nature/genetics or environment and often integrating contributions from both. How do innate characteristics of the child interact with environmental factors in determining how a child develops and who the child will become? Sameroff and Fiese's (2000) transactional model is a useful way of looking at this interaction (see Figure 1.2). This model acknowledges that both nature and nurture are important, that they interact in the individual, and that this interaction has a cumulative effect over time (Sameroff & Fiese, 2000). The following vignette illustrates the usefulness of the transactional model of development for understanding the sometimes complex cause(s) of disability and for determining multiple and repeated intervention opportunities.

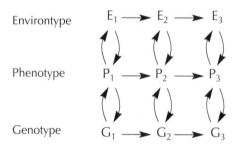

Figure 1.2. Regulation model of development with transactions among genotype (nature), phenotype (the individual), and environtype (nurture). (From Sameroff, A.J., & Fiese, B.H. [2000]. Transactional regulation: The developmental ecology of early intervention. In J.P. Shonkoff & S.J. Meisels [Eds.], *Handbook of early intervention* [2nd ed., p. 143]. New York: Cambridge University Press; reprinted with the permission of Cambridge University Press.)

 **PETER'S STORY** ─────────────────────────────

A social worker referred 30-month-old Peter to an early intervention program because "he doesn't talk." According to the limited medical notes that were available, Peter was born at 34 weeks' gestation but was small for gestational age, indicating that he was both premature and undergrown.

Peter's mother, Angela, is a single parent. She admitted to some drug and alcohol use during the pregnancy and sought no prenatal care. Since Peter's birth, she has moved numerous times and had another child named Eric. Peter, well behind in his immunizations, has had little routine health and developmental surveillance.

Dennis, the early intervention coordinator, visited the family at home and noted that their apartment was filthy and disorderly. Leftover food was lying on the kitchen counter. Two-month-old Eric was sleeping on a stained blanket on the floor. Peter was sitting in front of the television, intently focused on a cartoon show and paying no attention to Dennis.

Angela agreed that Peter does not talk much but indicated little concern. She said that Peter watches television most of the day and makes few demands on her except when he wants something. Then, he can be really difficult because she rarely understands what he wants. In addition, she remarked that she is only able to leave the apartment when her boyfriend watches the children.

When the problems and challenges are so overwhelming, as in this case, it may be difficult to know how and when to start intervention. According to the transactional model, the ideal point of intervention would have been well before Peter was 2 years old. Identifying the high-risk pregnancy might have encouraged Angela to cease drug and alcohol use, improve nutrition, and get good prenatal care—all measures that might have given Peter a better start in life. Angela entered a system of care at the time of Peter's birth. This was another opportunity for significant preventive intervention to help Angela find adequate housing, support her in parenting skills, inform her about pregnancy prevention, enroll her in a home visitation program, and develop her links with community supports.

Instead, the problems escalated. Peter has a significant communication disorder, reflective of a wide differential diagnosis including hearing impairment, psychosocial deprivation, mental retardation, and autism spectrum disorder. Regardless of the nature of his innate developmental challenges, success in facilitating his developmental progress must also address his environment. Improving his communication will improve his environment, and improving his environment will improve his communication skills—whatever the cause of difficulty. Furthermore, intervening now using a multidimensional approach will prevent worsening problems in Peter's development and in the lives of his family members.

Using the WHO model of disability, the first step is to identify the underlying *health condition* of Peter's communication disorder, if possible. Did he have a congenital cytomegalovirus infection that affected hearing? Are his communication difficulties related to fragile X syndrome? After a thorough medical evaluation, no specific health condition was identified.

What *body structure or function* is involved? Is the impairment a hearing loss? Sensorineural or conductive? Does he have an auditory processing problem or developmental apraxia? Does he have mental retardation or autism? Following a comprehensive team assessment, Peter was found to have age-appropriate skills in the motor, problem-solving, and receptive-language areas. His expressive language abilities were markedly delayed. Thus, his interactive *activities* are largely restricted to grunts, points, and tantrums. His *participation* in family life is typically negative with his mother either ignoring him or spanking him when he would cry and bang his head. The *environmental factors* complicating this scenario include poverty, stress, isolation, and desperation.

This approach also provides a framework for acknowledging strengths, such as Peter's curiosity or his supportive grandmother, and family needs. Building on strengths and targeting specific needs will enhance the likelihood of positive outcomes. The WHO approach also exemplifies the value of a multidimensional approach to early intervention, usually involving input from a variety of health, educational, and social professionals. It is obvious that the elements of family support and community inclusion emphasized in this chapter are key to successful intervention.

DOES EARLY INTERVENTION WORK?

To some people, asking whether early intervention works is like asking, "Is healthy food good for you?" or "Should serious infections be treated in the beginning of an illness or later when the bacteria have really taken hold?" The European Academy of Child Disability stated, "Certain services or facilities should be available as a basic right in a caring society, rather than these having to meet a strict scientific test of effectiveness" (McConachie, Smyth, & Bax, 1997, p. 5). This provocative statement presents a conundrum that is well put in further comments by the European Academy of Child Disability:

> Health providers have a responsibility to try to measure the effectiveness of any programs set up for children with disabilities and to identify which treatments are ineffective. On the other hand, the availability of certain services such as early intervention is now an accepted right, even though appropriate methods of evaluation may yet be lacking. (McConachie et al., 1997, p. 5)

Do early intervention methods need to have a proven scientific basis? In countries where disability laws exist, do they guarantee early intervention services as a right, even if the services are unproven? Early intervention legislation in the United States (PL 99-457, PL 101-476, and PL 105-17) defines essential elements, procedures, and safeguards for early intervention but does not require that a single study support the services that it mandates (see http://www.nectac.org/idea/idea.asp).

There are many examples of unproven practices that are implemented in education, medicine, and social services. For example, children with autism are commonly given dietary supplements, none of which have solid scientific evidence of efficacy for treating any aspect of autism. If one were to track an individual from each of these professions through a single day, much of what is done is based on minimal, equivocal, or perhaps, no evidence. Still, this is not a model that should be emulated in early intervention.

Some activities initially seem to have such obvious benefit that no evidence is deemed necessary, at least in the opinion of some people. Yet, practices that were once considered benign can prove to be harmful. For years, colds were treated with antibiotics, mainly because of patient demand. Now, widespread bacterial resistance to these drugs is an outcome of that mistaken notion. Certain therapeutic approaches, although not harmful in themselves, demand such intense time, effort, and financial resources that the family as a whole suffers. Danger is an important reason not to do something. However, intervention practices must be judged not on absence of harm but on their merits: efficacy, effectiveness, and cost justification.

Macroview

In assessing the value of early intervention, research studies have examined both efficacy and effectiveness. Efficacy studies investigate whether an intervention *can* work in ideal, highly controlled experimental situations in which, for example, all participants comply with all aspects of a treatment under investigation. Effectiveness studies are designed to determine if an intervention *does* work in real-life situations in which noncompliance is usually commonplace, either on the part of the provider or recipient (Cadman et al., 1987).

Even if efficacy or effectiveness of early intervention is demonstrated, an important question remains: Does an intervention warrant an investment of financial resources? In Peter's case, if an intervention at age 30 months for expressive language delay could avert the need for more intensive (and expensive) therapy and special education later on, then an argument could be made for cost-effectiveness of the early intervention. Furthermore, if the intervention for Peter includes help for his mother in developing parenting and home management skills and finding part-time employment, all of which keep the family intact and off public assistance, then, clearly, savings to the public would be realized. Other interventions, however, may not show cost benefit in the long run. Examples include physical therapy for an infant with benign congenital hypotonia (which would likely improve naturally) and intense individual speech-language therapy for a toddler with global developmental delay.

Several meta-analyses and reviews of early intervention have demonstrated overall positive benefits of early intervention, although many of the studies pose substantial methodological questions. The concept of early intervention has so many different dimensions, from the individual to the family to society. Therefore, it is not surprising that randomized, controlled studies of sufficiently large numbers of participants to allow statistical analysis of confounding variables and individual differences are expensive. They are also unpopular because it is difficult and perhaps unethical to provide no intervention for a true control group. Several widely cited meta-analyses of early intervention efficacy have been published (Casto & Mastropieri, 1986; Shonkoff & Hauser-Cram, 1987). Although no conclusions could be drawn about specific interventions, certain themes emerged. Programs that involved the parents, not just the child, were more effective than programs that had a planned curriculum and included children with varying types of disabilities (rather than a categorical program for children with, say, cerebral palsy or Down syndrome). Guralnick's (1997) book critically reviewing studies of early intervention effectiveness came to an overall conclusion that early intervention programs "work."

The RAND Corporation conducted an objective review of the scientific evidence available on early childhood interventions (Karoly et al., 1998). Early childhood interventions were defined as attempts by government agencies or other organizations to improve child health and development, educational attainment, and economic well-being.

The aim was to quantify the benefits of these programs to children, their parents, and society at large. Short-term benefits were typically developmental, such as increased cognitive performance, whereas long-term benefits tended to be social, such as increased rates of high school completion or economic independence. The important lesson from this review is that carefully targeted early childhood interventions can yield measurable benefits in the short run and that some of these benefits persist long after the programs have ended.

Microview

Results of research into the effectiveness of early intervention with respect to specific components, program features, and populations served are mixed. Guralnick's (1997) comprehensive volume on the effectiveness of early intervention contains an excellent summary of the literature on specific interventions and is used as the basis of the following discussions.

Children Who Are Disadvantaged

Bryant and Maxwell (1997) examined four home visiting studies that ranged from not effective to highly effective. Baseline differences among the populations in the level of disadvantage may account for these differences. Home visiting is, logically, more effective for families in communities with no services or extreme poverty. More frequent home visits or center-based programs extended over a prolonged period offer the most benefit to children and parents. The most comprehensive family-focused program that Bryant and Maxwell described, the Comprehensive Child Development Program, offered an early childhood program; parenting education; and classes for adult education, literacy, and job skills; however, it had almost no effect on attitudes or behaviors and meaningful cognitive effects for children.

In their review of early childhood education programs, Schaefer and Cohen (2000) concluded that for economically disadvantaged children, high-quality, out-of-home, child-focused environments seem to offer the greatest advantages. Policy makers hoped that home visiting programs could bring about changes in parenting practices, which would translate into developmental gains for children who are at risk. Unfortunately, the most reliable studies of such programs have not supported this assumption (Gomby et al., 1999).

Low Birth Weight Infants

Blair and Ramey (1997) noted that overall, low birth weight (LBW) infants exhibit increased rates of health, neurodevelopmental, and psychological problems. Since 1986, effectiveness in both center- and home-based programs for LBW infants has been reliably observed in a number of methodologically sound studies. Intervention attenuates the decline in IQ scores that typically occurs for LBW infants in relation to normal birth weight infants over the first few years of life. Comprehensive, intensive interventions that begin early are most likely to be effective. However, intervention effectiveness is moderated by birth weight and maternal education level.

The most significant of the early intervention studies for LBW infants was the Infant Health and Development Program (IHDP). Intervention included biweekly home visits beginning at hospital discharge, 5-day-per-week attendance at a child development center with a sophisticated curriculum, and emphasis on adult–child interactions in the home. Positive intervention effects on intelligence, health, and behavior were noted at 36 months. The larger LBW infants and those of mothers with lower educational levels benefited most from the interventions. Yet, these effects disappeared at age 5 years, except for effects on intelligence in children whose birth weights were between 2,001 and 2,500 grams (Brooks-Gunn et al., 1994). These results indicate that understanding of factors contributing to long-term intellectual outcomes is still quite limited (Baumeister & Bacharach, 2000).

Children at Risk for Neuromotor Problems

No discipline in the early intervention field has subjected its practices to closer scientific scrutiny than physical therapy. Unfortunately, there is no clear evidence that interventions for children at risk for motor disability are effective (Pakula & Palmer, 1997). Meta-analyses of studies of intervention for children with known motor disabilities showed only small to moderate treatment effects. In fact, the least positive effects were seen in motor outcomes, compared with cognitive and language outcomes (Harris, 1997).

In an excellent review of research on therapeutic interventions for young children with neuromotor disabilities, Harris (1997) stated that the focus of physical therapy, and the studies attempting to justify this focus, have been misdirected. Therapists have tried to change underlying impairments resulting from central nervous system damage (e.g., abnormal muscle tone, atypical movement patterns, joint contractures) or to speed up the attainment of motor milestones. Rather, Harris said that physical therapists should direct their interventions toward 1) enabling a child to be more independent and to participate in nonrestrictive environments and 2) teaching parents, teachers, and other caregivers techniques to enhance child participation and reduce family stress (i.e., the participation and environmental aspects of the WHO model).

Down Syndrome

Spiker and Hopmann (1997) remarked that no genetic syndrome has received more attention in the early intervention field than Down syndrome. Because Down syndrome has unique and easily identified features, children with this disorder were among the first to be included in emerging early intervention programs and subjected to empirical study. A rather sizable literature exists that traces the natural history of the developmental disabilities that accompany Down syndrome and the responses to various interventions. Although the overall impression is that children with Down syndrome respond positively to early intervention, some scholars dispute this claim. Gibson and Harris (1988) concluded that evidence has yet to confirm that children with Down syndrome receive greater benefits from early intervention programming than from "ordinary," prudent parenting. The question, then, is not whether children with Down syndrome (or any other disorder, for that matter) benefit from special attention in the language, motor, and cognitive domains, but, rather, whether specialized programming is superior to a nurturing family environment.

Unfortunately, nurturing family environments were not always available, not because parents were unwilling to provide them but because professionals, especially those in the medical field, gave pessimistic prognoses for these children during much of the 20th century. Parents were urged to hide their children or place them in institutions, even at very early ages. In such environments, it is not surprising that individuals with Down syndrome failed to develop to their potential.

The focus of early intervention for children with Down syndrome was to slow the rate of decline in developmental progress known to occur during the first decade of life. By giving these children an early boost, it was hoped that they might achieve maximal cognitive and adaptive functioning. Overall, the literature to date supports this notion, although there are many methodological problems with the studies. It is clear that early intervention offers short-term advantages for children with Down syndrome, but whether these benefits persist long term is less certain.

A better way to conceptualize early intervention for children with Down syndrome is the role of early experience—that is, initiating children into a set of experiences and expectations that will optimize their participation in community activities and relationships. In contrast to the fear and shame that families felt in the past, most families seek to normalize the lives of these children as much as possible, including them in all facets of family life and school, religious, and recreational activities. An early intervention program can assist families in understanding their child with Down syndrome, appreciating both his or her limits and potential, procuring assistance with the child's areas of developmental weakness, and including the child in all normal activities. Early intervention for Down syndrome provides a good model of how early intervention might be broadly interpreted and applied.

Autism Spectrum Disorder

The worldwide prevalence of autism spectrum disorder appears to be on the rise, although it is not known whether this is due to keener recognition or a true increase (Wing & Potter, 2002). Whatever the cause, early intervention programs are inundated with referrals of young children who have language delays and disorders, limited social gaze, restricted imaginative play and imitation, and stereotypic behaviors. It has become evident that this disorder is indeed a spectrum, ranging from minimal difficulties in these areas to severe functional limitations.

The literature on intervention for children with autism spectrum disorder is clear about several issues. Program methods must focus on learning contingencies, social gaze, turn taking, imitation, shared attention, and communicative intent. Furthermore, the programming must be consistent and intense, with families and professionals sharing the responsibility of maintaining the techniques.

Communication Disorders

Disorders of language and speech comprise a wide and heterogeneous range of difficulties complicated by developmental aspects of communication. Communication includes far more than verbalizations, suggesting complex brain function in a person's social interaction with the environment that goes beyond the areas of the brain traditionally associated with speech and verbal comprehension. However, communication disorders typically include only language, speech, and hearing disorders.

In a review of 56 studies, McLean and Cripe (1997) concluded that early intervention for a broad spectrum of communication disorders can be very effective in eliminating those disorders or at least mitigating their impact on a child's later speech and language development. In trying to answer the question of how early an intervention should occur, studies are confounded by natural developmental change. When intervention is started for a toddler, it is sometimes unclear whether the child had a disorder requiring intervention or a developmental lag that would have self-corrected with maturation.

There is little debate that hearing disorders should be detected and treated as early as possible. The later that hearing problems are detected, the more difficult secondary communication problems are to treat.

Some countries have initiated hearing screening in delivering hospitals, with the recognition that if congenital hearing impairment is not detected at birth, the average age of detection is likely to be greater than 18 months.

In general, for children with all types of communication disorders, intervention at an early age appears to be more effective and efficient than when provided at a later age. No one approach fits every child. Rather, specific treatment objectives, intervention environments (group versus individual), and procedures most appropriate for a particular child must be determined.

BIOLOGICAL RATIONALE FOR EARLY INTERVENTION

Regardless of the mixed results in evaluating early intervention efficacy and effectiveness, there are biological reasons why an intervention, if properly timed and implemented, can substantially improve the developmental outcome of a particular child. Much has been learned since the early 1990s about how the brain develops, both structurally and organizationally, during fetal and early postnatal life.

By the end of the second year of life, the brain has achieved four fifths of its adult weight and size. Obviously, the brain grows at a remarkable pace from conception through the first several years of life. This begins with five critical phases of prenatal brain development. The first phase is *neural proliferation.* By the fifth prenatal month, all of the neurons that the brain will ever have—approximately 100 billion—are created. In the second phase, *neural migration,* neurons begin to migrate to the outer cortex of the brain. This delicate process is completed by the end of the sixth prenatal month. These events create the basic "hardware and wiring" necessary for sensory input, information processing, and motor output. The third phase involves a process called *synaptogenesis,* by which the neurons develop interconnections (or *synapses*) that allow them to communicate with one another. More synapses are created than are really necessary. Thus, "pruning" occurs during the fourth phase, reducing the number of connections so that only those that are used and needed survive. In the fifth phase, the nerves are coated with *myelin,* a fatty sheath that accelerates the transmission time for electrical impulses, especially along the nerves that run from the brain down the spinal cord. The result is that commands are executed almost instantaneously. Primitive and survival-related cognitive structures are myelinated first during early postnatal life. Executive functioning structures are myelinated as late as adolescence

and early adulthood. This information alone could justify early intervention, although it is still necessary to find the best way to facilitate
typical brain development during critical periods, minimize the impact
of injury, and take advantage of the brain's attempts to self-repair
(Shonkoff & Phillips, 2000).

Critical Periods of Brain Development

In the 1990s, research on early learning and its relationship to brain
development exploded. During this time, President Clinton designated
the 1990s as the "Decade of the Brain" in the United States. Discoveries
were made not only in how readily newborns can learn but also in
how much they already know at birth. For example, Dr. Patricia Kuhl
at the University of Washington has demonstrated that the brains of
newborns are prewired to recognize every sound in every human language. They lose this capacity over the first year of life, maintaining
recognition only for those sounds to which they are exposed. For
example, Japanese infants distinguish between *l* and *r* at birth. By 9
months of age, they lose this ability (Kuhl et al., 1992).

Perhaps there are certain critical times for learning. It is known
that infants who are deprived of early visual experience will perma-
nently lose vision. In animal experiments, such deprivation results in
significant deterioration of the connections between nerve cells in the
visual cortex (Hubel & Wiesel, 1970). Once these connections are lost,
they do not repair themselves. Similarly, there may be certain aspects
of language for which the brain is prepared to acquire given the appropriate stimulation. If the stimulation is not present, those aspects (e.g.,
sound recognition) are lost. Bruer and Greenough (2001) referred to
this phenomenon as "experience expectant." Basically, it comes down
to "use or lose it!" For some functions, infants seem to have built-in
capacities that need to be exercised in order to be preserved.

Fortunately, the capacity to learn is lifelong, although infants and
toddlers do have the edge when it comes to speed. Young children
clearly are more adept at learning new languages than adolescents or
adults. Of course, foreign language curricula do not reflect this well-
demonstrated fact. Foreign language training rarely begins before middle school, often not before high school. Bruer and Greenough (2001)
referred to this type of learning as "experience dependent." Without
certain experiences, one simply cannot learn certain things. One cannot
learn what snowflakes feel like on the face unless one has been outside
while it is snowing. Similarly, an infant with spina bifida may not learn
shape and size relationships because he or she cannot get into the
kitchen cupboards to play with pots and pans.

Injury and Self-Repair

The amazing processes of brain development unfold in a prescribed, organized manner unless there is a disrupting influence, such as chromosome microdeletion (e.g., Prader-Willi syndrome), intrauterine infection (e.g., cytomegalovirus, rubella), hazardous chemical exposure (e.g., alcohol), or trauma (e.g., birth asphyxia). Even with these unfortunate events, there is evidence that the brain attempts to self-correct. In contrast to the adult brain, the developing brain initially develops redundant neurons that act as a neurological reserve against possible injury (Sarnat, 1996).

According to Farel and Hooper (1995), for this "plasticity" to be operative following injury, new neurons must be created or intact regions must compensate. Although advances are being made in the area of regeneration, this mode of recovery is quite limited. As noted previously, the absolute number of neurons and their migration to various areas of the brain is completed by the second trimester of gestation. Yet, research suggests that in a few areas of the brain (e.g., the hippocampus), new neurons are added, even in adulthood. The problem is that even if there were a way to replace lost neurons (and there may well be in the future), they would have to find their appropriate positions in the nervous system and reconnect with the complicated network of other neurons. Intense work at the basic scientific level may make this approach feasible someday.

Compensation may be possible but effective only during critical periods of brain development and only within certain biological limits. That is, neurons in the occipital cortex programmed to interpret visual images cannot take over for damaged neurons in the temporal cortex responsible for auditory comprehension. Stimulation enhances new neuronal connections, hemispheric dominance is changeable, and different areas of the brain can be used for the same task.

Figure 1.3 demonstrates the brain's capacity to self-repair. The left panel of the figure shows the computed tomography (CT) scan of a 4-month-old who sustained traumatic brain injury from child abuse. The CT scan shows diffuse and severe destruction of brain tissue. Examination of the child 1 month after injury suggested that she would likely have cerebral palsy and mental retardation. The chapter author conducted a developmental and neurological examination of the child at 1 year of age (see right panel of Figure 1.3), however, and the findings were completely normal. Despite the obvious damage shown on the CT scan, the child's brain was able to adapt and compensate for the injury. Although such a complete and unexpected recovery does not occur in all cases of traumatic brain injury in infancy and early childhood, this example illustrates the potential of plasticity even when

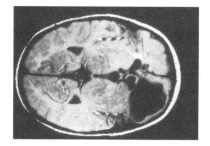 

Figure 1.3. Left panel: Computed tomography (CT) scan of the brain of an infant who sustained traumatic brain injury from child abuse at age 4 months. There are multiple areas of brain damage. Right panel: Same child at age 1 year, at which time a developmental and neurological examination produced completely normal findings.

the specific factors that facilitate such a dramatic improvement are not known.

Inconsistent results from studies of various interventions for children with specific disabilities or risk factors indicate that it is not yet known how to capitalize fully on the brain's plasticity and potential for recovery. The most obvious options are interventions that facilitate nature's determination to get it right the first time or to mitigate the effects of injury.

When the disrupting influence was not prevented, secondary preventive efforts can minimize further neurological deficits. Say that a mother did not take folic acid at the time of conception and her child developed spina bifida. Facilitation of the child's mobility will foster the development of new synapses because of increased opportunities for learning in an expanded environment.

In other words, doing nothing else in early intervention beyond removing barriers to typical brain development processes may be the most important and effective intervention. Perhaps no complex or expensive training programs are needed. Simply thinking about typical developmental processes and how these might be facilitated through interventions with the child, the family, and the environment almost guarantees effectiveness.

FROM SKILL MASTERY TO SOCIAL COMPETENCE

In the early intervention field, there has been a major philosophical shift away from focusing merely on acquisition and practice of developmental skills to developing functional and social competence. Zigler

(2000) criticized those who base their (often disappointingly negative) evaluations of early intervention on programs' ability to raise IQ points. He encouraged colleagues in the early childhood education field to look beyond the narrow cognitive focus to the broader basis of human functioning in society—the cluster of skills that make up the construct of social competence.

Early intervention programs that succeed in achieving long-term benefits are typically broad based and have strong parental participation. In studies of early intervention or preschool enrichment programs with comparison groups, motor and cognitive gains are transient. The persistent benefits of these programs seem to be in the social realm: reduced school drop-out, crime, and teen pregnancy rates.

Despite this philosophical shift, the bulk of early intervention services still tends to address cognitive and motor issues for three reasons. First, they are easier to recognize. Second, early childhood specialists have received more training for dealing with them than with other issues. Finally, health and education funding agencies often are more likely to pay for their treatment than for the treatment of social and emotional aspects. No one would suggest that cognitive and motor problems should not be addressed. Rather, it is suggested that they be addressed with the goal of optimizing emotional and social competence in the context of the family.

CONCLUSION: LINKING NEURONS TO PEOPLE AND COMMUNITIES

Scientific advances have increased understanding of how the brain develops, what can impede typical brain development, and which approaches have the potential to help the brain recover. Still, many children who fail to achieve their full potential do so not because of a faulty brain but because of the environment in which their brain develops. Thus, although early intervention works with one child at a time, the greatest challenges lie with the family, community, nation, and world in which the child lives.

The Committee on Integrating the Science of Early Childhood Development of the U.S. National Research Council and Institute of Medicine published an extensive report on scientific knowledge about the nature of early development (Shonkoff & Phillips, 2000). It sought to understand how early experience affects all aspects of development—from the neural circuitry of the maturing brain, to the expanding network of a child's social relationships, to both the enduring and the changing cultural values of the society in which families raise children. It examined the typical trajectories of early childhood, as well as the atypical developmental pathway that characterizes the adaptations of children with disabilities. The major findings of this report (pp. 386–403) include the following:

- All children are born wired for feelings and ready to learn.
- Early environments matter, and nurturing relationships are essential.
- Society is changing, and the needs of young children are not being addressed.
- Interactions among early childhood science, policy, and practice are problematic and demand dramatic rethinking.

The Committee's concluding charge to society was to blend the skepticism of a scientist, the passions of an advocate, the pragmatism of a policy maker, the creativity of a practitioner, and the devotion of a parent. The use of such knowledge will ensure both a decent quality of life for all children and a productive future for the world. As the proverb "a stitch in time saves nine" implies, intervention begun early for developmental problems has the greatest chance of preventing more serious problems later on.

REFERENCES

Amiel-Tison, C., & Grenier, A. (1986). *Neurological assessment during the first year of life.* New York: Oxford University Press.

Baumeister, A.A., & Bacharach, V.R. (2000). Early generic education intervention has no enduring effect on intelligence and does not prevent mental retardation: The Infant Health and Development Program. *Intelligence, 28*(3), 161–192.

Blair, C., & Ramey, C.T. (1997). Early intervention for low-birth-weight infants and the path to second-generation research. In M.J. Guralnick (Ed.), *The effectiveness of early intervention* (pp. 77–97). Baltimore: Paul H. Brookes Publishing Co.

Brooks-Gunn, J., McCarton, C.M., Casey, P.H., McCormick, M.C., Bauer, C.R., Bernbaum, J.C., Tyson, J., Swanson, M., Bennett, F.C., Scott, D.T., Tonascia, J., & Meinert, C.L. (1994). Early intervention in low-birth-weight premature infants: Results through age 5 from the Infant Health and Development Program. *Journal of the American Medical Association, 272,* 1257–1262.

Bruer, J.T., & Greenough, W.T. (2001). The subtle science of how experience affects the brain. In D.B. Bailey, J.T. Bruer, F.J. Symons, & J.W. Lichtman

(Eds.), *Critical thinking about critical periods* (pp. 209–232). Baltimore: Paul H. Brookes Publishing Co.

Bryant, D., & Maxwell, K. (1997). The effectiveness of early intervention for disadvantaged children. In M.J. Guralnick (Ed.), *The effectiveness of early intervention* (pp. 23–46). Baltimore: Paul H. Brookes Publishing Co.

Cadman, D., Chambers, L.W., Walter, S.D., Ferguson, R., Johnston, N., & McNamee, J. (1987). Evaluation of public health preschool child developmental screening: The process and outcomes of a community program. *American Journal of Public Health, 77*(1), 45–51.

Casto, G., & Mastropieri, M.A. (1986). The efficacy of early intervention. *Exceptional Children, 52*(5), 417–424.

Chan, S. (1998). Families with Asian roots. In E.W. Lynch & M.J. Hanson (Eds.), *Developing cross-cultural competence: A guide for working with children and their families* (2nd ed., pp. 251–344). Baltimore: Paul H. Brookes Publishing Co.

Clinton, H.R. (1996). *It takes a village—and other lessons children teach us.* New York: Simon & Schuster.

Dawson, G., & Osterling, J. (1997). Early intervention in autism. In M.J. Guralnick (Ed.), *The effectiveness of early intervention* (pp. 307–326). Baltimore: Paul H. Brookes Publishing Co.

Education of the Handicapped Act Amendments of 1986, PL 99-457, 20 U.S.C. §§ 1400 *et seq.*

Farel, P.B., & Hooper, C.R. (1995). Biological limits to behavioral recovery following injury to the central nervous system: Implications for early intervention. *Infants and Young Children, 8*(1), 1–7.

Gibson, D., & Harris, A. (1988). Aggregated early intervention effects for Down's syndrome persons: Patterning and longevity of benefits. *Journal of Mental Deficiency Research, 32,* 1–17.

Gomby, D., Culross, P.L., & Behrman, R.E. (1999). Home visiting: Recent program evaluations: Analysis and recommendations. *Future of Children, 9*(1).

Guralnick, M.J. (Ed.). (1997). *The effectiveness of early intervention.* Baltimore: Paul H. Brookes Publishing Co.

Harris, S.R. (1997). The effectiveness of early intervention for children with cerebral palsy and related motor disabilities. In M.J. Guralnick (Ed.), *The effectiveness of early intervention* (pp. 327–347). Baltimore: Paul H. Brookes Publishing Co.

Hubel, D.H., & Wiesel, T.N. (1970). The period of susceptibility to the physiologic effects of unilateral eye closure in kittens. *Journal of Physiology, 206,* 419–436.

Individuals with Disabilities Education Act Amendments of 1997, PL 105-17, 20 U.S.C. §§ 1400 *et seq.*

Individuals with Disabilities Education Act (IDEA) of 1990, PL 101-476, 20 U.S.C. §§ 1400 *et seq.*

Karoly, L.A., Greenwood, P.W., Everingham, S.S., Hoube, J., Kilburn, M.R., Rydell, C.P., Sanders, M., & Chiesa, J. (1998). *Investing in our children: What we know and don't know about the costs and benefits of early childhood interventions.* Santa Monica, CA: RAND Corp.

Kuhl, P.K., Williams, K.A., Lacerda, F., Stevens, K.N., & Lindblom, B. (1992). Linguistic experience alters phonetic perception in infants by 6 months of age. *Science, 255,* 606–608.

McConachie, H., Smyth, D., & Bax, M. (1997). Services for children with disabilities in European countries. *Developmental Medicine and Child Neurology, 39*(Suppl. 76), 5.

McLean, L.K., & Cripe, J.W. (1997). The effectiveness of early intervention for children with communication disorders. In M.J. Guralnick (Ed.), *The effectiveness of early intervention* (pp. 349–428). Baltimore: Paul H. Brookes Publishing Co.

Murray, T.R. (2000). *Comparing theories of early intervention.* Belmont, CA: Wadsworth.

National Early Childhood Technical Assistance Center. (2002). *The Individuals with Disabilities Education Act (IDEA).* Retrieved October 23, 2002, from http://www.nectac.org/idea/idea.asp

Pakula, A.L., & Palmer, F.B. (1997). Early intervention for children at risk for neuromotor problems. In M.J. Guralnick (Ed.), *The effectiveness of early intervention* (pp. 99–108). Baltimore: Paul H. Brookes Publishing Co.

Sameroff, A.J., & Fiese, B.H. (2000). Transactional regulation: The developmental ecology of early intervention. In J.P. Shonkoff & S.J. Meisels (Eds.), *Handbook of early intervention* (2nd ed., pp. 135–159). New York: Cambridge University Press.

Sarnat, H.B. (1996). Neuroembryology. In B.O. Berg (Ed.), *Principles of child neurology* (pp. 607–628). New York: McGraw-Hill.

Schaefer, S., & Cohen, J. (2000, December). Making investments in young children: What the research on early care and education tells us. *Issue Brief.* Washington, DC: National Association of Child Advocates.

Sharifzadeh, V. (1998). Families with Middle Eastern roots. In E.W. Lynch & M.J. Hanson (Eds.), *Developing cross-cultural competence: A guide for working with children and their families* (2nd ed., pp. 441–482). Baltimore: Paul H. Brookes Publishing Co.

Shonkoff, J.P., & Hauser-Cram. (1987). Early intervention for disabled infants and their families: A quantitative analysis. *Pediatrics, 80,* 650–658.

Shonkoff, J.P., & Phillips, D.A. (2000). *From neurons to neighborhoods: The science of early childhood development.* Washington, DC: National Academy Press.

Spiker, D., & Hopmann, M.R. (1997). The effectiveness of early intervention for children with Down syndrome. In M.J. Guralnick (Ed.), *The effectiveness of early intervention* (pp. 271–305). Baltimore: Paul H. Brookes Publishing Co.

Thomas, R.M. (2000). *Comparing theories of child development* (5th ed.). Belmont, CA: Wadsworth.

Wing, L., & Potter, D. (2002). The epidemiology of autistic spectrum disorders: Is the prevalence rising? *Mental Retardation and Developmental Disabilities Research Reviews, 8*(3), 151–161.

World Health Organization. (1980). *International Classification of Impairments, Disabilities and Handicaps.* Geneva: Author.

World Health Organization. (2001). *International Classification of Functioning, Disability and Health (ICF).* Geneva: Author.

Young, M.E. (1996). *Early child development: Investing in the future.* Washington, DC: The World Bank.

Zigler, E.T. (2000). Foreword. In J.P. Shonkoff & S.J. Meisels (Eds.), *Handbook of early childhood intervention* (2nd ed., pp. xi–xv). New York: Cambridge University Press.

Service Delivery Models

CHAPTER 2

Cultural Issues and Service Provision in Rural Areas

Summer Tsai-Hsing Hsia,
Helen McCabe, and Bao-Jen Li

PEOPLE'S REPUBLIC OF CHINA

Tian sheng wo cai bi you yong.

Heaven gives me my talent necessarily for some use.

The People's Republic of China (PRC) is slightly smaller than the United States, but its population is four times larger. At the beginning of the 21st century, the PRC governed 1.25 billion people, or close to 22% of the world's population (Becker, 2000). Its eastern provinces are among the world's most populous; its western provinces are among the world's least inhabited. With a history of 5,000 years, China is the only continuous ancient civilization. Its culture is rich, profound, and well documented. Although most Chinese people are deeply proud of their country—not only of its modern achievements but also of the long record of Chinese achievements—for more than 200 years, the intellectuals of the Middle Kingdom have been struggling with a complicated mix of traditional and Western ideas and structures. ("Middle Kingdom" is the old name for China, reflecting how its people have viewed the country: in the middle of the world.) An easy solution used to be a neat separation of the two elements in examining a dilemma: the East for values, the West for science and technology (Scalapino, 1999). The issue may not be this clear-cut when it comes to the provision of human services, especially in educating children with disabilities.

When designing intervention programs, the PRC, like many developing countries, has adopted the service delivery models developed by Western countries, especially the United States. Complete adoption may be problematic because the fundamental elements that make the models work elsewhere may not be readily available in many parts of China. Although the economy has been growing at an amazing speed, many people, especially those in inland provinces, remain poor. In areas where resources are scarce, successful implementation seems unlikely for services that require qualified interventionists from a variety of disciplines, interagency collaboration, and parent involvement.

This chapter first provides a description of early intervention practices in the PRC. This overview is followed by a depiction of how a program in Sichuan province meets the needs of young children with disabilities and their families. Strategies for enhancing the quality of the teachers, designing an effective curriculum, and encouraging family involvement are described.

QING QING'S STORY

Every day at dawn, Qing Qing and her grandmother Po Po cross the Yangtze River to attend a program for children with disabilities. On the street quite a few children, wearing school uniforms and backpacks, wave at her. Qing Qing follows the children to the schoolyard for the

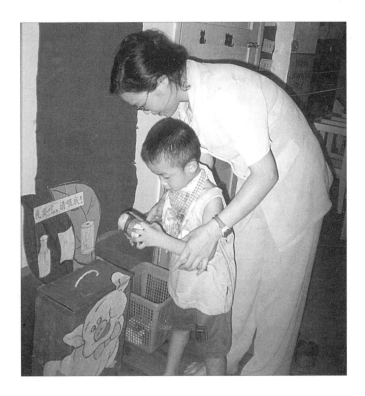

flag-raising ceremony and returns with her teachers to her school, right next to the elementary school. Qing Qing is 5 years old and has developmental delays and cerebral palsy due to a near-drowning accident in the Yangtze River when she was an infant. This happy and active little girl grows and thrives gradually under the insistence and protection of Po Po. Now, she attends the preschool program at a special school, wearing an identical uniform and name tag as the students next door. The special school was purposefully given the same name as the elementary school, Xiang Yang, so Qing Qing's Po Po can tell everyone, "My granddaughter goes to the school in town." The school is located on the second floor of a row of apartment buildings. The 560 square meter, accredited, privately operated school has better facilities than most of the educational programs in this agricultural town, especially with the support that it has from the local teachers' college.

With the help of a teacher, Qing Qing puts on her indoor shoes at the entrance and flips her name card hung on the door to signal "I'm here in school." She finds the chair with her name on it, sits down, removes a family communication book from her backpack, and puts it in a basket. Most of the time the family member who reads and signs the blue notebook is Po Po. Qing Qing's parents are divorced, and her father does not get along well with his new wife. Taking care of Qing Qing sometimes seems like a burden to the couple.

The classroom becomes increasingly lively as more children arrive. Qing Qing remembers to greet her best friend, Xiao Ma, who is sitting in an adaptive chair. The chair was specially designed by the teachers so Xiao Ma will not have to lie on his back all day long. When he sees Qing Qing, Xiao Ma smiles and sticks out his tongue. A teacher sees that and interprets for him. "Good morning, Qing Qing." Qing Qing giggles and goes back to her seat.

The classroom is divided into several areas for the children to practice their skills in all developmental areas. Qing Qing follows the routines of the day and enjoys being with her friends and teachers. At home, however, she refuses to listen to her stepmother and fights with a strong will that astonishes Po Po. Qing Qing's father avoids coming home.

The teachers have suggested that Po Po encourage her daughter-in-law and help her interact with Qing Qing more positively. They have also arranged for the stepmother to arrive at school a half hour earlier than usual so they can show her how to play Qing Qing's favorite games. Of course, the teachers must work very hard to find resources to support families like Qing Qing's, and this is not feasible in a lot of places in China.

There is a special event at the elementary school to promote Beijing's bid for hosting the Olympic Games in 2008. Qing Qing and four other young children in the classroom join the students from the elementary school and dance to the blasting music. The performance attracts a large crowd, including Qing Qing's family, and Qing Qing is not shy at all. Focusing on doing every move right, this little girl who almost succumbed to the gushing Yangtze River is happy and full of life.

NATIONAL CONTEXT

The PRC is a large developing country, divided into 22 provinces, five autonomous regions, four centrally administered municipalities, and one special administrative region. The Han Chinese, who make up 91.9% of the population, dominate culturally and politically. Fifty-five recognized minority groups—including Zhuang, Uigur, Hui, Yi, Tibetan, Miao, Manchu, and Mongol—represent the remaining 8%.

Since economic and political reforms began in 1978, the standard of living has increased in all areas of the country. The coastal areas have been very successful in improving their economy, with slower but visible progress in inland provinces. The national language is *Putonghua* (the common speech) or Mandarin, which is one of the five working languages of the United Nations. Most of the ethnic minorities have their own languages. As a written language, Chinese has been used for 6,000 years.

The Chinese traditional way of life is influenced by three systems of belief: the teachings of Confucius, Taoism, and Buddhism. Confucius laid great stress on the virtues of benevolence, righteousness, propriety, wisdom, and trustworthiness. He emphasized obedience and respect for elders. Taoism is the study of the "Way" and is concerned with remaining harmonious with the universe. Buddhism aims to teach its followers how to reach a state of nirvana through rejection of the material world.

The "Six Relationships" form the basis of all social interactions between individuals, and they are based on the fundamental relationship between parents and children. *Xiao,* or filial piety, means the complete and unquestioning respect and obedience children owe to their parents, and it is expanded to include the relationships between the ruler and subjects, elder and younger brothers, husband and wife, teacher and student, and friends.

Education Services Systems

In 1986, China passed the Compulsory Education Act, calling for 9 years of schooling for all children. To meet this requirement, a child attends either 5 years of elementary education, followed by 4 years of junior middle school or 6 years of elementary education, followed by 3 years of junior middle school. At the beginning of the 21st century, the second (or "6-3") system is more common. Although the Compulsory Education Law calls for each child to have 9 years of formal schooling, it is recognized that certain realities prevent this standard from being implemented. Therefore, a provision of the Compulsory Education Law is that the PRC shall be divided into three categories: 1) cities and economically developed areas, 2) towns and villages with medium development, and 3) areas with little or no economic development. The first two categories compose 91% of the population; in these places, the 9-year standard has become almost universal. However, in the areas with little or no development, which contain approximately 25% of China's population, a variable timetable for implementing compulsory education has been tied to each such region's local economic development.

The terms *preschool* and *kindergarten* (*xueqian ban*) are used inter-changeably. This period can last for up to 3 years.[1] Children enter as early as age 3 and attend until age 6, when they typically enter elementary school. The State Education Commission (SEC) is the chief administrative organization that oversees education. The SEC formulates and enforces policies and laws concerning education, and it coordinates the operation of the individual schools. When Deng Xiaoping came into power in 1978 and began the period of *gaige kaifang* (Reform and Opening [to the Outside]), opportunities for the education of children with disabilities began and have been increasing.

Statistics from the 1987 National Survey on the Status of Disabilities estimated that of 52 million people with disabilities, 2.46 million were children younger than age 6 (Epstein, 1992; Gargiulo & Piao, 1996). Education for children with disabilities in China began on a small scale in the late 19th century. Schools for children with sensory impairments were opened by American and European missionaries. The earliest special education school founded by Chinese alone was a teacher training school for teachers of students with visual and hearing impairments in 1912; a similar school for these students opened in Nantong, Jiangsu, in 1916. By 1937, there were almost 40 schools of this type, although many were closed during World War II (Epstein, 1988; Ye & Piao, 1995). With the establishment of the PRC in 1949, schools reopened and those that had been operated by foreigners became part of the public school system (Yang & Wang, 1994).

Education for children with disabilities became part of public education after 1949. The first class for children with cognitive disabilities was established in Beijing in 1958, and another school opened in Dalian in 1959. However, progress stopped during the chaos of the Cultural Revolution of 1966–1976 (Yang & Wang, 1994; Ye & Piao, 1995). Since *gaige kaifang* began in 1978, education opportunities for all children have been increasing in all parts of the country. Services for children with sensory and cognitive disabilities are currently provided in a variety of environments. Separate schools specifically for children with disabilities exist in most cities. By 1990, there were 746 state-run special education schools as part of the public education system. A second type of environment is special education classes attached to general education primary schools. In 1990, there were 1,885 such classes

---

[1]Translations of the term *early childhood programs* for children younger than 6 years in China use both *preschool* and *kindergarten*. Both refer to education for children between the ages of 3 and 7 years. In this chapter, the term *preschool* is used for programs for young children in this age range; *kindergarten* is used when it is clear that the program is only for the *xueqian ban,* which is a class that immediately proceeds first grade.

(Renmin Jiaoyu Press, 1991). At these schools and classes, students are provided with education in grades 1–9 (equivalent of elementary and junior middle school); some schools also have a kindergarten class for children younger than 7 years of age.

Since the early 1980s, a new educational placement has been available for children with disabilities. Children with sensory impairments and mild cognitive disabilities are increasingly being educated in general education environments (*suiban jiudu*). The first schools to implement *suiban jiudu* were in remote mountainous and rural areas, beginning in the early 1980s. Although cities and larger towns have special education schools and classrooms, rural and remote areas do not have the finances or the infrastructure to make separate schools feasible. The goal of providing 9 years of education to all students, including students with disabilities, has led to inclusive education as a practical and feasible way to provide education to all children (Chen, 1996, 1997).

KEY FEATURES OF EARLY INTERVENTION

Although special education policy and programs for school-age children in the PRC have been consistently developed and expanded since the mid-1980s, early intervention for children with disabilities younger than 6 years is a more recent development. Several reports have provided general information about overall numbers of early childhood classes and schools for children with disabilities. By 1990, Carter, Chen, Hwang, and Yu (1996) reported that more than 600 preschool classes were being run, largely by local communities, for children with disabilities. Young children with mild and moderate disabilities were included in general preschool programs. In addition to opportunities in preschool environments, since the late 1980s, many public and private early childhood special education programs have also been established and run by medical personnel and parents (Mu, Yang, & Armfield, 1993; Yang & Wang, 1994).

This information provides an overall sense of early intervention in the PRC as of 2002. It is obvious that efforts have been made and that some children are receiving services. Available enrollment percentage statistics, however, reveal the continued need: A 1997 report found that more than 85% of young children with disabilities still had no opportunity for early education (Zhao, Guo, & Zhou, 1997). A more detailed look at the specific programs and practices in these programs provides a better understanding of early intervention in the PRC today.

Curriculum and Classroom Practices

Early intervention services are provided for young children at both public and private schools and organizations. The Beijing Xinyun FORTUNE School, established in 1986, is one of the earliest and best-known early intervention programs in the PRC (Mao & Wang, 1994). At the FORTUNE School, children are taught both in groups and individually. The curriculum addresses social behavior, gross motor, fine motor, language, cognitive, and self-help skills, with a special emphasis on language and fine motor skills.

Many programs are located in medical facilities or in private organizations run by parents. Examples include the state-run Nanjing Child Mental Health Research Center, which has short-term intervention programs for young children with autism, and the Beijing Xingxingyu (Stars and Rain) Education Institute for Children with Autism, established and run by the parent of a child with autism.

Although several schools and programs are dedicated to educating young children with cognitive disabilities and autism, a large proportion of China's early intervention programs serve children with hearing impairments. These programs include classes attached to special education schools and classes for preschool children within nationwide rehabilitation centers for children with hearing impairments. Inclusive preschool education is a growing trend.

Overall, it is clear that China is making significant progress in the development of early intervention services. Both poor, remote areas and urban, developed areas have begun to establish programs for young children with disabilities. The service delivery methods range from early intervention classes at special education schools or rehabilitation centers to much more integrated placements within general education preschools.

Family Roles

Many programs in the PRC include parent participation in early intervention services as well as services that offer support and parent education. Family roles range from observation and occasional meetings with professionals to more comprehensive involvement. Programs that contain family components are described next.

The Beijing Xingxingyu Education Institute for Children with Autism is one of the most innovative programs for young children with disabilities and their families. Parents at Xingxingyu actively participate in their child's program for 3 months. They act as primary instructors under the guidance of the teachers and attend a weekly class taught by the director that focuses on specific techniques and principles of applied behavior analysis. At this early intervention program, families play highly active roles in the education of their children and also receive significant support.

The other previously mentioned program that serves children with autism, the Nanjing Child Mental Health Center, also includes roles for parents. At least one parent observes every class with his or her child. Parents also actively participate in the daily group music and movement classes.

The FORTUNE School has a parent component as well. It runs parent meetings once per month and before holidays. Work with parents focuses on enhancing parental observation skills, sensitivity, and responsiveness to their child's cues and behaviors (Mao, 1989).

The Save the Children Foundation project in Anhui Province has also stressed the importance of working with families. One of the project's goals is to promote a partnership between teachers and families. Teachers visit their students' homes, and families visit their children's schools. The family is encouraged to be involved with their child's individual learning program, to meet with other families, and to take part in seminars. Both parents and teachers believe the teacher training and new methods have led to an improvement in the educational experiences of all children—with and without disabilities (Holdsworth, 1993).

Early intervention programs in the Hongkou district of Shanghai also contain a family education component. Parents are encouraged to participate in discussions on goal setting and individual program content. It is believed that on the basis of participating in cooperative training, parents will be able to use the teacher's instructional methods at home and reinforce what the child learns at school (Gao, Xiang, & Jing, 1999).

Theoretical Influences

Western early intervention research and experience have influenced the development of early intervention in China. One example is early intervention for children with disabilities and children who are at risk, such as the Head Start program in the United States. Inclusive school and preschool programs abroad have also influenced the current direction of early intervention in PRC (Mao & Wang, 1994).

U.S. research on and experience with applied behavior analysis has had a significant impact on the instructional strategy used at the Beijing Xingxingyu Education Institute for Children with Autism. The director has visited centers in the United States to learn about using applied behavior analysis to teach young children with autism, both by observing and by collecting curriculum and research materials.

Political Influences

One of the most important political influences on the practices of early intervention in the PRC is the initiative to achieve universal compulsory education for all children. The Compulsory Education Act of 1986 specified that local governments at all levels should set up 9 years of compulsory education (at special schools or classes) for children who have sensory or cognitive disabilities (National People's Congress, 1986). Other legislation has also targeted the education of children with disabilities. The 1990 Law of the People's Republic of China on the Protection of Disabled Persons gives priority to compulsory education for school-age children with disabilities, but it also is the first law to encourage efforts for early childhood special educational opportunities as well (National People's Congress, 1990).

Although it does not mandate preschool education for children with disabilities, the Compulsory Education Law has been a major influence on the establishment of early intervention programs. Concern for meeting the national objective of 9 years of compulsory education for all children has led local education agencies to consider early intervention as a way to meet this goal.

The goal of universal basic education and the impossibility of building and staffing new separate schools and classrooms make inclusive education the most feasible solution to provide education for all children. Early intervention provides a child with a foundation for successful inclusion (Chen, Ye, & Peng, 1995; Zhao, 1996; Zhou & Cheng, 1995). Because of this rationale, compulsory education and disability policies have had a significant impact on the development of early intervention.

Leadership is another major political influence on overall services for people with disabilities. Deng Pufang, son of the late Chinese leader Deng Xiaoping, chairs the China Disabled Persons' Federation, the government organization in charge of assisting people with disabilities. Deng, who uses a wheelchair due to a spinal cord injury received in 1968, is also the leading advocate for China's estimated 52 million citizens with disabilities. In 1996, the official press reported that the State Council had completed the outline of a government program for people with disabilities. The program, which is a part of the government's ninth 5-year plan (1996–2000), is designed to solve food and clothing problems for people with disabilities and to guarantee the basic needs of the 3 million people believed to live in extreme poverty. The program also confirms goals previously established to provide rehabilitation services: Raise school enrollment rates for children with disabilities to 80%, and increase their employment rate to 80%. The government requires all state enterprises to hire a certain number of workers with disabilities, but authorities estimate that nearly half of these people are unemployed.

The political environment since 1978, which has approved of international exchange and cooperation, has also been a factor in the development of early intervention in the PRC. Knowledge about early intervention came from the West (Mao & Wang, 1994); several early childhood special education programs, such as Anhui Provincial Education Commission (APEC)/Save the Children and UNICEF community-based rehabilitation (CBR), have been established and are run jointly with international organizations. Exchanges and study trips to the United States and Germany have been beneficial for the progress of two early intervention programs for children with autism. Such exchanges and interactions have been made possible by the political atmosphere of reform and openness to the outside.

Cultural Influences

The Chinese consider education a stepping stone to success. Chinese parents are renowned for their willingness to sacrifice their own personal well-being to secure a good education—and, thus, a successful future—for their children. Teachers are generally highly respected, and school children seek conformity, obedience, and group dependence.

Strict enforcement of birth restrictions has had a two-sided impact on some children with disabilities and their families. To curb the fast-growing population, in 1979 the Family Planning Commission of the PRC implemented the one-child policy. The policy states that parents in urban environments are limited to having one child, and parents in rural areas are allowed to have two children if the first is a girl. Sons are highly valued in Chinese culture because when girls get married, they become part of their husband's family, leaving no one to care for the parents in their old age. This value especially applies to more rural areas, where added offspring provide field help to increase family income. Another exception to this policy is families whose first child has a disability, provided that parents have the necessary birth permit. Violation of the one-child policy may incur severe penalties, including denying educational and medical services to the second child and a fine equivalent to 10 years' wages (Strom, Strom, & Xie, 1995).

The government's birth planning restrictions have led some people to abandon daughters in their quest for a son, and the shame and hopelessness brought by the birth of a child with a disability has caused some parents to reject their offspring. Abandonment is a punishable crime, but most cases are overlooked and go unpunished. However, the policy also leads some families to care more about their child with a disability and to put more effort into educating the child. Because it is emotionally and financially difficult to have a second child, many families whose first child has a disability do not choose to have a second child. These families put all of their energy into helping their child obtain educational and other services. When four grandparents and two parents all care for one child with a disability, the care and support that he or she receives is enormous and positive.

There are multiple barriers in the development and implementation of early intervention services in rural China. A description of one program's effort to meet the challenges follows.

DESCRIPTION OF THE PROGRAM

With more than 20 years of experience working with children with disabilities in Taiwan, the third chapter author and her colleague established Xiang Yang Children's Development Center in Jiang Jin in 1996. Located in the southwestern part of China, Jiang Jin and Chongqing (the capital of Sichuan province) are 60 kilometers apart and connected by freeways, railroads, and the Yangtze River. The majority of the residents of Jiang Jin are farmers who seek work in coastal cities during slow seasons. The extra incomes and economic reforms have added to the prosperity of this city of 100,000.

Among the 20 students enrolled at Xiang Yang, seven of them are between 3 and 6 years old. When the center was founded, it was nearly impossible to enroll preschool-age children because most parents were not willing to send their young sons and daughters to a "school for the handicapped." Many more parents did not even know that special education and services were available in town.

Three strategies were used to locate the children in need of services. First, because adjustments in birth regulations are made for parents whose firstborn child has a disability, parents can obtain permission at the family planning office to have a second child. The records kept at the office provided information that helped the staff at Xiang Yang locate the families. Second, local hospitals do not keep patients' records, so the staff at Xiang Yang established a network with the physicians at children's hospitals and clinics so that referrals could be made once a child was identified as having a disability. Third, Xiang Yang opened a toy-and-book-lending library in Chongqing, targeting young children with developmental delays and disabilities and their families. Counseling and information services were offered to help parents recognize the importance of early intervention. As a result, a number of families have chosen to enroll their children at Xiang Yang.

Practices that Address Specific Challenges

Most of the Xiang Yang parents are farmers or laborers. Many seek out-of-town work, leaving their children in the care of grandparents; others have opened small businesses in town to make a living. Encouraging parents to actively participate in their children's education and instilling a sense of hope in their future has remained extremely difficult. An even more challenging task is the transfer of a well-established service delivery model developed in Taiwan to this location with limited resources and information.

Staff Recruitment, Training, and Ongoing Professional Development

Educational opportunities for young children with disabilities were relatively unheard of in Jiang Jin prior to 1996. An important initial step was recruiting, training, and retaining teachers who wanted to learn to work with children and their families. For Xiang Yang to become a truly local program and develop a personnel preparation model appropriate for a rural agricultural area, all of the teachers were people born and raised in Jiang Jin. The eight teachers who first joined the center were recent graduates from high schools or correspondence schools. With no background in special education or child development, they completed a month-long training and probation period. All of these teachers have remained at the school and have become the most valuable asset of Xiang Yang. Their experience and hard work have enabled them to implement instruction independently, to serve as consultants to other programs, to mentor practicum students, and to give talks on intervention strategies.

The in-service program at Xiang Yang is characterized by a systematic progression, and it allows the teachers to acquire knowledge in an organized manner and avoid fragmentation. During Xiang Yang's first 2 years, all of the teachers had a similar professional development plan. In the third and fourth years, center directors determined the areas on which individual teachers needed to concentrate based on careful performance evaluations. In the fifth year, teachers outlined their own goals for professional growth.

Each teacher's yearly professional development plan has a goal, and the goal matches the individual's current responsibilities. For example, during the first year, teachers learned how to establish satisfactory relationships with children and family members and to design and implement intervention activities. During the second year, the teachers were expected to accurately assess and understand children's characteristics and needs and to develop individual program plans. Gradually, the goals have come to focus on the ability to help families deal with various concerns; skills such as counseling, utilizing resources, and working with other professionals and agencies are emphasized. Strategies for teachers to grow professionally include reading books on special education or related fields and submitting reports, participating in case studies and conducting their own research, attending conferences given by both home and foreign experts, and giving presentations to families and the general public. The most challenging yet rewarding task is providing support to other special education programs. After visiting Xiang Yang, many agencies for children with disabilities request on-site assistance. Xiang Yang selected a few programs located in remote areas to train their teachers to become consultants. At first, a team of three trainers was sent; later, two more teachers went to share their knowledge and experience.

It is believed that after years of reading, learning, discussing, and—most important—providing direct services, teachers develop their own areas of interest and expertise and have explored other possibilities of meeting the needs of children and families. The program supports all teachers' efforts to combine their own interests and the resources available to improve the quality of life for the families they serve. For example, one teacher (also a parent of a child with autism) started at the toy-lending library and gradually created her own service delivery model.

Serving children with disabilities and their families in a rural area is the primary mission of Xiang Yang, and training a group of qualified interventionists who can promote high-quality special education in many similar places around the country is the center's long-term goal. In preparing themselves to be pioneers, the eight teachers have been constantly reminded that a well-rounded special educator asks fundamental questions such as "Why do we teach these children when so many people have given up?" and "How will this child use the skill he is learning to better his life?" Teachers are guided to find and shape their answers by first recognizing the value of their work.

In most parts of the world, early intervention and early childhood special education are provided by several agencies. However, an interdisciplinary professional staff and interagency collaboration are nearly impossible in this agricultural town. Obtaining needed physical, speech-language, and occupational therapy for the young children at Xiang Yang requires staff creativity and resourcefulness. Therapists from

Taiwan have been hired to evaluate the children and provide in-service training. Videotapes of the children's progress are mailed to the trainers, who develop intervention activities and strategies and then convey these to the teachers via videotapes and written instructions. To address this lack of specialists, Taiwanese professionals develop systematic training programs in Jiang Jin and establish referral networks among the hospitals in southwest China.

Curriculum Development

Since the late 1980s, special education has evolved from a medical remedial approach to a more developmental and functional approach. The usefulness of models developed in Western, industrialized countries in areas with underdeveloped economies is highly questionable. Simply following the footsteps of U.S. special educators cannot promote independence and quality of life for children in the PRC. It is essential that practitioners closely examine children's ecological environment and develop their own service delivery models and curricula.

Although many cities are becoming prosperous as a result of the economic reforms, more than 70% of Chinese people are peasants living in the countryside. An ecological approach that emphasizes utilizing the least amount of resources and fully includes children in their surrounding community may be the most cost-effective service delivery method. Specifically, the staff at Xiang Yang strive to help children successfully interact with the environment and integrate skills in all developmental areas. The process of learning—including content, location, and time—is carefully prepared to match the characteristics and needs of the environment. Learning is considered a process that requires long-term planning; fragmented, meaningless, and unrelated behaviors need to be avoided.

Individual Learning Objectives Before assessing a child by using the Developmental Checklists developed in China and the center-made Young Children's Learning Scale, teachers visit the child's home and community to have an understanding of his or her daily routine activities. Parents are encouraged to help develop individual learning objectives by expressing their long-term plans for their child.

Choice of Instructional Methods All of the learning objectives are taught by one or a combination of the following strategies:

- *Incidental learning:* Most learning objectives can be integrated in daily routine activities by using naturally occurring events to teach children the proper way to respond. For example, using a spoon to self-feed is taught at lunchtime, and pulling down one's pants is taught at toileting time. Activities throughout the day are carefully arranged to maximize the opportunity for learning. Requiring the children to remove their shoes and put on indoor slippers is an example. An effort is made to help the children acquire the skills in an environment where the behavior is needed, thus making the learning meaningful.

- *Repetition:* Routine activities, such as morning and afternoon gatherings, follow a certain format so that young children repetitively practice important concepts about self and others, space, numbers, and time.

- *Thematic learning:* Related learning objectives are connected by a theme reflecting significant events in nature or community. For example, during a 2-week lesson about celebrating the New Year, young children learn the color red, use drum sticks to make music, and paste couplets on the walls. An ecological approach emphasizes providing the child with a complete experience and enhancing the child's ability to recognize an event and participate in the creation of the event.

- *Remedial instruction:* Based on the special needs of the children, a few instructional objectives are taught by the use of adult-directed activities. However, all children have time every day to engage in free play, and self-initiation and creativity are encouraged throughout the day.

Environmental Design and Scheduling   The intervention environment is not limited to the center. The community, farm lands, river banks, and—especially for very young children—the home, are all possible environments for instruction. Children's activities are arranged and sequenced based on daily routines such as arrival, lunchtime, and naptime. On occasion, the routine activities need to be changed for special events. For instance, all of the children at Xiang Yang skipped their nap one summer day to join people in the community in watching a rehearsal of the dragon boat festival taking place at the Yangtze River.

Design of Activities   Activities are community based to foster full inclusion. The purpose is to facilitate the interaction between community residents and the children and staff at Xiang Yang and, as a result, enhance the quality of the children's environment. Xiang Yang is an isolated special education program in a community where most residents are posteconomic reform peasants, business people, and retired laborers. The sense of community awareness has not been developed among neighboring people, and Xiang Yang has taken steps to actively involve the community and invite the neighboring people to get to know the center. Cleaning and painting the alleys and the building's stairway are examples of initiating efforts to improve the quality of life. By participating in such activities, young children learn to be a part of their community early in their lives.

In an area where resources are scarce, it is a luxury to think about using technology in instruction. If shown models or photographs in catalogs, however, local carpenters can use inexpensive, locally available materials to build adaptive equipment for children with physical impairments. One parent has made two adaptive chairs, a stander, and many indoor climbing structures for the center. The staff is planning to import parts from Taiwan for local electricians to assemble augmentative and alternative communication devices. Economic hardships can be compensated by the ingenuity and craftsmanship of the Chinese people.

Family Involvement

In a society in which both parents must work and unemployment is a growing problem, learning how to address the needs of their children with disabilities is not the priority. A few of the parents who are more educated and resourceful travel long distances to large cities seeking help and counseling, but the results are often short lived and cannot help them handle all of the problems as the child grows. The staff at Xiang Yang strive to support the families so that parents maintain a positive outlook and do not get discouraged or give up on their child. The strategies focus on poor families living in rural areas, and they may not be appropriate for parents who have more resources and live in metropolitan cities.

Most of the services that Xiang Yang offers are free, and the teachers are not allowed to accept gifts from families. Therefore, trust is formed between the service providers and recipients. Also, services are designed to accommodate the families' needs and schedules. For example, meetings with parents are held at pick-up time, and child care is always available. Typically, two teachers go on a home visit together so that one can play with the child and his or her siblings while the other discusses issues with the parents. Before making suggestions, the teachers always inquire about what has been done at home. In a culture in which teachers are highly respected, Xiang Yang staff do not refrain from making direct recommendations when they see fit.

At pick-up time, parents are often asked to purchase school supplies for the teacher, for which they will be reimbursed later. This has created opportunities for families to become familiar with school activities and to expose their children to the community. The rewards that teachers use to reinforce children's learning are often household items that the families need. After the child has acquired an important skill and with the permission of the parents, the teacher helps the child demonstrate the skill using materials available at home. The child's and family's daily routines are closely examined to understand the nature and location of activities so that parents can be instructed to use what already exists to enhance the child's development. Parents need motivation to play a positive role in their child's education, and this can only be accomplished if what parents are asked to do is easily integrated in their typical activities. Parents are never asked to specially block out time for instructional purposes. For example, one family owns a fruit stand at the market, and their 4-year-old boy loves to be part of the family business. With the teacher's help, the boy's parents have successfully taught him to wipe the apples clean and to sort oranges and pears.

The services provided by Xiang Yang do not focus only on enhancing the child's development; the child is considered a part of a family unit whose members' needs have to be met for the child to grow positively. Workshops for parents sponsored by Xiang Yang have focused on spousal communication, financial management, recreation, home decorating, traveling, sports, and vocational training.

RECOMMENDATIONS FOR
PROFESSIONALS IN OTHER COUNTRIES

In searching for the most appropriate service delivery model for young children with disabilities and their families, one may consider two extremes in solving many problems in human services. The first is to employ the most advanced technologies and abundant resources to effectively eliminate the problem. The second is to allow the "problem" to become part of life and live with it harmoniously. Each country, based on its level of economic development and cultural orientation, may differ on the surface in the way that services are provided. In essence, however, all are searching for and using solutions on the continuum.

The beauty of China lies in its vastness; it can encompass these two extreme service delivery approaches. On the one hand, the PRC has cities with plentiful resources and progressive technologies to help children and their families to meet the challenges. On the other hand, huge lands and agricultural societies provide the best backdrop for accepting children with disabilities for who they are.

Coming from Taiwan, the founders of the Xiang Yang program have been struggling to find the best avenue to properly serve families. They do not want to interfere with society's way of viewing its members but wish to strengthen the support much needed by children with disabilities and their families. The founders have come to realize that nonlocal change agents need to take root by living with the native people, and it takes a long time for the locals to develop trust and acceptance. China has invited countless foreign special education experts to introduce various service delivery models, which have been proven successful. However, those models are of little help to Chinese practitioners in serving their own people in their own cities and villages. Instead of bringing in professionals from advanced countries, a better way to support the early intervention programs in remote Chinese areas is to inspire the local special educators to search for answers from anthropological and ecological perspectives. What is desperately needed is discussion of the connection between effective service and political, economic, and sociological orientations. Chinese special educators need to be inspired by such discussion to create unique services that reflect local social and economic characteristics. Only through exploring one's own values can the most suitable services be developed.

CONCLUSION

Recognizing the importance of early intervention and having finances to support programs in rural areas means that programs like Xiang Yang Child Development Center have the potential to stimulate program development and enhance the quality of existing services. To provide services for young children with disabilities and their families, the public has to recognize the value of early intervention. The staff at Xiang Yang Child Development Center work hard to provide high-quality programs by meaningfully involving the families and actively participating in the community, and the Center's success has attracted the attention of service providers in many provinces. In a country as big and diverse as the PRC, the experience of one center rarely provides an exact model that would work equally well in different locations. Practitioners are encouraged to use Xiang Yang's guiding principles to develop services to support teachers and to address the needs of both children and their families in their own communities.

REFERENCES

Becker, J. (2000). *The Chinese*. New York: The Free Press.

Carter, D., Chen, G., Hwang, T.Y., & Yu, X. (1996). Special education in the People's Republic of China: History, trends and challenges. *B.C. Journal of Special Education, 20*(3), 25–35.

Chen, Y.Y. (1996). Making special education compulsory and inclusive in China. *Cambridge Journal of Education, 26*(1), 47–57.

Chen, Y.Y. (1997). Mianxiang weilai mianxiang shehui de Zhongguo yitihua jiaoyu. [China's integrated education: Facing the future and facing the world]. In Y.Y. Chen (Ed.), *Zhongguo yitihua jiaoyu gaige de lilun yu shijian* [Theory and practice in China's integrated education reform] (pp. 3–17). Beijing, People's Republic of China: Huaxia Chubanshe.

Chen, Y.Y., Ye, L.X., & Peng, X.G. (1995). Ningxia huizu zizhiqu teshu jiaoyu xianzhuang de diaocha [Investigation of the situation of special education in Ningxia Moslem Autonomous Region]. *Teshu Ertong yu Shizi Yanjiu [Special Children and Teacher Preparation], 1*, 24–27.

Epstein, E. (1988). Special educational provision in the People's Republic of China. *Comparative Education, 24*, 365–375.

Epstein, I. (1992). Special education issues in China's modernization. In Ruth Hayhoe (Ed.), *Education and modernization: The Chinese experience* (pp. 285–303). Elmsford, NY: Pergamon.

Gao, M., Xiang, B., & Jing, G.Z. (1999). Xueqian teshu jiaoyu shijian: Yitihua jiaoyu de tujing [Practice of preschool special education: An approach of integration education]. *Zhongguo Teshu Jiaoyu [Special Education in China], 3*, 12–15.

Gargiulo, R.M., & Piao, Y.X. (1996). Early childhood special education in the People's Republic of China. *Early Child Development and Care, 118*, 35–43.

Holdsworth, J.C. (1993). Integrated education project, Anhui province. In United Nations Educational, Scientific, and Cultural Organization (UNESCO) (Ed.), *Making it happen: Examples of good practice in special needs education & community-based programmes* (pp. 9–15). Paris: UNESCO. (ERIC Document Reproduction Service No. ED 375556)

Mao, Y.Y. (1989). The FORTUNE training school in China: A support for mentally retarded children and their parents. *Early Childhood Development and Care, 50*, 189–196.

Mao, Y.Y., & Wang, S.Q. (1994). *Ruozhi ertong de zaoqi ganyu.* [Early intervention for children with cognitive disabilities]. Beijing, People's Republic of China: Huaxia Chubanshe.

Mu, K.L., Yang, H.L., & Armfield, A. (1993, April). *China's special education: A comparative analysis.* Paper presented at the annual convention of the Council for Exceptional Children, San Antonio, TX. (ERIC Document Reproduction Service No. ED 361947)

National People's Congress (1986). *Zhonghua renmin gongheguo yiwu jiaoyu fa* [Compulsory Education Law of the People's Republic of China]. Beijing, People's Republic of China: Law Publishers.

National People's Congress (1990). *Zhonghua renmin gongheguo canji ren baozhang fa* [Law of the People's Republic of China on the Protection of Disabled Persons]. Beijing, People's Republic of China: Legal System Publishers.

Renmin Jiaoyu Press. (1991). Man, longya, ruozhi xuexiao [Schools for children who are deaf, blind, or have mental retardation]. In *Zhongguo Jiaoyu Chengjiu, 1986–1990* [Educational Achievements in China, 1986–1990] (p. 84). Beijing, People's Republic of China: Author.

Scalapino, R.A. (1999). China: Between tradition and modernity. In E. Sand-schneider (Ed.), *The study of modern China* (pp. 1–15). New York: St Martin's Press.

Strom, R.D., Strom, S.K., & Xie, Q. (1995). The small family in China. *International Journal of Early Childhood, 27*(2), 37–45.

Yang, H.L., & Wang, H.B. (1994). Special education in China. *The Journal of Special Education, 28*(1), 93–103.

Ye, L.Q., & Piao, Y.S. (1995). *Teshu jiaoyu xue* [The study of special education]. Fujian, People's Republic of China: Fujian Jiaoyu.

Zhao, L., Guo, C.F., & Zhou, M. (1997). Jiankang youer yu long youer de duikou jiaoyu huodong shijian [The implementation of counterpart activities for healthy young children and young children who are deaf]. In Y.Y. Chen (Ed.), *Zhongguo yitihua jiaoyu gaige de lilun yu shijian* [Theory and practice of the reform of China's integrated education] (pp. 198–202). Beijing, People's Republic of China: Xinhua Chubanshe.

Zhao, T.Z. (1996). Wo guo canji ertong kangfu gongzuo de duice yu tujing [Strategies of rehabilitation of children with disabilities in China]. *Zhongguo Teshu Jiaoyu [Special Education in China], 1,* 28–31.

Zhou, J., & Cheng, X.Q. (1995). Lun xueqian jiaoyu jigou de teshu ertong jiaoyu [A discussion of special education within preschool organizations]. *Teshu Ertong Yu Shizi Jiaoyu [Special Children and Teacher Preparation], 3,* 2–5.

CHAPTER 3

Community-Based Inclusion

SoHyun Lee

SOUTH KOREA

Cho-cho-ik-son.
The earlier, the better.

A common saying in Korea is "da-da-ik-son" [the more, the better]. Early interventionists have changed this saying into "cho-cho-ik-son" [the earlier, the better] and use it to emphasize the importance of early intervention. This reflects how Korean people think of early intervention for young children with disabilities. Although there has been no research to prove the effectiveness of early intervention in South Korea, families, teachers, and other professionals who are involved in early intervention can see and realize the positive impact of education provided during the early years on children's development and learning. As reflected in the metaphor of "cho-cho-ik-son," it can be said that intervening early in life to prevent later problems and to produce better outcomes for children and families has become conventional wisdom in South Korea.

Programs for young children with disabilities are usually classified in two age groups: programs for infants and toddlers (birth to age 3 years) and programs for preschoolers (ages 3 to 6 years). In South Korea, most early childhood special education programs are for children between ages 3 and 5 years. Therefore, the term *early intervention* is used throughout this chapter to represent mainly services for the latter group of children, although many authors have used the term to define services for children from birth to age 3 years and their families (e.g., Meisels & Shonkoff, 1990).

In addition to the brief description of the key features of early intervention practices in South Korea, this chapter introduces the community-based inclusion in early intervention that has been developed and practiced in South Korea and describes details for the nature and specific features of the service. Examples of inclusive preschool and child care programs are given for a better understanding of community-based inclusion in South Korea.

 YOUNGHO'S STORY

Youngho is a 3-year old boy with Down syndrome. Because the disorder was not apparent when Youngho was born, his parents did not listen to the doctor's discussion of the associated complications and challenges. Youngho's parents are both professionals, and Youngho spends most days with his grandmother. It was not until after his younger brother was born, when Youngho's family began to compare his development and behavior with his brother's, that Youngho began to get attention

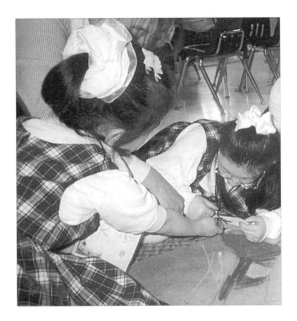

for his developmental delays. When he was again diagnosed as having Down syndrome, Youngho was already 2 years old.

Following the doctor's recommendation, Youngho's parents enrolled him in a private program for young children with disabilities. Youngho's mother had a hard time accepting that her son was somewhat different from other children. Although accepting and adjusting to her son's disability was hard, the most difficult thing for her was knowing that her son was being educated only with other children with disabilities. This led her to look for an inclusive program, which she and her husband found in a neighborhood child care center. Youngho was enrolled in a class with 17 same-age peers, including two other children with disabilities. One of the two classroom teachers had a certificate in special education, and her work focused on providing services for the three children with disabilities. An individualized education program (IEP) and lesson plans were written for Youngho and applied while he followed the general education preschool curriculum. Programs such as small group activities in the classroom to support Youngho's social interaction skills, home visits, a family support group, and a sibling day camp were developed to meet the various needs of Youngho and his family. Now, Youngho is not simply one of the children with disabilities in an early intervention program but, rather, a child who goes to a community children's house, just as many of his same-age peers do. Youngho's parents are optimistic about their son's future in the community.

NATIONAL CONTEXT

Korea is a peninsula that juts from the northeast Asian mainland in a southerly direction for about 1,000 kilometers. It is similar in size to the United Kingdom or New Zealand. Korea has been divided into two parts, North Korea and South Korea, since the ceasefire agreement ending the Korean War. North Korea is independently ruled by a communist government and has no connection to the government of South Korea, which is democratic.

The population of South Korea is approximately 47 million. The capital city of South Korea is Seoul, which is the country's political, cultural, commercial, financial, and educational center. Korea has a 5,000-year-old history and culture of which Korean people are very proud. The Korean language has its own alphabet, which was devised by a group of scholars in the 15th century. The original Korean alphabet is so effective that it remains largely unchanged today and is lauded by linguists for its simple clarity and ease of learning.

Koreans have great concern for education, and illiteracy is almost nonexistent. Children begin their 6 years of elementary school at the age of 6. After 3 years of middle school and 3 years of high school, students may advance to university for 4 years of higher education. At the beginning of the 21st century, parents are giving more attention to early education for their children, and the preschool educational system is growing rapidly to meet this need.

Education Service Systems

In South Korea, all children have the legal rights to elementary and middle school education. In addition, children with disabilities may receive a free education for 3 years of preschool and 3 years of high school. The Division of Special Education of the Ministry of Education and Human Resources is responsible for educational services within the school system. At the preschool level, the responsibility for services for young children with disabilities is shared by two ministries, the Ministry of Education and Human Resources and the Ministry of Health and Welfare.

Free education for preschoolers with disabilities is only for children from ages 3 to 5 who enroll in public school programs or private preschool programs that meet the standards and regulations specified by the 1994 amendments to the Promotion Law for Special Education (PLSE). There is no public support for early intervention programs for children younger than age 3. Infant and toddler programs are difficult to find, and if they are available, parents must pay for services.

Preschoolers with special needs are placed in one of several different educational environments, including preschool classes in special elementary schools, special preschools, special classes in general education preschools, nonprofit welfare centers, private institutions, community children's houses for children with disabilities, and inclusive children's houses. Table 3.1 shows the characteristics of each educational environment.

KEY FEATURES OF EARLY INTERVENTION

Early intervention in Korea has changed a great deal since the late 1980s. These changes can be seen in the number of children receiving educational services and the quality of the services provided. In the 1970s, there were few programs or services for young children with disabilities. Today, early intervention programs are available in more than 200 classes in special schools or general education preschools, more than 100 nonprofit welfare centers or religious centers, more than 200 private institutions, and some inclusive preschools or child care programs. Although the PLSE provides financial support for some of these preschool programs, as noted previously, this law does not provide for services to infants and toddlers with disabilities.

Curriculum and Classroom Practices

In Korea, the Ministry of Education and Human Resources has developed the general curriculum for school-age children and a specially tailored curriculum for children with disabilities. Children with disabilities follow either one or both curricula depending on their placement. Those in general education schools follow the general curriculum but also have a specially tailored curriculum. Those in special schools follow the special education curriculum.

Only one curriculum has been developed for typically developing children. Most children with disabilities who are enrolled in a general education preschool or a community children's house follow the national general preschool curriculum. This curriculum may or may not be supplemented by an IEP or adapted lesson plans, depending on

Table 3.1. **Characteristics of different educational environments for early intervention in South Korea**

Environments	Age of children	Special education teacher certification required?	Type of service	Cost	Government division responsible for program	Inclusive?
Preschool class in special elementary school	3–5 years	Yes	Education	Free	Ministry of Education and Human Resources	No
Special preschool	3–5 years	Yes	Education	Free	Ministry of Education and Human Resources	No
Special class in general preschool	3–5 years	Yes	Education	Free	Ministry of Education and Human Resources	Yes
Nonprofit welfare center	Under 5 years[a]	No	Education	Low[b]	Ministry of Health and Welfare	No
Private institution	Under 5 years[a]	No	Education	High[c]	None	No
Segregated children's house	Under 5 years[a]	No	Child care	Free	Ministry of Health and Welfare	No
Inclusive children's house	Under 5 years[a]	No	Child care	Free	Ministry of Health and Welfare	Yes

[a]Depends on the policy of the institution; [b]compared with private institutions; [c]compared with welfare centers

whether the institution has a special class or special education personnel. Special day schools or private early intervention centers sometimes develop their own curricula for young children with disabilities. In the past, developed curricula focused on readiness skills for academic achievement and were delivered in classroom activities in which all children participated. However, practices have changed to emphasize individual children' abilities and needs (e.g., daily life skills). Today, early intervention curricula usually include various developmental areas—such as social, communicative, cognitive, adaptive, and motor development—and instruction focuses on the unique needs of individual children. Also, many private early intervention centers use published curricula such as The Carolina Curriculum for Preschoolers with Special Needs (Johnson-Martin, Attermeier, & Hacker, 1990) and the Portage Guide to Early Education (Bluma et al., 1976), both of which have been translated into Korean.

According to a study in Korea, increased flexibility has been emerging in curriculum content and delivery, as well as the pace of instruction (Lee, Park, & Kim, 2002). These adaptations create better matches between instruction and each child's learning speed, style, and capacity. Teachers prefer to combine various available curricula, instructional contents, and methods than to follow one specific curriculum to fulfill each child's individual needs. Quality of education for young children with disabilities is judged by the appropriateness of instruction to the child's individual learning traits. Generally in Korea, the IEP is used as an individualized curriculum or a learning program that is based on a child's strengths and weaknesses, learning styles, and special needs. Even though the IEP is not mandatory in Korea, most teachers use IEPs for young children with disabilities. Based on children's IEPs, lesson plans are written or adapted (in inclusive classrooms) daily, weekly, and/or monthly.

Family Roles

Families play a critical role in early intervention for young children with disabilities. Unless parents learn how to work effectively with their child, the gains accomplished in an early intervention program may not be maintained (Turnbull & Turnbull, 1996). In Korea, the importance of including parents and extended family members in the whole process of the assessment and intervention practices is well recognized and accepted in the field. Despite this acceptance, it has not been put into practice well. The importance of family involvement and a parent–professional partnership has been emphasized in newer teacher training courses, and most teachers are beginning to apply the notion to their own practice with young children with disabilities.

The extent of family involvement depends on the policy of the individual institution or teacher. Some early intervention programs have specific guidelines for family involvement; others do not. When the institution does not have any policy for family involvement, the responsibility is left to teachers. Some teachers who consider family involvement important develop their own family involvement programs, guiding parents, siblings and other extended family members to participate in the program.

The most common form of family involvement in Korea is participating in a parent education program. In these programs, family members receive various sources of information about their child's disabilities and educational needs. Although most parent education programs follow a somewhat unidirectional provision of information rather than a reciprocal relationship-building process, the programs give many parents valuable information on their child's needs and education.

Although direct involvement of family members in early intervention is somewhat limited, they still may play important roles. Parents often are the first people who make referrals for their children's special education services. They also provide valuable and necessary information in the process of assessment and intervention. Some parents and teachers build good reciprocal relationships and work together to maximize educational outcomes for children. In addition, parents often serve in the programs in which their children are enrolled. They may be voluntary aides, prepare materials or special events, raise funds and awareness through advocacy efforts, and provide support and assistance to other parents.

Theoretical Influences

Departments of special education in Korean colleges and universities play a leading role in early intervention theory and research. The Korea Institute for Special Education, which is the only national special education institution operated by the government, also plays a major role in research. It provides in-service training to help teachers learn and put into practice recent theories and research findings. Although Korea's early intervention practices and research have followed those of other countries, practitioners in Korea also have been developing research and practices. Among them are the supporting systems for early inclusion in community preschool or child care programs (described later in this chapter), independent special schools for early childhood special education, and teacher training courses in early childhood special education that blend the theory and practice of early childhood education and early childhood special education.

The early intervention field in Korea has been enriched by the theories and practices contributed by disciplines including early childhood education, special education, and psychology of learning. Several theories play an important part in guiding assessment and intervention practices for young children with special needs. Curriculum and instructional models are based on theoretical perspectives such as developmental (Bayley, 1969; Gesell & Amatruda, 1947), behavioral (Skinner, 1953), cognitive (Piaget, 1971), and functional (Strain et al., 1992). Inclusive preschool programs use developmental or cognitive perspectives as a foundation; segregated programs usually take both developmental and functional perspectives. Starting in the late 1980s, some theoretical perspectives—such as ecological (Bronfenbrenner, 1974) or interactive/transactional (Sameroff & Fiese, 1990)—emerged in the country and are having a great impact on assessment and intervention for young children with disabilities. Many current approaches to improving children's development and educational achievements apply a wide range of theoretical assumptions depending on the program's philosophical and theoretical perspectives. Research and practice in early intervention emphasizes several important issues in Korea. These include early diagnosis, family involvement, developmentally appropriate practice, positive behavioral support, assessment-linked curriculum, activity-based intervention, and inclusion.

Political Influences

Changes in legislation and regulations are key to progressing the fields of special education and early intervention. Korea has been formulating legal bases for providing education for all children. Compulsory education was enacted in 1949, but children with disabilities were not mentioned specifically. Educating children with disabilities appears to have been an afterthought for policy makers. Korea developed separate policy documents for the education of children with disabilities, and the PLSE was enacted in 1977. However, this law did not include any clauses or regulations for preschoolers. At that time, only a small number of children with disabilities were receiving free education—those who were enrolled in the preschool programs of special day schools. Free education for young children with disabilities was expanded in the 1980s by the Ministry of Education and Human Resources' encouragement of preschool programs in special day schools. Yet, the legal basis for expanding free education did not exist until the 1994 amendments to the PLSE. Free education for children with disabilities ages 3–5 years is still limited to public school and private programs that are qualified according to the detailed regulations of the PLSE 1994.

However, changes in legislation have had a positive impact on increasing the number of children receiving free early childhood intervention services. Indeed, since the beginning of the 1990s, early intervention programs in special schools and special classes in general education preschools for children ages 3–5 have been increased a great deal.

Despite these developments, surveys conducted in the late 1990s indicated that no more than 20% of children younger than 5 years with disabilities were receiving appropriate special education services. Also, the number of children receiving services at no cost was much smaller. In Korea, there is a need for government leaders to enforce existing policies and to establish new policies that increase the number of children receiving services, as well as the quality of programs.

Cultural Influences

Two specific features of Korean culture might have an impact on education for young children with disabilities. First, as in some other cultures, there has been a long-standing negative perception of disability, resulting in cultural stigma for people with disabilities. People with disabilities often were treated as social failures and were not welcomed as equal members of society or their own communities. As a result, many family members were ashamed or afraid of taking their child with a disability into public. This stigma and hesitation on the family's part negatively affected the provision of an appropriate education for children with disabilities. In terms of early intervention, it prevented the early identification and diagnosis of disabilities and the provision of services. In the 1990s, the efforts of families, professionals, advocates, and policy makers led to changes in public perception of disability. People with disabilities are beginning to be accepted as equal community members, and their rights to education and quality of life are being respected. No longer afraid, most families now actively seek professional help for their children with disabilities. This, combined with the second cultural characteristic described next, plays an active role in improving the quality of early intervention services.

A second cultural characteristic that affects early intervention is Koreans' great interest in education. Most Korean mothers are enthusiastic about their children's education, especially early childhood education. The mothers of children with disabilities are no exception. They want their children to get the best education possible. For some children and family members, this may lead to burnout because of the many programs and therapies in which they are involved. However, as long as parents of children with disabilities are interested in and enthusiastic about finding better programs, they will continue to make a great impact on improving the quality of services provided.

DESCRIPTION OF THE PROGRAM

In Korea, many children with special needs attend general education preschool or child care programs. Parents enroll their children in these programs because of their belief in the importance of inclusive education and their unwillingness to send their children to separate classes where they will receive a diagnostic label. However, many of these children will not be successful in these classes without appropriate special education supports. These children, who may have a variety of impairments, may be at risk for failure because their needs are not identified and they have no early intervention support.

Until the late 1990s, it was true that young children with special needs who attended general education preschools or child care programs hardly received any special educational help in Korea. However, the government has begun to encourage special education professionals to support children with disabilities in these environments by facilitating community-based inclusion. This happens in two different ways. One is within educational service systems governed by the Ministry of Education and Human Resources based on the 1994 amendments of the PLSE. According to the PLSE 1994 and its detailed regulations for the application of the law, any preschool for children ages 3–5 can have a class for children with disabilities, which is funded by the government. It can be operated as a self-contained special class or an inclusive program. For either model, preschools are provided with tuitions and fees for a maximum of six children per class, salary for one special education teacher, and operational money. Compared with the typical teacher–student ratio of 1 to 20–30 in general early childhood education environments, the 1 to 6 ratio provides incentive to start programs for children with disabilities. This is especially true for preschools in which these children are already enrolled.

Children's houses make up the other system that facilitates community-based inclusion. Children's houses, supported by the Ministry of Health and Welfare, provide child care and educational programs for children younger than age 5. Until the mid-1990s, there was resistance from children's houses to enrolling children with disabilities; they treated children with disabilities as burdens if no professional support was received to care for those children. However, this tendency has been changing, influenced by the policy that programs in which three children with disabilities are enrolled can receive financial support from the government to hire a special education teacher. As a teacher–student ratio of 1 to 3 is highly encouraging, children's houses are increasingly accepting children with disabilities into their programs.

In both types of community-based inclusive programs, the qualifications of special education teachers are very important. In fact, the quality of the service provided depends on these teachers. They may develop and implement IEPs for each child with special needs, adapt and accommodate lesson plans and activities for a mixed group of children with and without disabilities, assist or cooperate with general education early childhood teachers, and involve parents and extended family members in their child's education.

Examples of Programs

The following examples illustrate these two types of programs: an inclusive preschool and an inclusive children's house.

Inclusive Preschool

"J Preschool" was founded in 1979 to practice the 3 Cs philosophy: Christian education, cooperative education, and creative education. It now has 168 students, divided into six classes. Each class includes a child with a disability. Six early childhood education teachers and two early childhood special education teachers work together to support the children's growth and development. For the children with special needs, teachers work cooperatively to apply various educational strategies, including developing and implementing IEPs, writing or accommodating individual/group lesson plans, and sharing their specific expertise. Various programs for children, teachers, and parents have been developed to improve the outcomes of inclusion.

Children Some programs facilitate relationships between young children with disabilities and their peers. One facet is having early childhood special educators teach periodically to help children to accept peers with disabilities. Another example is the picture exhibition ("First secret! Hidden camera"). Teachers use a hidden camera to take pictures of children helping or playing with peers with disabilities, then exhibit the photos on a school bulletin board. The children in the picture get a surprise reward for their exemplary behavior. In the vacation program ("I and my friends"), teachers facilitate social interaction between children with disabilities and their peers while they are playing together at swimming pools or amusement parks during school holidays.

Early Childhood Education Teachers Early childhood education teachers meet students with disabilities and their parents before the semester begins. This helps the teachers understand the needs of the children and their parents. Through in-service training programs, teachers are provided with information to understand children and their disabilities, as well as instructional strategies to teach them appropriately.

Parents   During an orientation at the beginning of the school year, parents of children with and without disabilities are provided with information about the school's educational philosophy and inclusion programs. Parent education is also a component. Parents are provided with information individually, according to their needs for caring for and educating their children more effectively throughout the academic year. Also, they are trained to work with children in the classroom as assistant teachers if desired.

Children's House

"G Children's House" was founded in 1992. The first facility in the country to successfully include children with disabilities, it received an award from the Samsung Welfare Foundation in 1993 and was also commended by the Seoul city government in 1994 for its inclusion program. The goal of G Children's House is to provide child care for children from low-income families whose parents both work. Children between 3 months and 5 years are enrolled. There are 252 children in 7 classes for toddlers and 5 classes for preschoolers, including 42 children with disabilities. G Children's House has 46 employees, including 35 teachers who have had special training and have acquired degrees in various fields, such as early childhood education, special education, social work, day care, nursing, dietetics, art education, and physical education. Descriptions of its programs for children, teachers, and parents follow.

Children   The children's house emphasizes a total-development education according to each child's development, individualized special education plans for children with disabilities, a program encouraging all children to get along with each other regardless of whether they have disabilities, a nutrition program also providing vaccination and safety-awareness training, and physical education.

Teachers   All teachers participate in 30–60 hours of in-service training programs each year. The training is designed to maximize the effectiveness of education by helping teachers strengthen their professional knowledge and enhance positive attitudes, creative thinking, and self-determination. The training also includes approaches that support successful inclusion.

Parents   G Children's House also has programs for parents that encourage their participation in the educational process and strengthen family functioning. The programs include parent orientation, parent education through parent effectiveness training, counseling and conferences, and workshops. Parents also participate in their children's education through various activities such as serving as teacher aides. Parents of children with disabilities usually find these activities very helpful. Also, parents of children without disabilities are encouraged to participate in the program to understand children with disabilities and their families.

Barriers to Inclusive Practice

Inclusion of young children with disabilities in general education environments is a feature of early intervention that exemplifies services in Korea. However, the success of inclusion depends on various elements, one of the most important being the quality of services provided by early childhood education and early childhood special education teachers. Co-teaching, the most widely used inclusion model (Lipsky & Gartner, 1997), is a critical factor influencing the quality of inclusion programs. In other words, a general early childhood education teacher and an early childhood special education teacher are partners, sharing a physical environment and responsibility for planning, arranging, and evaluating learning experiences (Friend & Cook, 1996; Pugach & Johnson, 1995). In Korea, however, teachers are prepared for their own field, with little preparation for collaboration with teachers from the other field. For example, college students in early childhood education programs are well trained to become good early childhood education teachers. Yet, most of them do not learn about children with disabilities, including how to teach them or how to cooperate with special education teachers. Students in the special education field receive too little training for working with early childhood educators. They do not learn how to work as a team member or to share roles and responsibilities for developing and meeting educational goals of children with disabilities in inclusive environments. Consequently, the responsibility for education of children with disabilities is usually placed on special education teachers, and sometimes children with disabilities are separated from the general education class activities to spend time with special education teachers. This separate instruction may minimize some of the outcomes sought for children with disabilities in these inclusive environments (e.g., development of social skills). To overcome this problem, preservice and in-service professional development should include information about how teachers from each field can collaborate with each other and use each others' expertise.

Another barrier to community-based inclusion occurs in the children's houses. Most of the inclusive children's houses have difficulty finding special education teachers. This is due partially to the division of responsibility for children's education between the Ministry of Education and Human Resources and the Ministry of Health and Welfare. These two ministries do not have joint policies. Because teacher certification and teaching career records are issued and managed by the Ministry of Education and Human Resources and children's houses are governed and supported by the Ministry of Health and Welfare, teaching at a children's house is not counted as an official teaching career. As a result, teachers who have a special education teacher certification and need an official teaching career record for promotions avoid working at children's houses. As it is difficult to find teachers with special education teacher certification, professionals from other disciplines, such as psychology, social work, or early childhood education, take the role of early childhood special education teacher. The professional role of early childhood special education teachers in developing, adapting, and implementing IEPs, as well as their relationship to other members in inclusive environments, is crucial to the success of education programs for children with disabilities. To solve this problem, it is important for the two different divisions responsible for child education, the Ministry of Education and Human Resources and the Ministry of Health and Welfare, to work together developing and implementing policy.

Finally, access to inclusive community-based programs may be a problem. Many parents want their children with disabilities in the community-based inclusive programs, but there are not enough vacancies. Especially in programs known for their high quality of inclusive education, competition for enrollment is very high. Parents of children with disabilities have become more active in searching for and finding good programs for their children. Most Koreans now accept the notion that inclusion is beneficial to young children with disabilities. The next step is to increase the number of inclusive programs to fulfill the demands of parents and their children with disabilities. However, there are barriers to increasing the number of inclusive programs: the difficulty in hiring early childhood special education teachers, administrative complications, and unwillingness by some staff and administrators to include children with disabilities in general education preschools.

Lessons Learned

Several lessons have been learned from the practice of community-based inclusion in Korea. Implications from these lessons are described in terms of three factors: 1) feasibility of inclusion, 2) incentive for inclusion, and 3) quality of inclusion.

First, the feasibility of inclusion is verified through the previously described programs. The efficacy of early intervention and early childhood special education, including the practice of inclusion, is reasonably well established in research (Richey & Wheeler, 2000). Experience with community-based inclusion in South Korea has shown that existing preschool or child care programs can include children with disabilities. Early childhood programs exist in most communities. They differ in size, location, school time, and funding. However, they share the common goal of providing qualified learning environments for all young children. Despite the barriers mentioned previously, the widespread availability of these early childhood programs make inclusion for young children with disabilities feasible.

Second, an incentive to start inclusive programs, provided by the government through financial support, has played a very important role in increasing the number of inclusive preschools and child care centers. Generally, education for children with disabilities requires more intensive intervention (e.g., a smaller student–teacher ratio, increased teacher-mediated instruction) than education for children without disabilities. Hiring a special education teacher for a small number of children can be a fiscal burden to the program and its administrator. However, this burden can be cleared through financial support by the government, which provides funding for the teacher's salary and operating money for the class if more than three (at a children's house) or six (at a preschool) children with disabilities are enrolled. Financial incentives have played the largest role in increasing the number of inclusive programs in South Korea. However, South Korea needs to go forward in strengthening the legal base for inclusion.

Finally, of the many preschools and child care centers in South Korea, some are already inclusive while others object to inclusion. The most important lesson learned from existing inclusive early childhood education is not whether the program is inclusive but whether effort is put into meeting the needs of children with disabilities and their families. Inclusion is influenced by a dynamic set of factors operating inside and outside of the classroom (Odom et al., 1997). To control program quality, it is important to know the elements influencing the quality of programs and how they are related to each other or to program outcomes. It also means that inclusion cannot be successful without continuous efforts to identify and apply those elements. For example, one study has found a significant relationship between the co-teacher and the quality of the environment (McCormick, Noonan, Ogata, & Heck, 2001). Another study, conducted in a children's house in Seoul, has shown that systematic application of the Activity-based Inclusive Preschool Curriculum (AIPC; Lee & Park, 2001a) increased the social interaction of children with disabilities and decreased negative behavior and isolation during free play (Lee & Park, 2001b). The results also indicated that without well-planned systematic help to promote social interaction, meaningful social integration may not occur for children with disabilities in inclusive environments. In sum, achieving goals for children with disabilities should be the most important goal in inclusive programs, and every research and practice effort should be made to meet this goal.

RECOMMENDATIONS FOR PROFESSIONALS IN OTHER COUNTRIES

Based on the successes and problems observed as well as lessons learned in Korea, there are several recommendations for professionals in other countries regarding community-based inclusion. First, some government incentives may be necessary for existing preschool or child care centers to include children with disabilities. All preschool or child care programs can become inclusive programs, but such financial support may be required for them to do so. Second, program access to qualified special education teachers is essential and may be one of the most important elements for successful inclusion. Administrative systems and supports may needed to be made to ensure an adequate supply of teachers. Third, to assist early childhood education teachers and early childhood special education teachers in collaborating as a team, preservice and in-service professional development should emphasize team building. Fourth, for community-based inclusion programs to be successful, every effort in research and practice must be made to identify and achieve the developmental and learning goals of children with disabilities. Fifth, a sufficient number of early childhood programs should be available so that any child with a disability can enroll in a program in his or her community. In that case, the programs can be considered real community-based inclusion.

CONCLUSION

Across countries, early intervention programs share an important common goal: facilitate the development and learning of young children with disabilities and children at risk for disabilities. The nature and manner of delivering early intervention services in South Korea may differ from those of other countries, but this may be simply another way of meeting the same goal. In South Korea, attitudes toward individuals with disabilities have been changing. Partly as a result, community-based inclusion in early childhood programs has been developing and expanding in South Korea. In addition to adopting the theories and practices of other countries, South Korea has developed its own unique way of delivering services. Although the approaches have developed uniquely in a Korean context, they are also similar to approaches developed in other countries. By sharing information about successes as well as barriers, it is possible that teachers from South Korea and other countries who are implementing community-based inclusion may learn from one another.

REFERENCES

Amendments to the Promotion Law for Special Education (PLSE). (1994).

Bayley, N. (1969). Behavioral correlates of mental growth: Birth to thirty-six years. *American Psychology, 23,* 1–7.

Bluma, S.M., Shearer, M.S., Frohman, A., & Hilliard, J. (1976). *Portage Guide to Early Education: Checklist, Curriculum and Card File.* Portage, WI: Cooperative Educational Service Agency.

Bronfenbrenner, U. (1974). *Is early intervention effective?* Washington, DC: Department of Health, Education, and Welfare, Office of Child Development.

Friend, M., & Cook, L. (1996). *Interactions: Collaboration skills for school professionals* (2nd ed.). New York: Longman Publishing.

Gabarino, J. (1990). The human ecology of early risk. In S.J. Meisels & J.P. Shonkoff (Eds.), *Handbook of early childhood intervention* (pp. 78–96). New York: Cambridge University Press.

Gesell, A., & Amatruda, C.S. (1947). *Developmental diagnosis.* New York: Harper & Row.

Johnson-Martin, N.M., Attermeier, S.M., & Hacker, B.J. (1990). *The Carolina Curriculum for Preschoolers with Special Needs.* Baltimore: Paul H. Brookes Publishing Co.

Lee, S., & Park, E. (2001a). *Activity-based Inclusive Preschool Curriculum (AIPC).* Seoul, Korea: Hakjisa.

Lee, S., & Park, E. (2001b, November). *Effects of Activity-based Inclusive Preschool Curriculum (AIPC) on social integration of Korean young children with disabilities.* Poster session presented at the 2001 TASH annual conference, Anaheim, CA.

Lee, S., Park, S., & Kim, K. (2002). A national survey of early childhood special education programs on using assessment and curriculum. *Korean Journal of Special Education, 36*(4), 191–212.

Lipsky, D.K., & Gartner, A. (1997). *Inclusion and school reform: Transforming America's classrooms.* Baltimore: Paul H. Brookes Publishing Co.

McCormick, L., Noonan, M.J., Ogata, V., & Heck, R. (2001). Co-teacher relationship and program quality: Implications for preparing teachers for inclusive preschool settings. *Education and Training in Mental Retardation and Developmental Disabilities, 36,* 119–132.

Meisels, S.J., & Shonkoff, J.P. (Eds.). (1990). *Handbook of early childhood intervention.* New York: Cambridge University Press.

Odom, S.L., Peck, C.A., Hanson, M.J., Beckman, P.J., Kaiser, A.P., Lieber, J., Brown, W.H., Horn, E.M., & Schwartz, I.S. (1997). Inclusion at the preschool level: An ecological systems analysis. *SRCD Social Policy Report, 18–30.*

Piaget, J. (1971). *Biology and knowledge.* Chicago: University of Chicago Press.

Pugach, M.C., & Johnson, L.J. (1995). *Collaborative practitioners, collaborative schools.* Denver, CO: Love Publishing.

Richey, D.D., & Wheeler, J.J. (2000). *Inclusive early childhood education.* Albany, NY: Delmar.

Sameroff, A.J., & Fiese, B. (1990). Transactional regulations and early intervention. In S.J. Meisels & J.P. Shonkoff (Eds.), *Handbook of early childhood intervention* (pp. 119–149). New York: Cambridge University Press.

Skinner, B.F. (1953). *Science and human behavior.* New York: Macmillan.

Strain, P., McConnell, S., Carta, J., Fowler, S., Neisworth, J., & Wolery, M. (1992). Behaviorism in early intervention. *Topics in Early Childhood Special Education, 12*(1), 121–141.

Turnbull, A.P., & Turnbull, H.R. (1996). *Families, professionals, and exceptionality: A special partnership* (3rd ed.). Columbus, OH: Charles E Merrill.

CHAPTER 4

ISRAEL

A Mediational Approach to Early Intervention

Pnina S. Klein

Each child should be taught
in his own way so when he grows
up he will still find it acceptable.
(Proverbs 22:6)

This chapter describes a general approach to early intervention (rather than one specific program) that is applied in Israel in early care and education of very young children. This approach requires the construction of an individual profile representing the nature and quality of adult–child interactions, including a focus on characteristics of the child and his or her family, community, and culture. The objective of the intervention is to improve the quality of interactions and, consequently, to enhance the quality of parental or other caregiver mediation (teaching behavior) that can affect the child's flexibility of mind—that is, his or her ability to learn from new experiences.

 ## TALY'S STORY

Three-year-old Taly wandered around the room aimlessly, touching various objects or looking at them in a fleeting manner. Taly's father tried to play with her, as he was asked to do by the educational counselor. He pulled a book off the shelf, sat down on the carpet, and tried to seat Taly close to him, preparing to read to her. Taly had no intention of sitting, let alone listening to the story. Her father tried again to engage her, pulling out a basket with toys and dumping its contents on the floor. Taly moved closer to the objects, taking one toy after another and dropping them immediately. Her father offered a little ball; Taly took it but quickly lost interest. Taly kept looking around the room. She then came close to her father, pulled him toward the door, and mimed her wish to leave.

Her father said that this was typical of Taly's everyday behavior, except that at home she is hard to manage and has tantrums when she does not get what she wants. Taly's parents were primarily concerned about her poor language development. They were following the advice of Taly's pediatrician: Stimulate Taly by showing her many items such as concrete objects and toys or pictures in books.

The overall objective for Taly's intervention program was to help her develop a set of needs (i.e., the need to focus on things and perceive them clearly, to find the meaning of what is perceived, to link or

The research presented in this chapter has been supported in part by the World Health Organization (WHO); the United Nations Children's Fund (UNICEF); the United Nations Educational, Scientific, and Cultural Organization (UNESCO); NORAD; and Red Barna supporting the implementation of the Mediational Intervention for Sensitizing Caregivers (MISC) in Ethiopia, Sri Lanka, Indonesia, Norway, Sweden, the United States, and Israel. Preparation of this chapter was supported by the Machado Chair for Research on Cognitive Modifiability, Bar-Ilan University, Israel.

associate between things, to plan before doing, to finish tasks, and to experience success). The concept of need is essential for understanding the intervention. The objective of the Mediational Intervention for Sensitizing Caregivers (MISC) intervention is to affect a child's need system. All other objectives, including development of understanding or skills, are only secondary to the effect on the need system that will enable Taly to

- Learn from new experiences (i.e., be driven by the need to focus on things and see, hear, smell, taste, and feel them clearly; to assign significance to things; and to relate or associate things and obtain more information about them beyond what is perceived through the senses)
- Seek approval and experience success in meaningful social contexts
- Plan ahead to regulate her behavior to experience success in meaningful social contexts

This multifaceted objective was met through improving the quality of Taly's interaction with others, specifically through the quality of teaching behavior (mediation) she received.

Taly was videotaped while interacting with her parents at home during play and during other caregiving situations. In a series of meetings with Taly's parents, practitioners analyzed these videotapes. Profiles of mediation were constructed and shared with her parents along with information regarding Taly's general development (language, cognitive, emotional, and motor), likes and dislikes in relation to her sensory integration dysfunction, and temperament.

At each meeting with Taly's parents, the practitioners used the videotaped interactions to identify one or more basic criteria of a quality interaction with very young children. The meetings with Taly's parents began with the practitioners providing encouragement (mediating competence) regarding some components of the taped interactions with Taly (e.g., the parents' concern about her development, their efforts to focus her attention). Based on the videotaped sessions, instances in which Taly attended to or looked at something—even briefly—were noted and discussed in relation to the parental behavior preceding or following it. In future meetings with Taly and her parents, the focus shifted to combining developmental landmarks, child-specific characteristics and difficulties, and criteria of quality interaction and mediation. The practitioners continued encouraging Taly's parents to invest in the process of quality mediation (as opposed to fragmented stimulation). The intervention was based on the ongoing interaction processes with Taly in her natural environment. All adults interacting with Taly at home and at her child care program participated in the intervention.

Following eight meetings with Taly's parents and three meetings with the staff at Taly's child care program, significant changes were noted in Taly's interactions with her parents and with her child care providers and peers. Her parents and caregivers have learned to refrain from using fragmented stimulation and an over-didactic approach, which led to focusing Taly's attention repeatedly without actually making any use of the attention captured. Instead, they were following Taly's lead by choosing objects or activities that she selected, sustaining her attention, and prolonging episodes of joint attention by expressing affect and associating things with meaning (e.g., "Wow, what a beautiful bird"). Taly's social engagement, level of play, and interest in the world around her improved considerably, leading to significant developments in her communication and language skills. She is now well on her way to having skills that match those of typically developing children.

NATIONAL CONTEXT

Israel was established as a state in 1948 to serve as a homeland for the Jewish people. It is a small country, 22,145 square kilometers, with a population of 6 million people. Israel has a proportionally larger population of children than most Western countries. Based on a 2000 public census, there are 841,000 children younger than 6 years and a steady growth of approximately 127,000 new births each year. The vast majority of young children living in Israel were born there.

Since its inception, Israel has been considered a melting pot for immigrants from all over the world. Most immigrants came from Europe, Asia, and Africa, and some came from the United States and Canada. Starting in the 1990s, there have been significant waves of immigration from countries comprising the former Soviet Union and from Ethiopia. Despite the common denominator of being primarily Jewish, the immigrants differ considerably in physical appearance as well as cultural and educational backgrounds. Immigrants from African and Asian countries tend to have lower incomes and education levels than those of Western origin. They tend to live in poor neighborhoods; their children's school achievement is lower, with a higher rate of school drop out. Although the differences between the immigrants from the East and West have tended to decrease with time, as many people integrated into Israel's core culture, they have left behind their parents' cultural and religious values without replacing them with others. This frequently leads to breakage points in cultural transmission to the young.

As professionals attempt to assist the immigrant families in dealing with their new world, they also transmit the tacit message, "We are locals. Do as we tell you; we know better." When this type of message is conveyed in relation to child-rearing practices, it may have a devastating effect on parents, reducing their trust in their own ability to help their child grow and develop. This perceived inability may be amplified when a child has a disability. Early intervention programs, such as the model described later in this chapter, have been developed to assist parents with concerns they may have about their child and to introduce ways in which they may promote their child's development without the use of structured materials or games imposed by "outsiders."

Education Services System

The Israeli educational system was established approximately 50 years prior to the establishment of the Independent State of Israel. In 1949, a compulsory education law was passed, committing the state and requiring parents to ensure that each child between 4 and 15 years attends school, free of charge. The compulsory education law was modified to include 3-year-olds; however, it is not yet nationally implemented.

The objectives of early childhood education in Israel, as proclaimed by the Ministry of Education, are "to ensure that all children are provided with the necessary conditions and opportunities for effective functioning and personal achievement." The public education system includes two main subsystems, Jewish and Arabic. Each system has its own curriculum and institutions that are analogous to each other but differ in language and culture. The Jewish educational system is further divided, based on religious observance, into Secular, Religious, and Independent (Ultra Orthodox) systems. These separate systems enable each sector to be independent, to use its language, and to practice its own culture; however, it also exacerbates disparities in educational attainment levels and may perpetuate social gaps between these groups. There are 8,300 kindergartens (not including the Ultra Orthodox ones) in Israel. The Ministry of Education supervises all educational programs for all children age 3 and older.

The Board of Education offers several programs for children between birth and 3 years. These programs—designed for people who are at risk (primarily very poor families)—are operated at children's homes, health centers, or community centers. They are designed to encourage parental involvement and quality interactions with their children. They attempt to enhance parental skills, general child development, and school readiness. Afternoon programs are offered either by the local authorities and the Ministry of Education, community centers, or the national women's organizations. Parents pay for these programs.

Child Care for Infants and Toddlers

Infants and toddlers are cared for either in child care centers, in family care units (child care provided to a group of four to six children in a private home), or by relatives or other caregivers at home. The child care centers are funded and supervised by the major women's organizations in the country and supported by the Ministry of Labor and Welfare. They are operated by a number of women's organizations. These programs usually operate 8 hours per day, 6 days per week. The objectives of the child care centers and the family care centers are nurturing general well-being, promoting and facilitating mothers' employment, and providing educational enrichment. Child care programs have gone through extensive changes caused by intensive preservice training of caregivers and in-service supervision.

Family child care programs for children ages from 3 months to 3 years are supervised by the Ministry of Labor and Welfare and are sponsored either by the local community center or by the local welfare department. This type of program is operated by one caregiver providing care and education to as many as six infants and toddlers in her home. The objective of family child care is to provide more individualized, developmentally appropriate care for infants and toddlers. Compared with Jewish children, a relatively higher percentage of Arab children attend family child care programs rather than child care centers. Many private caregivers are not licensed. This type of service is fairly common for children in their first and second years of life.

There is still much to be desired in the quality of care provided to Israel's very young children. The major difficulty appears to be reduced sensitivity and responsivity to each child's needs, which is primarily due to the relatively large child–caregiver ratio. In addition, several problems related to the quality of infant child care in Israel result from caregivers' difficulties in "translating" available knowledge into caregiving practices.

Nursery School and Kindergarten

The term *nursery school* refers to the care provided to children 3–4 years old. Then, children attend kindergarten through age 6. The attendance rate of Arab children in nursery schools and kindergartens is lower than that of Jewish children; however, it has increased since 1980. In 1992, the Ministry of Education began operating a special program to further promote education of Arab children (including the Druze sector, which is a Muslim sect living primarily in Lebanon, Southern Syria, and Northern Israel). The program includes adding classroom instruction hours, teacher training, and development of curriculum and textbooks.

Kindergartens in Israel are supervised by the division of Pre-primary Education of the Ministry of Education. The primary objective of kindergartens is to ensure the optimal growth and development of each child, with a special focus on individual differences as reflected by the cultural proverb "each child should be taught in his own way." One of the primary objectives of the kindergarten is to prepare children for formal school learning. To reach this objective, the Ministry of Education has defined guidelines for teachers of very young children in all kindergartens: Arab, Druze, secular, and religious.

The Ministry of Health is responsible for the education of children with physical or developmental disabilities up to the age of 3 years. The policy of the Ministry of Education for children with disabilities 3–6 years old is to include them into the regular kindergartens and support their program with a few hours of special services provided weekly within the regular educational framework.

KEY FEATURES OF EARLY INTERVENTION

Within the framework of the Jewish culture and the State of Israel, children are viewed as the main natural resource, and there is no question as to the centrality of the child in governmental decision-making processes. In Israel, there is no lack of early childhood intervention programs. To the contrary, there has been a proliferation of early intervention programs, which are implemented for short periods of time only to be replaced by others. The diversity in intervention programs may be related to the reality represented by a common statement in Israel, "If you ask three Israelis the same question, you will get seven different answers." Most intervention programs involve structured exercises or instructions for parents to do things with their children in a specific way and with designated toys. These programs may encourage parents to depend on specific toys or materials without learning how to generalize activities as the child grows older.

The Mediational Intervention for Sensitizing Caregivers

The objective of the Mediational Intervention for Sensitizing Caregivers (MISC) model is to support the development of More Intelligent and Sensitive Children (also MISC) through mediated learning—that is, learning that occurs in the presence of an adult who tries to mediate between the child and his or her environment to ensure that learning takes place. *Intelligence* is defined as the ability and need to learn readily and easily from one's experiences. The MISC model is the process through which this goal is achieved.

The MISC, a developmental mediation approach, is an integration of three major theoretical frameworks. Ecocultural theory highlights caregivers' objectives of child rearing, their long-term educational view of goals, and their perceptions of an ideal child and parent. The MISC approach introduces the necessity of clarifying the basic ethnocultural and ecological environment in which children are raised and matching them with the objectives of the intervention prior to designing any educational program (Hundeide, 1996; Klein, 1996). Developmental theory suggests that a match between adults' mediational behaviors and individual children's developmental needs is essential (Greenspan & Wieder, 1998; Klein, Wieder, & Greenspan, 1987). It begins by meeting the emotional need of a young child for a stable, affectionate relationship with one caregiver. Mediated learning theory, drawn from the work of Feuerstein (1979, 1980) and Vygotsky (1978), proposes that several basic characteristics of adult behavior are necessary to create experiences of mediated learning for young children. These mediational behaviors include

- *Focusing*—attempting to catch a child's attention or join the child and relate to that to which he or she attends

- *Exciting*—mediating meaning to raise the child's awareness of the affect or significance associated with objects, people, and actions in the environment

- *Expanding*—transcending (verbally or nonverbally) the concrete, immediate context of the interaction

- *Encouraging*—supporting and expressing the child's feelings of competence in a manner that is most appropriate for him or her

- *Organizing and planning*—regulating behavior to promote planning behaviors, including the considerations that precede actions, as well as actually demonstrating to a child how to do things

Empirical evidence (Klein, 1996; Klein & Alony, 1993; Tzuriel, 1999) suggests that these experiences may promote the chances for cognitive and emotional development of young children. See Table 4.1 for more information about these aspects of the MISC approach.

Children Who Could Potentially Benefit from the Mediational Intervention for Sensitizing Caregivers

In line with Feuerstein's (1980) Theory of Cognitive Modifiability, much of children's capacity to benefit from new experiences is linked to the type of interactions they have with adult caregivers. These differences are apparent in the way that children approach new experiences, integrate them with other experiences, and express themselves. Children deprived of mediation, regardless of their disability or special need, lack the desire to explore their environment, to search for meaning, to make connections between their experiences, and to seek "newness" and novelty. They are less inclined than other children to seek adults' assistance. These children experience their world in an isolated, fragmented manner that limits their capacity to benefit from future experiences. Feuerstein (1979, 1980) identified these characteristics as emerging from deficient cognitive processes that are related to poor mediation experiences. Children who have these limitations may be considered as lacking cognitive flexibility or having difficulties in benefiting from new experiences.

Learning Difficulties of Children Who Have Not Received Sufficient Mediational Experiences

The MISC has been used with children at risk due to poverty and neglect, as well as with special needs children, including children born at a very low birth weight (VLBW) (Klein, 1991; Klein, Raziel, Brish, & Birenbaum, 1987); children with Down syndrome; very young gifted children (Klein, 1996; Klein & Tannenbaum, 1992); and, more recently, children with sensory integration and communication difficulties.

Table 4.1. The Mediational Intervention for Sensitizing Caregivers (MISC) program: Intellectual and socioemotional needs developed following mediation

Mediation process	Examples of the process	Intellectual needs	Socioemotional needs
Focusing (intentionality and reciprocity)	Make the environmental stimuli compatible to the child's needs (e.g., bring closer; eliminate distractions; use repetition, sequencing, and grouping; help the child focus, see, hear, and feel clearly)	Need for precision in perception (versus scanning exploration) Need for precision in expression	Need to focus on and decode facial and bodily expressions of emotion Need to modify one's behavior or the environment to mediate to others (to make the other person see or understand)
Exciting (meaning) *Note:* Unlike the other mediational processes, Exciting does not have two needs columns, as there is no difference between needs in this context.	Express excitement (verbally or nonverbally) about experiences, objects, people, and so forth Name, identify	Need to search for meaningful new experiences that remind one of meaningful experiences in the past or of future expectations Relating to people, things, or events in a way that conveys meaning and excitement (sound, look, and feel excited) Need to invest energy in meaningful activities	
Expanding (transcendence)	Explain, elaborate, and associate between things; raise awareness to metacognitive aspects of thinking Relate past, present, and future experiences Relate to physical, logical, or social rules and frameworks	Need to go beyond what meets the senses, to seek further information through exploration Need to request information from other people and other sources Need to seek generalizations Need to link, associate, and recall past information and to anticipate future experiences	Need to think about one's own feelings and the feelings of others Need for cause-and-effect sequences in social interactions Need to associate experiences, recall past information, and anticipate future experiences

Mediation process	Examples of the process	Intellectual needs	Socioemotional needs
Encouraging and providing feelings of competence	Praise in a way that is meaningful to the child	Need to seek more successful experiences	Need to please others and gain more mediated feelings of competence
	Identify the reasons for success	Need to summarize one's own activities and determine what led to success	Need to identify what pleases different people
	Act in a manner that is well timed in relation to the experience		Need to provide others with mediated feelings of competence
Organizing and planning (regulation of behavior)	Provide regulation with regard to speed, precision, force, and a sequence of activity leading to successful completion of a given task	Need to plan before acting (e.g., consider possible solutions prior to responding)	Need to control one's impulses in social situations
		Need to clarify goals and meet subgoals	Need to learn acceptable ways of expressing one's emotions (e.g., regulate the pace and intensity of one's social responses to anger and joy)
		Need to pace one's activities	
		Need to regulate the level of energy invested in any given task	

Based on all of the research carried out on the subject (see particularly Klein, 1996; Klein & Alony, 1993; Klein & Rosental, 1999), two general patterns of parental mediation have been identified as not contributing to or potentially even harming children's development. One is related to parental lack of the motivation, energy, and positive affect needed for mediation. This results in low frequencies of all mediational behaviors. The other pattern is being overly motivated to mediate, which is characterized by the disproportionately high frequencies of focusing behaviors unmatched by high frequencies of other mediational behaviors (i.e., affecting, expanding, encouraging, and regulating behavior). It is as though these parents are energized to act in order to support their child's development. However, the parents do not know how to provide mediation that allows their children to focus on objects or people in their environment to obtain meaningful, expanded experiences and be successful. In their work with parents of low birth weight infants, Klein, Raziel, and colleagues found that even brief MISC interventions led to significant improvement in parental mediation and, consequently, to the enhancement of children's cognitive performance.

Analytic and Holistic
Styles of Mediation Across Cultures

Cross-cultural studies have contributed significantly to the identification of various styles of mediation and their effects on children. Most modern, Western, early intervention programs typically focus on specific skills; abilities or disabilities; and ways to train, exercise, or promote individual skills. These programs rarely touch the wider circles of the cultural meaning of life, the nature of values, parental philosophy of education, and parental perceptions of the ideal child or parent. Identifying and using this information in the intervention may improve both parental cooperation and the chance for long-term maintenance of intervention effects.

Understanding the meaning, values, and commitment level of parents and caregivers plays a key organizing role in early interventions. Based on research carried out in Israel, Europe, Africa, and the United States, Klein (1996) found two major styles of mediation: analytic and holistic. Analytic mediation is typically found in adult–child interactions in the so-called Western world. It includes the mediational sequence of focusing, affecting, and expanding, with various forms of encouraging and regulating behavior (e.g., "Look, look at this flower; it is a rose. Smell it; it smells nice."). The components within this group differ in frequency and form, but they are generally based on isolating fragments of the environment and focusing the child's attention on them.

Holistic mediation is typically found in non-Western, more traditional societies. Unlike the analytic style, it is not based on fragmenting experiences into small components and teaching them sequentially. Rather, it gives the child experiences that have cultural significance and are directly related to meaningful events in the life of the child and his or her family. For example, mediation occurs through repeated storytelling and dramatization of events related to the child's life. These may not necessarily pass the test of science or be true, but they help many children know their environment, as well as how to do things and why.

Features of Using the Mediational
Intervention for Sensitizing Caregivers in the Home

The MISC in Israel is carried out through Mother Infant Health Care Centers, child care centers, and kindergartens, as well as through the preservice training of child care workers, kindergarten teachers, and primary school teachers. The essence of this approach is sensitization and increased consciousness regarding key issues in the caregiver–child relationship. The objective of the MISC is to promote a sound, facilitative adult–child relationship as a means of enhancing the child's potential for learning. The program can be implemented with most children in a variety of contexts, from nursery schools and preschools to large-scale community-based projects involving professionals or resource individuals who conduct "home training" with parents. A successful application of mediation occurred in a kindergarten computer learning environment (Klein & Nir-Gal, 1992; Klein, Nir-Gal, & Darom, 2000). This chapter focuses on using the MISC with parents in the home.

The MISC project includes structured and unstructured components. The structured component relates to the training of the mediators who are expected to carry out the intervention. The unstructured component is related to the cultural interpretations of the objectives and the content through which the criteria of mediation are introduced and demonstrated in the home.

When the MISC is carried out at home, mediators are home visitors. Mediators must have a basic knowledge of general principles and milestones of child development, an appreciation of individual differences in development, and a deep understanding of the cultural and socioeconomic realities of a particular context. They should be capable of forming an empathic relationship with the mother or caregivers and function in an accepting nonauthoritative manner. They are expected to encourage rather than criticize or evaluate and to convey enthusiasm and hope regarding the role of the parent or caregiver in promoting child development.

It does not matter whether a child learns to associate meaning with one object or another as long as experiences are associated with meaning. Because the criteria of mediation are not highly culture or content specific, criteria may be demonstrated across families in relation to different cultural experiences, objects, or people.

Process of Using the Mediational Intervention for Sensitizing Caregivers at Home

The basic process for implementing the MISC in the home consists of several key features, which are detailed in the following subsections.

Conduct an Initial Visit   Home visits are conducted for every participating family prior to the program's onset. During these visits, mother–child interactions during feeding, bathing, and play are observed and videotaped (in most homes, the mother is the primary caregiver during early infancy). The mother is interviewed to assess her attitude toward the child, educational philosophy, and objectives of child rearing, as well as to obtain an overview of the child's daily routine. Based on the observations and interview, the home visitor constructs a typical profile of the mediation provided to the child. If possible, the type of mediation provided by each family member is described. In addition, a general outline of the plan of intervention is then drawn up.

Choose the Form of the Intervention Plan   In some families, the primary emphasis of the intervention may be to establish a positive cycle of expressive adult–child interaction. Such a relationship is necessary to form a sound basis for mutual acceptance and an affective bond between the adult caregiver and the child. This type of intervention is required to establish intentionality and reciprocity in adult–child relationships.

Mediate Feelings of Competence   With every family, the home visitor begins the intervention by mediating feelings of competence to the mother. This is done regarding the behaviors that she mediated most successfully to her child and for which she demonstrated the highest frequency of mediation criteria (as determined in the initial observation). That specific criterion is brought to the mother's attention and clarified using a technique that is described later in this discussion. Then, the mediator helps the mother find additional ways to demonstrate it in everyday life. The sequence in which the criteria are presented depends on the mother's strengths and weaknesses in mediation and always starts with her relative strengths to ensure that competence is mediated to her.

Review the Previous Session   Every session begins with a review of the mediation criteria and examples that were presented at the previous meeting, and it ends with a summary of mediational behaviors presented in the current session. Each family participating in the program is visited periodically (once per week or less frequently, as needed) by its assigned mediator. Each mediator reviews the session with an instructor (supervisor) and prepares a summary of the session as well as objectives and plans for the next session.

Conduct Parent Meetings   General meetings are held monthly or bimonthly for all participating parents. During these meetings, parents are asked to analyze videotaped mother–child interactions and to suggest alternative ways of mediating.

Suggested Practices for Home Visits

When using the MISC model in the home, mediators have followed several useful practices. These may differ from family to family, so the information that follows is for illustrative purposes only.

Parent guidance is most efficient when mother–child interactions are videotaped and the mother views the tapes with the mediator. Each basic criterion of mediation is used in the mother–mediator interaction, and the mother is helped to identify those criteria.

Mediating the criteria to caregivers (usually mothers) is focused on everyday situations. Following the initial stage, the criteria are identified as they appear in home routines and expanded to demonstrate other possible ways to generalize the interactions. For example, a mediator may say, "Your mother-in-law comes to visit, and you have put effort into cleaning the house, cooking a good meal, and washing and dressing the children. Your mother-in-law does not say anything. After all the work that you have done, you receive no mediated feelings of competence. How do you feel? There are other possibilities: Your mother-in-law says, 'Thank you; I enjoyed my visit,' or 'Thank you; I love to see you and the children looking so nice.' Both possibilities provide you with feelings of competence; it does feel good to hear good things said about yourself. However, only the second possibility is specific enough to provide input for the next visit. In other words, if your mother-in-law enjoyed seeing you and the children look nice, perhaps it is not necessary to put as much effort into cleaning the house or cooking."

Next, the same criteria are discussed as they appear in adult–child interactions. For example, a mediator may say, "When your child scribbles on a piece of paper and brings it to you, don't ignore the action. Provide mediation of competence. Tell her that the drawing is beautiful and why you think so (provided that you want her to do even better next time). You might say, 'It is very nice. I see that you have used many colors' (or 'you have filled the entire page'). Your comments depend on what you consider a desirable goal in your child's development and future behavior." It is easier for mothers to identify with and remember the criteria of mediation as they are represented in their lives and only later to view these regarding their own interactions with their children. It has also been found that mothers develop the ability to use the mediation criteria to evaluate the ongoing mediation among different family members and the child as well as between child care workers or teachers and their child.

Role playing is helpful, such as mediating to the mother the possibility of understanding the child's behavior if placed in his or her position. The mediator might say, "Suppose that you are the child. The entire family is in the living room, and you are taken away to a dark room and asked to go to sleep. How do you feel?" To help the mother realize how the child feels, it is sometimes necessary to role-play with her as the mother and with the mediator as the child. In the role of the child, the mediator can verbalize how the child might feel, helping the mother gain insight into her child's behavior. This procedure is primarily helpful when mothers believe that negative intentions underlie their child's behavior.

Sharing is the verbal or nonverbal demonstration of the thinking processes, overt behavior sequences, or methods that one uses in different situations (e.g., "When I look at this kind of question, I feel confused. So I ask myself . . . first and then . . . "). Sharing is primarily useful for focusing mothers' attention on their own feelings, causes, and consequences. Through this process, one can share "cultural wisdom" in the form of folk sayings, stories, efficient strategies for communication, expressions of affect, or information about cognitive processes such as memory, planning, or evaluation. For instance, the mediator might say, "When I want to remember something, I try to see it clearly and vividly in my mind, in full detail and in the funniest way. That helps me remember it later."

Stories, nursery rhymes, songs, dance, and music that are typical to a culture may be used to improve mediation to young children. Mothers are encouraged to tell stories or to sing and dance with their children, and mediators help them identify elements of quality mediation within such interactions.

Affecting Caregivers' Perceptions of and Attitudes Toward the Child

Parents' normative conceptualizations of their children are part of a cultural tradition and practice and need to be respected. In fact, it is impossible to expect long-term sustainable intervention effects if practitioners do not work within these cultural norms. Still, it can be assumed that there are certain universal conceptions, feelings, and attitudes in the caregiver–child relationship that are crucial for optimal child development in any culture. Examples of these basic attitudes and feelings are "I gave birth to a wonderful human being," "I am very important to my child, who loves and needs me," and "I can help my child develop physically and cognitively." The following paragraphs discuss activities that home visitors from the MISC program have used to foster caregivers' positive perceptions.

Compliment the parent on his or her child (*parent* is used because the objective of the intervention is to invite all family members to interact with the child), pointing out special features such as beautiful and lively eyes, shiny hair, soft skin, delicate hands, and so forth. In some cultures, however, compliments should be given carefully. In Ethiopia, for example, compliments are considered dangerous because they may elicit jealousy and the "evil eye." In addition, praise is viewed as unnatural in an authority-based adult–child interaction. Thus, when working with Ethiopians in Israel, special care must be given to avoid mediating competence in the presence of strangers.

Indicate positively any physical appearance similarities between the child and the parent. If the parent has photos of the baby, these also may be used to enhance positive feelings for the child and to demonstrate how much the child has grown since the picture was taken. While doing so, it is important to stress the parent's role (e.g., "You are a good mother—see how well he is developing").

Provide parents with basic information about the sequential development of children in various areas so they are aware of and can enjoy even small steps in their child's development. Avoid overwhelming parents with information by being aware of which areas of child development they consider important. Relate primarily to these areas.

Demonstrate to the parent that the infant responds to him or her more than to anybody else. For example, let the mother call the baby, and point out the response. Ask the mother if her child would go to anyone else while she is holding him or her. Again, stress the special relationship between the two. Also point out the positive qualities that may be found in the parents' existing child-rearing practice and interactions with their child.

Establishing a Positive Cycle of Early Caregiver–Child Interaction

Establishing a cycle of positive expressive interaction is a necessary condition for mediation. It is important for an infant to learn that the world around him or her is predictable and responsive to his or her signals of distress as well as to behaviors expressing positive excitement (i.e., vocalization, facial expressions, and other bodily signals). The infant needs to learn that it is worthwhile "to do something," or to be active rather than to be passive, frightened, uninterested (not initiating any behaviors indicating interest), or apathetic (not responding to any attempt to catch the child's attention)—all of which are behaviors found in children who lacked responsive human contact in infancy. Most infants are equipped to learn the basic signs for human interaction, but they need mediated learning experience to further develop these communicative skills and attach meaning to such communication.

Sample Activities for Establishing a Positive Cycle of Interaction
To establish a communicative cycle with an infant or an adult, it is necessary to interpret a partner's behavior as intentional—namely, expressing the wishes, needs, and ideas of the communicative partner—rather than accepting it as accidental. Awareness of the child's intentions is an important trigger of the adult's interactive behavior, thereby determining the quality of interaction with that child.

One of the best ways for a caregiver to start such a cycle of expressive communication with an infant is to assume that the baby is intentionally expressing a message through his or her gestures and that he or she somehow understands sensitively adjusted replies from the caregiver. Such an interpretive attitude, which is intuitive for many mothers, makes communication with a baby natural and easy.

Parents are encouraged to ask questions such as "What is your child doing now?" "What is he trying to tell you?" and "What are his initiatives?" Infants want to experience human warmth and closeness to a loving person and to receive confirmation of this contact through the adult's expressive behavior. Mediators help parents identify the specific message that their child may be trying to convey at any particular moment.

In addition, parents are encouraged to respond to their child's initiatives with particular behaviors. One is to maintain eye contact with the baby, smile at him or her, and respond to his or her behavior with movements and vocalizations (e.g., pat the child, imitate the sounds that he or she makes). Another is to reflect the child's behavior in a positive, confirming, and reassuring way. It is suggested that while interacting vocally or otherwise, parents tune in and "dance in rhythm through turn taking" (once the child has a turn, then the parent takes a turn, following the child's initiative). It is also recommended that parents express their happiness and excitement in being with the child, responding to him or her by making happy faces or sounds. It should be noted, however, that these examples relate to the establishment of a positive communication cycle and are not sufficient for quality mediation. The latter includes the additional elements of exciting, conveying meaning, expanding, associating, encouraging, and regulating behavior.

Terminating the Intervention

The intervention is terminated when caregivers can explain in their own words the mediation criteria as well as demonstrate this understanding in their daily interactions with their children. In most of the participating families in Israel, mothers demonstrated a change in behavior toward their children before they could verbally explain what they were doing. This was confirmed in other countries as well. If the natural sequence is action before conceptualization, should one initially concentrate on modeling techniques rather than on explanations?

The basic idea behind the MISC intervention is not to teach mothers and educators specific behaviors but to help them identify behaviors existing within their own repertoire that may help their child develop. The objective is to overcome the difficulties of generalization and transfer that plague many educational programs. By clarifying to parents behaviors that are essential for a quality mediational interaction and by mediating competence to them, parents learn to use these behaviors more frequently and to internalize them as decontextualized knowledge that can be applied in many situations.

Parents not only use these behaviors more frequently, but also learn to match their own behaviors with signs of initiation or reciprocity from their child. Explaining, demonstrating, and focusing the child's attention may be a "wasted" educational experience or, worse, a disturbing experience if the child is uninterested, tired, or overexcited. Parents learn to act in synchrony with the child's behavior, which cannot be readily learned by repeating modeled behavior. It is learned through a process of developing insight about one's own behavior in relation to the child's. Parents first express this insight through improvements in mediation quality and only later through verbally expressed insights. The objective of the intervention is to reach this verbal stage and not to be satisfied with a change in behavior only. Caregivers who can verbalize clearly what constitutes quality mediation (independent of specific contexts) can be expected to use it in different situations as their child grows and encounters new experiences.

RECOMMENDATIONS FOR PROFESSIONALS IN OTHER COUNTRIES

The MISC has been adopted for use in a number of countries, including Norway, Sweden, Belgium, Holland, Ethiopia, Sri Lanka, Indonesia, and the United States (Klein, 1996). Cross-cultural adaptation of the program was possible because it is based on basic elements of adult–child interaction, which can be identified and enhanced in most interactions with young children anywhere. The mediation (teaching) behaviors identified and enhanced were not imported from outside the context of everyday life with the children at their homes. Rather, mediation behaviors were identified within the context and content of life within each family, community, and culture. Thus, the basic criteria of an adult's teaching behavior (focusing, affecting, expending, encouraging, and regulating behaviors), as well as behaviors leading to a positive affective communication, can be assessed. Consequently, they can be enhanced in any culture for the benefit of typically developing children as well as children who are at risk. In addition, the use of mediation behavior enhances potential learning in a computer environment in any country.

CONCLUSION

Infants and young children require adult mediation to develop the potential to benefit from new experiences. Various patterns of mediation are related to characteristic behaviors of infants and young

children, reflecting the needs to seek clarity in perception, search for
meaning, seek information beyond what is perceived directly through
the senses, link between experiences (i.e., make spontaneous associations), and experience success, especially in social contexts. Mediation
has been applied in a variety of educational programs for young children
in Israel.

Developmental mediation is suggested as a possible approach for
the identification of sensitive periods in adult–infant mediational interactions. Research confirms that it is possible to modify caregiver mediation and that this kind of intervention significantly affects the development of infants' and young children's learning. Specific patterns of
mediation may differ for children with certain disabilities. Being aware
of such patterns is essential for planning early intervention for young
children and their families.

REFERENCES

Feuerstein, R. (1979). *The dynamic assessment of retarded performers.* Baltimore:
University Park Press.
Feuerstein, R. (1980). *Instrumental enrichment: Redevelopment of cognitive functions
of retarded performers.* Baltimore: University Park Press.
Greenspan, S.I., & Wieder, S. (1998). *The child with special needs.* Reading, MA:
Addison-Wesley.
Hundeide, K. (1996). Facilitating cultural mediation: Indonesia. In P.S. Klein
(Ed.), *Early intervention: Cross-cultural experiences with mediational approach* (pp.
113–133). New York: Garland Publishing.
Klein, P.S. (1991). Improving the quality of parental interaction with very
low birth weight children: A longitudinal study using a mediated learning
experience model. *Infant Mental Health Journal, 12*(4), 321–337.
Klein, P.S. (1996). *Early intervention: Cross-cultural experiences with a mediational
approach.* New York: Garland Publishing.
Klein, P.S., & Alony, S. (1993). Immediate and sustained effects of maternal
mediation behaviors in infancy. *Journal of Early Intervention, 71*(2), 177–193.
Klein, P.S., & Nir-Gal, O. (1992). Effects of computerized mediation of analogi-
cal thinking in kindergartens. *Journal of Computer Assisted Learning, 8,* 224–
254.
Klein, P.S., Nir-Gal, O., & Darom, E. (2000). The use of computers in kindergarten, with and without adult mediation; effects on children's cognitive performance and behavior. *Computers in Human Behavior, 16,* 591–608.
Klein, P.S., Raziel, P., Brish, M., & Birenbaum, E. (1987). Cognitive performance
of a 3 year old born at very low birth weight. *Journal of Psychosomatic Obstetrics
and Gynecology, 7,* 117–129.

Klein, P.S., & Rosental, V. (1999). *Developmental mediation for children with special needs.* Paper presented at the biannual meeting of the International Association for Cognitive Education, Calgary, Alberta Canada.

Klein, P.S., & Tannenbaum, A.J. (1992). *To be young and gifted.* Westport, CT: Ablex Publishing.

Klein, P.S., Wieder, S., & Greenspan, S.L. (1987). A theoretical overview and empirical study of mediated learning experience: Prediction of preschool performance from mother-infant interaction patterns. *Infant Mental Health Journal, 8*(2), 110–129.

Tzuriel, D. (1999). Parent–child mediated learning interactions as determinants of cognitive modifiability: Recent research and future directions. *Genetic, Social, and General Psychology Monographs, 152*(2), 109–156.

Vygotsky, L.S. (1978). *Mind in society: The development of higher psychological processes.* Cambridge, MA: Harvard University Press.

CHAPTER 5

Early Intervention Practices

Tirussew Teferra

ETHIOPIA

Lejen be tut ehilen be tikimet.

As the month of October is the right time for crop harvest,
so is breast-feeding the right time for molding a child's behavior.

Ethiopia is a country with diverse sociocultural dimensions and languages, and people use many sayings to reflect understanding, knowledge, and thoughts about issues surrounding early childhood experiences. These metaphors are taken from the Amharic language, which is the official language of the Federal State of Ethiopia and the most widely spoken among the different ethnic groups in the country. As noted in this chapter's opening quote, *"Lejen be tut ehilen be tikimet"* expresses the idea that the best time to modify a child's behavior is early in development. The metaphor applies also to illness, habit, conflict, and other situations. For example, it is always advisable to get treatment for a disease before it reaches the stage in which no cure is possible. Other popular sayings that suggest the importance of early intervention are figuratively associated with trees and animals. For instance, *"Zaf beljenet yetarekal"* means that it is easy to straighten a tree during its nursery stage, just as early childhood is conducive for modifying human behavior or curbing the escalation of any problem. An attempt to make the tree straight after it has reached a certain level of maturity may cause it to break. An associated saying is *"ebabin be einchechu,"* which means that you can deal with a snake during its early stage of development (zygotic phase), while later on it is not only difficult to handle, but also a threat to one's life.

In Ethiopia, as in many other countries, one of the major difficulties encountered by people with disabilities is social. This chapter discusses ways to address that issue, and the following vignette portrays the nature of early familial experiences and modes of early intervention for people with disabilities in Ethiopia. This story describes a person with disabilities who has a high level of achievement and a resilient personality. However, the vast majority of people with disabilities in Ethiopia do not have access to intervention, education, or health care; they live in poverty, constituting the poorest of the poor in the country. A different life course occurred for this individual because of his education and family experiences.

 ## KEBEDE'S STORY

Kebede was born in a town of a distant province to a local tradesman's family. In the following account, he describes himself as one of the luckiest individuals with disabilities in his country and emphasizes the importance of his early childhood experiences.

"I was born, reared and educated until grade 3 with sight. Then, the devastating situation came afterwards; one evening while I was in

my sleep a certain insect entered through my ear. I was entirely disturbed by the voice of the insect. I screamed, shouted, jumped and my family did not know what to do. This lasted for about three days without any help. My parents consulted many people in the neighborhood and finally decided to take me to a local traditional healer. The healer prepared some herbal leaf, poured the liquid into my ear, and then sucked it out. The disturbance of the insect ceased but the color of my eyes became as red as blood and from then on my eye balls started to diminish in size. Gradually, I became unable to see things at a distance. From day to day my vision deteriorated. My father took me to a known modern eye specialist in Addis Ababa (capital city of Ethiopia), which is about 320 kilometers far from my hometown. After a thorough examination, the doctor told us that it was too late for any form of treatment. He advised my father to take me to the Blind school as early as possible to get education to my future career.

"Since the occurrence of losing my sight was a gradual process and since I was child, I didn't consider the impairment as a serious one. However, my father was always talking to me about the problems I was going to face and how to solve them. He developed my insight and helped me to accept myself. He let me know so many people so as to develop my social interaction, which helped me to be a social person throughout my life. He also advised me not to speak anything against myself even when I carelessly broke some household utensils while walking here and there. He also ordered my younger brother to help me walk to distant places, and I found my brother to be very co-operative and helpful.

"I was always playing with the children in the neighborhood. I was not looked at as bizarre and different. These and many other childhood experiences helped me very much to have a clear self-concept, to accept myself positively, to have a positive attitude towards people, to develop patience, to work hard, and finally to be a successful and self supporting individual like sighted persons. At present, I am happy not only because I am self supportive but am also contributing my share to the society.

"I would like to underscore that almost everything should be done for a child with visual impairment at his/her early years of development. It is a foundation for the psychological, social, and career well being of future of the child. It is crucially important to guide and protect the child to lead a proper life. To do this, so much is expected, starting from the family, neighborhood, and the society at large." (From Teferra, T. [1998]. *Persons with disabilities of high achievement profile and resilience in Ethiopia* [p. 46]. Addis Ababa, Ethiopia: Save the Children Sweden; reprinted by permission.)

NATIONAL CONTEXT

Ethiopia is located in East Africa, west of Somalia, with an area of 1,127,127 square kilometers. By African standards, it is a medium-size country that is as large as France, Spain, and Portugal combined (Redie, 1998). Ethiopia borders Kenya, the Republic of the Sudan, the Republic of Djibouti, Somalia, and Eritrea (Gold Mercury International, 1982).

Ethiopia is a breathtakingly beautiful country and is full of contrasts. The country's altitude ranges from 125 meters below sea level (at Dankail, one of the hottest locations on earth) to more than 4,500 meters above sea level. As a result, a range of climates is found in the highlands and tropical zones along the borders with Sudan, Somalia, and Kenya (Pankhurst, 1988; Redie, 1998). The country's terrain is characterized by a high plateau with a central mountain range divided by the Great Rift Valley. In Ethiopia, the land is used for various purposes. Estimates in 1993 showed that 40% of the land was planted with permanent crops, 25% was composed of forests and woodland, 12% was arable land, and 22% was characterized as "other" (Central Intelligence Agency, 2002). Natural hazards occur primarily in the geologically active Great Rift Valley, which is susceptible to earth-quakes, volcanic eruptions, and frequent droughts. Current issues related to environmental problems of the country are deforestation, overgrazing, soil erosion, and desertification.

People and Culture

Ethiopia is the oldest independent country in Africa and one of the oldest in the world. The population is estimated to be 61,672,000 people, of which 52,598,000 live in rural areas and 9,074,000 live in urban areas. The population is growing at 3% annually and predicted to reach 86 million in 2005. Individuals younger than 15 years make up 45% of the population; 51.4% of the population is 15–64 years old, and only 3.2% is older than 65 (Central Intelligence Agency, 2002). This age structure, characterized by high proportions of young and old individuals, is typical of developing countries.

The people of Ethiopia are multiethnic, multicultural, and multilingual. There are more than 83 different languages with 200 dialects spoken in different regions. Although Amharic, with its unique alphabet, is the official language, there are other local languages such as Oromiffa, Tigrigna, Sidamagina, Wolaitagna, Guragigna, Somaligna, Kembatigna, and Hadiyigna (Central Statistical Authority, 1999; Wondimu et al., 1997). The 1994 census identified 80 ethnic groups that make up the national mosaic (Befekadu & Berhanu, 1999/2000).

Ethiopians are generally religious people (Befekadu & Berhanu, 1999/2000). According to the 1994 census, the overwhelming majority (50.6%) are Orthodox Christians, followed by Muslims (38%), and Protestants (10.2%). Traditional religion is practiced by a small percentage of the people (approximately 5%), mostly in the rural areas.

Ethiopia is one of the poorest countries in the world. With a real gross domestic product per capita of $427 and a human development index of 0.244, it ranked 173 of 175 countries (National Committee on Traditional Practices in Ethiopia [NCTPE], 1998). Poverty in Ethiopia is multifaceted. Measured mainly in terms of food consumption (set at a minimum nutrition requirement of 2,200 calories per adult per day) and also including nonfood consumption requirements, a 1995/1996 estimate showed that 45.5% of the population lived below the poverty line. Poverty was prevalent both in rural (47%) and urban (33%) areas. In 1994, life expectancy at birth was 50.6 years; the infant mortality and child mortality rates were 118 and 173 per 1,000, respectively; and the maternal mortality rate was 700 per 100,000 (Ethiopia/Country Paper, 2000). Agriculture is the backbone of the country and its economy. Rural life is dominated by small-holder farmers, constituting close to 80% of the rural occupation (NCTPE, 1998).

A new constitution was approved in 1994 by a constituent assembly that had been elected in 1993. A coalition of ethnic political parties under the banner of the Ethiopian People's Revolutionary Democratic Front (EPRDF) is the leading political party. In June 1995, the Federal Democratic Republic of Ethiopia was established and the new government, led by EPRDF, was sworn into office (Redie, 1998).

Education Service Systems

With the onset of modern education in Ethiopia, the goal was to produce personnel who can speak a number of foreign languages (particularly French, English, and Italian) and who have the skills to fill positions in the growing modern government bureaucracy and to engage in limited development activities. According to the 1994 census, of the total population age 5 years and older, 11% of the males and 8% of the females attended school at various levels. The literacy rates for urban and rural areas were 69% and 15%, respectively (Central Statistical Authority, 1999).

The educational system was reformed in 1994, with the existing systems described in Table 5.1. The aim of grades 1–4 is achieving functional literacy while that of grades 5–8 is preparing students for further education (general secondary education). Grades 9–10 are meant to enable students to identify areas of interest for further training. The next tier of secondary education (grades 11–12) is targeted toward preparing the students for higher education (Advance Research and Training, 2002).

KEY FEATURES OF EARLY INTERVENTION

In Ethiopia, both governmental and nongovernmental services respond to the needs of people with disabilities. Among the millions of people with disabilities, however, only very few have access to special services. The types of services that operate in the country include special day schools, special residential schools and special classes, treatment centers, sheltered workshops, orthoses and prostheses production centers, homes for the children, and homes for "the aged" (Teferra, 1995). Community-based rehabilitation centers (CBRs), operating through nongovernmental organizations (NGOs), have started door-to-door, home-based early intervention programs.

The vast majority of people with disabilities in the country do not have access to such services. They either engage in begging and looking

Table 5.1. Categories of education in Ethiopia

	Age	Level
Kindergarten	4–6	Preparatory for Grade 1
Primary school	7–14	Grades 1–8
General secondary	15–16	Grades 9–10
Second tier of secondary school	17–18	Grades 11–12
Postsecondary education	19–20	1–2 years for diploma
Higher education	21–25	3–5 years for undergraduate degree
Higher education	26–28	1–3 years for postgraduate degree

Source: Advance Research and Training (2002).

for alms or live out of public view. They constitute the poorest of Ethiopia's poor. Also, it is not uncommon to find in the urban centers people without disabilities who generate their daily income by having individuals with disabilities to beg for alms. This can be referred to as "double dependency syndrome."

Even NGOs once gave little attention to the importance of early intervention for children with disabilities. The Ministry of Health does have various immunization programs for young children and offers primary health care for mothers to possibly prevent disabilities. Childhood "crippling diseases" such as poliomyelitis have not yet been controlled, although encouraging results were reported by the Ministry of Health.

Curriculum and Classroom Practices

In Ethiopia, there are 7 residential special schools, 8 day special schools and 42 special classes (Ministry of Education, 1997). The programs are for school-age children with visual or hearing impairments or mental retardation. Located in urban areas, the programs provide services to a small percentage of all children with disabilities (Teferra, 1993). As such, the country does not have an early intervention curriculum. In fact, only one course on early intervention is available for graduate students in the field of special needs education. Since 1998, this course has been offered by the Faculty of Education in the Department of Educational Psychology at Addis Ababa University.

In the Education and Training Policy of Ethiopia, the first general objective is developing the physical, mental, and problem-solving capacities of individuals by providing basic education (Transitional Government of Ethiopia, 1994). Furthermore, the policy indicates that

Ethiopia's educational structure starts from preschool, focusing on all-around child development in preparation for formal schooling. Teachers, starting from the kindergarten level, must have the necessary qualifications and competence in the media of instruction, which is provided through preservice and in-service training (Transitional Government of Ethiopia, 1994). In addition, the New Social Security Development Policy explicitly expressed the need to expand early childhood education and family support programs (Federal Democratic Republic of Ethiopia, 1997).

These policies reflect the government's recognition of the importance of early childhood development, education, and care. With this encouraging action, early intervention programs for children with disabilities could be included in the education system. As of 2002, modern early childhood education establishments were highly concentrated in the urban sectors, primarily serving children from middle- and upper-income families. Most children from rural and poor urban areas attend traditional Priest and Koranic preschools because of their accessibility and affordability. Except in a few early childhood educational establishments, neither teachers' backgrounds nor school programs provide the educational experiences that children require at this period of development. There is a need to reorganize the present establishments and to introduce a curriculum that is oriented to early childhood. In light of the cost-effectiveness and accessibility to children from rural and poor urban areas, the Ministry of Education has considered upgrading the traditional early childhood establishments through in-service teacher training programs and resource provision. Because the trend is to educate young children with disabilities in inclusive classrooms, their needs should be incorporated when designing the early childhood curriculum and teacher training program, and additional family-based intervention should be provided.

Sociocultural Perspective

As a traditional and religiously oriented society, some Ethiopians attribute disabilities to supernatural powers, evil deeds, wrong actions, and/or possession by evil spirits. This is illustrated in the following excerpt of an interview with a father whose child has cerebral palsy:

> The father attributes the cause of his son's physical disability to his wife. He said, "My wife is the cause for our child's disability. Once I remember my wife during her 5th term in her pregnancy, came home highly agitated and angry. She complained that on her way back home, she saw a person with distorted and ugly physical features walking on the street. The sight of the person causes my wife to say bad things about him. Then, she was punished for her behavior." (Abedella, Asrat, & Tadesse, 2000)

Similar attributions occur in the general public, particularly in uneducated sectors of society. Therefore, great shock, bewilderment, and anger arise when parents discover that their child has a disability. Families may experience feelings of guilt and a lack of equilibrium. Parents often try to cope with the problem without professional help or counseling. Some may prefer to hide the child at home to avoid social stigma and the risk of social exclusion. In most cases, however, parents try to find treatments for their child.

Parents sometime visit religious institutions and secular traditional healers. Particularly in rural areas, the Ethiopian Orthodox Church has been the center for remediation for various diseases. Remediation efforts are purely based on religious belief, such as engaging in deep prayer, reading religious texts, receiving a sprinkling of holy water, drinking holy water, eating and drinking blessed materials, eating food prepared in monasteries, fasting, and putting *eminet* (an ash-like substance) on the affected part of the body. It is not uncommon to hear individual reports of children making progress or being cured after going through the required religious treatment. As the treatment is based on faith, it seems to be more therapeutic or psychological in nature, with changes affecting the child's physical well-being.

With regard to the secular traditional treatment, individual healers hold different levels identified as *awaki, metsehaf-gelach, debtera, wegehsa, qalecha, tsenkoy,* and *bale-zar.* Three types of treatments exist. The first is herbal medicines that are administered internally or externally. The second is a type of indigenous psychotherapy in which a person who is possessed by a *zar* (special spirit), is capable of communicating with supernatural powers and secures possible solutions for the problem (i.e., the child's disability). The third is a traditional form of physiotherapeutic treatment provided by *wegeshas* (traditional physiotherapists) when a child has a problem related to motor performance (e.g., sitting, walking, coordination). The traditional physiotherapy treatment is reported to be very effective. It has a positive reputation in both rural and urban areas.

In the absence of professional support and early intervention programs, the parents of children with disabilities have no treatment options other than the traditional forms. After trying the different forms of traditional treatment, parents often seek modern medical treatment for their children. When this pattern occurs, the critical and sensitive early years of development often pass without treatment, eroding the family's resources and hopes.

In many cases, children with disabilities in Ethiopia do not have access to early intervention programs. The combination of traditional beliefs and misconceptions may lead to emotional deprivation, ranging from passive neglect to active rejection. Consequently, sensory, physical, cognitive, and psychomotor impairments that could be addressed through early intervention may well develop into permanent and severe disabilities.

Theoretical Influences

At present, the general trend regarding provision of professional support to children with disabilities focuses mainly on family-based programs and CBRs. This approach entails the mobilization of local resources, which may involve parents, siblings, community leaders, or professionals utilizing all forms of informal networks in promoting intervention for children with disabilities. Furthermore, strategy is shifting from segregated education (educating children with disabilities in special schools) to inclusive education (education of children with disabilities in "regular schools") (Teferra, 1999).

The provision of educational and other services in special centers tends to focus on "within individual factors" and special professional support for the child, with little attention to restructuring the child's learning and living environments. Professionals assume that problems lie exclusively within the individual and solutions consist of attempts to change the individual (Teferra, 2000). This view has been sharply challenged by an alternative, which stresses that development proceeds through reciprocal interactions between children and environments so that both individuals and their environments undergo change (Mitchell & Brown, 1991). In this model, the child's development is seen as a product of continuous dynamic interactions between the child and the experiences provided by his or her family and social context (Sameroff & Feise, 2000).

In Ethiopia, nongovernmental CBRs on early intervention are emerging. These programs as well as new government policies target not only the child with disability as a point of intervention or rehabilitation, but also the ecology in which the child lives and learns. For instance, topical issues of governmental and nongovernmental organizations include raising the awareness of the family, the community, and general public about the causes of disability; the importance of early detection and intervention; and protection of the child's rights. Generally, special needs education and early intervention in particular seem highly influenced by the ecological approach. This approach has gained momentum in the academic circles of special needs educators in Ethiopia.

Specific Features of Early Intervention Services

From the foregoing discussions, it is clear that early intervention services in Ethiopia are a rather new and mainly urban phenomenon, focused primarily in the capital city Addis Ababa. Several CBRs, carried out by international and local NGOs, have been established since the 1990s. Most of them collaborate with the Ethio-Swedish Clinic of the Black Lion Hospital, which is mainly responsible for the medical treatment of children with health and physical impairments. As a rule, children receive free medical service in government health centers and hospitals if their parents can prove financial need.

Studies confirm that the CBR projects adopt a holistic approach that encompasses educational, social, and medical issues. For instance, they organize a series of short-term training programs for fieldworkers on sign language, braille, mobility and environmental orientation, adaptive skills, physiotherapy, and primary health care. This has equipped the fieldworkers with the knowledge and skills to work with children with disabilities and their families as well as with the community. The major areas of CBR services include health, education, training, advocacy, disability awareness, and income-generating activities (Desta, 2000). The CBR projects appear to be having a positive effect.

Yet, ongoing resistance and indifference appear to occur sometimes, even from families who are direct beneficiaries of CBR services. Parents' and family members' responses appear to fall into three groups. The first consists of families that are highly involved and receptive to the CBR program. Families in the second group are not as interested in the CBR activities but, rather, are looking for information about financial or other forms of support for their children as well as themselves. They consider other activities (e.g., promoting child development) of CBR as basically the responsibility of the CBR workers. The last group of parents shows a strong resistance to early intervention; these parents close their doors to any form of CBR program activity (Desta, 2000). These family members often keep their children hidden at home because they fear social stigma or exclusion. Such parents, particularly from upper-income families, often incorrectly believe that they will lose their social status if their child's disability is disclosed. It is not unusual for these parents to seek placement for the child outside the family (e.g., an institution, a distant relative's home).

Because early intervention is just beginning in Ethiopia, it will not be easy to expand services. However, Desta (2000) found encouraging changes occurring. In communities where CBRs had been providing services, there have been positive changes in the attitudes of parents and community members toward children with disabilities. With time and continued positive results, it is anticipated that early intervention services will grow, but along with this growth will come new challenges. An example follows of early intervention services begun through the Cheshire Home Foundation.

DESCRIPTION OF PROGRAM[1]

The Cheshire Home Foundation, one of the oldest NGOs in the country, was established in 1962 by Ethiopian and foreign philanthropists to care for children with mental retardation. After a decade, it was shifted to serve as a center for rehabilitating children with polio and to operate in collaboration with Black Lion Hospital. The Cheshire Home Foundation Center, Community, and Outreach Early Intervention Project provides short-term rehabilitation through intensive physiotherapy and surgical intervention for children from all over Ethiopia. The Cheshire Center has a follow-up program for children who are discharged after treatment. In this follow-up program, workers change assisting devices as children grow and check the intervention practices undertaken by parents. The Cheshire Center provides the follow-up activities through its Mobile Outreach Programs, which go deep into the country's rural areas.

In 1994, the Cheshire Home Foundation started an early intervention CBR program for young children with mental retardation, visual impairment, and hearing impairment. Intervention for motor disorders is also included, but mainly in Addis Ababa. As of 2003, they are working with the communities of Woreda 8 and 25 in Addis Ababa. The CBR workers are given 3 months training as practitioners before they go into the community. Field supervision and follow-up is conducted by the CBR coordinator.

The Cheshire Outreach Early Intervention Project consists of several key activities. Children with disabilities are provided with individual, home-based assistance in areas such as stretching contracted limbs, bathing with warm salt water every night and morning, massaging legs and hips, and providing access to the outdoors every morning. Parents receive counseling for their emotional reactions to having a child with a disability. Parents are also advised to look for any additional sensory, physical, or developmental delays and to report them to nearby health centers instead of traditional healers. Prospective mothers and parents of children with disabilities are educated on practices that promote development and prevent future delays. So that parents with low incomes can care for their children's needs and support the family, loans are identified and provided for income-generating activities. Children with disabilities are encouraged to accept their disabilities and

---

[1]This program description is extracted from papers written by graduate students (Abedella et al., 2000; Berta, 2000) for a course in early psychosocial intervention as part of the special needs education program at Addis Ababa University, Ethiopia.

build their self-esteem. Methods are sought to reduce the impact of environmental hazards, such as drought, war, poverty, malnutrition, air and water pollution, and poor sanitation. Primary health care and medical follow-up is promoted for prospective mothers. Community awareness about disabilities is heightened, particularly by working with local elders to help eradicate the social stigma attached to disability. Finally, parents of children with disabilities are taught how to use local materials to help their children, such as providing walking sticks to enhance mobility.

In addition to individual home visits and community meetings, the following strategies were found to be effective in carrying out these key activities. In Ethiopia, the coffee ceremony is an informal gathering of the ladies in the neighborhood. They sit for approximately an hour, chat, and drink coffee. The community workers educate parents during coffee ceremonies, especially if they are hosted by mothers of children with disabilities. This is the best occasion for raising the mothers' awareness. In addition, parent support groups have been organized so that parents of children with disabilities can share their experiences and emotions and help one another. Furthermore, child-oriented programs have been implemented that focus on accident prevention and personal and environmental sanitation.

Feedback from Parents

To get feedback on the impact of the Cheshire Home Foundation's CBR early intervention activities, parents were interviewed, and their interviews were summarized. In general, parents reported that before the program, they had consulted community elders and the *awakies* (traditional healers) and had carried out all the rituals and medicines prescribed, including tying an amulet on their child's neck. When this failed, the parents took their children to the holy water of the different Christian saints. As a final step, they took their child to the hospital. Families and children were referred to the CBR project through the hospital and began participating in the project. Excerpts from several family interviews follow (Abedella et al., 2000):

- One father said, "The CBR workers came and convinced us to bring our child to the project. We are seeing change in the movement and control of her body. Now she tries to walk by herself, though with great difficulty and help."

- A mother reported, "The project people came and convinced me to bring my child to this therapy room; now I see very little but good changes in her. And I believe this is God's way of answering to my prayer. . . . My husband and I are hoping that our child will improve if we continue this treatment for her. Within 6 months, 'T' [will] have strong neck muscles and [try] to move by creeping on the floor using her seat. For us this is a great mercy of God."

- A second mother said, "Now he is improving a lot after he came to the project."

- A third mother reported, "My daughter was not able to eat, drink, and walk by herself. She cannot also speak. . . . After she started the treatment here, she is able to eat, drink and walk by herself. Talking is still difficult for her but she understands everything we say and tries to communicate. . . ."

These are positive and encouraging outcomes of the CBR early intervention programs. The need to share experience with other CBR early intervention programs as well as professionals is essential to enrich this new and important undertaking in Ethiopia. To promote the holistic development of children with disabilities and to curb negative social and emotional consequences, the early intervention programs should incorporate a psychosocial component focusing on the quality of parent–child, caregiver–child, teacher–child, and peer–child interactions. In fact, these factors should constitute the major segment of the early intervention programs for children with disabilities. In a country where myths and misconceptions surround disabling conditions and people with disabilities, educating and sensitizing caregivers to promote quality interaction with their children should be the top early intervention priority.

RECOMMENDATIONS FOR PROFESSIONALS IN OTHER COUNTRIES

From the Ethiopian experiences of early intervention, it is suggested that professionals in other countries educate the public on preventive health care services through conveying information on primary health care, factors that cause disability, and disability-related interventions. In addition, it is recommended that family- and community-based early intervention programs be launched as early as possible (in the first 6 years of life). Moreover, rehabilitation programs should focus on adjusting the social environment and on enhancing the assets of people with disabilities rather than dwelling on deficits. Furthermore, it is suggested that professionals promote indigenous knowledge in the areas of disability treatment, cure (when applicable), and rehabilitation.

Finally, it is recommended that professionals work closely with parents and associations for people with disabilities.

CONCLUSION

The incidence and prevalence of childhood disability is high in Ethiopia. The primary factors contributing to disabilities include lack of personal and environmental hygiene, lack of immunization, infectious diseases, malnutrition, harmful cultural practices, lack of proper prenatal care, improper child health care, and genetics. In spite of these facts, many people attribute disability to supernatural powers and evil spirits and do not understand the needs of children with disabilities and their families. These factors have influenced the types of treatment that parents seek for their children and the way that they care for their child with a disability. Parents often take their children to religious or secular traditional healing places. The search for proper care, the psychological shock of learning an infant has disabilities, the fear of societal stigmatization, and the lack of adequate knowledge about disabilities affect the way that parents interact with their children. There is a need to educate the public on preventive and rehabilitative health care services. Workshops, seminars, and the media could be used to convey information about primary health care, factors that cause disability, disability-related intervention, and medical treatment. As mentioned in the beginning of this chapter, certain societal metaphors have relevance for early intervention, education, and child care. A productive approach might include using these metaphors as a way to engage community participants in a dialogue about disability and early intervention.

In Ethiopia, early intervention practices are concentrated in urban areas, mainly in Addis Ababa, and have a very short history. Almost all of them are CBRs initiated by NGOs. They are all in their early stages of development and require extensive professional input and resources. Their coverage is negligible when compared with the magnitude of the problem in the country at large. Their achievements, however, are positive and noteworthy, and the government as well as the community should encourage these programs.

Above all, to make a difference in the status of early intervention programs in Ethiopia on a large scale, the government and the community need to be highly involved. The government must enforce health, education, social development, and security policies that promote activities of primary health care, early childhood education, and family support in child care. Early intervention programs for children with disabilities could be included in this effort. If the goal is to create an inclusive society, then making inclusion a natural circumstance must be based in family and community everyday beliefs and practices.

REFERENCES

Abedella, R., Asrat, M., & Tadesse, S. (2000). *Early intervention strategies on children with cerebral palsy.* Unpublished dissertation, Special Needs Graduate Program, Addis Ababa University.

Advance Research and Training. (2002). *A project profile on the establishment of kindergarten and primary schools in Addis Ababa.* Addis Ababa, Ethiopia: Author.

Befekadu, D., & Berhanu, N. (1999/2000). *Annual report on the Ethiopian economy: Volume I.* Addis Ababa: The Ethiopian Economic Association.

Berta, F. (2000). *The situation of early intervention programs for physically handicapped children in Ethiopia: The case of Cheshire Home and parents of children with motor disorder.* Unpublished paper, Special Needs Education Graduate Program, Addis Ababa University, Ethiopia.

Central Intelligence Agency. (Ed.). (2002). *The Worldfact Book 2002.* London: Brasseys.

Central Statistical Authority. (1999). *The 1994 population and housing census of Ethiopia results at country level: Volume II—analytical report.* Addis Ababa, Ethiopia: Author.

Central Statistical Authority. (1999). *The statistical report on the 1999 National Labor Force survey.* Addis Ababa, Ethiopia: Author.

Desta, D. (2000). *Attitudes toward disability and the role of community based rehabilitation programs in Ethiopia.* Dissertation, University of Joensuu, Finland.

Ethiopia/Country Paper. (2000). *Interim poverty reduction strategy paper 2000/2001–2002/2003.* Addis Ababa, Ethiopia.

Federal Democratic Republic of Ethiopia. (1997). *Social Security development policy.* Addis Ababa, Ethiopia: Author.

Gold Mercury International. (1982). PANA African Conference, Addis Ababa, Ethiopia.

Ministry of Education. (1997). *Education statistics (1995–1996).* Addis Ababa, Ethiopia: Educational Materials Production and Distribution Agency.

Mitchell, D., & Brown, R.I. (Eds.). (1991). *Early intervention studies for young children with special needs.* London: Chapman and Hall.

National Committee on Traditional Practices in Ethiopia. (1998). *Baseline survey on harmful traditional practices in Ethiopia.* Addis Ababa, Ethiopia: Author.

Pankhurst, R. (1988). *Ethiopia engraved: An illustrated catalogue of engravings by foreign travellers from 1681 to 1960.* London: Kegan Paul.

Redie, A. (1998). *Ethiopia: Country profile.* Addis Ababa, Ethiopia.

Sameroff, A.J., & Fiese, B.H. (2000). Transactional regulation: The developmental ecology of early intervention. In J.P. Shonkoff & S.J. Meisels (Eds.),

Handbook of early childhood intervention (2nd ed., pp. 135–159). New York: Cambridge University Press.

Teferra, T. (1993). Problems and prospects of persons with disabilities in Ethiopia. *The Ethiopian Journal of Development Research, 15*(1), 67–87.

Teferra, T. (1995). Reflections on the status of persons with disabilities in Ethiopia. *Proceedings of the symposium on Dignity for All* (pp. 76–89). Addis Ababa: Ethiopian Red Cross Society.

Teferra, T. (1998). *Persons with disabilities of high achievement profile and resilience in Ethiopia.* Addis Ababa, Ethiopia: Save the Children Sweden.

Teferra, T. (1999). Inclusion of children with disabilities in regular schools: Challenges and opportunities. *Ethiopian Journal of Education, 19*(1), 29–64.

Teferra, T. (2000). *Inclusive education: An international perspective of the education of children with special educational needs.* Paper presented at the SAHER workshop, Addis Ababa, Ethiopia.

Transitional Government of Ethiopia. (1994). *Education and training policy of Ethiopia.* Addis Ababa, Ethiopia: Educational Materials Production and Distribution Agency.

Wondimu, H., et al. (1997). *Ethnic identity, stereotypes and psychological modernity in Ethiopian young adults: Identifying the potential for change.* Unpublished report, Addis Ababa, Ethiopia.

Working with Families

CHAPTER 6

Working with Families to Implement Home Interventions

Sudha Kaul, Swapna Mukherjee, Asis Kumar Ghosh, Madhabi Chattopadhyay, and Utsab Sil

Shubhasya Sheegram.
Good work should begin as early as possible.

Ethos, values and aesthetics are shaped in childhood and reinforced by the verbal and nonverbal milieu in which the child is nurtured. To understand Indian children, it is important to study India's culture, its written and oral traditions. To understand children with disabilities, it is equally important to acknowledge the deeply instilled social attitudes of communities and the support systems available in the environments where they live. Children with disabilities are instinctively loved and cared for regarding basic needs, but parents often do not know the importance of early stimulation and early intervention. They have little access to information on parenting and most of their support comes from within the family itself. This chapter discusses how families of children with disabilities can be an important part of the intervention team. It demonstrates, through examples, the strong cultural beliefs and strengths of the Indian family—beliefs that can be practically nurtured to augment the quality of life of children with disabilities.

 BISH'S STORY ————————————————————————

Bish comes from an economically poor background. His father is a mason and his mother is a maidservant in a private house. Neither parent has formal education, but Bish's older brother attends a local school. The family speaks Bengali.

Bish's grandmother lives with the family in a *kuccha* (nonpermanent) house, made of *dorma* (woven bamboo sheets) and bricks with a tiled roof. It is a one-room structure with a verandah in the front, where they cook. Sometimes Bish's mother bathes at the home of her employer. Water is obtained from a tube well, a 2-minute walk from the house. The family members share a common toilet with their neighbors, who also live in a *kuccha* house. Approximately 50 families live very close together in this *bustee* (slum dwelling), which is on government land, adjacent to a main road; the residents can be ousted at any time. There is no playground, and the children generally play in an open space near the *bustee.*

Bish was referred by a pediatrician to the early intervention clinic when he was approximately 2 years of age. His mother was not sure of his exact date of birth. She had fallen during the seventh month of her pregnancy and was immediately taken to the hospital, where she had a normal delivery. Bish did not cry immediately after birth and had to be given oxygen. He was in an incubator for 3 days, after which he and his mother were released from the hospital. He has since been diagnosed as having cerebral palsy with athetosis and spasticity.

Bish had bright eyes and a ready smile for anyone who spoke to him, but at age 2, he still did not use clear speech to communicate. He

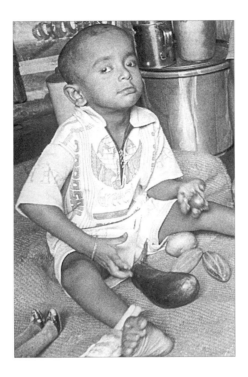

shuffled around his home and could reach for and grasp toys. The early interventionists asked Bish's mother about her primary concerns to prioritize Bish's needs and individualize the program. She expressed concern about her son's toileting accidents and his inability to self-feed, as well as concern about her time constraints for implementing intervention. The interventionists explained a program that could be incorporated into the family's routine. Thus, a detailed assessment of Bish's daily routine was the first step of the intervention. Along with teaching Bish toileting and self-feeding skills, it was suggested that a physical and communication intervention program would facilitate Bish's learning. His parents were eager to assess Bish's learning potential and were willing to bring him to the clinic regularly. They had great hope and faith in his future progress.

Bish's intervention plan revolved around the family's routine. His physical intervention program was aimed at increasing his trunk rotation and stability and helping him move from sitting to standing. His mother was shown how she could conduct such exercises through play activities. Bish would practice standing in the corner of the room while his mother cooked; therefore, she could also encourage him to comment on what she was doing.

To promote toileting skills, the interventionists suggested using a corner of the verandah as the toileting area. They showed Bish's mother how to make a toilet with a pot between two bricks. Bish soon learned to use the improvised toileting area.

Daily routines like bathtime and mealtime became learning periods. Bish learned to drink water independently by using a straw. By teaching him to use a spoon to eat rice (rather than his fingers, which is the customary Indian way), Bish was able to spill less food while eating. The interventionists also recommended that Bish's mother teach the names of objects that Bish used during routines (e.g., food, toys), thereby providing him with opportunities to talk about his activities. Bish soon began to realize that he could control his environment by using language. He learned words for the names, colors, shapes, and sizes of the vegetables and fruits that he ate. He began to label and name objects, present demands, and even make jokes. He was soon given a special picture book, with the words written above each picture to help him communicate more efficiently not only with his family but also with other people in his community.

Once Bish and his family realized that there was so much he could and did learn, they became more confident. Bish now interacts more with his peers. The children in the *bustee* accept him more. He has made some friends who come to the house to play with him. His knowledge about the world has increased so he has a lot more to talk about!

Bish was progressing so well that his Mother arranged for a private "tutor" from the *bustee* to teach Bish to read, as she herself could not read. The social worker who regularly visited Bish's family met the tutor to discussed Bish's intervention program. The social worker also advised the family about low-cost healthy food. She also emphasized the need for a clean and safe environment, as the house was on a busy road.

Although family members remain concerned about Bish's future, they are more relaxed. His father has taken more interest in Bish's progress. Bish's mother has made friends with other mothers at the clinic. She says that she feels less isolated now. Bish enjoys his weekly visits to the clinic, with its bright atmosphere and numerous toys. He says that it is like a picnic!

NATIONAL CONTEXT

The heart-shaped country of India stretches from the magnificent Himalayan range in the north to the waters of the Indian Ocean on the west and the Bay of Bengal on the east. From the northern-most peak of the Himalayas down to the southern-most tip the coastline measures 3,280,543 kilometers (Gandhi, 1980). The country contains every type of climate, with temperate zones as well as the flora and fauna of the tropics. The geological, geographical, and natural environments have profoundly influenced food, clothing, lifestyle, and cultures. The moods of the people are reflected in the different traditions of fine art, music, dance, and sculpture.

India has been described as a mosaic of people from various origins and cultures blending together. As Indira Gandhi noted, "India is a world in itself, it is too vast, too diverse for any complete description" (1980, p. 7). To understand India, one has to accept the plurality of both its culture and context. Nothing exemplifies India better than the variety of languages: 723, with 544 dialects (Ramanujan, 1991). There are 18 regional languages (Census of India, 1991).

The Official Languages Act (1963) allows the use of English in addition to Hindi, the accepted national language. Although India achieved independence in 1947, even 54 years later, English is considered the language linking the educated elite across India. Higher education institutes and universities use English as the medium of instruction. The present education policies set out by the national government, however, emphasize the development of regional languages and the use of Hindi.

Dharma, or the ethical mode of life, has greatly influenced Indian thought, and all major religions are found in India. The 1991 census report indicated the following statistics: 82% Hindu, 12.12% Muslim, 2.34% Christian, 1.94% Sikh, 0.76% Buddhist, and 0.40% Jain. The national census completed in February 2001 included disability for the first time. The provisional census report placed the population of India at just over 1 billion (Census of India, 2001), of which an estimated 10% have disabilities (Status of Disability in India Report, 2000).

India is the largest democracy in the world. Sadly, the disparity between economic groups and classes, both urban and rural, is enormous and complex. With the growth of industry in the urban areas, a steady influx of people from the rural areas has become inevitable. Although the profile, beliefs, and lifestyles of the Indian people changed over the millennium, there is an amazing degree of continuity in Indian culture. One of the major themes that has transcended time and regions is family solidarity. At the beginning of the 21st century, changes in family structure and size are evident, but the basic inherent family values—family cohesiveness and "familism" (Anandalakshmy, 1998)—have stood the test of time. Family context is provided by the social group and the community, and kinships are legitimized by the use of language. Deference to older people is the most consistent part of socialization within Indian families. This aspect cuts across all of India's regional boundaries, religions, and cultures.

Although the Indian woman has been revered from ancient times as *ardhanarishwara* (a half female, half male combination that makes a perfect whole) who enjoys full freedom and equality, her status has changed over the years, relegating her to a secondary position in society. She is seen as the conserver of tradition and the family member who must bear the burden of shock and tragedy. Although India has had a female Prime Minister, Indira Gandhi, and many Indian women in the forefront of different spheres of life and work, modern Indian women continue to fight for equality.

Child-rearing practices differ across regions, but there are certain common factors. The birth of a child is seen as a "gift from God," and illness or disability is sometimes considered the result of previous sins or of a stranger or neighbor giving the "evil eye." Therefore, parents of children with disabilities tend to expect a life of sacrifice rather than to focus on rehabilitation. In many families, there is traditionally more than one caregiver, and a grandparent, uncles, or aunts share responsibilities with parents. Strict rules are not usually imposed, and looking after the child's basic needs is usually the responsibility of older siblings or cousins. With the changing family structure, single-unit families are emerging, and young urban parents increasingly share child-rearing responsibilities.

Nonetheless, tradition still plays an important part in raising children (Swaminathan, 1998). In the *kanethur* ceremony (among Kashmiris) or the *namsanskara/namkaran* ceremony (in most Hindu communities), the family begins establishing a newborn's identity by giving the baby a name. The *annaprasan or kheer chatana* (rice eating ceremony) occurs when the child is 6 months old and is given solid food for the first time. It is typically an occasion to celebrate the presence of the child within the family and to share this joy with other family members and friends. These *sanskaras* (traditions) create a bond between the family and the community.

Education Services Systems

The notion of child care and commitment to educating children is not new in India. Stories of adult–child interaction can be seen in innumerable fables and religious and mythological stories.

Pre-schools (or nursery schools, as they are popularly called) in urban India have been greatly influenced by the philosophy of Friedrich Froebel. Maria Montessori visited India in the 1930s and initiated several Montessori education centers. Good nursery schools of today are very much the product of this method. In addition, the role of the teacher as the facilitator and the concepts of self-exploration, self-initiation, and learning are seen in the teachings of Mahatma Gandhi, Rabindranath Tagore, and J. Krishnamurthy—all thinkers and philosophers who greatly influenced the Indian education system.

Critics of India's present early education system state that the pedagogic function of play is totally overlooked. Anandalakshmy, supporting this viewpoint, stated, "The cultural underpinning of karma and rebirth is that every action has its consequences" (1998, p. 282). Often, the focus is not on age-specific activities but on how the activity will affect the child's future. Childhood is seen as a time for inculcating proper habits, and playfulness is not seen as a means of learning. Therefore, the "play way" teaching method (or learning through play), based on Froebel's belief that play is the highest form of self-development, often does not get the credibility that it deserves. The child is treated like a mini-adult, and parents endure traumatic periods of tutoring their 4-year-olds to sit for entrance examinations as the fear of failure looms over their heads. Parents want their children to learn how to read and write as quickly as possible. A school is considered to be a serious place of learning and often a teacher's "play way" or informal teaching method is viewed with misgiving.

In urban areas, most parents want their children to attend "English Medium Schools," so children struggle with learning in a language that they do not use at home. It is slowly being accepted that the beginning years are crucial for learning in an atmosphere that is conducive for development. Thus, progressive schools and teaching centers are emerging. There are excellent examples of good practice in urban areas and villages, but they are still the exception and not the rule.

KEY FEATURES OF EARLY INTERVENTION

Early childhood care and education in India dates back to the 1890s, when the first kindergarten was opened by a Scottish missionary (Swaminathan, 1998). The sociopolitical climate has been positive and in the postindependent era, which began in the 1950s, various education policies have been formulated. This point is illustrated by legislation that demonstrates commitment to early childhood care and education: the National Policy for Children (Ministry of Human Resource Development, 1974), the National Policy for Education (Ministry of Human

Resource Development, 1986), and the National Primary Education Programme (Ministry of Human Resource Development, 1993).

Yet, the target of serving 70% of children (birth to 6 years) by the end of 2000 has fallen drastically short. The Indian government initiated a massive Integrated Child Development Scheme (ICDS) in 1975. The ICDS is a holistic early childhood and development program that addresses the interrelated needs of children, adolescent girls, and women from disadvantaged communities. At *Aganwadi* centers (literally, "centers run in courtyards"), paraprofessionals serve 20–40 children for several hours each weekday by providing supplementary feeding, health checkups, and educational activities. This program is the largest in the world of its kind. In 1987–1988, there were more than 88,400 centers, reaching 4.8 million children birth to 6 years (Swaminathan, 1998). The main objective of this program is to provide a healthy learning environment for the development of children. This is done through the education of mothers about nutrition and health-related issues (including immunizations), enabling them to take care of themselves and their children. In several states of India where the literacy level is high among women, the ICDS program has been successful. According to 2000 government data, the ICDS reaches 4.8 million expectant and nursing mothers and 22.9 million children younger than 6 (Ministry of Human Resource Development, 2000). Nonetheless, a UNICEF report noted,

> Education at all levels is a critical challenge in India, where only about 50% of the children enrolled in school complete the first year, in part because child labor remains prevalent, and girls often stay home to care for their younger siblings. These stark conditions provide the context into which Indian preschool programs must fit. (Kolucki, 1999, p. 10)

Educational Services for Children with Disabilities

In her study on disability and policy in India, with a specific focus on the ICDS policy, Alur stated, "Although the Integrated Child Development Scheme (ICDS) states that it is for all children, in practice, it does not include disabled children" (2000, p. 20). There is a dichotomy between policy and practice. Education of children with disabilities continues to remain in the purview of the Ministry of Social Justice and Empowerment while the Ministry of Human Resource Development, the nodal ministry responsible for education policy, has remained silent on the education of children with disabilities. However, the government has set up a number of specialized institutions at national and state levels for the development and improvement of education. The major organizations are the National Council of Educational Research and Training (NCERT), the National Institute of Educational Planning and Administration (NIEPA), the National Institute of Public Cooperation and Child Development (NIPCCD), and the National Council of Teacher Education (NCTE).

In 1994, the national government launched the District Primary Education Programme (DPEP), with its special focus on making education accessible to children with disabilities, the girl child (a commonly used term in India), and children who dropped out of school to work. This is under the larger framework of the government policy of Education for All—Sarva Shiksha Abhiyan (SSA). The SSA program aims to provide elementary education for all children (including children with disabilities) between 6 and 14 years of age, with the active participation of the community in the management of schools. According to government reports (Rehabilitation Council of India, 2000), some 60,000 children with disabilities have been enrolled in general education schools. It is estimated that 30 million children in India have disabilities. Nongovernmental organizations (NGOs) continue to take the major responsibility in imparting education to children with disabilities, but their reach is limited. Government statistics reveal that only 2% of people with disabilities are being served (Rehabilitation Council of India, 2000).

In 1992, the Rehabilitation Council of India (RCI) was set up to regulate manpower development programs in the field of education for children with special needs. In 1995, the historic Persons with Disabilities (Equal Opportunities, Protection of Rights and Full Participation) Act proposed free education for all children with disabilities and an accessible environment for full participation in the community. However, despite the passing of this act, its implementation remains a struggle.

Under its national health programs, the government of India has undertaken several initiatives to prevent disability. The need to provide services at the grass roots level has been addressed by initiatives to spread the concept of community-based services. A national community-based program was introduced in the ninth Five-Year Plan (1997–2002). The concept of providing two multipurpose rehabilitation workers to serve a cluster of villages (total population of approximately 5,000) was also initiated. The program has been successful only in a few states where it was supported by local NGOs.

Early intervention programs focus on prevention rather than education. They do not form part of the existing early childhood care and education program. The medical model of intervention is still a priority for infants with disabilities, particularly for those with multiple disabilities. Early intervention clinics or services for children with disabilities are limited to a few specialized centers, which are usually in cities.

DESCRIPTION OF THE PROGRAM

The Indian Institute of Cerebral Palsy (IICP), based in Kolkata, is one of the country's major specialist centers focusing on cerebral palsy. IICP's history is a reflection of the success of partnerships between parents and professionals and other like-minded organizations. IICP was established in 1974 by a group of parents and their motivated friends who wanted to provide a school for their children with cerebral palsy. Since then, IICP has emerged as a nationally and internationally recognized training institute specializing in the education and rehabilitation of children and adults with cerebral palsy. It provides a range of comprehensive services—an early intervention clinic, a special school, and an adult training center. The organization has an implicit belief in the concept of partnership training to enhance and ensure the quality of education. IICP runs community-based training courses at the grass roots level; family and parent education programs; and postgraduate training courses for professionals in the fields of education, medicine, and therapy. The impact of its training is seen by the rural- and urban-based community services that have been initiated in different parts of India, from the remote hilly states in the northeast to the villages of West Bengal and the coastal regions in the south.

The Early Intervention Clinic run by IICP is unique in its approach. Its main philosophy is based on the intrinsic belief that parents or family members are the primary caregivers and equal intervention partners. The equal partnership model has resulted in building exceptional relationships between families and professionals.

IICP has five primary early intervention goals. The first goal is to augment the development of children with cerebral palsy (or suspected neuromotor problems) in all spheres—physical, cognitive, communicative, and self-care—mainly through play, physiotherapy, and daily routine activities. The second goal is to give parents information about cerebral palsy and its management. The third intervention goal is to educate parents about working with their children with cerebral palsy. The fourth goal is to empower parents so they can ultimately work for their children's rights as well as the rights of other children with disabilities. IICP's fifth intervention goal is to motivate parents to start support programs according to their needs so they can initiate services, leisure groups, and self-help groups in the community.

Early Intervention Clinic Routine

IICP's early intervention clinic follows a specific routine, which is described in the following subsections.

Diagnosis and Referral

Doctors, hospital staff, other parents, or organizations generally refer children to the weekly diagnostic clinic run at IICP. If children are diagnosed as having cerebral palsy, then they are referred on the same day to the early intervention clinic that serves children between birth and 2 years. Children older than 2 years are served in an outpatient department. In the early intervention clinic, one professional from the team (i.e., the physiotherapist, the special educator, or the social worker) records the child's background data. Parents are told about the services provided by IICP. They are encouraged to discuss their concerns and problems regarding their child. Most parents are naturally anxious about their child's future and often seek a "cure" for his or her "ailment." With sensitivity, IICP staff explain their child's condition. To identify the parents' primary needs, the child's daily routine is discussed. Parents are then given weekly, biweekly, or monthly appointments, according to their schedules. Because most parents are generally worried about the child's physical development, staff demonstrate a few exercises on the first day, allowing parents to leave the clinic with a positive beginning step for intervention. Parents are encouraged to carry out the exercises from the first day. Simple suggestions also are given for feeding. In Bengal, most children are fed in a lying position; therefore, the importance of feeding the child in a sitting position is explained. Parents are asked to bring food to the next clinic visit so that clinicians can help with eating problems.

Individual Assessment

At the second visit, assessment is initiated. Assessments generally take two to three sessions. During assessment, the child's physical development is discussed with his or her parents. Clinicians demonstrate for them different positions that the child can practice during daily activities such as bathing, feeding, and playing. Parents are encouraged to learn how to do the exercises because they are the best teachers and therapists for their children.

Group Sessions

Group sessions demonstrate how parents can carry out the exercises through play activities like doll play or sing-alongs or daily routines like feeding, bathing, and dressing. The child's daily routine is discussed, and the parents encouraged to detail their routines. The key questions are presented in Table 6.1.

Creating Family Support Groups

Parents from a particular area of the city are encouraged to attend the clinic on the same day so they can meet each other and, in the future, perhaps start support groups. However, parents are also told to select the most convenient day. Counseling sessions are a crucial part of the intervention program. Parents are encouraged to voice their concerns and discuss their views in both individual and group sessions. Social workers make home visits to understand family needs and provide appropriate support to mothers. Family counseling sessions are taken whenever required. In particular, mothers usually require a great deal of emotional support to cope with having a child with a disability. The importance of mother–child interactions in early developmental stages is emphasized, and the significance of attachment reiterated. Social workers advise family members on the various needs that they express. These needs may range from employment to health or nutrition issues. Sometimes, the family requires specific guidance regarding family planning or drug abuse.

Table 6.1.   Questions to discuss the daily routines of the child and primary caregiver(s)

Child	Primary caregiver(s)
How does the child participate?	What do you do during each routine activity?
Does the time of day make any difference to the child's participation?	When do you do a particular activity? Is it a convenient time of the day? How much time is available to you?
Does the use of any particular item (e.g., utensil, toy, article of clothing) make a difference to the child's participation?	What items do you use to perform a particular activity (e.g., during mealtimes, which utensils do you use)?
Does the child enjoy performing an activity with a particular person in the family or community?	With whom do you perform an activity? Do (or can) any other family members help (e.g., spouse, other child, extended family member, neighbor)?
Does the place make any difference to the child's participation?	Where do you do these activities? Is it in any particular part of the home or neighborhood (e.g., is there a community toilet if there is not one within the house)?
How does the child respond?	What do you say while with your child? Do you talk, or are you too pressured to finish the activity?

Parent Training Workshops and Discussion Groups

An important objective of the early intervention clinic is not only to accelerate the child's development through intervention, but also to empower parents by providing them with information and knowledge. This is done through group workshops on various issues according to parental priorities and needs. Parents are encouraged to voice their concerns and question professionals about the program. Senior faculty from IICP, the intervention team, and experienced parents conduct these workshops, sharing basic parenting information and their experience with honesty and simplicity. These focused group discussions cover a wide range of issues from health and nutrition to genetic counseling and child-rearing practices. Community prejudice and superstitions are discussed, and ways of harnessing community support are suggested. Parents are given information about existing governmental facilities for people with disabilities and are encouraged to exercise their rights.

Teaching and Learning Materials

Even families who are nonliterate want written information, as there is generally someone in their neighborhood who can read the material to them. This is also an ideal and natural way to involve people from the community. An ordinary exercise book is often used to record in pictorial form exercises and advice given by the clinic. Written information is also available for parents in the form of simple booklets in three languages (Hindi, Bengali, and English). These booklets are well illustrated, and even parents with limited literacy skills can use them. For instance, an exercise booklet contains drawings to explain sitting and standing exercises. Titles of other booklets include "You and Your Baby," "Infant Assessment," "Play," and "Feeding."

Reaching Out to the "Unreached" in Rural Communities

The state of West Bengal has 17 districts, and IICP has a network of partners in each of district. The partners have undergone a series of training courses to help them start services in their villages. They have also initiated some early intervention programs. Using community resources is an integral and crucial part of intervention in the outreach community. Therefore, IICP is involved with conducting awareness seminars and basic training for workers from Primary Health Centres,

Aganwadi centers, and other NGOs. In some districts, the response has been encouraging, and some trainers have come to IICP to attend short training programs in basic management of cerebral palsy. A concerted effort to integrate disability in existing community services is being made by IICP and its partners, a challenge in community work.

Key Feature of the Intervention Program

The key feature of IICP's intervention program is acknowledging the roles and responsibilities of all involved in the intervention process. This includes the child, the family, and the clinic staff. By empowering parents to augment their child's learning and development and by demonstrating where and how this learning best occurs, an early intervention program can definitely succeed. The strategies used to put the program into practice are practical and feasible. The family's environment, time, and financial constraints are always considered before a program is suggested. Working around the family routine is the first strategy for providing intervention.

IICP staff begin intervention by identifying the immediate and current needs of the family and the child. These include the family's economic and survival needs. Also identified are the family's structure, the family's economic level and resources, and the parents' education level and employment status. The family's child-rearing practices, availability of time and knowledge, and attitude toward disability are noted as well. Furthermore, the structure of the community in which the family lives is noted, including attitudes, knowledge and perception of disability, beliefs, and practices. It is important to include community resources, too, such as transportation, education, and health services for children with disabilities. Based on this information, the intervention team helps the family to prioritize its needs. Family and environmental constraints and support systems are discussed, and parents are encouraged to select achievable goals for their children. The intervention team has to carefully and sensitively identify the primary caregiver (generally the mother or grandmother) and build on that person's strengths and willingness to learn. In addition to meeting the child's immediate needs, suggested programs must be feasible within the caregiver's personal time constraints and the family's routines. The initial selection of the routine context for intervention must be left to the caregiver.

A physical management program is reinforced through the daily routine by positioning the child for his or her activities to facilitate more normal postures. The prime consideration is to provide good positioning or seating, which gives the child sufficient support to perform activities. Good support during skilled activities such as eating or drinking allows a child to concentrate solely on the activity, not on maintaining his or her balance as well. Play activities provide opportunities to reinforce the physical program, and balance and movement can be practiced. Early learning skills also are taught through the child's everyday routine activities. The following vignette illustrates the efficacy of using the environment and family routines to implement an intervention program.

Priya's Story

Priya is a 3-year-old girl with athetosis. Because she had poor sitting balance, the clinicians provided a floor seat that allowed Priya to join her family when they sat on the floor to eat. As Priya had no access to a regular school, the IICP staff showed her mother how she could help Priya learn simply by talking to her during mealtimes (e.g., pointing out and naming foods and utensils). Priya reacted with such enthusiasm that her mother began to teach different things during the routine. For example, portions were used to present the concepts of *more, less, big,* and *small.* As is the practice in Bengali households, the father's meal was served in a big *thali* (plate). Priya learned that *Baba* (father) was served *more* rice than her, as she ate *less* than her father. Her father's *thali* (plate) was *big* and hers was *small.* Every time Priya's mother served food, she asked Priya to get her the bigger *thali* for *Baba,* and Priya always chose the right one!

When her mother brought fruits and vegetables home from the market, Priya enjoyed removing them from the shopping bag and putting them in a basket. Through this activity, Priya learned to identify and name the fruits and vegetables. She also learned their shapes (beans are thin and long) and colors (potatoes are brown). In addition, Priya learned concepts through touch: She could squash a tomato but not a gourd; she had to chew hard sugarcane but could merely swallow a soft piece of papaya. Furthermore, her mother learned to provide Priya with opportunities to communicate by requiring Priya to ask for what she wanted before she was served. Priya began to decide what she wanted to eat and expressed her opinions about the food that she ate. She learned new words, such as *bhalo* (nice) or *theekha* (hot), which could be generalized to other contexts and conversations. These opportunities for natural interactions added to the quality of life of the family, fostering social closeness between Priya and her parents. Priya was able to actively participate in the daily family routine and take some control of her life.

RECOMMENDATIONS FOR
PROFESSIONALS IN OTHER COUNTRIES

To summarize, one first must identify the immediate and current needs of the family and the child. These include the family's economic and survival needs, structure (family members), economic level and resources, parental employment status, and parental education level. The family's child-rearing practices, availability of time, and knowledge and attitude toward disability are noted. The community structure—such as beliefs; practices; and attitude toward, knowledge of, and perception of disability—are noted as well. Resources available in the community are identified in terms of transport facilities, education and health services, and services for children with disabilities (health clinics, child guidance clinics, diagnostic and therapeutic facilities, special schools, social service organizations, Aganwadi centers). Based on this information, the intervention team helps the family prioritize its needs. Family and environmental constraints and support systems are discussed, and parents are encouraged to select achievable goals for their children. The intervention team has to carefully and sensitively identify the primary caregiver—generally the mother or grandmother—and build on her strengths and willingness to learn. In suggesting a program, the caregiver's personal time constraints and family routine must be carefully examined. The initial selection of a routine to carry out any intervention program must be left to the caregiver. An intervention program that is easy to follow at home and will meet the child's immediate needs is selected. Several steps are suggested in planning an intervention program using a daily routine:

1. Choose a routine that is followed daily.

2. Analyze the routine. Find out what the child does during the selected routine activity by asking the family and/or caregiver, observing the family during the routine, listing what happens and what each person does during the routine, and noting the caregiver's time constraints.

3. Decide what the child needs to learn during the activity.

4. Note the child's present participation skills during the activity.

5. Decide what the child needs to learn NOW (immediate goal).

6. Plan which skills the child can learn over a period of time (long-term goals).

7. Determine the child's likes and dislikes (reward assessment).

8. Find out whether other family or community members would be interested in helping the child and the primary caregiver in carrying out the program (the community intervention team).

9. Work out specific steps to teach the present goal. The steps should be simple enough and small enough for the caregiver to follow the program, initially with professional guidance and then independently. Always welcome suggestions from the family.

10. Plan the specific strategies you will use to teach the goal. These will depend on *family characteristics* (resources, time constraints, economic/educational status, routines, perceptions and knowledge about disability) and *child characteristics* (cognitive ability, physical ability, chosen daily activity/routine).

11. Teach the caregiver facilitation strategies.

12. Demonstrate the teaching strategies during the routine. Always encourage the caregiver when small successes are attained and reward the child for his or her achievements.

CONCLUSION

The increasing challenge for practitioners is to suggest practical intervention programs that meet child *and* family needs. In their study of parental involvement with children with disabilities attending an intervention clinic in Calcutta, Goldbart and Mukherjee (1999) noted that the roles and responsibilities of mothers vary according to the type of family structure. They also observed that parents believe teaching can affect their child's development and progress, so practitioners must be sensitive to individual family practices and constraints. Involving the family in the intervention process is crucial for the success of any intervention program. Parents need to understand that all children with disabilities can learn and that the best learning environment is the home because it is a place for sharing and learning. Mothers and especially grandmothers, who are already skilled in parenting, can serve well as primary teachers. Although a clean and healthy home is important, a stimulating learning environment is not dependent on expensive objects. The home itself can be an enriching environment.

The key features of IICP's early intervention program are related to the home. The family routine and the environment are used to create an environment for learning and intervention. Sensitivity regarding the family's needs is ensured. A team approach is used, giving parents equal participation in the intervention program by sharing roles and responsibilities. While existing parental strengths are acknowledged, efforts are made to augment the family's quality of life. One way of doing this is to help create support groups within and outside the family.

It is difficult to capture the infinite variety of India in words. This chapter has shared one Indian experience. The authors do not claim that the practices in early intervention discussed in this chapter are representative of India. Yet, they share an implicit faith and belief in India's people, parents, and children that cuts across all regions, cultures, and religions. Given opportunity and knowledge, parents of children with disabilities can and should be catalysts in this enormous process of development in India.

REFERENCES

Alur, M. (2000, October). *Exclusion of children with disabilities in India: A policy perspective*. Paper presented at the 6th International Conference for Children, Edmonton, Alberta, Canada.

Anandalakshmy, S. (1998). The cultural context. In M. Swaminathan (Ed.), *The first five years: A critical perspective on early childhood care and education in India* (pp. 272–284). Thousand Oaks, CA: Sage Publications.

Census of India. (1991). *India at a glance*. New Delhi, India: Ministry of Home Affairs, Office of the Registrar General and Census Commissioner.

Census of India. (2001). *Provisional population totals: Census of India*. New Delhi, India: Ministry of Home Affairs, Office of the Registrar General and Census Commissioner.

Gandhi, I. (1980). *Eternal India*. New Delhi, India: B.I. Publications.

Goldbart, J., & Mukherjee, S. (1999). The appropriateness of Western models of parent involvement in Calcutta, India. Part 2: Implications of family roles and responsibilities. *Child: Care, Health and Development, 25*(5), 335–347.

Kolucki, B. (1999). Overview: Early childhood and disability. *Disability World, 1,* 1–14.

Ministry of Human Resource Development. (1974). *National Policy for Children*. New Delhi, India: Author.

Ministry of Human Resource Development. (1986). *National Policy on Education* New Delhi, India: Author.

Ministry of Human Resource Development. (1993). *National Primary Education Programme (Education for all: The Indian scenario)*. New Delhi, India: Author.

Ministry of Human Resource Development. (2000). *Education for all. The year 2000 assessment report*. New Delhi, India: Author.

Ramanujan, A.K. (1991). *Folktales from India*. New Delhi, India: Penguin Books India.

Status of disability in India: 2000. New Delhi, India: Rehabilitation Council of India, Ministry of Social Justice and Empowerment.

Swaminathan, M. (1998). Learning from experience: An overview of the Suraksha studies. In M. Swaminathan (Ed.), *The first five years: A critical perspective on early childhood care and education in India* (pp. 272–284). New Delhi, India: Sage Publications.

CHAPTER 7

The Right to a Good and Supportive Start in Life

BRAZIL

H. Garren Lumpkin and Maria Salete Fábio Aranha

Direito de ter direitos
The right to have rights

Since the early 1990s, governments, key institutions, nongovernmental organizations (NGOs), civil society entities, and international agencies in the Latin American and Caribbean (LAC) region have developed and implemented strategies to guarantee the rights of children and adolescents to survive, develop, participate in society, and be protected. Combined advances have been in direct response to individual country efforts to achieve World Summit for Children (WSC) and Education for All (EFA) goals. Increased emphasis has been given to children younger than 6 years of age. The May 2002 United Nations Special Session of the General Assembly on Children gathered world leaders, government institutions, civil society organizations, media, international agencies, and youth. They discussed and reconfirmed their commitment to creating a world fit for children, in which

> All girls and boys can enjoy childhood—a time of play and learning, in which they are loved, respected and cherished, their rights are promoted and protected, without discrimination of any kind, where their safety and well-being are paramount and where they can develop in health, peace and dignity. (United Nations, 2002, p. 6)

The global plan of action aims to achieve this "child-friendly world" guarantee:

> All children get the best possible start in life and have access to a quality basic education, including primary education that is compulsory and available free to all, and in which all children, including adolescents, have ample opportunity to develop their individual capacities in a safe and supportive environment. (United Nations, 2002, p. 8)

Notable improvements have occurred in the LAC region. However, not all countries have made the necessary political and financial commitments to policies and programs that link specific interventions throughout the life cycle, especially those that focus on the first years of life and address the needs of children who are at risk and/or have disabilities. In addition, the family unit has not been truly considered or supported, even though all agree that family members and other caregivers play a key role in guaranteeing the child's survival, promoting his or her development, and assisting in the timely and targeted protection against risk situations.

The purpose of this chapter is to describe some emerging early intervention and childhood disability experiences in Brazil that promote

---

The findings, interpretations, and conclusions expressed in this chapter are those of the authors and do not necessarily reflect the views of UNICEF and the State University of São Paulo "Julio de Mesquita Filho" (UNESP–Bauru), Brazil.

the values and goals of the international forums previously discussed. The approaches and strategies included are part of a more global and innovative construction process that is underway, with its expanded alliance approach that includes multiple government and civil society partners and varying geographic levels of intervention (i.e., interventions at various levels, including local, municipal, state, and national).

 ## MARIA'S STORY[1]

I made a home visit with an Infant Development Promoter (ADI) and child care assistant to the slum area near the child care center. Our goal was to enroll children who were eligible or registered in our zone. In a barely accessible shack, we discovered a child tied to a baby cart. We perceived that the girl, named Maria, had some type of disability and verified that she was not registered in our zone. When we asked Maria's mother if she had looked for child care services, she responded no, because she thought that these centers never took children with disabilities. We explained her rights to her and asked her to visit the center.

---

[1]The experiences described in this vignette are based on an interview with a child care center director who is actively participating in the development of pilot experiences for the inclusion of children with disabilities in local child development centers.

We anxiously waited for Maria and her mother, who appeared a week later. The mother was quite scared to leave her baby at the center and unsure of what to do, so the team arranged for her to meet the professional staff. She felt more enthusiastic and was advised to go have Maria's doctor complete a health form after completing an examination.

Maria's mother noted that her child has motor disabilities and seizures. Maria has already received neurological follow-up and medication for her seizures.

The "big day" arrived for Maria to attend the child care program. Despite the fact that we had received training on inclusion, we did not know for sure which procedures to use. Thus, we asked the occupational therapists and Maria's mother to attend as well. At first, Maria was very excited. She crawled and grabbed all the children, who were scared of the "different" child. At feeding time and in agreement with the mother, the ADI positioned Maria's head to place the food in her mouth. Only through this positioning and method could she eat. The rest period was a disaster. Maria did not sleep and kept hitting the door, crying, and waking up the other children.

Now, all of us in the daycare center are happy to see her advances. Maria eats cookies, bread, and desserts. Food is still placed in Maria's mouth, but it is no longer necessary to position and hold her head. What is more surprising is that she sits at the table throughout the snack period. She sleeps during the rest period, and for the duration of the activity time, she participants at her own speed. During the free period, she plays with other children. Our objective is to provide additional stimulating experiences that lead her to independence.

She is not "more different" (from others), and we learn a lot from her, such as her will and effort to walk and to express herself without words as well as the happiness to live. (Adapted from Inclusão Melhora Vida de Deficientes, 2000.)

NATIONAL CONTEXT

Brazil, a federal republic, is the world's fifth largest country, with an area of 8,511,970 square kilometers (3,286,472 square miles). The land mass represents 47.7% of South America and 20.8% of the Americas. Brazil is comprised of three main geographical regions. The most internationally known is the Amazon basin in the north, which covers more than half of the country. The Amazon basin contains the world's largest rain forest and second longest river, the Amazon. The second region is the Northeast, which consists of a coastal plain and the *sertão*, the inland plateaus and hill country. This is the country's poorest region. The third region is the Southeast, made up of the plateaus. This region, which covers approximately a quarter of the country, is the most economically developed and densely populated. According to preliminary 2000 national census results, Brazil has reached an estimated population of more than 170 million. At the end of the 20th century, Brazil experienced a rapid urbanization process. Census data from 1999, which then estimated a population of 163 million, showed that 78% of Brazilians lived in urban areas. The country's ethnic diversity is notable: 87 million white; 64 million people of mixed races; 8.6 million blacks; 742,000 individuals of Asian origin; and 261,000 people from native or indigenous populations. The cultural diversity in Brazil is also great. The country is undergoing an age and demographic population shift due to decreases in the fertility rate, which fell from 5.2 children per woman in 1980 to 2.4 in 1999. The number of children and adolescents younger than 18 years of age was 60.4 million, or 37% of the total population (Instituto Brasileiro de Geografia e Estatística, 1997).

In relation to the economic characteristics, 77 million Brazilians are considered economically active. Included in this number are 31 million women or 40% of the population and, representing glaring child labor abuses, 2.9 million children 5–14 years of age (Instituto Brasileiro de Geografia e Estatística, 1997). In U.S. dollars, Brazil's gross national product is 557 billion. It has the largest economy in Latin America and the ninth largest in the world, with an annual per capita income of U.S. $3,401 (Brazil Ministry of Education, 2001b; this amount varies among different information sources).

Although Brazil is considered an important country in terms of economic influence, its existing economic and social disparities continue to be a concern. According to the United Nations Development Programme's Human Development Report (1999), Brazil has the greatest income disparity in the world. In 1998, the richest 10% of Brazilians earned 48% of all personal income in the country while the poorest 40% earned only 7%. This means that the average income of the wealthy is 20 times greater than that of the poor. In most Latin American countries, this income differential is about 10 and in the industrialized European countries it is not quite 4.

Although poverty is present in every city, it is most prominent in the Northeast region. Of the 20 million children younger than 17 years who are poor, more than half (53.4%) live in the Northeast, followed by the Southeast (21.8%), the South (9.7%), the North (6.0%) and the Central-West (6.2%). Poverty affects some groups more than others. Women generally have higher educational levels than men, but they earn at least 30%–40% less than men for the same type of employment.

Those who are not white or who live in rural areas tend to be poor, as both groups have decreased access to a complete, quality education and, therefore, have lower educational levels. As noted previously, millions of children and adolescents also live in poor households, which often means that their rights to health, education, recreation, a name (families were and sometimes still are charged to register children at birth; those that cannot afford to do so have children that officially do not exist), and other items are denied or blocked.

Since 1988, Brazil has been establishing and strengthening a growing democratic process. The previous political structure has been changed. Following 21 years of military rule, the 1988 Constitution was approved. The new Constitution initiated a rapid decentralization process, giving greater political, administrative, financial, and legislative autonomy to municipalities. Brazil has more than 5,500 municipalities and of that number, 4,077 have fewer than 20,000 inhabitants.

The process of decentralization and community participation proposed in the Constitution carries a series of problems and challenges. The most critical follow:

- Community participation is not a common practice in all areas of Brazil.
- Roles and rules for executive power between the councils and the municipalities are poorly defined.
- Local administrations still face limited technical and operational capacity.
- Social control over financial resources is restricted.
- Insufficient participation of local entities nongovernmental organizations (NGOs) remains.

Nonetheless, existing challenges are often offset by significant opportunities and emerging successes that highlight more local involvement and ownership to achieve children's rights. In fact, a longer metaphor for this chapter could be Article 227 of the 1988 Brazilian National Constitution, which reflects a new vision growing in Brazil—that rights are important and that children should be a priority to guarantee the future of the country. Article 227 of the Constitution reads,

> It is the responsibility of the family, of society, and of the States to ensure that the child and adolescent have absolute priority to the rights to life, health, food, education, recreation, training, culture, dignity, respect, liberty, family and community, and to ensure that these rights are guaranteed in a manner free of all negligence, discrimination, exploitation, violence, cruelty and oppression.

This article and the ratification of the Convention on the Rights of the Child (CRC) paved the way for a strengthened importance and recognition of Estatuto da Criança e do Adolescente (ECA; "Statute of the Child and Adolescent"), based on the principle of "holistic protection." With the promulgation of the ECA in July 1990 (Brasil, 1990a) and the ratification of the Lei Orgânica da Saúde in September 1990 (Brasil, 1990b), Brazil clearly entered an era in which children and adolescents have "the right to have rights."

People and Culture

Portuguese is Brazil's official language and is spoken by almost all who live there. The past Spanish domination in the region was rather limited in Brazil. Portuguese explorer Pedro Alvarez Cabral claimed Brazil for Portugal in 1500. While Spain occupied western South America, the Portuguese began to develop their colony, which was more than 90 times as large as Portugal. To do this, they enslaved many local Amerindian people and introduced approximately 4 million African slaves to work on plantations and in mines. Brazil declared itself an independent empire in 1822 (when a monarchy was established), adopted a federal system of government in 1881, and became a republic in 1889. The diverse cultural setting of Brazil, thus, is based on a complex historical background. The native populations were gradually forced to share the massive territory with the Portuguese. The practice of slavery—including "importing" African slaves—introduced unique cultures, with different foods, religions, forms of art expression, and languages.

Slavery was abolished by the end of 19th century, and the country needed workers to substitute for the freed slaves. The government offered jobs and land to whomever wanted to start a new life in Brazil. This initiated a 50-year period of intense immigration from Portugal, Germany, Italy, Czechoslovakia, Spain, Syria, Lebanon, Palestine, Armenia, and Japan. Many German-speaking people settled in the southeast region. Most immigrants were sent to the inner areas of the country. Based on 1997 Instituto Brasileiro de Geografia e Estatística census estimates (with a total population of 168 million), approximately 54% of the population was considered of European descent, primarily Portuguese. *Mestizos* (people of mixed descent) of African-European and European-Native American ancestry totaled 39%. People of Native American, African–Native American, and Asian descent formed much smaller parts of the population. Results of the Pesquisa Nacional por Amostra de Domicílios (PNAD; Brazilian National Household Survey) by the Instituto Brasileiro de Geografia e Estatística (1997) show that

45% of the Brazilian population declared themselves *Black* or *Colored* (terms from the PNAD survey).

Education Services Systems

Compared to most countries in the LAC region, the Brazilian educational system is highly decentralized. Important steps have been taken to establish clear lines of responsibility for the federal, state, and municipal governments. Perhaps the most critical step was the passage of a constitutional amendment (No. 14), which was approved by the National Congress in September 1996 and in December 1996 as Law No. 9,424—the Guidelines and Foundations of National Education (LDB). The clear involvement and commitment of all three government levels is critical, especially considering the size, diversity, and political structure of Brazil—a federal republic comprised of 26 states, a federal district, and more than 5,500 municipalities. As designed in the constitutional amendment of 1996, as well as clarified by the LDB and a new funding system for primary education, lines of responsibility were established and/or reinforced:

- The provision of primary education is still divided between states and municipalities, but the funding strategy supports the increasing role of municipal governments to manage primary schooling.

- Municipalities have the responsibility to guarantee early childhood development services (including child care programs, preschools, and kindergartens).

- States are assigned the responsibility for secondary education.

- The federal government's responsibility remains establishing guidelines and standards, combined with a focus on attacking regional and social disparities through material and funding distribution. In terms of education services, the federal government concentrates on higher education and some technical schooling.

The educational system in Brazil is predominantly public and free (including universities), except for some private higher education institutions. The federal government, in partnership with states and municipalities, has undertaken critical steps to guarantee a quality primary education for all children. Perhaps the most critical steps are those directed toward achieving universal enrollment and inclusion of all children—including those at risk—in primary education services. Educational services for children younger than 14 is concentrated at the municipal level and is combined with targeted primary health care services for mothers and children younger than 6.

During the 1990s, Brazil achieved significant improvement in primary school coverage and made important advances in key educational problems: hidden exclusion (within and outside the classroom) and the poor quality of primary education that promotes failure and dropout. Primary school enrollment is massive, totaling more than 35 million students and representing an estimated 97% net enrollment. In relation to education for children with disabilities, a gradual shift is under way to focus on inclusive models. In 1998, 87% of children with disabilities enrolled in educational services were in traditional special education settings while 13% were attending inclusive models. In 2000, education in special schools and classes was reduced to 78.9%; 21% of children with disabilities were served in general education classrooms.

KEY FEATURES OF EARLY INTERVENTION

In the education field, significant advances have been made by the federal government and some individual state and municipal administrations to support and better assist children and families who live in poverty. Through use of innovative family-based financial incentives that are linked to primary school attendance, steps are being taken to eradicate child labor and to guarantee full enrollment, permanence, and learning success, especially for working children or those who are most at risk for exclusion.

Under the direction of the Secretaria de Estado de Assistência Social (SEAS; Federal Secretariat of Social Assistance) within the Ministry of Pensions and Social Assistance, a wide range of programs and projects are being implemented through joint cooperation with states and municipal governments. The main focus is strengthening the family's role and capacities. Within a wide range of social assistance initiatives, the SEAS is supporting specific early interventions for children who are at risk or who have disabilities and their families.

One example is the Roda Moinho project, undertaken collaboratively by the different levels of government and with the participation of the Catholic church's Pastoral da Criança (Child Pastoral) volunteer organization. This project addresses three main elements:

1. Improvement of health and nutrition for young children and their families

2. Promotion of child development principles that stimulate social interactions and cognitive development

3. Social promotion of families and improved conditions through the implementation of work and income-generating projects

For people with disabilities, the main SEAS objective is to coordinate; technically support; and financially assist states, municipalities, and institutions in their efforts to develop protective actions and to promote social inclusion. This support targets families that have a monthly income of less than half the minimum salary and a child with a disability.

The SEAS also works in partnership with other funding sources to improve institutional capacity and to expand existing institutional or center-based child care services for children of working mothers. This is represented by the joint partnership between the SEAS and the Workers' Support Fund (FAT), which focuses on training staff, purchasing equipment, and constructing or remodeling child care centers and preschools.

Multiple efforts continue to receive federal, state, and municipal government support to expand primary health care initiatives at the community level for expectant mothers and children younger than 6 years old. Locally paid health promoters, combined with community health volunteers of the Pastoral da Criança continue to play a key role in prevention, early detection, and family support and education efforts in the poorest regions.

Family Roles

As in most countries in the region, the extended family is considered a young child's key provider. This has been reinforced by the legal position the family has received from the 1988 National Constitution and the ECA. Since the ratification of the Constitution, key initiatives have been undertaken to support the family's role, especially for families that are at risk. However, increased political will, civil society participation, and private sector support are needed to overcome lingering disparities and the impact of poverty.

Women are typically the primary caregivers. Their situation has gradually changed. Women are increasingly part of the work force. In 1997, an estimated 40.4% of women were in the work force—up from 21% in 1970. In addition, women are increasingly assuming head-of-household responsibilities. According to 1997 Household Survey (PNAD) data, women represented 24% of all heads of families. This situation is often associated with unemployment or underemployment and/or loss of a partner, all leading to a reduction in family income.

Although the situation of women has improved since the 1980s, discrimination continues to affect the lives of women. Compared with men, women have higher levels of education (7 years compared with men's 6 years), and they have progressed in the work market. Nevertheless, negative situations remain:

- Women are paid 30%–40% less than men for the same type of work (even with most women's higher level of education).
- Women are more prone to lose their jobs, and situations such as pregnancy and children's illnesses are seen as "women problems."
- Women have fewer opportunities for training compared with men, who are considered more stable and are generally placed in decision-making positions.

In addition, the past and accumulated neglect in education for the poorest sectors continues to place a significant burden on families living in poverty. According to 1997 PNAD data, 62.6% of active workers (44 million) have less than the officially guaranteed 8 years of primary schooling, thus reducing their capacity and opportunities to earn an income adequate for fulfilling basic needs.

Political and Cultural Influences

As previously mentioned, education was targeted as a government priority during the 1990s. The EFA mobilization process during 1993–1994 provided the basis for a long-term mobilization and participation process. This entailed institutional involvement at all political levels and was supported by an expanded civil society partnership including the private sector, NGOs, trade unions, and media. With the arrival of the Cardoso government in 1995, further steps were taken to expand joint efforts by the federal, state, and municipal governments. Education was one of the new administration's priorities: "The Government's educational program, founded upon the principal of seeking equality of opportunity, incorporated the principles of universalization, decentralization, municipalization, community participation in the management of schools and greater social control of public expenditure and its outcomes" (Brazil Ministry of Education, 2001a, p. 7).

As in most Latin American countries, the existing cultural influences in Brazil include aspects that have or can have a direct impact on the relationships within families, especially in those that have children with disabilities. Relationships are often strained between parents, between siblings, and between parents and their children. As previously mentioned, Brazil has a wide range of cultural foundations based on a rich history of immigration. Most Brazilians are Roman Catholic, but other religions play important roles in Brazil. In particular, rather strong Afro-Brazilian beliefs predominate in certain regions, and Native Americans generally follow traditional religions.

Although one cannot underestimate the impact of the cultural and religious backgrounds of Brazilians, a growing "child rights culture" will probably be influential for promoting and guaranteeing the systematic provision of quality family-based services and support for children who are at risk and/or have disabilities. For the LAC region, Brazil has advanced legal frameworks on child and adolescent rights. Clear results have been made in child labor eradication and the promotion of the right to quality primary education for all. In terms of the rights of children with disabilities, inclusion of all children in primary schooling is emerging. However, limited progress has been made for the expanded promotion and implementation of the key aspects of early intervention for children who are most at risk. Parents still lack information pertaining to the rights of their children. Most parents, especially mothers, lack the confidence and self-esteem to carry out a long-term process to demand their rights and those of their children.

Since Brazil's return to democracy and the 1988 Constitutional ratification, new opportunities are available for greater family, civil society, and local government participation. Yet, those participating in the disability movement tend to remain isolated within their own circle of interest, distant from the more global child rights movement (covering issues such as street children, child abuse, child labor, and indigenous rights). Brazilian organizations like the National Association of Parents of Exceptional Children (APAE) have demonstrated an impressive capacity to mobilize and organize services for children with disabilities. Nevertheless, marked limitation remains in terms of expanding integral early intervention efforts and childhood disabilities initiatives with existing global child rights frameworks.

DESCRIPTION OF THE PROGRAM

This section describes and analyzes an innovative package of Brazilian experiences, supported through a partnership approach involving NGOs, governmental entities (federal, state, and municipal), an international agency, and other nontraditional partners. The Brazilian approach is perhaps one of the best examples in the LAC region, as it attempts to respond to multiple issues and utilize a wide range of entry points. These entry points include

- Promotion of children's rights
- Building the family's capacity for participation and support
- Promotion of wide-reaching public information on disabilities
- Development of inclusive models for child care, preschool, and primary school services
- Building the capacity for increased municipal-level approaches

This information, taken from a 2000 Sorri-Brasil and UNICEF cooperation report, covers a wide range of initiatives developed and supported by Sorri-Brasil, a nonprofit NGO based in the state of São Paulo. It is a Brazilian federation of nonprofit organizations that work together to promote the vocational rehabilitation and social inclusion of people with physical, sensory, cognitive, and social disabilities. The system is made up of the central Sorri-Brasil unit (in the city of São Paulo) and five other local centers. The first center was established in 1976 and focused on people with physical, cognitive, auditory, visual, and social impairments. Special attention was given to individuals with leprosy. Sorri-Brasil has expanded its interventions to include a strong community education program and to increase efforts to support governmental initiatives (federal, state, and municipal) aimed at inclusion. This expanded vision reflects Sorri-Brasil's global dedication to promoting inclusive contexts and developing a society that upholds dignity, justice, and equality. It has proven to be an important example of how NGOs can work through a wide range of strategies and projects that

- Reach a larger public through community education and public awareness actions
- Promote links and collaboration between organizations and sectors around a common interest, goal, or initiative
- Design and field-test new models and/or modified approaches for future expansion through the use of public and private funds
- Assist in placing new disability issues on the public agenda
- Promote operational links between NGO and government entities working in the disability field

Challenges Addressed

As with any country, the design of early intervention programs requires an expanded vision of partnerships, multilevel interventions, family and societal support, and participation. Sector involvement and collaboration, public mobilization, and capacity building are also critical elements. In addition, specific attention must be given to actions that guarantee quality and child/family-friendly services, as well as long-term expansion and sustainability. Early intervention services for children who have or are at risk for developing disabilities should be designed in light of Brazil's unique characteristics, continental size, marked economic and social disparities, increasing decentralization of responsibilities and service development, and emerging respect for child and adolescent rights.

Numerous challenges in Brazil influence the development, quality, expansion, and sustainability of family-based early intervention programs. The following subsections highlight issues common to countries in the LAC region and issues that are unique to Brazil.

Issues Similar to Other Countries in the Region

There is a lack of coordination among the health, education, and social service sectors—all partners critical to designing, implementing, funding, and expanding prevention and early intervention programs with a family-based focus. Also lacking are opportunities and support for increased participation of and capacity-building efforts for families that are at risk and those that have children with disabilities. Public information and services that support early intervention and families—and thereby reduce dependency on restrictive institutional services—are limited. Children's rights are not stressed, as opposed to the prevalent emphasis on continuation of a more "public" charity vision or approach. Furthermore, there is duplication, isolation, and/or conflict among NGOs, government services, parent organizations with government services, and so forth. Finally, there is a lack of continuity or linkages between early intervention initiatives and more formal primary school inclusion efforts, causing breaks in service planning across the life span.

Issues Unique to Brazil

One important issue that is unique to Brazil is rapid decentralization, with greater responsibilities given to more than 5,500 municipalities for a wide range of health, education, and social services. Most municipal governments lack the internal technical capacity and funding to implement all levels of education responsibilities and to support early intervention and educational inclusion actions. A positive factor unique to Brazil is the existence of a legal framework (ECA) that promotes and advances local implementation and guarantees child rights. Another positive issue is an emerging emphasis on providing financial and technical support to families living in poverty, especially to promote complete and sustainable primary school enrollment and to eradicate child labor.

Specific Program Features

The following individual program features represent the key elements of Sorri-Brasil initiatives. Although each program area has individual value, the overall feature is this package of initiatives based on the combined efforts and coordinated strategies of the multiple interventions presented. This integrated approach addresses the wide-ranging rights and needs of children with disabilities and their families while creating new strategies, thereby mobilizing new partners and promoting increased public capacity and awareness.

Public Information and Networking

Sorri-Brasil has recognized the importance of undertaking or supporting numerous public information, mobilization, and networking initiatives in collaboration with other partners. One of the main work areas is the Turma do Bairro public awareness program, which uses puppets and is based on the Kids on the Block model. Chief topics of awareness building include preventing disabilities, promoting a better understanding of disabilities, and organizing a nonaggressive environment that allows individuals who do not have disabilities to indirectly feel the impact of disabilities. This public information effort concentrates on child care, preschool, and primary school environments within the greater São Paulo area. Sorri-Brasil joined forces with the National Education Ministry and UNICEF to expand mobilization, public information, and municipal capacity-building efforts regarding child rights and inclusion of children with disabilities. The following specific actions were undertaken:

- A child rights video was prepared, promoting ECA by using the Kids on the Block model.

- A national media campaign was developed on disabilities and inclusion of students with disabilities in the general primary school system. This involved spots on national television that included Kids on the Block figures, two nationally famous television stars, and one internationally known singer. The campaign was broadcast on national television and radio with an estimated daily audience of 3.2 million. The enrollment of students with disabilities in the following year (1997) increased by 67.5% nationally as a result of the campaign (Aranha, 2000).

- Orientation and training materials were prepared for the national municipalization plan for special education. There were three guides to prepare teachers for inclusion, along with three videotapes for the national distance-education teacher training program (TV Escola). This represented the first joint project of the special education and general education systems.

Programs for Community Education and Inclusion of Children with Disabilities

In 1995, experiences gained and lessons learned from previous community education initiatives were incorporated in an expanded effort to include children with disabilities in early childhood and primary school services. As done previously, the Kids on the Block model was used to dialogue with children, parents, and professionals. The goals of such dialogue were to reduce fears and ignorance about disabilities and to prepare individuals to share the common space of school life with children who have disabilities.

In 1996, a pilot project was initiated to develop in-depth strategies and materials for promoting the inclusion of children with disabilities in creches (child care). A municipal resolution (Decree 034/97) was passed that allocated 5% of municipal child care center enrollment for the inclusion of children with disabilities. Child care workers—the agents and promoters of infant development—were motivated by the satisfaction, recognition, and support they received to expand this process. (They were also motivated by the fact that a decree was passed, which, in a sense, recognized the good work that they were undertaking.) In addition to the new law, important technical and operational materials and instruments were prepared.

Based on pilot experiences undertaken with two municipal governments and supported by Sorri-Brasil, further efforts were taken to expand the Integration of Children with Disabilities in Creche Program. Capacity-building efforts were supported by the prepared training strategies and materials. The initial training for municipal-level multipliers (i.e., the individuals responsible for training other individuals) was extremely important for promoting the sustainability and quality of intervention.

Sorri-Brasil participated in "Re-definition of Educational Attention for Children in Risk and with Disabilities" (Inclusive School—School for All), an experimental program in the São Paulo state. The main objectives were to 1) improve conditions to correct existing problems in serving children who demonstrate learning disabilities, 2) reduce the high levels of school dropout and grade repetition, 3) reduce the elevated number of students sent for psychological evaluations, 4) increase primary school completion, and 5) increase specialized education possibilities for children with disabilities in public school contexts without cutting their participation in general education classrooms.

New Efforts Focusing on Family Contexts and Support

In its work in other initiatives, Sorri-Brasil found that most families had significant problems gaining access to services, either because they lacked service knowledge or because the required services were nonexistent. The disappointment of not having an "ideal" child combined with abrupt lifestyle changes and family dynamics also was seen to affect Brazilian families. The overwhelming impact on mothers is clear, especially when they are heads of household. The degree of impact on fathers is still unclear due to the predominately cultural vision that fathers are not sensitive to the needs of young children and generally are not involved in child rearing.

Based on this situation, a new project was aimed at developing strategies for the orientation and support to families having children and adolescents with disabilities. The initial focus was preparing families to manage their child's disability and to appropriately intervene while reducing dependency on formal or institutional-based services. Two levels of strategies were targeted for design and implementation: 1) increased family support through peer group involvement and 2) reduced family stress.

Increased Family Support   The first component, increased family support, has targeted groups of parents, groups of siblings, and groups of children and adolescents with disabilities. Interactions between all family members are emphasized, and siblings—rather than simply parents—are included. Family empowerment components are also emphasized to 1) increase the capacity to understand and defend child and family rights and 2) improve skills for parenting children with disabilities. Furthermore, family-based initiatives are targeted as opposed to service-generated responses.

Preliminary results showed advances and learning experiences for the three groups. Parents were able to identify and share problems or to share existing solutions. This opportunity started a process for addressing existing social isolation, and specific service-related needs were discussed (i.e., the identification of community services and the processes required to use them). For the first time, siblings of children with disabilities could share experiences, frustrations, and lingering feelings of rejection by peers. Children with disabilities were given opportunities to share experiences and play together outside the formal education environment.

Although progress has been made over the course of project implementation and experimentation, numerous difficulties remain that jeopardize the sustainability and impact of the models being developed. For most families, frequency of participation is influenced by poverty and daily challenges to meet the most basic needs. In addition, the long-term frustration and rejection that many families have faced has caused skepticism about any changes resulting from group meetings. In fact, many families want their children in special education environments and are not convinced that inclusive models are the best for their children. Similarly, many municipal-level workers, who are responsible for multiplying or expanding project actions, are not truly committed to inclusion. This is a common situation in countries that take a joint NGO–government approach. Municipal government changes also tend to increase feelings of job insecurity among public workers, affecting their level of commitment to and participation in project development.

Reduced Family Stress   During the initial stages of development, program objectives were established for the second component, reduced family stress. One objective was to give family members times in which they are free to pursue private or individual interests and to complete common family routines. Another was to promote specific actions that reduce stress for families of people with disabilities. A third goal was to promote the mental health of people with disabilities through social interaction, rest, and recreation.

In addition to objectives directed toward the family unit, Sorri-Brasil aimed to share with other organizations (public and private) the "know-how" that it developed or expanded. This was accomplished by training professionals in other organizations to develop and duplicate this type of program and creating conditions for the implementation of this program by other organizations and in other São Paulo municipalities.

Based on respite care service models in the United States of America, this innovative effort in Brazil has attempted to combine a volunteer approach for family-based workers under the network of formal supervision. Although this component is new and experimental, initial results are clearly consistent with other international experiences.

Entre Amigos (Between Friends)

Sorri-Brasil had the goal of reaching a larger portion of society with critical and timely information of a legal, technical, and informative nature. Thus, existing information-network models were explored. The network of the National Information Center for Children and Youth with Disabilities (http://www.nichcy.org), operating out of Washington, D.C., and serving the United States, was used as a model and starting point for the Brazilian model, Entre Amigos (http://www.entreamigos.com.br). In the initial planning process, a wide range of groups were targeted, such as people with disabilities, families, service providers, universities, governmental entities, and NGOs.

The main goals of this initiative were to offer information, orientation, and referral for children and adolescents with disabilities, their families and circles of friends, professionals, and society in general. This was to be accomplished through fax, e-mail, the Internet, and direct attention (i.e., going directly to one of the participating organizations for support or orientation). Specific objectives included

- Provide information to families of children and adolescents with disabilities and to society regarding people with disabilities, services, and related products
- Refer children and adolescents with disabilities, as well as family members, for rehabilitation, education, health, work opportunities, and other services
- Produce informative printed materials regarding frequently asked questions
- Support other existing disabilities information networks by disseminating their experiences and knowledge on related subjects
- Stimulate the integration of and mutual cooperation between institutions involved in the project to construct an expanding interinstitutional network

The initial steps in 1998 were dedicated to the design, creation, and implementation of the network's diverse elements: web site; data bank; and direct attention. Perhaps one of the most important results of the initial period was the identification of a strategy that included 21 institutional partners from different governmental, NGO, and civil society sectors. This initiative promoted a common effort but allowed each organization to maintain its autonomy.

The Entre Amigos web site provides access to a wide range of features: an events calendar, news, direct attention, a chat room, a forum, information on specific themes or topics, a guide on where to go for support, a bulletin board, institutional links, and legal advice. This combined information and support program was initially directed to the local São Paulo population. Due to the nature and capacity of the system, however, a wide range of national and international users are now taking advantage of the web site.

RECOMMENDATIONS FOR PROFESSIONALS IN OTHER COUNTRIES

The direct transfer or application of external project or service models in different political or cultural situations often leads to frustration and failure. In only a few cases has success been achieved in applying models in their original form without modifications. However, a number of the program's aspects are usable, and lessons learned and strategies tested by Sorri-Brasil can be applied within different situations if appropriate adjustments are undertaken.

Within this context and based on emerging results in Brazil, there are several considerations for other countries that want to design, develop, implement, and/or expand the early intervention initiatives described in this chapter. The following recommendations respond to lessons learned through the previously mentioned experiences (including the use of a multiple-strategy approach) and building on other regional efforts in the early intervention field.

A multiple-component or project focus, as developed in Brazil, can lead to an integrated approach that covers all critical stages of the life cycle and focuses on both internal and external factors that directly affect the lives of children and their families. Although a long-term strategy with multiple components should consider the relationship among all elements during the initial stage, applying a staggered approach is recommended, beginning with components or projects that have the strongest potential to mobilize new partners and political will.

When developing model projects, consideration initially should be given to elements that ensure financial and technical sustainability, expansion, and service quality. In particular, the following four elements should be considered:

1. The promotion, design, and approval of targeted legislation is essential to guarantee the legal framework for sustainable interventions and funding, as well as to reduce the impact of political/governmental changes.

2. A field-tested, systematic, and decentralized staff training system—with the necessary training materials—is critical for ensuring sustainable and flexible training for a wide range of service providers and partners.

3. For long-term service development and expansion, it is important to evaluate and document experiences in using the modified approach, to calculate financial requirements, and to train staff and other partners.

4. Incorporating new partners (some nontraditional) in the process and undertaking a wide-reaching dissemination process for the public assist in promoting expanded ownership, sustainable public demand, and new levels of participation.

As experienced in Brazil and elsewhere, care must be given to evaluating and considering the multiple factors that can promote or block successful early intervention initiatives. The most appropriate way to guarantee the responsiveness and cultural appropriateness of the strategy while maintaining a technically sound approach is to include key beneficiaries (i.e., children with disabilities and their families) and service providers in project design, implementation, monitoring, and evaluation.

Finally, a partnership approach including governmental, nongovernmental, civil society, and international participants has been critical to the success of early intervention efforts in Brazil. The strengths and weaknesses of each partner must be considered and evaluated in the design and implementation of the long-term strategy.

CONCLUSION

This chapter has described initiatives undertaken by Sorri-Brasil and other key government and civil society partners. All efforts have been directed toward increasing public sector capacity to implement a wide range of prevention, early intervention, and inclusive service models. Another objective of the efforts has been to promote the transformation of Brazilian society to be more committed to supporting and improving the lives of children with disabilities and their families. This chapter's descriptions of project components probably will not provide the required in-depth information for other institutions or countries to fully develop similar models. However, this material may promote an integrated vision for early intervention, which incorporates multiple indispensable strategies that strengthen families, promote social inclusion, and guarantee the right of all children to a good and supportive start, quality education, and preparation for life.

REFERENCES

Aranha, M.S. (2000). *Analise da Produção Resultante da Parcereia entre Sorri: Brasil e UNICEF 1995–2000* [Analysis of results of the Sorri-Brasil and UNICEF partnership 1995–2000]. Unpublished document, Brazil.

Brasil. (1988). *Constituição da República Federativa do Brasil* [Constitution of the Federal Republic of Brazil]. Brasília: Promulgada em 05 de outubro de 1988.

Brasil. (1990a). *Estatuto da Criança e do Adolescente.* Brasília: Lei no. 8.069, 13 de julho de 1990.

Brasil. (1990b). *Lei Orgânica da Saúde.* Brasília: 19 de setembro de 1990.

Brazil Ministry of Education. (2001a). *Bringing universal primary education to Brazil: A success story.* Brasília: Author.

Brazil Ministry of Education. (2001b). *Education in Brazil (1995–2001)*. Brasília: Author.

Durham, E.R. (2001). *Educação*. Retrieved February 2002 from http://www.mec.gov.br

Inclusão melhora vida de deficientes: Antes isolados, portadoes são agora incluidos no processo educacional [Inclusion improves the life of the disabled: Before isolated—the disabled are now included in the educational process]. (2000, July 11). *O Estado de São Paulo (Cidades) [The State of São Paulo (Cities)]*, p. C4.

Instituto Brasileiro de Geografia e Estatística. (1997). *Pesquisa Nacional por Amostra de Domicílios (PNAD)*. Rio de Janeiro, Brazil: Author.

UNICEF Brasil. (2001). *Situação da Infância Brasileira 2001*. Brasília: Author.

United Nations. (1989). *Convention on the rights of the child*. New York: Author.

United Nations. (1990, September). *World declaration on the survival, protection and development of children*. Declaration made at the World Summit for Children, New York.

United Nations. (2002, May). *A world fit for children: Declaration and plan of action*. General Assembly Special Session for Children, New York.

United Nations Development Programme. (1999). *Human development report 1999*. New York: Oxford University Press.

CHAPTER 8

A Family Partnership Model of Early Intervention

EGYPT

Naguib Khouzam, Eglal Chenouda,
and Georgette Naguib

Learning when young is like carving in stone.

This chapter begins with a vignette to illustrate the work of the Seti Center, Caritas–Egypt. The chapter continues with descriptions of Egypt's national context and early intervention features. It then describes how the Seti Center's parent-partnership model of early intervention accounts for such context characteristics. The community's role in early intervention is discussed as well.

  ## RAHMA'S STORY

Every morning, Rahma (whose name means "mercy") wears her uniform and goes to school like hundreds of thousands of other Egyptian school children. However, Rahma was born with Down syndrome, and children with Down syndrome usually are not admitted to general education schools in Egypt. Rahma's inclusive education results from the tenacity of her mother, who is a firm believer in the Egyptian proverb, "Learning when young is like carving in stone." In fact, Rahma was just a few months old when she and her mother joined the early intervention program at the Seti Center, Caritas–Egypt. As the letters *SETI* stand for Support, Education and Training for Integration, the center's objectives are training professionals who work in the disabilities field and presenting pilot models of intervention and rehabilitation for people with disabilities and their families.

By actively participating in Rahma's sessions and attending parent education programs, Rahma's mother was able not only to develop her daughter's abilities, but also to help other families of children with Down syndrome by showing them what Rahma has achieved. Moreover, she is head of the newly established Learning Disabilities Unit in Rahma's school. Being a full partner in her daughter's educational process gave her knowledge and skills to be a guide for other families and an advocate for the rights of children with disabilities in Egypt.

NATIONAL CONTEXT

Since ancient times, Egypt has been recognized as the gift of the Nile. Its more than 60 million inhabitants cram the Nile's riverbanks, maybe

The authors express their thanks to all members of early intervention teams in Cairo and Alexandria. Their dedication, flexibility, listening capacities, and concern about the welfare of children and the satisfaction of parents allowed them to develop, adapt, and innovate the program described in this chapter. In turn, the program is now a model for other institutions in Egypt, Jordan, Syria, Morocco, and Palestine that want to present similar services.

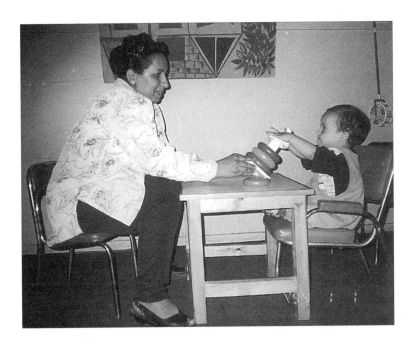

as a sign of eternal gratitude to this great benefactor. However, the overpopulation in this narrow green strip leaves miles of desert unoccupied.

Situated on the northeast coast of Africa, Egypt's geographical position has exposed it to the influence of three continents: Africa, Asia, and Europe. Considered a developing country, moderate in both a political and religious sense, Egypt gained its independence in the early 1950s. Three successive wars in the subsequent 30 years consumed most of the country's yearly budget. After the peace treaty was signed at the end of the 1970s, attention was finally given to improving the country's deteriorating infrastructure and to upgrading services such as health and education.

People and Culture

Settled, nonadventurous, and agrarian by nature, Egyptians, like their millenary crops, do not easily uproot. Often, they work, marry, have children, and ultimately die within the same area—sometimes even within the same neighborhood.

Family members, even distant relatives, are most always within reach, and the extended family is an established and influential structure. The family is always available for help, support, advice, or occasional criticism on every matter of life, including child-rearing practices.

This type of popular wisdom is especially important because illiteracy is widespread: 35% of the population is illiterate, and women make up more than two thirds of that number (National Council, 2000). Profoundly religious by nature, Egyptians consider all that happens to them—good or bad—as God sent, and they have learned to be grateful for it. Loaded with their cultural heritage, Egyptians have proven responsive to the polish of modern science and civilization. A land of contradictions, state-of-the-art inventions in all fields exist alongside millenary practices. These practices stem from centuries of Pharaonic, followed by Christian, and then Islamic civilizations.

Disability Services Delivery System

As in all developing countries, children constitute a vast segment of the population: 45% of Egyptians are younger than 18 years (National Council, 2000). Prevalence rates of disability for children younger than 15 years lie somewhere between 5% and 10%. Discrepancies in the results obtained from various studies are due to a lack of reliable statistics (Mansour, 1997), misunderstandings about the international classification system for disability, and the high cost of undertaking studies on a national scale based on truly representative samples.

Regarding intervention for children with disabilities, there is a wide gap between needs and available services. Despite the long heritage of institutional systems—both governmental and nongovernmental—in Egypt, only 1% of people with disabilities receives any form of rehabilitation services (El Sherif, 1996). The gap in the present system has various causes. There are personnel shortages; the number of individuals with training covers only 10% of the need. There is a shortage in the number of centers providing intervention services, too, as well as the impossibility of extending existing centers. Even with the existing centers, the prohibitively high cost of certain services deprives most families of access to them. The uneven geographical distribution of existing services also limits access: 80% of the services are in large cities, mainly Cairo and Alexandria, while the suburbs, slums, small towns, and other areas suffer from serious shortages. In addition to distance, the cost of transportation, difficulty of traveling with a child with a physical disability, and inconvenient services schedules and operating hours represent major inhibiting factors for most families (French Center, 1997).

Aside from such concrete reasons, there is poor public and parental awareness concerning disabilities, the types and locations of available services, and the efficacy of intervention. Moreover, physicians do not sufficiently recognize the role of families—a situation that leads to mistrust, a serious lack of communication, and a poor exchange of information between parents and professionals. Attitudes toward disability also differ greatly according to the type of disability, being more positive for physical disabilities than for sensory ones and the least positive for mental retardation. As a result, most services are either health-oriented, especially for young children, or designed on the basis of charity rather than from any legally acknowledged rights (Magdi, 1995).

Furthermore, many children are ineligible for services according to the conditions of admission imposed by centers. Children with multiple disabilities, who constitute 33% of total incidence of disabilities, are refused admission by most centers (French Center, 1997). Centers and special schools affiliated with the Ministry of Education accept children at school age (6 years), while those affiliated with the Ministry of Social Affairs may accept children as early as 4 years. Thus, there is no formal system of intervention for infants and children younger than 4 years of age.

Finally, certain types of services simply do not exist. The Ministry of Health, the primary coordinator of services for people with disabilities, has a huge network of services that covers not only towns, but also more than 4,000 villages and is considered one of the largest in the Middle East. In addition to institutes for poliomyelitis, ophthalmology, and hearing and language, it established Mother and Child Health Units, which have made considerable efforts in covering vaccinations, nutrition, and medication. Yet, the percentage of children with disabilities who receive health assistance is still very small, and the partial role of many existing programs does not include intervention. A great deal remains to be done in the areas of prevention, detection, and intervention. Efforts in these three areas have been undermined by several difficulties. In rural areas, a higher number of children per family is considered an asset. Therefore, prenatal examinations and genetic counseling pose real problems of feasibility and acceptability among parents. In particular, cost and feasibility problems exist for neonatal screening for disorders such as phenylketonuria, hypothyroidism, and thalassemia. In addition, a large percentage of pregnant women in both rural and urban areas still give birth at home with untrained help. This results in numerous cases of motor disabilities and mental retardation. Furthermore, a lack of awareness among medical personnel regarding the early symptoms of disabilities means that many disabilities are not detected before 2 years of age (French Center, 1997).

Most of the limited early intervention services that exist, including the Seti Center's model, were initiated by nongovernmental organizations (NGOs). These services have spread to a few training institutes (e.g., genetics units in the National Research Center and in some medical schools) and to the Mother and Child Health Units in the Alexandria governorate.

KEY FEATURES OF EARLY INTERVENTION

Early intervention in Egypt has been shaped by political as well as theoretical and cultural factors. These influences are described in the following subsections.

Political Influences

To improve the disastrous situation of people with special needs in Egypt, a 5-year plan was designed in 1997. This plan has supporting strategies and programs that cover most domains pertaining to disability, from early detection to public awareness and the roles of families, media, and NGOs. The political will is very much in favor of radical changes. President Mubarak declared the decades 1990–2000 and 2000–2010 to be the first and second "Decade[s] of the Egyptian Child." Egypt also has ratified the world convention on the Rights of the Child (National Council, 2000).

The 5-year plan is a component of The National Strategy to Combat Handicaps in Egypt, which was designed by the cabinet, the highest executive authority in the country. Moreover, the First Lady, Mrs. Mubarak, has chaperoned many events in relation to children with disabilities. She is conscious that doing so automatically publicizes the events, raises public awareness, and gives considerable support to endeavors aimed at improving the existing situation.

The difficulty still resides in allocating enough resources and in coordinating different sectors and entities. Despite a stable and well-established legislative framework, parallel uncoordinated plans exist, as does dichotomy between NGO and public health services.

Theoretical and Cultural Influences

Rehabilitation in Egypt traditionally has been characterized by a medical approach. Three distinct sectors within the health assistance services have emerged: a popular sector, a professional sector, and a folk sector.

The popular sector, although seldom recognized, is the largest and probably the most immediate determinant of care. It includes the entire nonprofessional popular culture at the individual, family, and social network levels (neighbors, extended family members, friends, and acquaintances). In this circle, illness is first defined, and health care activities are started. Within this sector, choices are made about when and whom to consult, whether to comply with instructions, and when to switch treatment alternatives (Cook, 1997). This sector is particularly important because health care is not always solicited. Treatment recommendations often are not carefully followed, the utility of prostheses is underestimated, and there is sometimes little confidence in health service personnel and the care that they offer (Hussein, 1997).

This attitude is partly caused by the second sector, the professionals themselves. Professionals often start with the presumption that they possess all of the knowledge and that people outside the medical circle should have little say in matters of health (Cook, 1997). As a result, communication between clinicians and families is often inefficient, and their perceptions of service delivery characteristics overlap very little (French Center, 1997). Complaints abound on both sides. On the one hand, professionals complain that families never seem to realize the extent or severity of the problem, talk too much, do not understand what is required of them, do not persevere, "shop around" for other professionals, or are passive and unresponsive. On the other hand, families complain that professionals do not listen to them, are always in a hurry, and ask them to achieve unrealistic or complicated goals. They often feel that professionals want to use their children for research purposes. Families also indicate that professionals sometimes charge too much for their services, use jargon that nobody understands, hold back the truth or give it in a blunt and inconsiderate manner, or falsely reassure parents that children will "outgrow" their problems.

This situation of mutual distrust often leads families to consider the third level of health services, namely the folk sector. This sector acquires its prominence from the fact that much of the population believes in occult causes of disability: bad spirits, the "evil eye," fate, God-inflicted trials, reparation for sins committed by the parents, or punishment for not desiring the baby (Hussein, 1997). Folk medicine is easier to use and cheaper than professional medicine. It includes spiritual healers, sheikhs, priests, and herbalists. A different set of beliefs and values governs the understanding and management of illness and health issues at this level. For instance, epileptic seizures are not addressed by medication but by spiritual healers, as from this perspective, seizures are considered an indication of possession by demons. If folk medicine proves ineffective, families can still look upon their child with a disability as a *baraka* (grace) from heaven, and they can "accept God's will without murmur" (Hussein, 1997).

The service delivery situation is further complicated by the fact that pediatricians and general practitioners sometimes miss early signs of disability because disabilities are not covered adequately in medical school. In cases of established diagnoses, some physicians may evade the issue, not having been trained at breaking the news to parents. Thus, they leave this burden to another physician on the basis that parents will eventually find out. Physicians also may intentionally ignore the issue when they do not know where to send the families for intervention. A head nurse working for a governmental hospital as part of its mobile health team related such a dilemma. During a visit to a remote area, a mother brought a 5-month-old boy with Down syndrome to the mobile clinic for routine vaccination. It was clear that the mother did not know about her child's condition. The head nurse believed that it was no use telling the mother, as there were no services nearby and she did not know how to counsel parents in such cases. Finally, although no medical treatment has been approved for cognitive disabilities, some physicians still prescribe anabolic and stimulant drugs, which at times are responsible for seizures.

The role of psychologists and social workers in the service delivery system is not sufficiently clear. Furthermore, the scarcity of physiotherapists and speech-language pathologists, the absence of occupational and psychomotor therapists, and the lack of communication among different specialists working with the same child all contribute to fragmented and incomplete intervention.

Family Roles and Early Intervention Services

The ambivalent feelings parents may have for their child with a disability is further complicated in Egyptian society by gender, succession, and heritage issues. The birth of a baby with a disability creates great disappointment when he or she is the first child of previously sterile parents or when he is the much-valued baby boy—a potential inheritor of the family's name and wealth. When a daughter is born with a disability, there is fear of her being sexually abused in the future. All these factors, together with social pressure, may increase feelings of shame, embarrassment, and social isolation. This may result in rejecting or simply neglecting and not sufficiently stimulating the child.

Other factors may challenge early intervention teams: fathers who are unwilling to cooperate, siblings who have their own problems in coping, extreme poverty and low socioeconomic status, illiteracy, and low educational level. In fact, epidemiological studies have shown that the educational level of mothers of children with disabilities is significantly lower than that of mothers whose children do not have disabilities. Moreover, anthropological studies have shown that mothers' attitudes concerning disability were more negative among those with lower educational levels (French Center, 1997).

Furthermore, certain aspects of disabilities and chronic illness necessitate the use of health resources over time. In a developing country like Egypt, the choice and continued use of services may be hindered by parameters such as accessibility—especially transportation, cost, and communication with medical personnel (Cook, 1997).

There are some positive features of early intervention in Egypt. First, in the majority of cases, health care is free. Moreover, families do not commonly seek boarding institutions for their child with a disability. Families generally are willing to keep the child in their care. Great support can be expected from extended family, neighbors, and community members; all are ready to help when they are shown how.

DESCRIPTION OF THE PROGRAM

The Seti Center runs one of Egypt's few early intervention programs. In 1987, Caritas–Egypt, an NGO affiliated with Caritas Internationalis, established the Seti Center. Caritas Internationalis typically works in the fields of health, youth, women's promotion, refugees, and children's welfare.

Given the lack of infrastructures that facilitate access to intervention and the scarcity of services, the solution for Egypt is to rely on families and the support of institutions or communities. Thus, the Seti Center has been developing a model of early intervention services in partnership with families. This model assists families in ensuring that their children with disabilities develop to their full potential while accounting for the Egyptian context, with its strengths and weaknesses. The model is aimed at

- Helping children from birth to age 4 years who have disabilities such as Down syndrome, cerebral palsy, cognitive disabilities, chromosomal anomalies, or metabolic deficiencies
- Helping to develop children's motor, social, and cognitive abilities, as well as their communication and self-help skills
- Supporting families to help them understand their child's disability and overcome feelings of shame and embarrassment, as well as to show them how to carry out the intervention plan
- Supporting and training pediatricians, health professionals, and community health workers to raise awareness of disability characteristics and services and the importance of early screening
- Training the staff of NGOs and governmental organizations on the strategies and techniques of early intervention in order to expand

the model, thus replicating the model and increasing the number of beneficiaries

The Seti Center's model of service delivery is built on the belief that creating true partnerships with parents is not only desirable but is also essential to the success of any early intervention program. Studies have suggested that active therapy, when coupled with counseling, produces significant improvement in children's abilities in areas such as communication (Rustin, 1995). Bronfenbrenner stated that without family involvement, "any effect of intervention, at least in the cognitive sphere, appears to erode rapidly once the program ends" (cited in McConkey, 1985, p. 20). Thus, one of the aims of the early intervention program is to restore parents' confidence in their parenting skills (Rustin, 1995). This approach can be contrasted with packaged "recipes" for action prepared without parental involvement, which risk increasing rather than decreasing parental dependence on specialists and eroding parental autonomy and self-confidence (Cunningham, cited in McConkey, 1985). Moreover, programs that respect home environments and routines have a better chance of success than those that ignore family structures of child care or impose too many changes in daily routines (McConachie, cited in McConkey, 1985). Parents should not be viewed as passive recipients of information from others who know better; rather, services should be characterized by the full sharing of knowledge, skills, and experience between parents and professionals. Such focus provides an ongoing support system for the child that reinforces a program's effects while it is in operation and maintains its benefits after it ends (Bronfenbrenner, cited in McConkey, 1985).

Practices that Ensure Partnership

The Seti Center's model is based on the importance of family involvement for optimal child outcomes and on belief in the capability of parents to act as intervention partners. This model of service delivery has six main objectives:

1. Ensure parent involvement.
2. Provide parents with knowledge and skills.
3. Ensure program structure and continuity.
4. Make equipment available.
5. Maintain motivation and participation.
6. Spread awareness and improve service accessibility.

Specific strategies have been adopted to attain these objectives. A description of each follows.

Ensure Parent Involvement

The program is designed to involve parents in assessment, objective setting, and intervention using the methods illustrated next.

User-Friendly Assessment Tools The program utilizes developmental checklists with simple terminology, such as the Portage Guide to Early Education (Bluma, Shearer, Frohman, & Hilliard, 1976) translated into Arabic and adapted to Egyptian culture. Such checklists have proven successful in explaining to parents the process of assessment, the kind of information needed, the features of child performance to observe, and the levels of functioning to identify. Sometimes these charts are given to parents to complete at home, thus involving fathers and other family members as well. A system of drawings and checkmarks is adopted for parents who cannot read. It is explained that assessment is ongoing and that sharing of information can be done anytime during the intervention process.

Clear, Accessible, Simply Formulated Objectives After identifying the child's level of functioning, parents are helped in selecting objectives for intervention according to their child's capabilities and their own priorities. Objectives are formulated in simple, clear words. They are directly applicable to the home, making use of equipment and materials that are already available. Home visits are planned at this stage to ensure the home environment is accounted for while further planning the intervention.

Parent Input in Adapting Activities Parents are invited to express their opinions as to whether suggested activities are appropriate for their child. They are also asked to help modify and adapt the activities to improve them. Parents' suggestions are welcomed, valued, and put into practice. This collaborative model enables professionals and parents to generate creative solutions to various problems collaboratively.

Provide Parents with Knowledge and Skills

In true partnerships, both partners possess equal information to ensure efficient action. This is accomplished through the following activities.

Parent Education Program The parent program runs parallel to the child's intervention program. It is designed for groups of parents whose children have similar needs. This provides parents with the theoretical background to understand typical child development in various domains, the nature and causes of disability, the rationale for intervention, and suggested action when faced with delays in certain areas. Audiovisual aids, such as videotapes and drawings, are used to make information accessible to parents from various educational backgrounds. Written material is distributed, complete with charts and illustrations, for parents' future reference.

Practical Demonstration in Addition to Counseling   Professionals demonstrate methods for teaching the child. Parents practice these procedures with the professionals so that they can continue the support at home.

Information and Feedback   A specific time is set within each session for both parents and professionals to comment on what occurred, to determine whether the activity was a success, and to make recommendations for future sessions or home activities. In achieving this objective, professionals learn to give away their knowledge and skills—indeed, whatever power they have. This empowers parents to actively perform these activities. This is not an easy task for professionals. In fact, it is "one of the most difficult skills that (highly trained professionals) have to learn" (Mittler, cited in McConkey, 1985). Moreover, setting aside a time for sharing information and feedback greatly improves communication between parents and professionals, which in turn has a positive effect on the morale of both and on their interaction with the child. A mother commented, "No matter how slowly my child is progressing, at least I know that once a week, someone is there to listen to me and share my burden." Her statement is reminiscent of another Egyptian proverb: "I'd rather have you greet me nicely than offer me lunch." This is in accordance with the results of the study by Huang and Heifetz (cited in McConkey, 1985), which found that parents first assess a professional's warmth, interest, concern, and understanding when classifying him or her as helpful. This criterion is followed by the professional's ability to allow parent participation in decision making. Experience and efficiency come in third place!

Ensure Program Structure and Continuity

Some well-conceived programs have failed for lack of follow-up or because schedules are either too lax or too busy. Sometimes, parents also have complained that activities were too time consuming. To ensure a balanced schedule, several procedures were adopted.

Weekly Sessions   One-hour weekly sessions have proved successful because they allow ample time for home practice of the objectives and for close follow-up and monitoring if problems arise. In addition, professionals can serve more children per week than they could before parents began carrying out activities at home.

Short, Clear Home Assignments   Activities for selected objectives are agreed on jointly, and parents indicate the frequency at which they will perform these activities throughout the week. On the weekly assignment sheet, they mark which activities were completed and include their comments, which are to be discussed in the following sessions.

Follow-Up at the Program's End   Monthly sessions for follow-up are scheduled to give parents support when needed.

Make Equipment Available

Parents frequently complained that materials or equipment used in traditional services are not readily available or are too costly. The following components address this issue.

Low-Cost Materials   Toys, books, and materials used during the sessions either are inexpensive and easily obtainable or can be made with materials available at home. Empty cheese boxes, colored clothespins, and wooden spoons, for instance, have been used to produce attractive and durable toys. Parents are allowed to borrow such toys from the center or are shown how to make their own.

Custom, Low-Cost Aids   Adapted aids and equipment for children with cerebral palsy or other motor disabilities can be custom made at low cost in a workshop attached to the early intervention unit. Standing frames, adapted chairs, and special eating utensils are manufactured out of inexpensive but durable material.

Maintain Motivation and Participation

Involving additional family members and showing parents how others can benefit from their experience proved instrumental in maintaining parent interest and enthusiasm. Various factors helped achieve this.

Family-to-Family Support   Meetings between families are arranged for sharing experiences, exchanging useful addresses, discussing particularly helpful activities, or simply expressing feelings. Families new to the Seti Center are encouraged to attend these meetings to get valuable support from people who have already been through it all and who can counsel them. As these Egyptian proverbs say, "To ask advice from an experienced person is better than to ask a doctor," and "One whose hand is put in fire will advise you better than one whose hand is in water."

Fathers' Involvement   By arranging meetings on Fridays (day off) and scheduling excursions for the whole family, the early intervention service tries to engage fathers. The aim is for fathers to meet together and feel that they have an important role in the lives of their children and wives. Fathers seem passive because they do not know what to do or are afraid of doing it awkwardly. The Seti Center has found that allowing fathers to express their feelings and talk about their children, as well as explaining to them how they can help their children and share their feelings with their wives, helps fathers take a more active role with their families and other families that need support. Meeting other fathers who have succeeded in taking this active role is more effective in changing fathers' negative attitudes than advice and directions given from the best of professionals.

Siblings' Program   In answer to parents' requests, a siblings program was started and proved to be quite successful. Group activities for brothers and sisters are organized to explain the nature and causes of disability, to allow siblings to express and discuss their feelings, and to suggest ways in which they can help their brother or sister and their parents. They get the chance to meet other siblings who have overcome their feelings of shame, embarrassment, or rejection, and they form among themselves groups of mutual support. In addition, they have subsequently exerted a positive impact in their schools and among their friends. For instance, the brother of a boy with Down syndrome indicated suitable services to his teacher, who himself had a baby with Down syndrome and did not know what course of action to follow.

Family Outings   As previously mentioned, extended family is still a significant unit in Egyptian culture. Extended family members may undermine parents' efforts through constant pressure or criticism, or they may support these efforts if the objectives are understood. To ensure this support, grandparents and aunts or uncles living with the family are invited to excursions and summer camps.

Spread Awareness and Improve Service Accessibility

The pediatricians or existing health services from whom parents initially seek help are often disappointing. However, instead of creating new structures, it is more important and economical to revitalize existing ones—especially those of primary health care—through training for physicians and personnel (French Center, 1997). Three programs were implemented to accomplish this goal.

Physician Awareness Program   Awareness meetings for pediatricians, physicians, and health care workers are organized to increase their knowledge about disability, increase their ability for early detection, give them information about existing services, and modify their attitudes toward disability. During these meetings, parents share with physicians their experiences of first being told about their children's disabilities. Painful versus reassuring ways of breaking the news are discussed. Medical professionals with a positive attitude toward children with disability are invited to share their knowledge and experience. This "expert" opinion is often instrumental in modifying physicians' negative attitudes because it comes from people in "the privileged circle." Pamphlets containing useful information and typical development charts (to help detect early signs of disability) are distributed.

Professional Training Programs Professionals in primary health care units or pediatric hospitals are offered training on early intervention service delivery in partnership with parents. Such service networks have good coverage and are reasonable in cost. Adding early intervention makes it accessible to the tens of thousands of families already visiting these units for examination or routine vaccinations. The National Research Center, Ain Shams University Hospital, and Primary Health Care Units in the Alexandria governorate are already providing these services.

Volunteer Training Programs The World Health Organization launched a worldwide program of community-based rehabilitation (CBR) especially suitable for developing countries. Services for people with disabilities are provided in the environment where they live, at minimal cost, and using resources available in the community. Volunteers are recruited from the community and trained to pass their experiences to families. Information on providing early intervention services has been incorporated into their training programs. Families living in slums and poor communities and those of low socioeconomic background are the main beneficiaries of CBR programs. Many volunteers are themselves parents or siblings of children with special needs.

Effectiveness of Seti Center Services

In addition to children showing improvement in various domains of development after attending the Seti Center, many of them have been accepted in general education schools. That achievement would not have been possible had they not received early intervention services. Furthermore, the program has successfully been adapted to suit various types of disabilities and delays. Families from different socioeconomic and cultural backgrounds also have benefited from the numerous components of these services.

Parents have been able to reestablish their parenting role as well as the lost link with their child. They also have been able to play the roles of educators for their children, guides to other families, and advocates for the rights of people with disabilities. Groups of mutual support have been established, with parents exchanging services or passing to others adapted equipment or toys that their child no longer needs. For example, one mother made a head covering for another woman's child to protect his head during epileptic seizures. Fathers have been collecting, translating, photocopying, and distributing useful information found on the Internet. Members of the newly established "League of Early Intervention Parents" have distributed their names and telephone numbers to pediatricians and gynecologists/obstetricians. The hope is that they will be contacted by other parents who have just discovered their child's disability and need the support of experienced families. Many families also have participated in seminars, conferences, meetings with volunteers or officials, and television or radio programs to raise societal awareness, modify wrong attitudes, or advocate for additional rights for children with disabilities. Several mothers with no previous professional experience have found work and a much-needed, stable source of income due to the training that they received through the early intervention program. Referrals from pediatricians who have attended awareness meetings have increased, and the referred parents have indicated that these pediatricians were considerably supportive. Some of these pediatricians have even started early intervention services in the clinics or hospitals where they work.

RECOMMENDATIONS FOR PROFESSIONALS IN OTHER COUNTRIES

The role of families in early intervention for children with special needs should be stressed. Not only do families know how to use their child's positive aspects and skills, but they also can modify and adapt program characteristics to better suit their child's individual needs. In addition, they can achieve this at minimal cost—an important dimension, especially in developing countries.

Thus, involving families as essential partners can be seen as the most effective and most economical approach to intervention. However, it is a challenge for which professionals are not always prepared. Professionals must respond to this challenge by making the necessary efforts to accompany families during their mourning stages and to continually aim, through parents' training programs, at improving parents' capacities. They also should be prepared to listen to parents, observe, and learn from them—to "consult them as often as they consult you" (McConkey, 1985). Professionals should include parents in decision making, taking into account their opinions to strengthen acceptability of proposed measures (French Center, 1997).

Not all of the team members working in such programs need to be medically qualified. In fact, the program can run efficiently provided that at least one member of the team has such qualifications (e.g., a pediatrician, a nurse). Highly specialized staff (e.g., speech-language pathologists, physiotherapists, occupational therapists) are scarce in developing counties; in other instances, such professionals do not consider working with infants a prestigious enough job. Yet, as done at the Seti Center, programs still may have recourse to train people from other backgrounds to provide early intervention services. Early childhood educators, psychologists, social workers, or even individuals who have specialties unrelated to the disabilities field but show interest and motivation, have been trained as team members (called "generic workers"). They acquire practical, on-the-job skills from various disciplines that enable them to work with children with disabilities. Skills such as supporting communication, positioning a child with cerebral palsy, or adapting the home environment to suit children with disabilities have been successfully passed on from specialists to early intervention team members. The challenge facing professionals is not only to involve and empower parents in a realistic and appropriate partnership (Rustin, 1995), but also to do this with nonspecialized workers. Success of this partnership is beneficial for the child, the families, the professionals themselves, and society as a whole.

Family members can take an active part in their child's intervention program, allowing gains in self-esteem and confidence about parenting skills. They learn to better formulate family needs, to be true advocates for their child, and to be more "critical" in a positive sense of the services presented to their child. Professionals learn to listen more, to show empathy, and to view parents as consumers who have the right to comment on the services offered. By so doing, they become even better professionals. Mutual trust is built, and mutual enrichment results from sharing experiences and information.

CONCLUSION

Faced with the scarcity of early intervention services in Egypt, the Seti Center initiated a model in partnership with parents. It takes into account Egyptian context characteristics, with both weak and strong points. It addresses challenges such as lack of resources, negative attitudes, poor awareness, parents' illiteracy, high cost, and low accessibility. At the same time, the program uses and develops parental competencies and behaviors that may contribute to healthy child development. It also identifies and activates latent resources within the community. Thus, early intervention is no longer the responsibility of professionals alone. Families and communities share this responsibility—a fact that greatly promotes the quality, continuity, coverage, and cost-effectiveness of this early intervention service.

REFERENCES

Bluma, S.M., Shearer, M.S., Frohman, A.M., & Hilliard, A.M. (1976). *Portage Guide to Early Education: Checklist, Curriculum and Card File.* Portage, WI: Cooperative Educational Service Agency.

Cook, J. (1997). People's perception and habits in making use of health services. In proceedings of the seminar *Childhood and Handicap: Concepts and Strategies* (pp. 23–24). Cairo, Egypt: United Nations Development Program.

El Sherif, H. (1996). The national strategy to combat handicaps in Egypt. In proceedings of the seminar *Childhood and Handicap: Concepts and Strategies* (p. 64). Cairo, Egypt: United Nations Development Program.

French Center for Culture and Cooperation. (1997). *Handicapped children in Egypt: Past and present work of the French cooperation* (pp. 2–5). Cairo, Egypt: Author.

Hussein, A. (1997). Anthropology of handicaps. In proceedings of the seminar *Childhood and Handicap: Concepts and Strategies* (pp. 40–41). Cairo, Egypt: United Nations Development Program.

Magdi, S. (1995). Current situation and services. In *Report on Childhood Disability Workshop* (p. 47). Cairo, Egypt: UNICEF.

Mansour, E. (1997). Policy of the Ministry of Health for the benefit of handicapped children. In proceedings of the seminar *Childhood and Handicap: Concepts and Strategies* (p. 24). Cairo, Egypt: United Nations Development Program.

McConkey, R. (1985). *Working with parents: A practical guide for teachers and therapists.* London: Croom Helm.

National Council for Childhood and Motherhood. (2000). *National report on follow-up to the World Summit for Children* (pp. 2–17). Cairo, Egypt: Author.

Rustin, L. (1995). Parents and families of children with communicative disorders. *Folia Phoniatrica et Logopaedica, 47,* 123–139.

Training and Personnel Preparation

CHAPTER 9

Creating a Team Around the Child Through Professionals' Continuing Education

SWEDEN

Eva Björck-Åkesson and Mats Granlund

Lekarna, ja hur de fyllde våra dagar! Vad skulle min barndom ha varit utan dem! Vad skulle förresten alla barns barndom vara, om inte leken fanns i deras liv?

Play, how it filled our days! What would my childhood have been without it! Anyhow, what would all children's childhood be, if there was no play? (Lindgren, 1992, p. 2)

The ecology of early intervention in Sweden consists of the family, the preschool, Child Health Services (CHS), and the Child Habilitation Center (CHC). Consensus on philosophy and principles for early intervention is important. Education for professionals focusing on the theoretical foundation for early intervention is needed in Sweden. This chapter describes early intervention in Sweden and how further education for professionals can be designed and implemented. The following vignette illustrates the importance (for the child and the family) of collaboration based on a common frame of reference in early intervention.

  KARL'S STORY ————————————————————————

Karl is 5 years old. He lives with his mother, father, and younger brother in a small town in the southern part of Sweden. His grandparents live close by. His mother is expecting a new baby soon.

Karl was 6 weeks premature. From birth, pediatricians at the children's medical ward and a pediatric nurse at CHS followed him closely. At the age of 6 months, it was evident that his motor development was delayed. Karl received the preliminary diagnosis of cerebral palsy at the age of 14 months. Karl received special support from a CHC physiotherapist starting at 6 months and later from a preschool consultant (special education teacher) and a speech-language pathologist.

Because Karl was their firstborn child, his parents had no previous experience with raising children. They thought that Karl's development was typical—maybe just a little slow. He was a very sociable child and had good communication skills from an early age. Karl's parents were shocked when they learned that he had cerebral palsy. They believed that professionals only looked at Karl's deficiencies and never acknowledged his capacities. His parents also were disappointed that the support offered at the time did not fully include them as intervention partners.

During his first 5 years, Karl received a variety of educational, medical, and therapy services. His parents were quite satisfied with the support they received but wanted greater inclusion in decisions and interventions that were planned for Karl. They also wanted to meet with all involved professionals at the same time to discuss and determine interventions. They believed that all interventions should be adapted to their lifestyle and integrated into their everyday life. What they requested was collaboration among all involved, including

themselves, and good documentation of the interventions. However, it took time for both to be accomplished.

By the time Karl was 5 years old, his parents finally believed that they were fully involved in interventions and decision making. The intervention team consisted of Karl's parents, a physical therapist, a personal assistant, the preschool teacher, the pediatric nurse, and a speech-language pathologist. Other professionals were brought in when needed.

A number of lessons emerged from working with Karl and his parents. First, parents often are not considered partners in the intervention process. They think that their experience with and knowledge about their child is sometimes neglected and that interventions are not always adapted to their everyday life. Second, parents prefer professionals from the different organizations to have more contact with each other and to work from a common philosophy and theory of action (as evidenced in the Swedish Support and Service Act [LSS, SFS:1993:387] and the Health and Medical Services Act [HSL, SFS:1982:763]). Third, parents believe that good documentation enhances the intervention process. Perhaps the use of new technology, such as a personal web page for a child and family, can help in the future.

NATIONAL CONTEXT

The Swedish philosophy of childhood considers childhood a unique period in the life of human beings. Childhood has its own value and is not merely seen as a time of preparation for adult life and an investment in the future. Children are allowed to live in the here and now. Play is highly valued, as seen in the chapter's opening quote from Astrid Lindgren, an internationally known Swedish author of children's books. In her books, Lindgren catches the "national soul" of Sweden, in which nature and close relationships between people are important, as are fantasy, thoughtfulness, and enjoyment of the small things in everyday life. Adults can create possibilities for children through supporting and challenging them in their development, play, and learning.

Sweden is a modern, industrial, and democratic country. Situated in Scandinavia in the north of Europe, it is part of the European Union. It is a long and narrow country: The distance between the most northern and southern parts is 1,574 kilometers, and it is 499 kilometers at the widest point. Despite its northern location at the polar circle, the climate is tempered with four distinct seasons. The Gulf Stream from the west gives warm summers. The winters may be long and cold. Sweden's counties vary from flat, cultured landscape to very isolated landscape with high mountains. Half of Sweden is covered with forest, and less than 10% is cultured landscape. Whereas the northern inland is scarcely populated, most people live in the southern and middle parts of Sweden. Sweden has a hereditary monarchy and a parliamentary government lead by a prime minister. It has approximately 8.9 million inhabitants (Statistiska Centralbyrån, 2000).

Swedish is the native language. Children start learning English in elementary school, and most children also learn another foreign language later (e.g., French, Spanish, German). Citizens are interested in civic matters, as demonstrated by the fact that 81% of the population voted in the 1998 election. Stockholm is the national capital, with about 2 million people living in the larger Stockholm area. The 289 municipalities in Sweden have great freedom to shape their own policy-making bodies. The municipalities are responsible for basic services to all people, including child care, school, and social services. School is free for all children and youth. Sweden is divided into regions with 20 counties governed by county councils. As of 2002, there is a trend toward integration of counties to larger regional entities. The county councils are responsible for health and dental care, which is free for children and youth. The primary communities provide social services and are also responsible for child care and education.

People and Culture

Sweden has a rather short modern history of cultural diversity. Until about 1960, Sweden had a unitary culture based on values and traditions rooted in Scandinavian history. For many years, the Sami of Lapland in the north were the main group of people in Sweden with a culture of their own. In the 1960s, Sweden invited skilled people from other European countries (e.g., Yugoslavia, Finland, Italy) to immigrate and be part of the industrial work force. Sweden has a liberal immigration policy, and immigration has increased since the 1990s, with many people coming from Middle Eastern and Balkan countries. As of 2002, immigrants formed approximately 10% of the population and 24% of children birth through age 17 years had at least one parent with a foreign background (Barnombudsmannen [BO], 2002). In previous time periods, many immigrants came from Eastern Europe. At the beginning of the 21st century, a large number of immigrants are refugees and have come in extended families. Most live in the larger cities.

Sweden is changing into a diverse, multicultural society. Many children now have their roots in cultures other than the traditional Swedish one. Child care and school have become places for multicultural integration, cultural inclusion, and bilingualism. The changes in Swedish society create a demand for new areas of knowledge in early intervention.

In Sweden, 75% of the children grow up in intact families, with both parents in the workforce (70% of mothers and 73% of fathers). The majority of parents with young children, especially mothers, work part time (BO, 2002). New types of families are emerging due to new cultural influences, the increasing number of one-parent families, and blended families following remarriage. The latter may be defined as *link-families*, or families that are linked through their children. Many children live with one biological parent who has started a new family with someone who also has children from an earlier marriage or relationship. This means that children may grow up in extended families with different groupings. When the extended family agrees on basic attitudes toward child rearing and communicates well, this can be an asset to children (Larsson Sjöberg, 2000).

The social insurance system governed by the Swedish state guarantees that one parent is entitled to stay home and care for a child younger than 18 months. The days can be divided between parents. One parent can draw the child benefit for the first 360 days following birth with 80% of his or her wages. In addition, one parent can stay home for 90 more days with a lower payment. The system is flexible, and parents can save the time until their child is 8 years old. For example, a person's workday can be shortened from 8 to 6 hours. The parents themselves decide how to distribute the time off work. Mothers typically stay home, but approximately 10% of fathers stay home for longer periods with their child (BO, 2002). The *contact days* concept entitles parents to 1 day per year to visit their child at school. When the child has a disability, his or her parents have 10 contact days and can also receive support from the social insurance system to stay home for longer periods. This system also guarantees that one parent can stay home when a child younger than 12 years is sick, with 80% of his or her wages. This is limited to 60 days per year, family, and child, but it can be extended. All families receive a monthly child benefit (approximately $100) from the state until the child is 16 years of age (2002). When a family has more than two children, the monthly benefit per child increases.

KEY FEATURES OF EARLY INTERVENTION

Early intervention in Sweden can be defined as intervention practices with children in need of special support from birth to the start of school at age 6 or 7. Children in Sweden grow up almost exclusively in a family environment, and most children are enrolled in child care from 1–2 years of age. Thus, early intervention services are directed toward the child in a family/proximal environment context. Both the communities and county councils are responsible for early intervention, with different goals and groups to be served. Table 9.1 presents these objectives in terms of Simeonsson's (1994) levels of prevention concept.

From the perspective of levels of prevention, the community has the basic responsibility for the well-being of all children and families and for securing acceptable conditions of living for everyone. At the secondary level, the community has the responsibility for intervention in preschool and in child care programs. A child who needs special support may have a personal assistant. Included in the services from the community is respite care to families with children with disabilities (Brodin, 1995). At the tertiary level, the community is responsible for creating a healthy environment for children and families.

Table 9.1. Description and objectives of early intervention in Sweden

	Primary prevention	Secondary prevention	Tertiary prevention
Definition	Reduce new cases by identifying children at risk	Reduce severity by intervention that is focused on the child and the family	Reduce complications by intervention that is focused on the environment
Focus	Well-being and health of all children and families	Well-being and health of children with disabilities and their families who need special support	Creation of a good social and physical environment for the developing child and his or her family
Organization County council	Child Health Services (CHS) provide an immunization program, surveillance, and general medical care	Child Habilitation Center (CHC) provide specialized medical care (e.g., physical therapy, speech-language therapy)	CHS and CHC provide staff supervision and consultation on environmental design
Community	Social services and preschool activities	Special support in preschool, personal assistance, special education, and respite care	Staff in-service training and environmental adaptation

The county council is required to provide health and medically related services at the primary prevention level. Since 1937, all children birth to 6 years old have been offered free health care provided within CHS. Goals for CHS were stated in the general advice given by Sweden's National Board of Health and Welfare in 1981:

- Decrease mortality, illness, and disability among children.
- Decrease harmful and distressing influences on parents and children.
- Support and activate parents in their parental role, thereby creating a positive living environment for all children.

The most common health problems in children are illness in newborns, congenital disabilities, sudden infant death, accidents, psychosocial problems, infections, malignant tumors, and asthma. Many of those conditions can be influenced by the preventive work of CHS. With changing living conditions, the focus of CHS has been altered to include more work regarding psychosomatic and socioemotional problems, changing parental roles, and support to immigrant families. The goal to support and activate parents has increased in importance, especially for families that are in crisis (with social and economical difficulties) and have children with disabilities (Aurelius, 2000). Parent groups and parent education are arranged as part of this service.

To strengthen the social network around families in need of support, CHS collaborates with social services, preschools and schools, medical services, and child habilitation services. CHS offers a basic program of surveillance for all children and families, consisting of screening and clinical identification (Aurelius, 2000; Larsson, 1996). The child's growth, health, and general development are monitored with regular checkups by a pediatric nurse. Child health records are established in a standardized, nationally used form. The checkups start from birth to 10 days of age, with a home-visit by a pediatric nurse who gives advice about nursing, caregiving, and child safety. During the first 2–3 months, the infant and parents usually visit CHS once per week. The parents choose when to visit CHS, and most parents decide to go there often. After the first 3 months, visits become less frequent. The visits consist of advice, immunizations, and health surveillance. At regular occasions, a pediatrician meets the child for structured assessment of development, often using the BOEL-test (Stensland-Junker, 1995). Thereafter, developmental screening is carried out at regular intervals. The family also may see a psychologist or a speech-language pathologist through CHS. From the age of 3 months to 6 years of age, a child and his or her parents visit CHS for checkups and immunizations more than 15 times. CHS is one of few systems in the world for regular recording of child health and provides a valid source for epidemiologic studies. When children have acute infections or illness, they are referred to physicians in general family practice that provides services to all age groups. If CHS suspects that a child has a disability, the child is referred to the Children's Medical Clinic and/or a CHC, also governed by the county council.

At the level of secondary prevention, the county council has the responsibility for giving advice and support to children with disabilities and their families. Services given to a child with a disability and his or her family are coordinated through an individual service plan at the family's request. The family is required to ask for services based on its perceived needs of support. Early intervention for young children with disabilities is mainly conducted within a CHC, although there is a trend toward more community involvement and collaboration in all kinds of services (Björck-Åkesson & Granlund, 1997).

At the CHC, advice and support to families of children with disabilities are based on the concept of *habilitation*. This term originates from the Latin word *habile* which means "to make skilled." The habilitation process encompasses contributions from the medical, social, psychological, and educational fields to support and help children with disabilities in their development and daily life (Bille & Olow, 1999). The traditional goal of habilitation has been to enhance the development of the child by building on his or her resources and to give the child optimal possibilities for an independent life in the future. The medical perspective has dominated in Sweden (Björck-Åkesson, Granlund, & Simeonsson, 2000), but at the beginning of the 21st century, the family's role in the child's development is becoming more pronounced. This is leading to a changed perspective on intervention. A transition toward a more social/educational perspective may be discerned.

At the habilitation centers, an interdisciplinary team—including a pediatrician or neuropediatrician, physical therapist, psychologist, occupational therapist, speech-language pathologist, social worker, and special educator—works in collaboration with the family and the child. Typically, the habilitation process involves a meeting to determine procedures for assessment by different team members, a team meeting for decision making, and implementation of an intervention program. This may be followed by an evaluation and then the process is repeated with varying degrees of emphasis on the different elements (Björck-Åkesson et al., 2000).

Tertiary prevention is provided by both the municipalities and the county councils. The municipalities are responsible for making all public places available for people with disabilities as well as for providing education-related in-service training and supervision to preschool staff working with children with disabilities. CHCs are responsible for providing in-service training and supervision on topics other than education to preschool staff working with children with disabilities (e.g., physiotherapy, occupational therapy).

Theoretical Bases for Early Intervention

A transactional model (Sameroff & Fiese, 2000) that builds on ecological theory and systemic theory can be seen in practices at all levels and gives support for providing family-centered services. In this model, the child is seen as active in creating his or her developmental environment. At the same time, there is an emphasis on the child as part of the family and the proximal environment—both influencing and being influenced by these environments. Thus, characteristics, needs, and strengths in the child, the family, and the proximal environment are important in the assessment and intervention processes. Even if consensus exists regarding the very broad principles of early intervention, different perspectives and professional cultures prevail in the three organizations involved.

Sweden's official philosophy for support to children with disabilities is based on a perspective corresponding with the *International Classification of Functioning Disability and Health* (ICF; World Health Organization, 2001). An interactive model is used, in which the interaction between the individual child and the social and physical environments contributes to the impact of the disability on the everyday life of the child and the family. Yet, the medical perspective is gaining importance, especially regarding new knowledge and experiences of neurological assessment.

A family-centered perspective implies that intervention is carried out in naturalistic situations, in everyday life. It also implies that it involves both the child and the parents/caregivers. When the proximal environment is involved in the intervention process, changes will occur both in the child and in other people in the environment. To adapt to the child and family's needs, it is important to acknowledge the expertise of all involved in early intervention, including the family.

Returning to the vignette at the beginning of this chapter, support and services to Karl and his family were provided by the three organizations (see Table 9.2). First, the CHS gave Karl's parents advice on general medical and everyday care. After a disability was suspected, the family was referred to a CHC, where a preliminary diagnosis was confirmed and therapeutic interventions were provided. Later, Karl was enrolled in a preschool near his home, and a personal assistant was employed. All three organizations carried out the interventions as expected but failed, at least initially, to form a team around the child and his parents. This problem may have resulted from lack of interorganizational service coordination, different theories about what to accomplish in intervention, different professional cultures (and cultures

Table 9.2. Interventions for Karl

	Child Health Services (CHS)	Child Habilitation Center (CHC)	Preschool activities
Focus of assessment	Surveillance, screening	Body function and structure; assessment of motor, language, and neurological development	Everyday functioning, proximal processes, play
Focus of intervention	General medical care, advice to parents about everyday care and functioning, immunization	Optimal, maximal level of performance; care in specific domains (sensory, cognitive, social)	Social competence, engagement, and inclusion
Goal	Developmental and functional goals for the child, empowerment for the family	Developmental and functional goals for the child, quality of life for child and family	Child as an active participant in creating learning experiences and social relationships
Professional roles	Expertise on child health, disability prevention, and child development in the everyday context	Expertise on child development and disabilities	Expertise on group activities for children and creating a good environment

within those organizations), and a lack of general principles and theories underlying early intervention. Karl's parents emphasized that the interventionists needed further professional development and training in working in a family-centered fashion and engaging in parent–professional collaborative problem solving. One way for early interventionists from CHCs, CHS, and preschools to obtain basic family-centered professional knowledge and skills is continuing education or interdisciplinary in-service training.

Since 1997, Mälardalen University has offered the master's-degree level International Program for Early Intervention and Family Support. In Fall 2002, a master's program based on earlier experiences in this area was implemented. Called "Children: Health, Learning, Development and Intervention," this program is described in the following section.

DESCRIPTION OF THE PROGRAM

When the content and form of university-based continuing education programs in early intervention are compared across countries, several common features emerge regarding the goals of education (Peterander, 1996). These include an interdisciplinary approach, providing support to the whole family, and involving parents in the decision-making and implementation phases of assessment and intervention. Regarding the format of continuing education, common features include an interdisciplinary approach, mixing lectures with practical applications, and individual feedback to participants (Granlund & Björck-Åkesson, 2000; Winton & McCollum, 1997). Common features include family systems theory, consultation and collaborative problem-solving models, and assessment and intervention theory.

Children: Health, Learning, Development and Intervention is an interdisciplinary program in which students enroll in courses with faculty and students from special education, health psychology, and preventive health. The program assumes certain common goals for professionals in early intervention:

1. Work from a sound theoretical foundation for early intervention
2. Promote children's overall development and functioning
3. Promote children's development and functioning in special areas
4. Support the development of proximal processes and children's social competence

5. Support families in facilitating their young children's development
6. Empower families in the intervention process

This program is closely connected to the research program CHILD (Children, Health, Intervention, Learning, Development) at the Department of Social Sciences of Mälardalen University. Children: Health, Learning, Development and Intervention has a research base in system theory, developmental ecology, transactional theory, and ICF (World Health Organization, 2001), emphasizing multidimensionality in early intervention.

The Children: Health, Learning, Development and Intervention program recruits students with a professional background in the areas of child health, child habilitation, social services, preschool, and school. Requirements include prior experience in intervention for young children, a bachelor's degree in the field of early intervention with a major in a relevant field, and prior basic courses in scientific methods.

The program's form is modified distance education, which means that the students meet at the university 2 consecutive days per month during semesters. The program is web-based, so it has a homepage and a web-based conference system is used. The conference system is used for collaboration between the students in smaller groups and for distribution of information in the larger group. It is also used to post assignments so that students can read each other's work before seminars.

The students, who come from different parts of Sweden and also from other Scandinavian countries, typically spend half of their time working in early intervention. The content and assignments are closely connected to students' everyday working experiences. The 2-year, part-time program is equivalent to a 1-year, full-time program. It totals 40 Swedish credit points, which are equivalent to 60 European Credit Transfer System credits.

Program Courses

The structure of the program contains four core courses, two independent courses, and a master's thesis (see Table 9.3). The courses comprise lectures, seminars, and applied coursework (i.e., accompanied by individual or group-based feedback/supervision). Participation in all coursework is mandatory. The examination consists of written papers, composed individually and as part of a group, that are presented at seminars.

The Ecology of Early Intervention

This course provides an overview of European and international perspectives on the ecology of early intervention and family support, as

Table 9.3. **Structure of the master's degree program Children: Health, Learning, Development and Intervention**

	Fall semester	Spring semester
Year 1	The Ecology of Early Intervention (5 points)	Systems Theory: The Child, the Family, the Team (5 points)
	Research, Methods and Application in Intervention Research (5 points)	Assessment and Intervention: The Intervention Process (5 points)
Year 2	Independent study (5 points)	Independent study (5 points)
	Master's thesis (10 points)	

well as a theoretical understanding about intervention and family support. Students learn to analyze models for intervention and to apply those models. The content covers perspectives on intervention, theories and principles of early intervention, philosophy, policy, ethical aspects, assumptions and context, cultural diversity, developmental ecology, empowerment, models of intervention, ICF, and principles for family-oriented support (World Health Organization, 2001). The literature consists of internationally established books, such as Guralnick (1997) and Shonkoff and Meisels (2000), combined with European and Swedish literature and articles in international scientific journals.

Research Methods and Application in Intervention Research

This course allows students to reach an understanding of major theories and current research related to early intervention and family support. The students acquire deepened knowledge about research methods, especially methods useful for research in the area of early intervention. The content focuses on research methods, qualitative and quantitative methods of analysis, and meta-analysis. Dissertations, scientific reports, and articles that are relevant to the field and represent different scientific orientation and design of study are analyzed in relation to definition of problems, methods of analysis, and interpretation of results. Research drawn from different cultures and ethical aspects of intervention research are discussed. The literature covers both quantitative and qualitative research methods. There is an emphasis on mixing methodologies in approaching complex, multidimensional phenomena. Assignments require critical review of scientific work in the area of early intervention.

Systems Theory: The Child, the Family, the Team

In this course, students acquire basic knowledge in general systems theory and dynamic systems theory, then relate these theories to child development and children's environments for growing up. The students gain in-depth understanding of the relationships and influences among the systems of which children with disabilities and children at risk are a part. They also attain an in-depth understanding of teamwork in a systems theoretical perspective. The content covers general systems theory, child development from a systems theory and environmental perspective, a transactional model, families and other close environments as systems, and relationships between different close environments affecting the child and system. The literature involves basic books on general systems theory, such as Bateson (1987) and van Bertalanffy (1968), as well as modern literature such as Wachs (2000).

Assessment and Intervention: The Intervention Process

This course gives students advanced knowledge about the assessment of development and function in children who have disabilities or are at risk and the assessment of resources and support needs in the family and proximal environments. In addition, the student acquires advanced knowledge regarding collaborative problem solving in the intervention process. The content covers theoretical perspectives on the intervention process, the assessment of development and function in children who have disabilities or are at risk, the assessment of resources and needs in families and other proximal environments, and the assessment of the physical environment. Also included are analyses of different types of assessment information and integration of information in planning and implementing intervention, collaborative problem solving, and evaluating intervention outcomes. The literature included in this course is international (i.e., North American and European publications on intervention and assessment). Many articles in scientific journals are used as well.

Independent Study

In the independent study courses, each student designs his or her own syllabus with the teacher or supervisor. The content can vary from pure theoretical issues to something approaching a special scientific method. The thesis consists of a theoretical framework and an empirical study. It is connected to research questions actualized in the student's professional area and/or actualized in the CHILD research program.

Summary

The high degree of similarities among countries in the goals, form, and content of continuing education indicate an opportunity to develop international collaboration around continuing education in early intervention. A common course syllabus for continuing education in early intervention has been developed collaboratively by five European and three U.S. universities through a Transatlantic Consortium on Early Intervention Studies that is financed by the U.S. Department of Education's Fund for the Improvement of Postsecondary Education (FIPSE).

Most participants in this master's degree program have an executive or leading position within their organization. A transition towards a family-centered perspective does, however, require that all members within the organizations move in the same direction and have a common base. Therefore, the continuing education of a small number of professionals needs to be supplemented by in-service training for all members of teams and organizations.

IN-SERVICE TRAINING PROMOTING FAMILY CENTERED SERVICES IN EARLY INTERVENTION

Health services and child habilitation professionals often have much training and experience in working directly with the child but less expertise working as consultants to parents, preschool staff, and other care providers. Frequently, assessment and intervention is focused on the child without any deeper consideration of the child's environments. As consultants, it is important to fulfill two different working tasks: 1) support the family in developing skills necessary for self-sufficiency in expressing needs and coordinating and utilizing services for the child and the family and 2) function as an expert in child-focused intervention within a specific domain. The first task applies to all professionals. It is, in the long run, the most important one if the child is going to function well within the family system (Guralnick, 2001). The second task has different form and content, depending on the professional category and organization involved.

The service coordination content is the actual services provided over time. Each service provided contains the following steps:

1. Identify problems to be solved
2. Explain problems
3. Prioritize problems and determine goals for intervention
4. Design and implement intervention
5. Evaluate the effects of intervention

Perceived problems will vary over time. Because of this variability, the interventionists as well as the service organizations involved will vary over time. The only stable team members are the child and the family. Thus, a key issue is how professionals can help parents become self-sufficient in service coordination to ensure continuity and relevance in the services obtained by the child and the family. To support parents in becoming self-sufficient professionals need knowledge and skills in 1) relating to the family and the proximal environment members in a proactive and emphatic fashion, 2) collaborative problem-solving strategies, and 3) systems/family theory. In addition, they must know how to apply these skills in a collaborative problem-solving process that includes parents, proximal environments, and professionals. That is, they must know how to work in a "team around the child" with family-centered services (Björck-Åkesson & Granlund, 1997; Peterander, 2000; Pretis, 2000). Table 9.4 illustrates the working tasks and necessary competencies of professionals in collaborating with families and proximal environments in early intervention.

In a series of quasi-experimental control-group studies, Granlund and Björck-Åkesson (2000) evaluated the outcome of in-service training for professionals in family-centered practices. They reported that if integrated into ordinary services, in-service training is an effective tool for changing practices in early intervention to a more family-centered approach. Several factors, however, can positively or negatively influence the effects of training. In-service training is just one of several possible change activities; it often needs to be supplemented by other activities (e.g., changes in organizational routines, changes in

Table 9.4. Working tasks and required competencies of professionals

Working tasks	Required competencies
Working tasks basic to family-centered services	*Basic knowledge and skills*
Surveying the needs of the child, family, and proximal environments	Skills in relating to families and direct-care providers
Service coordination	Skills in collaborative problem solving
Evaluation of the total outcome	Knowledge of systems theory and families
Supporting parents in the development of problem-solving skills	Skills in the basic aspects of the assessment process
Goal setting	Skills in surveying the needs of proximal environments
Designing methods to optimize adherence to interventions	
Profession-specific tasks	*Profession-specific knowledge and skills*
Domain-specific, child-focused assessment	Skills in domain-specific assessment
Diagnosis and goal setting	Skills in profession-specific intervention goals and methods
Domain-specific intervention methods	
Intervention-specific evaluation	Skills in profession-specific intervention evaluation

resource allocation). Change must be seen as a process of which in-service training is only one phase. The effectiveness of training seems dependent on factors related to the organizational framework for the training activity, the preparatory work before training, and the implementation of training and follow-up activities.

In-service training activities must be related to the organizational framework within which the training takes place. In a goal-governed system, different change activities and other factors affecting the organization need to pull the system in the same direction. In-service training must be linked to the overarching value base and the explicit goals of the organization and coordinated with other steering tools, such as required documentation of services. This necessitates a clearly publicized value base for the organizational goals.

In preparatory work, the current practices of the participants must be related to a desired effect and desired value base. The larger the discrepancy between the current state and the desired state, the more effort is required for surveying the participants' skills, knowledge, and concerns about change on an individual basis. It also might be necessary to introduce the change on an individual basis. The desired state (i.e., the desired effects on families and children) should be the focus, rather than the behavior of the professionals. This allows the professionals participating in change activities to have input on the form and content of the training activities.

In the implementation of training, it is important that theory and practice be connected and interrelated. One important means for achieving the appropriate level of interconnection is to view evaluation as an ongoing process directed toward enhancing the effects of training. A core training activity is individual feedback to participants on their application of family-centered practices.

Follow-up activities must ensure that opportunities and resources are available to maintain changes, practices, and skills in ordinary work contexts. Movement in the direction of family-centeredness will occur slowly if changes are expected on team and organizational levels. Therefore, in-service training must be a part of a long-term plan, which encompasses changes in, among other things, supervision, organizational routines, and resource allocation.

RECOMMENDATIONS FOR PROFESSIONALS IN OTHER COUNTRIES AND CONCLUSION

In Sweden, the general systems of child care provide all children and families with basic support and services (i.e., CHS and preschool). This implies that less effort is placed on early intervention services for specific groups of children. The negative side of this model is that sometimes professionals in basic support and services do not have the skills to provide necessary support to children with special needs. Professionals in CHCs traditionally have the necessary expertise in working directly with children with special needs but less expertise working with families and proximal environments. Families and preschools are the natural environments for children with special needs in Sweden; thus, early intervention focused on the child within his or her proximal environments is a key issue.

As consultants, professionals need to relate to the family and the proximal environment members in a proactive and emphatic fashion. They need to solve problems in collaboration with families and preschools. In-service training for professionals in CHS, CHCs, and preschools is one means to this end. The effectiveness of such in-service training depends on a clear and outspoken values base for training as well as on factors related to the organizational framework, such as opportunities for preparatory work before training and time and resources to implement training.

It is hoped that continuing education and in-service training of professionals in CHS, CHCs, and preschools will enhance early intervention practices in Sweden. Such actions would cause services to be provided in an environment in which professionals and parents can collaborate based on a common frame of reference. In turn, this would allow children like Karl, along with his family, to experience well-coordinated services focused on both child and family needs.

REFERENCES

Aurelius, G. (2000). Barnhälsovård [Health care in children]. In T. Lindberg & H. Lagercrantz (Eds.), *Barnmedicin* [Child medicine] (pp. 75–80). Lund, Sweden: Studentlitteratur.

Barnombudsmannen [The childhood ombudsman]. (2002). *Barndom i förändring* [The changing childhood]. Retrieved October 14, 2002, from http://www.bo.se/captest/barndom.asp

Bateson, G. (1987). *Steps to an ecology of mind: Collected essays in anthropology, psychology, evolution, and epistemology.* North Vale, NJ: Jason Aronson.

Bille, B., & Olow, I. (1999). *Barnhabilitering vid rörelsehinder och andra neurologiskt betingade funktionshinder* [Child habilitation for children with physical impairments and other neurologically based impairments]. Stockholm: Liber.

Björck-Åkesson, E., & Granlund, M. (1997). Changing perspectives in early intervention for children with disabilities in Sweden. *Infants and Young Children, 9*(3), 56–68.

Björck-Åkesson, E., Granlund, M., & Simeonsson, R.J. (2000). Assessment philosophies and practices in Sweden. In M.J. Guralnick (Ed.), *Interdisciplinary clinical assessment of young children with developmental disabilities* (pp. 391–411). Baltimore: Paul H. Brookes Publishing Co.

Brodin, J. (1995). *Avlösarservice för familjer med barn med funktionsnedsättningar* [Respite care for families to children with disabilities]. Stockholm: Lärarhögskolan i Stockholm, Institutionen för specialpedagogik.

Granlund, M., & Björck-Åkesson, E. (2000). Integrating inservice training in family centered practices in context: Implications for implementing change activities. *Infants and Young Children, 12*(3), 46–60.

Guralnick, M.J. (Ed.). (1997). *The effectiveness of early intervention*. Baltimore: Paul H. Brookes Publishing Co.

Guralnick, M.J. (2001). A developmental systems model for early intervention. *Infants and Young Children, 14*(2), 1–18.

Health and Medical Services Act of 1982 (HSL:SFS:1982:763). Sweden.

Larsson, J.-L. (1996). *Aspects of health surveillance at child welfare centres*. Doctoral dissertation, Department of Woman and Child Health, St. Göran's Children's Hospital. Stockholm: Karolinska Institutet.

Larsson Sjöberg, K. (2000). *Barndom i länkade familjesystem: Om samhörighet och åtskillnad* [Childhood in linked family systems: About being together and being apart]. Doctoral dissertation, Örebro Universitet, Sweden.

Lindgren, A. (1992). Skulle kunna flyga [Could be able to fly]. In H. Medelius, *Leka för livet* [Play for life] (p. 8). Stockholm: Nordic Museum.

National Agency for Education. (2001). *Beskrivande data om barnomsorg, skola och vuxenutbildning* [Descriptive data about early education, school and adult education]. Report No. 206.

Organisation for Economic Co-operation and Development. (2001). *Starting strong: Early childhood education and care*. Paris: Author.

Peterander, F. (Ed.). (1996). *Helios II final report—Early intervention: Information, orientation and guidance of families: Thematic Group 1*. Munich, Germany: LMU Munich.

Peterander, F. (2000). The best quality cooperation between parents and experts in early intervention. *Infants and Young Children, 12*(3), 32–45.

Pretis, M. (2000). Early intervention in children with Down's syndrome: From evaluation to methodology. *Infants and Young Children, 12*(3), 23–31.

Sameroff, A.J., & Fiese, B.H. (2000). Transactional regulation: The developmental ecology of early intervention. In J.P. Shonkoff & S.J. Meisels (Eds.), *Handbook of early childhood intervention* (2nd ed., pp. 135–159). New York: Cambridge University Press.

Shonkoff, J., & Meisels, S. (Eds.). (2000). *Handbook of early childhood intervention* (2nd ed.). New York: Cambridge University Press.

Simeonsson, R.J. (Ed.). (1994). *Risk, resilience, and prevention. Promoting the wellbeing of all children*. Baltimore: Paul H. Brookes Publishing Co.

Statistiska Centralbyrån [Statistics Sweden]. (2000). *Population and welfare: population*. Retrieved October 14, 2002, from http://www.scb.se/eng/index.asp

Stensland-Junker, K. (1995). *Den lilla människan* [The young child]. Stockholm: Natur & Kultur.

Support and Service Act (LSS, SFS:1993:387). Sweden.

von Bertalanffy, L. (1968). *General systems theory.* London: Penguin Books.

Wachs, T.D. (2000). *Necessary but not sufficient: The respective roles of single and multiple influences of individual development.* Washington, DC: American Psychological Association.

Winton, P.J., & McCollum, J.A. (1997). Ecological perspectives on personnel preparation: Rationale, framework, and guidelines for change. In P.J. Winton, J.A. McCollum, & C. Catlett (Eds.), *Reforming personnel preparation in early intervention: Issues, models, and practical strategies* (pp. 3–25). Baltimore: Paul H. Brookes Publishing Co.

World Health Organization. (2001). *International Classification of Functioning, Disability and Health.* Retrieved August 6, 2002, from http://www3.who.int/icf/icftemplate.cfm

JAMAICA

Paraprofessionals in Low-Cost Early Intervention Programs

Marigold J. Thorburn

Weh no dead, nu dash wey.
A child who looks dead, you don't give up; it may turn around.

"Weh no dead, nu dash wey" is a Jamaican Creole comment that community rehabilitation workers (CRWs) often hear from passers-by when they see how a child has progressed during the course of home-based early intervention. This chapter explains the reason for this program's success in Jamaica, starting with an illustrative vignette.

 ## SHEILA'S STORY

Sheila was born 2 months premature to a 17-year-old mother in a district hospital in Jamaica. The pregnancy was complicated by severe anemia. The birth was normal and she weighed 4 pounds, 8 ounces. She was discharged from the hospital at an unspecified time shortly after birth. (In Jamaican hospitals, the normal length of stay is one day.)

At 2 weeks of age, Sheila was readmitted with severe jaundice and was treated with phototherapy. She was reported to have fallen off a bed at age 7 months, but before that, at 6 months, she was not yet sitting up.

She was referred to 3D Projects, a community based rehabilitation program (CBR) in Jamaica, by a community health aide (a primary health care worker) at age 1 year, 4 months because of developmental delays, which were subsequently diagnosed as choreoathetoid cerebral palsy. At that time she was not able to sit or use her hands. She had involuntary movements and did not say any words.

She was enrolled in the early intervention program and assessed by the CRW according to the Portage checklist (Bluma, Shearer, Frohman, & Hilliard, 1976). This showed severe delays in all areas of development except socialization. Home-based intervention was started using the Jamaica-Portage Guide to Early Intervention (Caribbean Institute on Mental Retardation, 1986) and balancing exercises. The following is the story of Sheila according to her CRW, who has been visiting Sheila since 1997:

"She could not talk or roll over, neither could she follow objects across mid-line. It was very difficult working with Sheila's mother even though she attended parent orientation. Sheila's mother believed that her daughter's disability was caused by a *duppy* (a spirit of a dead person, which can be put on a person by an ill-wisher). She said that one day she sat her daughter in a wash pan under a tree in the yard and went inside the house. On her return, she saw a "duppy lady" moving away from her daughter. When she looked at Sheila, her head was leaning to one side and she was drooling. I reminded Sheila's

mother that Sheila had fallen from a bed when she was 7 months old and did not get medical attention. The mother gave a deaf ear to me.

"There were days when she would take Sheila to the *obeah* woman (medicine woman) for her daughter to get a bath and rub down with oil. She told me how the *obeah* people would pass lighted candle and a Bible around Sheila. Sometimes, when I visited Sheila, she was clad in a red dress with red string tied on her hands. This is to protect the child from the duppy. I was dismayed but decided to use a different strategy to get the parent's interest. I told Sheila's mother that what they said about the duppy might be true; however, we should try to address the disability by doing exercises with the child.

"Eventually, after nearly 2 years, the mother realized that Sheila needed help and began to participate in the program. A corner chair was built, and Sheila was placed in it daily. When I visited, the child would be in her chair. This helped Sheila a lot, as she can sit with little support now.

"She can now point to all body parts, put her hands together, pull to stand, feed herself with spoon, speak short sentences, put a hat on her head, indicate when she needs to go to the toilet, and draw vertical lines. Sheila's head still lags and she drools a little. Sheila started attending a special school for children with cognitive impairments in September, 2001. People look at Sheila and say, 'Weh nu dead, nu dash wey.' "

When last seen at the 3D clinic in 2000, Sheila had learned 135 new skills from the Portage checklist in 3 years, an average of 3.6 per month.

NATIONAL CONTEXT

Jamaica is a subtropical island, $1^1/_4$ hours' flying time south of Miami, Florida. It has a population of 2.7 million. It is mainly known as a tourist destination and the home of reggae singer Bob Marley.

The official language is English, but the majority of Jamaicans speak a Creole form of English. Jamaica was a British colony until 1962 and is the largest in population of the English-speaking territories of the Caribbean basin. The main income earning industries are tourism, production of bauxite, sugar, and bananas.

It has a democratically elected government and there is freedom of speech and the press, but the country is plagued by domestic, drug-related, and political violence. Administratively, the country is divided into 14 districts known as parishes, with populations varying from approximately 90,000 to more than a million (Kingston).

People and Culture

The Jamaican population originates from migration from other parts of the world. Through the diaspora brought about by the slave trade, 95% of the population is of African origin. Minority ethnic groups are European, originating from planters during Jamaica's time as a British colony. Other minority ethnic groups from more recent immigration include Arabs (mainly Lebanon and Syria) who came as traders, Indians who were brought in as indentured laborers after slavery was abolished, and Chinese who came mainly from Hong Kong. There has always been intermixing of ethnic groups, but this has probably increased and is a positive facet of national life. However, the history and abominations of slavery have had negative influences on many aspects of the national character.

The country is nominally Christian, with many different churches, and many Jamaicans are very religious. However, this factor is contradicted by the high number of children born out of wedlock and the frequency of multiple partners, especially in the lower socioeconomic groups. The last 60 years have seen the development of Rastafarianism, a religious subculture that has strongly influenced the music, dress, and even the food of the country. During the 20th century, the arts flourished, and there is a rich culture in indigenous music, dance, and fine art.

Education Services Systems

According to the Progress of Nations (UNICEF, 1998), 100% of children in Jamaica attend primary school, although the level of literacy is only about 70%. School attendance is not compulsory and tends to be irregular, depending on the financial ability of the family to provide bus fares, shoes, and lunch money, as well as whether children are needed to help in cultivation.

Formal education begins at 3–4 years of age in "basic schools," most of which are run by churches or other private organizations and receive some government support for training, food, and subsidies. By age 6 years, 95% of children attend school. It seems likely that at least part of the remaining 5% are children with disabilities. Government-supported education covers primary schools for children ages 6–12 years, secondary and comprehensive schools for students ages 12–15, and high schools for those with better academic performance who are 12–18 years old. The majority of children stop attending school at 15 years. Tertiary education is no longer free. Jamaica has three universities, approximately 10 teacher-training colleges, and a number of technical schools and community colleges.

Special education programs are mainly financed by the government but are run both by nongovernmental organizations (NGOs) and the Ministry of Education. Most of these programs are segregated, but the Ministry is moving toward inclusive education and will probably discontinue support of segregated facilities. There are approximately 2,500 children in special education programs and a higher but unknown number attending general education schools.

KEY FEATURES OF EARLY INTERVENTION

Early intervention for children with disabilities began in 1975 with the Early Stimulation Project in Kingston. It was established under what was then called the Jamaica Council for the Handicapped, the government body appointed to manage a program for adults with disabilities. Critical issues in the development of this program were cost, addressing the lack of skilled personnel, the need to reach children in their homes, and the need to involve parents. As a result, a model was developed that subsequently was used in CBR programs as well. More than 1,300 children in Jamaica receive early intervention (see Table 10.1).

Curriculum and Classroom Practices

As of 2003, virtually all early intervention in Jamaica is home based. It is available in most parts of the island, though with variable and mostly inadequate coverage. There are four organizations providing this service, including the original Early Stimulation Project—the only one that is not part of a CBR program.

The curriculum used varies. Three programs—the Early Stimulation Project, 3D Projects, and Private Voluntary Organisation Ltd.—use the Jamaica-Portage Guide to Early Intervention (Caribbean Institute on Mental Retardation, 1986). This consists of three parts: a checklist for assessment of development, a curriculum guide, and a manual to guide users. Jamaica was one of the first countries outside the United States to use this curriculum model. It was adopted in 1975 and adapted in 1976. Subsequently, it has been taught and used in different projects in various parts of the Caribbean, including Curaçao, Barbados, Trinidad, Antigua, and Grenada. It is also used in Haiti and the Dominican Republic. However, it is used differently in Jamaica than in many other countries, and use even varies a bit within Jamaica. In many countries, the assessment of the child and the individual program plan are completed by a professional (usually a teacher) along with a parent. Then, the teaching is done in the home by the same teacher with the mother. In Jamaica, the assessment, planning, and home teaching are all completed by the CRW, with intermittent supervision by a professional (see the section "Multifunction Community Workers: A Special Component of Jamaican Early Intervention Services"). In the Early Stimulation Project, only the home teaching is done by the CRW.

Table 10.1. Numerical breakdown of early intervention in Jamaica

Service provider	Number of children served
Early Stimulation Project	155
3D Projects	approximately 300
Clarendon Group for the Disabled	202
Private Voluntary Organisation Ltd.	650
Total	1,307

Family Roles

The family plays a crucial role in all of these programs. In fact the program could not succeed without its involvement. It was realized very early on in the Early Stimulation Project that additional work would be needed with families to overcome the various and frequent barriers to family involvement. Some of these barriers include lack of information; misconceptions about the nature of the child's disability; lack of awareness that a disability is even present; lack of acceptance; hope in other, possibly quicker treatments (e.g., going to the United States for medical treatment, using herbal remedies, visiting an *obeah* woman); and poverty.

These issues had to be tackled, and four main strategies were developed: 1) parent education, 2) the use of parents as CRWs, 3) the formation of parent groups, and 4) income-generating projects (Thorburn, 1991). All of these are integral parts of most early intervention programs in Jamaica. There are now thriving parent organizations in all of the parishes, and a National Parent Advocacy Group is in existence. Curricula have been developed with manuals and videotapes for parent training (3D Projects, 1995), and the majority of CRWs in most of the programs are parents. However, one weakness is the lack of involvement by fathers in the majority of families.

Theoretical Influences

There have been six main influences on the development of these projects. Five of these were manifested from the beginning of early intervention in Jamaica:

1. Use of the Portage model (Shearer & Shearer, 1972)
2. Use of the behavioral approach that is explicit in the Portage model
3. Use of a manpower model
4. Mobilization of parents
5. Use of paraprofessionals as CRWs

Professionals in Jamaica in the special education field were exposed to the behavioral approach in 1974 and 1975 through short courses conducted by psychologists from New York state through the Partners of the Americas program. The manpower model came from Canada (National Institute, 1971). It stratifies personnel required for disability programs to 4 levels, with the main workforce coming from people with minimum training (6 months to 1 year) but the right personality (i.e., the CRWs). This chapter has already outlined the mobilization of parents. The use and training of paraprofessionals is detailed in the section "Multifunction Community Workers: A Special Component of Jamaican Early Intervention Services."

Political Influences

It is hard to think of any political influences, as the programs have survived and been acknowledged since 1975 despite changes in government. However, in broader terms, there has been a total lack of policy development on this crucial area of human service. A much more serious and related influence is economic, which has had a very negative effect from the beginning. The only program that is supported fully by government is the Early Stimulation Project, and support for that program has so dwindled that it has only a quarter of the staff it had in the 1970s. The other programs are all run by NGOs and get some of their financial support from the government. They mainly rely on private and international funding, which is becoming increasingly difficult to obtain. With the economic recession in the Third World since the 1980s, these programs are struggling to survive, as it has not been possible to get much support from the beneficiaries. The closing of home-based programs, with their low profile, does not have the same impact as the closing of an institution.

Cultural Influences

Two main cultural influences can be identified: the use of a U.S. model and the role of child-rearing practices in Jamaica.

Use of a U.S. Model

From the initiation of tne Early Stimulation Project in 1975, the decision was made to use a curriculum model from the United States, the Portage model (Shearer & Shearer, 1972). This has its advantages and disadvantages.

Advantages   Advantages include the availability of a ready-made curriculum, assessment materials, and instruction manual. Also, advice and assistance could be sought from the Portage Project itself. Later, other countries started projects using the Portage model. This allowed the exchange of information between Third World, as well as First World, countries, and led to a regular international congresses and a newsletter.

The curriculum is easy to learn and can be used by paraprofessionals. One does not have to be a psychologist to use it. This has the advantage that people with less training can deliver this service in the program. Other advantages are the model's flexibility and, because of its objective character, the ease with which progress can be evaluated.

Disadvantages There are two main disadvantages: the language and the culture on which the model is based. The language is standard English and is very terse. For Creole-speaking people, both CRWs and parents, this is difficult to understand and use. Considerable time must be spent during training to explain the meaning of many items in the checklist, especially the language section. The latter requires an understanding of basic grammar. The solution was to adapt the language to the vernacular, which has already been attempted.

The Portage curriculum is also based on a U.S. lifestyle, which is very different from that of Jamaica (although with the countries' close proximity and the influence of American television, the gaps are closing). The question of cultural appropriateness has been considered, and it was decided that the benefits of the program outweigh its disadvantages. Certainly, the use of the behavioral approach helps considerably in emphasizing the need for positive reinforcement, which is often lacking in Jamaican child-rearing practices.

Role of Child-Rearing Practices in Jamaica

Child-rearing practices in Jamaica have been very much influenced by the breakup of the family during slavery and its legacy of unstable families. Many families are characterized by early pregnancy in unmarried girls; children born out of wedlock; lack of toys, books, and writing materials; absent fathers; domestic violence; and the necessity for mothers to work. Children are often brought up by other family members, sometimes elderly great-grandmothers or aunts, who are often less flexible and frequently have superstitions (Thorburn, 1998).

Child-rearing patterns include the perpetuation of gender roles, so that boys are expected to go outside the home while girls are often confined to the "yard." Boys are often spoiled, and this carries over to adulthood for many of them. At least one apparent outcome is that many boys perform poorly in school. Also, a much higher proportion of boys receive disability services than girls (Thorburn, 2000).

Management of children's behavior tends to be negative, with failure to use positive reinforcement, much attention given to negative behaviors, and frequent use of corporal punishment (Barrow, 1996). Sometimes, withdrawal of food is used as punishment (Sobo, 1993).

As in most Third World countries, there are belief systems in Jamaica that may have a negative impact on the child or adversely influence the effectiveness of intervention. Supernatural beliefs affect 15%–17% of people's understanding of disability. They may think that the disability is a form of punishment from God, is due to the pregnant mother seeing a person with a disability, is from feeling sorry for an animal, or is the manifestation of a duppy that was put on the child (Thorburn, 1998). An even more widespread belief is that of divine intervention, either in the cause of or deliverance from disability. All of these beliefs are more common in the older and youngest age groups, as well as among the least educated (Thorburn, 1998). Other beliefs are that children with disabilities will come to nothing and be a burden, should always be put in "homes" or institutions, and do not have the same rights as other people. All these concepts affect the acceptance of people with disabilities, the motivation of caregivers to participate in intervention programs, the placement and attendance of children in school and adults in jobs, and the inadequate provision of services.

Finally, a special cultural practice that probably originated in West Africa is widely practiced in Jamaica and very likely in other Caribbean islands. This is an infant-handling routine that mothers and grandmothers use with infants after their baths (Hopkins & Westra, 1988; Werrij, Voeten, Adriaanse, & Thorburn, 2000). It includes stretching, tossing, molding, range-of-motion exercises, and propping in the sitting position. It is used for longer periods of time and more frequently for babies with disabilities (van der Putten, Finkenflugel, & Thorburn, 2001) and has potential therapeutic value.

Multifunction Community Workers: A Special Component of Jamaican Early Intervention Services

The special feature of Jamaican early intervention programs that has contributed to their success and sustainability is the use of multifunction community workers. As mentioned previously, the majority of these workers are women with no previous training, and many of them are parents or family members of children with disabilities. They are always recruited from the communities of the children to be served. The idea for this model had two sources: the Community Health Aide Programme in Jamaica and the experience of training personnel who care for children with disabilities in day nurseries.

The Community Health Aide Programme was pioneered in 1970 by Professor Sir Kenneth Standard of the University of the West Indies as a means of providing primary health care at low cost. Women with minimal education recommended by the community are given 3 months training to provide common, basic, and simple health-related tasks in their communities under the supervision of public health nurses and midwives. This initial project was accepted by the Government of Jamaica and is now a national program. Community health aides in one district of Kingston were also subsequently trained to provide early stimulation for malnourished children.

In 1974, while working in Professor Standard's department at the University of the West Indies, the author trained a group of school leavers from a government program to do developmental screening (Thorburn & Brown, 1976). At that time, she also had her first experience of training a group of women from a government special employment program to work in child care centers. She decided to use women from this program in the Early Stimulation Project.

One of the major problems facing programs for people with disabilities in Third World countries is lack of expertise (i.e., professional staff trained for the specific type of work). Positions in disability services, especially CBR programs, do not pay well, and it is difficult to attract professionals. In addition, there is no specific training for early intervention staff in standard training programs at the university or community college level. A further problem is that there are not many intervention programs offering employment because of the difficult financial situation of most NGOs and the lack of government programs. When the Early Simulation Project started in 1975, the staff consisted of the author (a doctor), a public health nurse, and a Peace Corps volunteer elementary school teacher. It was only because of the Portage Guide that the project was able to start at all!

To overcome this lack of expertise, the staff decided to adopt the Canadian Manpower Model, which calls for a four-level pyramid structure. Level 1 is the CRW, making up approximately 60% of the staff. Level 2 is the supervisor—usually a CRW who has been promoted because of experience, competence, and the respect of other workers— making about 20%. Level 3 is the professionals (10%), and Level 4 is the director.

The Early Simulation Project had a small team of two professionals and a larger team of CRWs, in a ratio of 1 to 8. The professional team would ideally be multidisciplinary, and the CRWs also had to be multidisciplinary—in one person!

The development of the CRW role was crucial to the functioning of the program. As the CRWs are usually women with a limited level of education, the training had to be made appropriate for them to understand and learn. This means initially using practical and participatory types of training with minimum theory and breaking up the training into modules spread out over a period of time, usually a year.

Training was designed based on the functions and tasks required of CRWs. Both have been revised a number of times since 1975. Previous training has been detailed in several publications (Thorburn, 1976, 1990, 1992b). The modules for training were

1. Basic: 3–4 weeks
2. Use of the Jamaica-Portage Guide to Early Intervention: 2 weeks
3. Child-rearing skills (behavior management): 1 week
4. Simple physiotherapy and adaptive aids: 2 weeks
5. Speech and language: 1 week
6. Vision and hearing screening and management: 2 weeks
7. For selected CRWs, use of the Denver II test (Frankenburg et al., 1992): 1 week

This program of training resulted in a multifunction worker who, when she gained experience, could be remarkable and caring. Professional visitors to 3D Projects were always impressed by CRWs' range of skills and interest in learning more. Two of them were promoted to the position of coordinator, a position previously only given to professionals.

In 1999, a new revision of tasks and training objectives was undertaken, with a view to developing a training manual for preparing community staff at the Ministry of Health to provide early intervention. The training was also used for a new group of staff for 3D Projects early in 2000. The objectives for these two groups for the basic training were

1. Children with disabilities will be identified at the earliest possible time by developmental screenings and the use of at-risk criteria in postnatal and child welfare clinics.
2. Refer children identified as having disabilities to a special clinic for assessment and treatment of any medical problems. They will then be assigned to a CRW in their own district.
3. CRWs will provide home-based intervention by instructing caregivers in appropriate activities and exercises for the children. The parents will carry out the training in their homes between visits by the CRWs.
4. Children with disabilities receiving intervention will be re-evaluated periodically to ensure that progress is taking place. If there is no evidence of progress, the child can be referred to another professional or agency.
5. At age 3 to 4 years, children with disabilities will be assessed with a view to placement in a local preschool for inclusive education. The CRW will provide support to the teacher and child until this is no longer needed. For children not considered ready for school, the CRW will continue to provide home-based intervention until it is no longer needed.
6. Detailed training objectives based on the preceding five objectives were also developed (see the appendix at the end of this chapter).

Training was conducted on site by the staff of 3D Projects, both professionals and experienced CRWs. In the case of the 3D CRWs, 4 weeks of training were conducted. In the Ministry of Health training, a 3-day course was given for nurse practitioners and public health nurses. The community health aides had already received 1 week of training in a previous year, allowing the rest of the training to be completed in 3 weeks.

Training of Professionals

In Third World early intervention and CBR programs, much discussion centers around which types of professionals are needed for supervisory and directing positions. The World Health Organization proposed an intermediate-level professional, but only a few programs prepare such individuals (Mendis, 1995). Colleagues involved in CBR agreed with the chapter author that probably the most useful and easily available professionals are occupational therapists and physiotherapists. However, they must be prepared to be flexible and learn new skills, especially in supervision, management, and training.

In the four-tier system of the Manpower Model, Level 3 consists of professionals. In 3D, the position is that of coordinator. There is one coordinator for each parish program. In the past, 3D Projects was able to use a specialist, such as a physiotherapist, for supervision and training, but current financial constraints have limited this approach.

The coordinator is also a multifunction staff member. She needs the same skills as the CRW but with more depth, both in knowledge and judgment. She also needs management, supervisory, and training skills. This combination is not generally available in Third World countries, so the various professionals who have been hired for these positions have had to be trained. The background of the latter has included teachers, public health nurses, nurse practitioners, and social workers. From 1991 to 1993, 3D Projects conducted a part-time, in-service program to provide the in-depth background for a group of its coordinators and supervisors, called Intermediate Level CBR Training. Twelve staff members participated for 4 days per month. There is clearly a need for this type of training to be offered as a degree course in Jamaica. Current and future training issues in CBR are detailed in papers by Wirz (2000) and Thorburn (2000).

Lessons Learned

Over the years, various evaluations have been conducted for early intervention and CBR programs in Jamaica. For a number of reasons, evaluation is one of the more difficult aspects of low-cost, home-based programs. By the very nature of being low cost and having limited professional expertise, evaluation becomes problematic. Evaluation of early intervention programs also is difficult because of the wide variety of program components and disabilities involved.

3D has attempted two evaluations. The first was an impact evaluation of parents' views of the program in two separate parishes in two different years (Thorburn, 1992a). There was no control group. The results in the two areas were almost identical, consistent, and favorable. Home visits were very much appreciated, as the parents derived comfort and attention from sympathetic listeners. Understanding and knowledge about their child's disability was good, especially compared with a group of parents who had never been in a CBR program: 92% of the parents participating in 3D were able to state their child's disability, as compared with 11%–45% in the second group. Among the parents surveyed, 67% of those participating in 3D admitted to positive attitude change and 72% to changes in practices toward their children. Furthermore, 76% felt their child had improved as a result of the program, and 93% said that they would recommend the program to other parents.

In 1995, 3D decided to use OMAR to evaluate its program, along with two other community based services in Jamaica. OMAR was the outcome of an effort made by the United Nations Development Programme to develop a low-cost, user-friendly evaluation package called Operations Monitoring and Analysis of Results (OMAR; Jonsson, 1994). OMAR evaluates 5 areas:

1. *Effectiveness: Is the program making satisfactory progress? Is it achieving its objectives?* This was evaluated by using a questionnaire called the Activities of Daily Living Questionnaire (Thorburn, Desai, & Davidson, 1992), which assesses the person's problems and reassesses them at chosen intervals (in this case, 1 year later).

2. *Impact: What effect has the program had on the people with disabilities and the community at large?* This was evaluated by several questionnaires administered with parents, people with disabilities, and members of staff.

3. *Relevance: Is the work done relevant to people's needs?* This was assessed from the overall responses to the various questionnaires.

4. *Efficiency: Have the personnel and other resources been used in the most efficient way?* This should have been derived from questionnaires given to 3D Projects administrative staff.

5. *Sustainability: Can the program continue without outside support? Have local capacity and interest been developed?* This was also assessed from questionnaires to senior staff.

With the help of two Dutch university students who spent 6 months in Jamaica, an OMAR evaluation was conducted and the first part was reported in 1996 (unpublished work). To conduct the effectiveness component, a second pair of students had to complete the evaluation the following year.

The evaluation proved to be a difficult exercise, requiring computer expertise. Such expertise is not necessarily available in CBR programs until they become fairly sophisticated (the students provided it for the evaluation). Another problem was that the effort to simplify the questions in the questionnaires resulted in difficulties in parent understanding, recording, and analysis. What was intended as an easy, quantitative analysis did not give useful, clear results in relation to OMAR's five components, and it was believed that a qualitative approach would be more effective. However, this would be even more difficult to record and analyze. A third problem was that the questionnaires used did not identify which questionnaire or which questions were intended for which component of the evaluation.

As a result, although useful feedback was provided for the project managers, specific results for impact, relevance, and sustainability were not obtained. They had to be inferred. The students felt that they did not get the information necessary for evaluation of efficiency. Effectiveness proved to be the most difficult to evaluate because of the inadequate follow-up in the second year for clients seen in the first year. The drop-out rate made the final numbers inadequate for drawing valid conclusions, and the questionnaires used to assess progress were not sensitive enough.

The most useful tool for assessing effectiveness is the Portage checklist to quantify developmental gains. This was utilized to evaluate the progress of children in the Early Stimulation Project in Kingston in 1978 (Thorburn, Brown, & Bell, 1979). This method would probably not be acceptable in Western programs because of its lack of psychological testing and the absence of a control group. This type of sophisticated research, however, is beyond the means of low-cost community services.

In addition, several lessons have been learned from experience. Professionals tend to be elusive and upwardly mobile, resulting in a high turnover rate. In particular, difficulty has been encountered in recruiting physiotherapists. The reason for this is as yet unknown. CRWs—especially those who are parents—are very dedicated and become skillful and experienced workers. Even in the difficult times, they remain loyal to the program.

RECOMMENDATIONS FOR PROFESSIONALS IN OTHER COUNTRIES

One reason for the program's success is its use of parents as CRWs. These parents have vested interest in children with disabilities. Through firsthand observation, staff have been able to select parents whose exceptional dedication shows in the ways they deal with their own children.

Second, the program's training is successful because it is based on participatory methods and practical work, including exposure to children with disabilities. The courses are always evaluated and greatly enjoyed. Training is based on a task analysis of the job to be performed. A "training of trainers" course, conducted in Haiti, used a participatory approach to task analysis and planning training for a new CBR program. This was also successful. Professionals learned and planned simultaneously.

Third, the behavioral approach is a component of the program's success. This is influential in implementing home-based training and in helping change the negative child-rearing practices that are common in Jamaican society.

CONCLUSION

This chapter has described features of the low-cost, home-based, early intervention programs that are used in Jamaica, which reach approximately 1,300 children in the pre-school age group. Most of these are part of larger CBR programs and are mediated by women from the community who have a basic education. Many of them are themselves parents of children with disabilities. The first program has been in existence since 1975, evidencing that its sustainability is related to the appropriateness of its training, cultural, personnel, and financial features. However, more research needs to be done to determine the long-term outcomes of children who have been through the program.

Perhaps the most disappointing aspect has been the failure of the government to incorporate the early intervention programs into governmental programs. All of the existing early intervention programs except one are run by NGOs, with small government subventions and main support from overseas donors. Ideally, the early intervention programs should be incorporated into the community health program or early childhood education. Two efforts have been made to do the former but both were unsuccessful. Training of community health workers was conducted, but the home-based intervention was not implemented. The Ministry of Education has taken on the responsibility for child care and preschool education for children 3–6 years old. Perhaps it is now appropriate to attempt to get the ministry to include early intervention as well.

REFERENCES

Barrow, C. (1996). *Family in the Caribbean: Themes and perspectives.* Kingston, Jamaica: Ian Randle Publishers.

Bluma, S.M., Shearer, M.S., Frohman, A., & Hilliard, J. (1976). *Portage Guide to Early Education: Checklist, Curriculum and Card File.* Portage, WI: Cooperative Educational Service Agency.

Caribbean Institute on Mental Retardation and Other Developmental Disabilities. (1986). *Jamaica—Portage Guide to Early Education.* Spanish Town, Jamaica: 3D Productions.

Frankenburg, W.K., Dodds, J.B., Archer, P., Bresnick, B., Maschka, P., Edelman, N., & Shapiro, H. (1992). *Denver Developmental Screening Test II (Denver II).* Denver, CO: Denver Developmental Materials.

Hopkins, B., & Westra, T. (1988). Maternal handling and motor development: An intra-cultural study. *Genetic, Social and General Psychology Monographs, 114,* 377–408.

Jonsson, T. (1994). *OMAR in rehabilitation. A guide on operations monitoring and analysis of results.* Geneva: United Nations Development Programme Interregional Programme for Disabled People.

Mendis, P. (1995). Education of personnel: The key to successful community-based rehabilitation. In B. O'Toole & R. McConkey (Eds.), *Innovations in developing countries for people with disabilities* (pp. 211–220). Lancashire, England: Lisieux Hall.

National Institute on Mental Retardation, Canada. (1971). *A national mental retardation manpower model.* Toronto: Roeher Institute.

Shearer, M., & Shearer, D. (1972). The Portage model: A model for early childhood education. *Exceptional Children, 36,* 210–220.

Sobo, E.J. (1993). *One blood: The Jamaican body.* Albany: State University of New York Press.

Thorburn, M.J. (1990). Training community workers for early detection, assessment and intervention. In M.J. Thorburn & K. Marfo (Eds.), *Practical approaches to childhood disability in developing countries* (pp. 125–140). Spanish Town, Jamaica: 3D Projects.

Thorburn, M.J. (1991). Mobilising parent involvement in Jamaica. In V.R. Pandurangi & P.A. Woods (Eds.), *Early intervention for pre-school children in developing countries* (pp. 63–67). Bangalore, India: Sri Suhindra Printing Press.

Thorburn, M.J. (1992a). Parent evaluation of a community based rehabilitation programme in Jamaica. *International Journal of Rehabilitation Research, 15,* 170–176.

Thorburn, M.J. (1992b). Training community workers in a simplified approach to early detection, assessment and intervention. *Journal of Practical Approaches to Developmental Handicap, 16,* 24–29.

Thorburn, M.J. (1998). Attitudes towards childhood disability in three areas in Jamaica. *Asia Pacific Disability Rehabilitation Journal, 9,* 20–24.

Thorburn, M.J. (2000). Advances in the provision of services for children with disabilities in Jamaica (1988–1997). *Asia Pacific Disability Rehabilitation Journal, 11,* 69–79.

Thorburn, M.J. (2001). *Manual for training community workers in early intervention and community based rehabilitation for children with disabilities.* Spanish Town, Jamaica: 3D Projects.

Thorburn, M.J., & Brown, J.M. (1976). Para-professionals in early detection and stimulation. In M.J. Thorburn & C.A. Tucker (Eds.), *Proceedings of the Fourth Caribbean Congress on Mental Retardation* (pp. 125–134).

Thorburn, M.J., Brown, J.M., & Bell, C. (1979, August). *Early stimulation of handicapped children using community workers.* Paper presented at the Fifth Congress of the International Association for Scientific Study of Mental Deficiency, Jerusalem, Israel.

Thorburn, M.J., Desai, P., & Davidson, L.L. (1992). Categories, classes and criteria in childhood disability. *International Disability Studies, 14,* 122–142.

3D Projects. (1995). *Parent training. A manual for training parents in disability issues* [Book and video]. Spanish Town, Jamaica: Author.

UNICEF. (1998). *The progress of nations 1998.* New York: UNICEF Publications.

van der Putten, A.A.J., Finkenflugel, H.J.M., & Thorburn, M.J. (2001). Formal handling routines: Child-rearing practices in Jamaica. *Asia Pacific Disability Rehabilitation Journal, 12,* 52–62.

Werrij, M., Voeten, C.D., Adriaanse, H.P., & Thorburn, M.J. (2000). Formal handling routines in Jamaican infants: Knowledge, attitudes and behavior. *West Indian Medical Journal, 49,* 38–42.

Wirz, S. (2000). Training of CBR personnel. In M. Thomas & M.J. Thomas (Eds.), *Selected readings in community based rehabilitation: Series 1. CBR in transition,* 96–108. Bangalore, India: Asia Pacific Disability Rehabilitation Journal.

Chapter 10 Appendix

TRAINING OBJECTIVES
FOR COMMUNITY WORKERS

This appendix is adapted from a portion of *Manual for Training Community Workers in Early Intervention and Community Based Rehabilitation for Children with Disabilities* (2001), by Marigold J. Thorburn. The manual is available from 3D Projects, 14 Monk Street, Spanish Town, Jamaica.

GENERAL TOPICS

Community workers will

1. Be completely familiar with the operation of the program
2. Be able to establish and maintain good relationships with parents and children and to understand family dynamics
3. Be familiar with community attitudes, beliefs, and practices that may affect the success of program operation
4. Know the rights of children with disabilities and be able to advocate for them
5. Have an understanding of typical child development

SPECIFIC DISABILITY TOPICS

1. Know the nature, terminology, and frequency of the most common disabilities in Jamaica
2. Know the causes, manifestations, and essential anatomy of the following:

   - cognitive disabilities
   - motor disabilities
   - speech impairments
   - hearing impairments
   - seizures
   - visual impairments

PRACTICAL SKILLS IN SCREENING AND ASSESSMENT

Be able to administer

1. The developmental screening checklist
2. The Ten Questions
3. The Activities of Daily Living Questionnaire (Thorburn, Desai, & Davidson, 1992)
4. Basic hearing screening
5. Basic vision screening
6. An individual program plan

EARLY INTERVENTION SKILLS

1. Have overview of early intervention and an understanding of its rationale
2. Know how to assess and reassess a child's level of development using the Early Stimulation Manual
3. Know how to plan an intervention program
4. Be able to plan and teach lessons and activities
5. Be able to teach a child the following groups of skills

   - play/learning
   - motor
   - language
   - social
   - self-help

6. Be able to make appropriate teaching and adaptive aids to facilitate the preceding objectives
7. Be able to embed training into normal, everyday activities.
8. Be able to use the home-teaching process to show the caregiver how to teach the child
9. Be able to give basic advice on behavior problems
10. Be able to use the group problem solving approach

OTHER

1. Be able to work with teachers to facilitate the inclusion of children with disabilities into general education schools
2. Know the resources in the local and larger community that can assist children with disabilities
3. Be able to make community presentations on certain aspects of disability

RECORDS AND FILES

1. Be able to correctly use and maintain case files
2. Know the criteria for admission to and discharge from the program

CHAPTER 11

A Comprehensive Early Intervention Training Approach

José Boavida and Leonor Carvalho

PORTUGAL

Mais vale prevenir do que remediar.

It's easier to prevent than to remediate.

In 1989, implementation began for a community-based interagency program of early intervention in the Coimbra district in central Portugal (Boavida & Borges, 1990). The transdisciplinary interagency team model chosen in Coimbra allowed professionals from different disciplines and agencies to work together to provide integrated services to children and families. Developing a competent work force was considered critical from the beginning, the cornerstone of the Coimbra Project's development. A major goal of training was to create among professionals a common conceptual and philosophical framework (Boavida, 1992). The lack of preservice preparation, the child-focused (versus family-focused) professional training, the lack of teamwork skills, and a shortage of experienced Portuguese trainers were some of the difficulties encountered. How could an in-service training program be developed that would be effective in enhancing the knowledge and skills of personnel with limited or no experience in the field?

Although early intervention is relatively well established in Coimbra as of 2003, it has only recently emerged in most of Portugal. Since the mid-1990s, a wide array of programs and services have developed across the country. Thus, the Coimbra Project team faced a second question: How would a training team be developed that would provide ongoing support to practitioners from the Coimbra Project and from around the country?

In addition, the passage of early intervention legislation in 1999 (Despacho Conjunto 891/99, 1999) created further personnel preparation needs at a national level. Developing preservice and in-service training programs that consider all of the changes in the service delivery models that occurred since the 1990s will be a major challenge for universities, higher education institutions, and early intervention programs. To help others understand the Coimbra Project's challenges and responses to those challenges, this chapter begins with a vignette, which is followed by a discussion of the demographics, social context, health and education services systems, and key features of early intervention in Portugal. Also included are descriptions of the Coimbra Project, the development of the training and personnel preparation program within the project, future directions, and recommendations for professionals in other countries.

The authors express their warmest thanks to Marilyn Espe-Sherwindt, who gave valuable time to provide helpful comments and guidance that greatly influenced the development of this chapter. They are also indebted to their many colleagues who helped develop early intervention services in Coimbra and elsewhere in Portugal.

JOAQUIM AND PAULA'S STORY ————————

Paula, an Afro-Portuguese woman in her early thirties, left a former Portuguese colony, seeking a better life and medical care for her particular health condition. A childhood illness had left her with a serious motor disability. Living in poverty in a place with poor health care negatively affected her ability to receive intervention. Like many people in her country, she chose Portugal because of its better living conditions and because she spoke the language. Paula had to leave her 3-year-old daughter, Sandra, in her mother's care, promising to bring the child to Portugal as soon as possible.

António, Paula's partner, was already living in Portugal when Paula arrived. The couple resided in a small industrial town near Coimbra. António easily found a job in a factory. This was not the case for Paula due to her physical limitations. Depending almost exclusively on António's small salary, the couple had enormous economic difficulties.

Some months after her arrival, Paula became pregnant and gave birth to Joaquim. The pregnancy and delivery were normal. After a couple of months, Paula noticed that Joaquim looked "floppier" and less alert than other babies. Paula and António tried to get medical help in the nearest local health center.

The doctor confirmed Paula's suspicions that her child was not developing typically, although the reasons for the delay were unclear. Joaquim was referred to the children's hospital for developmental and pediatric evaluation in its child development center. At the same time, Paula and her partner were informed of the Coimbra Project's early intervention program and were asked if they would like to be contacted by a local team member. They immediately agreed to the idea.

The local team received the referral and a report describing Joaquim as having "possible genetic problems" and "at social risk." A special educator and a social worker were immediately chosen as the professionals to provide services to the family and child. By the time the first contact occurred, 4-month-old Joaquim had received a genetic diagnosis: Down syndrome. Diagnosis had been delayed because the traces of trisomy 21 were not easy recognizable in Joaquim.

During the first visit, the professionals explained to the family how the program worked, and most of the family concerns were explored. Paula, sweet but strong and determined, openly talked about her priorities and problems. Her first concern was the current and future development of her child. Despite the absence of the usual associated disorders seen in babies with Down syndrome, a motor delay was already quite evident.

Paula was also worried about her own physical disability. She wanted to buy an orthopedic device that would improve her mobility and quality of life, as well as find a job to contribute to the family's income. To do these things, she would have to legalize her immigrant status in Portugal. Paula also dreamed of bringing Sandra to live with the family in Portugal. She explained to the professionals that after being in Portugal for more than a year, her economic and health problems were worsening, and she had no idea who else to ask for help.

Paula agreed to receive weekly home visits for Joaquim. In collaboration with the professionals, Paula defined some objectives and strategies for Joaquim's development and for the family overall. Following some contacts with the proper authorities, Paula was able to legalize her residence in Portugal, opening new opportunities to reach her goals. After an orthopedic appointment, Paula received a new assistive device and started to attend physiotherapy sessions. Yet, because of her continued physical limitations, the search for a job was still difficult. With the help of a professional training agency, Paula was admitted to a paid professional training course. Joaquim had to be admitted to a child care center, where the service coordinator started to visit him on a weekly basis. Home visits, made whenever possible, continued to be an important aspect of the intervention.

In spite of legal and bureaucratic difficulties encountered during the attempt to bring her daughter to Portugal, everything else seemed to be falling into place for the family. Paula started to get excited and very motivated by her new career; she was considered the best attendee in her training class. With excellent collaboration among the service coordinator and all professionals, Joaquim was easily included in the child care program, where he was with other children the same age. Then, the situation began to worsen. With the approach of winter, contact with other children and the family's poor housing conditions, Joaquim had frequent respiratory infections with several hospital admissions. The family kept searching for a new home, but the rent was very expensive. With the help of the service coordinator, they applied to social housing. To care for Joaquim, Paula missed her classes several times, then began to fall behind. She decided to abandon the course just a few months before it ended so that she could give Joaquim more attention. Consequently, the family economic situation worsened.

Fortunately, a few months later Joaquim's health improved. Paula started looking for a job again. She wanted to proceed with her career, so with the help of the team, the training agency was contacted again.

Paula re-enrolled in the course and finished a practical internship in a factory that gave her some good chances for a job.

Joaquim is 2 years old now and has just started to walk. His mother's greatest concern for the last couple of months has been his ability to talk. Paula says Joaquim is "as lazy to talk as he was to walk." Because of this situation, the service coordinator proposed contacting a speech-language therapist. Paula agreed, and after the first appointment, strategies for using gestures to improve communication were added to Joaquim's plan.

In less than a year, Joaquim will be 3 years old. It is necessary to start working on his transition plan, as most children in Portugal go to a new type of child care center after age 3. Some contacts with the new child care center have already been initiated. A file containing all relevant information that the family is willing to share will go with Joaquim to the new child care center. Only one of the family's top priorities has not been successfully addressed. Legal red tape has been a barrier to bringing her daughter Sandra to Portugal. Attempts to deal with the proper authorities will continue. Right now, a faint light can be seen at the end of the tunnel.

Throughout the family's involvement in the Coimbra Project, Paula and professionals have been working together all of the time, identifying priorities and concerns, developing a plan for incorporating the family goals and objectives, gathering resources to solve problems, and—above all—giving the family members a chance to command their own lives.

NATIONAL CONTEXT

Portugal is the older and smaller of the two independent countries on the Iberian Peninsula in southwestern Europe. About the size of the American state of Indiana, the country occupies an area of 36,390 square miles, including the Azores and Madeira islands. Continental Portugal is rectangular in shape; roughly 360 miles long and 125 miles wide. All of its 10.5 million people speak Portuguese. Almost 60% of its population lives in rural areas.

Independent since 1143, Portugal's location at the edge of Europe, between Spain and the Atlantic Ocean, at first left it isolated from the great commercial centers and the major routes of land transportation. Eventually during the medieval period, however, Portugal experienced unparalleled maritime expansion and trade, when its navigators sailed to explore approximately two thirds of the world. The ocean continues

to play an important role for the country. The largest cities, such as
Lisbon and Oporto, are seaports. The population is densest along the
coast, where the best farming areas, chief industries, and main transportation routes are located.

From 1933 to 1974 Portugal was ruled by a conservative authori-
tarian regime. On April 25, 1974, a military movement, exasperated
by the long wars in colonial Africa and repressive policies at home,
overthrew the regime and started a new era in Portugal's history.
Portugal is a parliamentary democracy and has been a full member of
the European Union (EU) since 1986.

Traditional Portuguese industries include textiles, clothing, foot-
wear, cork and wood products, beverages (wine), porcelain and earth-
enware, and glass and glassware. Although Portugal is thought of as
an agricultural country, Portuguese agriculture has declined greatly in
importance since the end of the 20th century. As of 2003, the country's
income is heavily dependent on manufacturing and on the expanding
tourist trade. Portugal is a major European tourist destination, with
approximately 25 million visitors arriving every year from Spain, the
United Kingdom, Germany, France, and the United States. The 500
miles of coast, a mild climate, and the excellent food and wine are
some of the reasons for the success of the tourist industry.

Significant progress has been made since the 1980s in raising the
Portuguese standard of living closer to that of its EU partners. The
unemployment rate is 4.4%, the lowest in the EU (Instituto Nacional de
Estatística, 2000) and is expected to decline as the economy continues to
strengthen. The average per capita income is $10,824 (in U.S. dollars).
On a purchase power parity basis, it rose from 53% of the EU average
per capita income in 1985 to more than 70% in 1998.

People and Culture

Portuguese society remained traditional throughout the first three
quarters of the 20th century for two primary reasons: 1) a low level
of industrialization and 2) a massive emigration of the most innovative
and ambitious citizens, who fled to other European countries and
America to escape Portugal's colonial wars and dictatorship. After the
1974 revolution, many of those who had emigrated returned to Portugal, bringing substantial renovation to the society. With the 1986 entry
into the EU and the great improvement in living conditions, disparities
between classes started decreasing, and Portuguese society increasingly
began to resemble that of other European countries.

At first glance, Portugal may appear homogeneous. For example,
97% of the population is Roman Catholic. (Portugal is known for

several pilgrimage sites, the most famous of which is Fátima.) Among the "original" Portuguese population, other than a small African minority, there are no different ethnic or cultural groups. Portugal has no extremist or separatist movements engaged in terrorism; Portuguese people are generally regarded as being very tolerant and pacific.

Nevertheless, regional and local variations can be seen even in small regions; these variations basically reflect the nature of Portugal's economic activities. Maritime Portugal is a society of fishing and tourism, while Portugal's interior is largely agricultural. The greatest contrast is between the cities and the rural areas, where society is simpler and more traditional. Beyond this rural–urban division, there are no other significant contrasts.

Since the 1990s, the increasing public investment in construction, together with net transfers from the EU, has led to an increase in salaries. This increase has attracted thousands of foreign workers, especially from former Portuguese African colonies and from Eastern European countries. This migratory flow is a relatively new and challenging social problem, affecting housing, education, and social integration in general.

Health and Education Services Systems

Portugal has a National Health Service (NHS) that provides free health care to most of the population through a network of primary care health centers and local, secondary, and tertiary hospitals. Maternal and child health care services have improved significantly since the 1980s, with the infant mortality rate decreasing from 17.8 per 1,000 in 1985 to 5 per 1,000 in 2001 (Instituto Nacional de Estatística, 2002).

NHS services for children with developmental disabilities are provided by 1) child development centers in children's hospitals in Lisbon, Oporto, and Coimbra and 2) developmental clinics in pediatric departments in secondary hospitals. These services include a pediatric neurodevelopmental assessment as well as evaluations from professionals in special education, psychology, social work, speech-language pathology, and physical and occupational therapy. Laboratory investigations, imaging techniques, genetic and metabolic tests, and consultations from other medical specialists are performed whenever appropriate.

Education has been steadily improving as well. Illiteracy decreased from 34% of the population ages 15–64 in 1960 to 7% in 1991 (Barreto, 2000). Although school enrollment is only mandatory for children ages 6–16, preschool attendance (ages 3–5 years) increased from approximately 30% in 1987 to 64.7% in 1998 (Ministry of Education, 2000).

Meanwhile, the number of students attending universities and institutions of higher education has also risen steadily, from 24,149 in 1960 to 84,173 in 1980 to 344,868 in 1997 (Barreto, 2000).

Under Public Law 319/91, passed in 1991, the public school system is required to provide a full appropriate education for all children with disabilities. The education agencies are required to evaluate all children with special education needs and to prepare and implement individualized education plans for them. Placement in the least restrictive environment is also a key requirement of the law. "Related services" are also to be provided. These include transportation, counseling, psychological services, and even some assistive technology.

Despite a very good legal framework defining the provision of services for school-age children with disabilities, the reality is sometimes different. Public resources (financial and human) are frequently allocated to private institutions (e.g., parents' associations), which run segregated schools. However, a strong inclusion movement, supported by parents, professionals, and policy makers, is gradually shifting the educational situation to a more inclusive one.

KEY FEATURES OF EARLY INTERVENTION

The passage of early intervention legislation (Despacho Conjunto 891/99) in October 1999 was a landmark. Prior to this legislation, free and appropriate education to children with disabilities was only regulated after age 6. However, the urgent need for some kind of regulation arose due to the proliferation of early intervention programs in Portugal.

Since the early 1990s a wide array of programs and services, all calling themselves "early intervention," have developed across the country: some child centered; some professional centered; some resulting from the work of a single professional, a group of professionals, or even teams. Some programs have depended on the departments of education and health; others have depended on the social security system or are the result of an articulation of public and private agencies (Almeida, 2000). Conceptual frameworks; delivery models; target populations; goals; outcome measures; level of parental involvement; and the type, intensity, or duration of services have been extremely variable from program to program and even within the same program. Consequently, the overall picture of early intervention in Portugal has been so heterogeneous that only now, with the help of legislation, are there expectations for a possible but certainly slow movement toward nationwide consistency.

Through the efforts of committed professionals, the new legislation contains an important change: Rather than focusing only on the education of the child, it clearly identifies the family as the locus for planning and delivering community-based early intervention supports and services. The legislation also provides a reminder that early intervention is a multidisciplinary and interagency field. It is made of professionals from education, health, and social services who should provide comprehensive developmental services to children with disabilities from birth to age 6 and their families. The need for an individualized intervention plan is also a central feature of the Portuguese legislation. This plan is to be developed and implemented according to a family-focused philosophy.

The legislation defines a structure including local community teams, managed by a coordinating team in every district. Professionals from different education, health, and social security public agencies, as well as from private institutions, are included in these teams. Supervision and evaluation of implementing the law are provided by five regional groups—one in each of the country's regions. At the national level, supervision and evaluation are provided by an interdepartmental group with representatives from the three departments involved: health, education, and social security.

A critical shortage of qualified personnel to serve young children at risk and with disabilities will be a key challenge to the successful implementation of the new legislation. As a result, the purposes of early intervention, the age of children to be served, the needs and problems of families, team-based service, and delivery are all relevant issues that must be considered for future preservice and in-service personnel preparation at a national level.

DESCRIPTION OF THE PROGRAM

The Coimbra Project began in 1989, with the articulation of five regional agencies representing health, education, and social services. In 1994, a working party was created at the national level to develop national legislation on the provision of early intervention services. A member of the Coimbra Project was invited to participate in this group. In 1999, despite interruptions due to changes in the government, the efforts of the working party came to fruition: the early intervention legislation was passed. Most of the goals and assumptions and even the structure that constituted the basis of Coimbra Project were included in the legislation.

Coimbra is Portugal's third-largest city. It is the capital of the Center Region, which has six districts. The Coimbra District has an area of 1,600 square miles and a population of approximately 450,000. Like the whole country, the Coimbra District reflects different geographical contexts, ranging from isolated communities in the mountains to coastal villages thriving on tourism, as well as different social contexts, ranging from extreme poverty (alcoholism often a serious problem) to middle-class families.

The city of Coimbra itself is of moderate size, with a population of 150,000. The University of Coimbra, one of the four oldest in Europe, was founded in 1290 by King Dinis and is situated on a hill overlooking the oldest part of the city. The distant seas sailed by the Portuguese brought treasures that are attractions to the university's visitors: the portals in Manueline style (a Portuguese gothic architectural style from the period of the discoveries), St. Michael's chapel, and the exotic woods and Brazilian gold in the King John library. The old tower, which at 34 meters tall dominates the city's skyline, still strikes every hour. In May, the city is vibrant with each university department's color during the students' festivities and parade. All year long, university students are often seen walking the narrow streets in their traditional black capes, bringing to Coimbra *fados* (typical Portuguese national songs) and ballads, books and poems, dreams and nostalgia.

Health and education services in the Coimbra District are some of the finest in Portugal. For example, the infant mortality rate is the lowest in the country (3.8 per 1,000) (Instituto Nacional de Estatística, 2002). It also has one of the highest levels of preschool attendance in the country (Ministry of Education, 2000). Unlike other areas of Portugal, the Coimbra District has a long tradition of collaboration among different agencies.

Coimbra Project Goals and Assumptions

Six main goals have guided the development of the Coimbra Project since its beginning in 1989 (Boavida & Borges, 1994; Boavida, Espe-Sherwindt, & Borges, 2000):

1. Develop an interagency, multidisciplinary system of early intervention.

2. Use resources already existing in the community (both human and material) and involve health, education, and social services, as well as other formal and informal resources.

3. Be district wide and community based, with an early intervention team in each of the district's 17 councils.

4. Provide individualized comprehensive services to children younger than age 3 who are at high risk or have disabilities and their families.
5. Provide training to all the professionals involved in the Coimbra Project and promote collaboration with other programs in Portugal and abroad.
6. Contribute to the development of early intervention legislation in Portugal.

Certain assumptions constitute the basis of the Coimbra Project. The first is that early intervention helps the family in the process of adapting to a new member with a disability. Early intervention also optimizes the environment, thereby helping the child reach his or her potential and preventing secondary disabilities (Bennett & Guralnick, 1991). In addition, every family, regardless of socioeconomic status, has strengths and resources that should be used to enhance the development of the child (McGonigel, Kaufmann, & Johnson, 1991). Moreover, no professionals can substitute for the family's caregiving role. Helping families increase and enhance parenting skills has a lasting effect that is beneficial beyond early intervention years (Dunst & Trivette, 1987; Dunst, Trivette, & Deal, 1988; Simeonsson & Bailey, 1990). Finally, early intervention has a positive impact on society, increasing its awareness of the need for early support to young children and their families (Moor, Van Waesberghe, Hosman, Jaeken, & Miedema, 1993).

Project Structure

Choosing an ecological and transactional framework (Bronfenbrenner, 1977; Sameroff & Fiese, 1990), the Project team believed that early intervention services should involve the family and should be community based, with the family as a whole being the target for service delivery. Whenever possible and appropriate, services were to be provided within the context of the home, using resources available within the family and the community. Rather than promoting a standard setting or single location for early intervention, the Project focused on natural environments: a child care center, the home, or elsewhere in the community according to family preferences and child needs (Boavida, 1993).

During a period of 4 years, a local intervention community team was created in every council of the Coimbra District. Since the beginning, all 17 teams have included a core set of professionals: a primary care physician, a nurse, one or more special educators, a social worker, and a psychologist. Therapists are only available in the biggest councils.

Due to a shortage of specialized professionals in small communities, the Project makes available an occupational therapist and a speech-language pathologist on a consultant basis. The diagnostic and therapeutic services of Coimbra Children's Hospital and its Child Development Center, as well as its Cerebral Palsy Center, are also available (Boavida & Borges, 1994; Boavida et al., 2000).

Team members are professionals from different agencies operating in the community. Only a small number of professionals work full time in the Coimbra Project. In most cases, early intervention is only part of their job. They still perform their regular work in their employing agency.

Physicians and nurses come from the local health center. Special educators are from the public school system. Psychologists and social workers come from a private institution, the health center, or any other local agency that makes them available. All team members have experience working with families and children younger than 3 years.

Each team has a fully equipped room provided within the facilities of one of the agencies involved, where assessments, meetings, and sometimes parent support groups take place. The team uses a transdisciplinary approach that attempts to transcend the boundaries of the individual disciplines, maximizing parental involvement as well as sharing in skills among professionals and families. The team member designated as the primary service provider becomes the service coordinator. Usually, the case coordinator is an educator, a social worker, a psychologist, or a nurse, and, whenever possible, is from the discipline most closely related to the needs of the child and family.

At the district level, a coordinating team with one representative from each of the signing agencies provides coordination among the different services. Even more important, the coordinating team provides all the organizational support to the Coimbra Project, including planning, supervision, training, regular meetings with community teams, project development, and implementation.

The agencies involved at district level that are represented at the coordinating team include the following: Coimbra Children's Hospital; the Regional Primary Care Administration, which coordinates local health centers; the Regional Special Education Department; Coimbra's Social Security Center; and the Association of Private Special Education Institutions. The coordinating team as a whole is responsible for the development of the activity report and the negotiation of the budget on a yearly basis. Based on written agreements regarding roles and responsibilities that have been developed between the Coimbra Project and the service providing agencies, each participating agency is asked to allocate specific resources—professionals, funding, or facilities (Boavida & Borges, 1990).

The Coimbra Project has created a supervision team, which functions at an intermediate level between the coordinating team and the 17 early intervention community teams (Boavida & Violante, 1993). The supervision team is made up of five professionals with recognized knowledge and experience in providing direct services to children and families. Their role is to help and support the professionals in the field and to make sure that the adopted philosophical and conceptual framework is respected. In addition, they function as a bridge between the coordinating team and the community.

Children and Families

The Coimbra Project serves approximately 210 children and families each year. A retrospective look at the children supported since the beginning of the project indicates that 33% had an established developmental delay, 45% had not only developmental problems but also belonged to high-risk groups, and the remaining 22% received intervention on a preventive basis due to environmental risk factors (Boavida et al., 2000). Children with all kinds of developmental delays and disabilities have been served. Major groups include the following:

- Global delay: 68%
- Down syndrome: 8%
- Congenital malformations (including different dysmorphic syndromes): 7.5%
- Hearing impairment: 7%
- Cerebral palsy: 6%
- Visual impairment: 5%

Poverty has been the primary environmental risk factor, representing 40% of the total population served. Alcoholism comes second with 17%, followed by nutritional problems, 15%; social isolation, 14%; depression, 13%; illiteracy, 11%; and mental retardation in the family, 9% (Boavida et al., 2000). Since the late 1990s, children at environmental risk have been the focus of special attention within the Coimbra Project (Bryant & Maxwell, 1997). Usually living in deprived environments with substandard housing and overcrowded conditions, frequently rejected by the community, these families tend to be distrustful of services. They present high rates of absenteeism to clinics, especially developmental clinics. In an atmosphere of depression, discouragement, and helplessness, the child's development is clearly not a priority. Psychological and physical energies are usually spent in tasks of mere survival. In addition, professionals tend to attribute any delay only to poor living and environmental conditions.

    With these concerns in mind, Coimbra Children's Hospital and the
Coimbra Project started the Developmental Clinic in the Community
in 1998 (Boavida, Carvalho, & Carvalho, 1998). Exclusively for children
and families at environmental risk, clinic visits must be agreed to by
the family and organized by the service coordinator. A team including
a developmental pediatrician, a psychologist, and a clinical special educator meets the family and child in the most convenient place for them,
which, if possible, is the home. The service coordinator or any other
local team members chosen and desired by the family are present
during the evaluation. The evaluation includes 1) a pediatric and neurodevelopmental assessment of the child and 2) an identification of
strengths, priorities, needs, and risk factors—made by the family, with
the help of instruments developed for this purpose. At the end of
meetings, family members and professionals from the clinic and the
local team gather to address and discuss all the information that is
considered relevant for the intervention process. Formal and informal
resources available, strategies, outcomes, activities, as well as other
issues to be included in the plan, are outlined.
    Data from the first 2 years indicate that the clinic evaluation took
place in the home in 65% of the 75 cases assessed. Alcoholism was
present in one or both parents in 70% of the families; mental retardation was present in at least one of the parents in 25% of the cases.
Regarding pregnancy and childbirth, 17.5% of the mothers did not
attend any prenatal care clinic and 15% delivered the babies at home.
(In the general population, 2% of pregnant women fail to seek prenatal
care and 1.3% deliver at home.) These figures give a general idea of
the families attending this clinic and the challenges faced in providing
services (Boavida et al., 1998).

Mild developmental delays were present in 60% of the children seen at the Developmental Clinic in the Community. In some cases, a visit to Coimbra Children's Hospital for laboratory investigations or imaging studies became part of the plan. Some nonspecific brain malformations were identified, as well as fragile X syndrome. Most of the children were considered "normal" by local professionals, and were labeled as "at risk." When children with mild developmental delays live in poverty, the tendency to focus on the environment as the sole underlying cause of delay is in itself an extra risk factor. That is, a medical explanation is overlooked and the child is deprived of the necessary medical investigations and interventions. In these particular cases, evaluating the child in the natural environment (in the context of the family and community) and having an extended discussion involving family, local professionals, and developmental specialists have proved to be very helpful in planning and implementing intervention (Meisels & Fenichel, 1996).

The Role of Families

Until the late 1990s, parents were not directly involved in Coimbra Project management activities at a district level. With the 1999 constitution of the National Early Intervention Association (Associação Nacional de Intervenção Precoce, or ANIP), which includes two parents on the management board and has its central office in Coimbra, this situation began to change rapidly. The aims of ANIP are to administrate the Coimbra Project's public funding and to organize and provide training, information, and support for parents and professionals involved in early intervention.

Before ANIP, parental involvement had only taken place within the local teams, particularly in relation to activities regarding their own children as well as occasional parent support groups. Parent support groups are not particularly consistent with Portuguese culture; sharing experiences with other parents with similar problems is not traditionally a common practice in Portugal. Nevertheless, the few exceptions in this area have been relatively successful and rewarding.

The Coimbra Project itself has made significant progress in involving families. Despite its initial awareness of the need to target families for services delivery, the level of parental involvement was comparatively low in the beginning years. Since the late 1990s, the Project has moved steadily from a family-allied and family-focused approach toward an approach that is truly family centered. Two factors have facilitated a totally different level of parent participation in the early intervention process: 1) the adoption of a transdisciplinary team model and 2) the use of a Portuguese version of the Individualized Family Service Plan (Plano Individualizado de Apoio à Família, or PIAF) as a process to be developed and implemented in a way that supports families' goals and objectives (Espe-Sherwindt & Boavida, 1997).

Unlike multidisciplinary or even interdisciplinary teams, transdisciplinary teams, by their function and structure, create opportunities for families and professionals to work together (McGonigel, Woodruff, & Roszmann-Millican, 1994). Families are considered team members, involved to whatever level they choose in developing and implementing the PIAF. Their role of sharing information in their discipline—being a parent of a child with a disabilities and being aware of their own priorities, strengths, and needs—makes them a priceless resource in the intervention process.

This change in traditional family–professional roles and relationships has not always been easy to implement with some conservative professionals. The development and implementation of the transdisciplinary team approach has been facilitated in Portugal by the reality of budget constraints and the usually understaffed and underfunded teams.

Coimbra Project Results and Future Directions

A crucial question remains to be answered. Has the Project been able to minimize or prevent developmental problems in the children served so far? Knowing the children and families, it would be easy to say "yes." Scientifically, however, a definitive answer cannot be given due to methodological constraints. The heterogeneity of the population served, all of the variables that can influence development, the inability to separate neuromaturational from intervention influences, and the lack of control groups pose challenges that are beyond the Coimbra Project's means to solve.

In 1997, a parent satisfaction survey conducted with parents of 30 children who had been supported by the Project for more than 2 years provided some rewarding results. Ninety percent of the parents were satisfied with their child's progress, 89% thought the intervention met their child's needs, 81% felt as though they were active team members, 85% had better understanding of their child's problems, and 70% reported they had gained knowledge and skills and felt better able to use community resources (Boavida et al., 2000).

Parent satisfaction with the Coimbra Project was measured again in 2002 using the European Parent Satisfaction Scale about Early Intervention, or EPASSEI (Eurlyaid, 1997). The EPASSEI, developed within the European early intervention working party Eurlyaid, was translated into Portuguese by an independent research team supported by ANIP. The scale contains 57 items that measure parent satisfaction along eight dimensions: 1) parent-centered intervention, 2) child-centered intervention, 3) social environment, 4) partnerships between parents and professionals, 5) model of intervention, 6) parents' rights, 7) localization and network of the service, and 8) structure and administration of the service. Scoring for each item ranges from −2 (*strongly dissatisfied*) to +2 (*very satisfied*).

The survey was distributed, collected, and analyzed by the independent research team. The mean satisfaction score, based on results from 158 families, was +0.93, a score comparable to or higher than other European countries, even those with more resources than Portugal (Lanners & Mombaerts, 2000). The dimension receiving the highest average rating was partnerships between parents and professionals (+1.66). The dimension receiving the lowest average rating was localization and network of the service (+0.27). This concerns variables like flexibility of the working timetables, accessibility for parents and children, some functional aspects of the organization of the program, and recognition within the social structure. In general, satisfaction was highest among families who had children with mild developmental disabilities and families from low socioeconomic backgrounds; parents whose children had significant developmental disabilities and parents from high socioeconomic backgrounds were less satisfied (Cruz & Fontes, 2002). These results must be carefully analyzed and need to be taken into consideration for future directions.

Some results cannot be quantified, however. These include a big shift in the ways that families are regarded by practitioners. They also include increased awareness of the need to develop regulations on the provision of services; this awareness was partly responsible for the development of early intervention legislation in Portugal. Training was certainly part of the answer as far as creating a common collaborative perception and maintaining a common conceptual framework among different professionals from various disciplines and agencies. This specific feature of the program is detailed later in the chapter.

From the beginning, an ecological model of intervention was adopted (Bronfenbrenner, 1990), maximizing intervention efforts through a comprehensive and integrated program of services. The child, but also the family, the professionals, and the larger social contexts have been the focus for delivering early intervention services (see Figure 11.1). Training/supervision and support to starting programs, adaptation and development of instruments and procedures, and participation in national and international working parties have always been important parts of the Coimbra Project.

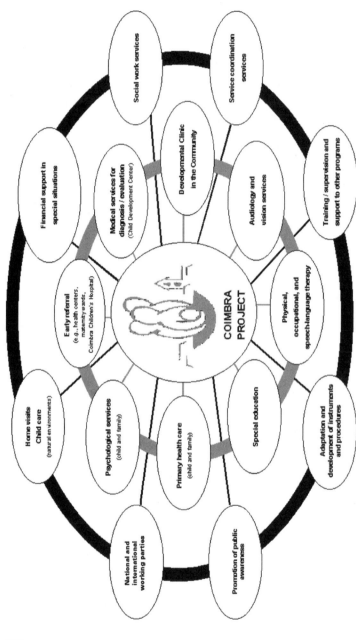

Figure 11.1. Diagram of the Coimbra Project's ecological model of intervention.

The Project is committed to investing very early in young children who have or are at risk for developmental disabilities. This commitment is reflected in an emphasis on increasing parental involvement at all levels—from local teams to national organizations; from contributing to the development of training programs or program evaluation.

When it started in 1989, the Coimbra Project was a totally new experience. It created a model for collaboration among multiple community agencies that was highly evaluated by families, was subsequently implemented in different ways and locations throughout the country, and eventually became the conceptual framework of Portuguese legislation.

TRAINING AND PERSONNEL PREPARATION

The delivery of early intervention services is a complex task requiring a combination of knowledge, skills, and experience that enables practitioners to select and use the best intervention techniques (Gallacher, 1997). From the beginning, personnel preparation was considered the cornerstone of the Coimbra Project's development (Espe-Sherwindt & Boavida, 1995). However, the task of preparing personnel in Portugal in 1989 was not easy. Issues faced included

- Professional training that was primarily child focused (versus family focused)
- A lack of regulations on the provision of services
- A lack of preservice preparation in early intervention issues
- A shortage of trained and experienced professionals and faculty in the field
- The continuing evolution of concepts and recommended practices

As a result, creating a common conceptual and philosophical framework among professionals from different agencies and disciplines was one of the major goals of training. In retrospect, this was critical in enabling the ability to adopt a new approach.

To address these challenges, a variety of strategies for continued personnel development had to be considered. Consultations with visiting experts (especially from the United States), interaction with programs in Europe and in the United States, short-term conferences and workshops, coursework, and supervision were provided to build and refine early intervention skills and to encourage continued professional support and growth (Boavida & Borges, 1994). This part of the chapter explores personnel preparation issues within the Coimbra Project. These issues include the evolving face of early intervention in Coimbra and Portugal, personnel training program design, program effectiveness, and future directions and considerations.

Evolving Face of Early Intervention in Coimbra and Elsewhere in Portugal

As discussed previously, when the Project started its activities in 1989, no legislation or recommendations for the provision of services existed in Portugal. In most cases, services were child centered, using the same methods as special education programs for older children (Boavida & Borges, 1994). Similarly, no specific early intervention professional training existed, either preservice or in-service. Early intervention topics were not widely included in the existing professional training; if early intervention content did exist, it typically was incompatible with what was considered best practice internationally. The fast-evolving field of early intervention, with new roles and visions of service delivery, was the single most important factor that influenced the content and process of the Coimbra Project training program. The implementation of the Coimbra Project—whose assumptions, goals, and philosophical framework were very much inspired by American legislation but adjusted to fit the project's own reality and creativity—constituted the starting point of a no-return process of early intervention development in Portugal. The decision to move toward a family-centered, community-based, interagency, transdisciplinary model created significant training needs for the Project.

Target Populations and Goals of Early Intervention

When planning professional preparation, one of the first relevant issues to be addressed was the nature of target populations (Klein & Campbell, 1990). As well as serving children with disabilities, the project started including services for children at high risk—particularly those with multiple environmental risk factors, with poverty being the common denominator. In addition, providing support and instruction to families and contributing to their autonomy, independence, and empowerment was considered a goal as important as enhancing child's development, minimizing developmental delays, remediating existing problems, or providing therapeutic services to children. Identifying the family as the target for delivering services and supports presented a radical change for providers.

Level of Family Involvement

From the beginning, the Project moved steadily toward a family centered approach. The changing point from a family-allied philosophy to an increasingly family-centered one was represented by the introduction of the PIAF (Espe-Sherwindt & Boavida, 1996). The PIAF was seen as a process to be developed and implemented by families and professionals, according to family priorities, concerns, strengths, and needs (McGonigel et al., 1991). Services were seen from the perspectives of families, the constant in the child's life and the primary unit for service delivery. Professionals also were required to work with the family as an integral part of the team, abandoning traditional prescriptive models. As at all levels of the intervention process, collaboration and partnership between family and professionals were the keys to the successful implementation of family-centered services. This particular philosophical change proved to be the most difficult to adopt and implement with some conservative child-focused trained professionals, and, as a result, became central to personnel preparation planning.

Location Where Intervention Occurs

The Coimbra Project did not prescribe a standard setting for early intervention. Every child has unique needs and lives in a family that is unique, with distinctive resources and priorities. The same principle applies to the community where the child and family live. A variety of factors have to be considered when choosing the optimum service environment for a child with disabilities or at risk. These include the family's home, a child care center, the health center, or elsewhere in the community, provided that they are natural environments (Stayton & Bruder, 1999). Consequently, practitioners had to learn to deliver services in settings that were perhaps not typical and traditional (and at times uncomfortable) for them.

Collaboration Among Agencies

According to the Coimbra Project organizational structure, teams were to include professionals from different health, education, and social security agencies as well as professionals from private institutions. This model was an approach to coordinate services across agencies. The need for a model to integrate services from multiple agencies was particularly important for families with complex, intense service and support needs.

The transdisciplinary interagency team model created a structure for professionals from different disciplines and agencies to work together to provide integrated and comprehensive services to children and families. It was seen as enhancing the possibility to coordinate services across both discipline and agency boundaries (McGonigel et al., 1994). The absence of such coordination among local teams would make support to families and their infants and toddlers with disabilities an unfulfilled promise. The need to create among professionals a shared philosophy and common language and goals—in other words, the need to create a team—was one of the most important issues considered in planning and development for personnel training (Boavida et al., 2000).

New Values and Roles in Early Intervention

The child's developmental needs were viewed as integrated across the major developmental domains, with the child's program preferably implemented by a single professional with assistance provided by other team members on a consultant basis. The Coimbra Project model required a dramatic reconceptualization of the traditional role of service providers: from decision makers to facilitators; from multidisciplinary to transdisciplinary; from direct services provided to children to indirect, consultative services to children and families (Stayton & Bruder, 1999). All of these shifts in service provision would be possible only if the new attitudes, skills, and competencies necessary for working with families were integrated into the training curriculum (Roberts, Rule, & Innocenti, 1998).

Personnel Training Program Design

Preservice preparation of the different professionals involved in the Coimbra Project did not include family-centered collaborative approaches to service delivery. Therefore, they were not prepared to function in a system that required practitioners to work with the child and the family, usually during home visits, and to tailor intervention strategies to the family's routines and priorities. What did professionals in the community need to know to effectively serve children and families? How could in-service training enhance the awareness, knowledge, and skills of personnel who had limited or no experience in the field? How could in-service training shift their definition of intervention from a set of activities for eligible children with disabilities to a broader concept influencing the child's development and the family's ability to care for the child? In addition, how difficult and possible would it be to create a system of in-service training and ongoing support that would be appropriate across disciplines and practices? How could local needs be defined and, whenever possible, local solutions be provided? These were some of the questions that had to be answered before planning personnel preparation.

The description of the program design contains aspects related to the content and the process. The content includes broad and specific areas of competence considered important for the provision of early intervention services according to recommended best practices. The process refers to the way that the content is delivered (McCollum &

Catlett, 1997). Supervision, by its importance in the provision of ongoing training and support to practitioners, is presented separately.

Program Content and Process

Knowledge and skills in a wide range of critical areas are important for
professionals to be appropriately qualified to provide early intervention
services (Thorp & McCollum, 1994). The Coimbra Project identified
four broad content areas for training purposes: 1) children, 2) families,
3) team functioning, and 4) philosophy and values (not only the
Coimbra Project's own conceptual framework, but also accepted best
practices identified in the literature). Content subareas of the training
curriculum were

1. Child development and behavior (typical and atypical)
2. Specific developmental problems (vision impairments, hearing
   impairments, motor impairments, autism, Down syndrome, fragile X syndrome)
3. Developmental screening and assessment
4. Use of the Portage model and curriculum (Shearer & Shearer,
   1972)
5. Use of Growing: Birth to Three curriculum (Copa, Lucinski,
   Olsen, & Wollenburg, 1999a)
6. Work with families
7. Home visiting
8. Family-centered early intervention
9. Transdisciplinary team work
10. Development and implementation of the PIAF
11. Philosophical and conceptual framework of early intervention
12. Supervision

Although not very "rich" in terms of addressing all of these content
areas, the Project's first year was still extremely important as far as
founding the development of a comprehensive training program. First,
an extensive search in Portuguese universities and higher education
institutions made clear the paucity of early intervention issues included
in the students' curricula and the lack of trainers in the field. Several
highly reputed center-based early intervention programs were
observed, but their practices appeared to be too child-centered. The
Coimbra Project was able to establish an articulation with Direcção
de Serviços de Orientação e Intervenção Psicológica (DSOIP), a social
security agency in the Lisbon area that for some years had been conducting early intervention, using the Portage model on a home-visiting

basis. This collaboration with DSOIP professionals was initially helpful and productive. Along with Centro São José, a social security early intervention program from Oporto, the Coimbra Project and DSOIP were able to create a team of trainers and provide several courses on the Portage Model for professionals around the country. The Portuguese Portage Association, a national association based in Lisbon, was also formally created in Coimbra in 1992 following the same collaborative efforts.

A second concern in the first year was the late identification of children with disabilities. Early referral was considered critical to intervention success. Health professionals are usually the best situated to identify very young children with disabilities or with risk factors (Boavida & Borges, 1994). The delay in the referral process was related to a lack of awareness among primary care physicians and nurses, who often were more concerned with growth than development in the first months of life (Boavida et al., 2000). As a result, health professionals became a particularly important target for training. From the beginning, the involvement of health care providers and the collaboration between health and educational and social services (a specific feature of the Coimbra Project) were considered extremely important for the success of its implementation. To increase the participation of primary care physicians and nurses, an extensive training program was developed. The main issues included were

1. The identification of biomedical and environmental risk factors for developmental disabilities

2. The systematic use of developmental screening techniques in the regular follow-up of children

3. The importance of good health care in family functioning

4. The importance of early identification in eligible children and families

5. The need to change traditional medical attitudes toward developmental problems and early intervention

This training for health professionals was provided by Coimbra Children's Hospital, in particular by its Child Development Center. The training consisted of theoretical and practical courses and workshops. Meetings and conferences took place in each of the district's 17 health centers, with a standardized package of developmental screening and assessment materials distributed to all physicians and nurses involved in the local teams. In addition, all the involved healthcare providers participated in a 2-week observation training in the developmental clinic of the Child Development Center, where they had contact with different developmental disorders and the interdisciplinary evaluation process. Given the purpose to increase identification by health care providers, it was decided that this specific content, with a breadth and depth tailored to physicians and nurses, was essential to create in these two disciplines a strong knowledge base and clinical skills. The discipline-specific process for delivering this component of the training program differed from subsequent personnel preparation, which was consistently cross disciplinary and team based. Physicians and nurses were also included in all the later cross-disciplinary training.

Also during the first year of the Coimbra Project's activity, this chapter's first author attended a 3-month intensive interdisciplinary training program in developmental disorders at the University Affiliated Cincinnati Center for Developmental Disorders. During this period, he had the Coimbra Project's first contact with American experience in the field and American legislation; he also was able to visit and establish contacts with early intervention programs and professionals. This was the beginning of an extensive exchange of materials and ideas, as well as visits to Coimbra by many outside consultants. Various agencies and professionals have been involved at different levels, from a one-time involvement to continuous participation in the training program: the Family Child Learning Center (FCLC) in Tallmadge, Ohio; the Altamira Project in Albuquerque, New Mexico; the Frank Porter Graham Child Development Institute in Chapel Hill, North Carolina; the Cooperative Education Service Agency 5 (CESA 5) in Portage, Wisconsin; Marilyn Espe-Sherwindt; Karen and Pat Gallagher; Jacqueline Van Horn; Julia Herwig; Karen Wollenburg; Donald Bailey, Jr.; Rune Simeonsson; Carl Dunst; and James A. Blackman.

Examples of two ongoing relationships with the U.S. agencies— CESA 5 and FCLC—demonstrate the impact that international collaboration has had on personnel preparation for the project. The collaboration with CESA 5, the agency that created the Portage model, has been particularly important as far as implementing a new curriculum is concerned. The Coimbra Project's first contact with CESA 5's Growing: Birth to Three occurred in Norway in April 1993. This new curriculum clearly did not have the limitations of the Portage curriculum version being used in Portugal at that time. Six months later, a more practical observation of this new product was possible when three Coimbra Project supervisors visited Wisconsin and attended a training by the Portage Project. The Growing: Birth to Three curriculum was presented as a set of materials and a philosophic framework for an early intervention process that underlies a relationship-based intervention. The term "growing" recognizes that child development from birth to three occurs in the context of relationships, and the curriculum's materials support an ecological, strengths-based and family-centered intervention (Doan-Sampon, Wollenburg, & Campbell, 1993). This new curriculum was much more consistent with what was already considered good practice in the Coimbra Project, possibly helping interventionists observe and record not only child development, but also the importance of the environment and relationships for child development (Bronfenbrenner, 1979; Sameroff & Chandler, 1975; Sameroff & Fiese, 2000).

Certain that this new curriculum would be extremely helpful to professionals in the Coimbra Project—and later to professionals all over Portugal—the coordinating team from the Coimbra Project was proud to accept an invitation from the Portage Project to translate, use, adapt and later publish the Portuguese version of Growing: Birth to Three. Regular training on the use of the curriculum, provided by Portage staff to Coimbra Project professionals, started in mid-1995. Due to lack of funding, translation and adaptation of the materials were delayed for a couple of years. The process restarted in 1997, with a new basic training program and a training program for trainers (Carvalho, Fidalgo, & Carvalho, 2000). As of 2003, the Coimbra Project developed a team of trainers, supervised by the Portage staff. All the materials are translated and have been used and adapted to the Portuguese population since 2001. Information on this new resource has been presented in meetings and conferences all over the country. The materials were released in January 2002, and the Coimbra Project trainers have started providing training on the curriculum to interventionists from all over Portugal.

A second example of international collaboration that has influenced the Coimbra Project's personnel development is its relationship with FCLC. Regular collaboration with FCLC started in the early 1990s. The turning point from a family-allied to a family-centered philosophy began with the first training activities provided by FCLC staff. Since then, ongoing support by the same FCLC trainer, provided yearly through workshops and conferences, has been extremely important. Working with families (in particular, families in which the parents themselves have special needs; Espe-Sherwindt & Kerlin, 1995), transdisciplinary team skills, family-centered services, and the PIAF have been the focus of collaborative training efforts. Due to collaboration with FCLC, the Coimbra Project was able to redesign its PIAF form in a way that reduced the importance of the written product and increased the process of collaboration and partnership between families and professionals (Espe-Sherwindt & Boavida, 1997).

This ongoing relationship has affected not only the content provided, but also *how* training is delivered. As a result of what has been seen and learned, trainings for and by the Coimbra Project are typically characterized by the provision of team-based training, the involvement of family members in the delivery of training, the involvement of participants as active learners, and responsiveness to team decisions and needs. In fact, the collaborative training activities with CESA 5 and FCLC are now considered training resources on a national basis.

Given the Coimbra Project's significant training needs, starting in the 1990s, it had to design a personnel development system that is comprehensive, yet creative, flexible, and adaptable to local needs and resources. The overall structure of the general in-service training program includes courses, field experiences, workshops, small conferences, interteam meetings (quarterly meetings of all the teams for case study presentations or relevant theoretical topics), and a large national conference each year. All professionals involved in the Coimbra Project are required to attend training. Agencies send their providers as part of the articulation agreement. A 3-day intensive initial training package has been developed, which includes the philosophical framework and PIAF development and implementation. In addition, all professionals attend a 2-day developmental assessment course and a 4-day "Growing: Birth to Three" workshop. On a regular basis, professionals also attend a large 2-day annual conference and the quarterly interteam meetings, not including the ongoing support provided by supervision. Other training activities provided throughout the year tend to be responsive to professionals' identified needs. Usually, another 4–6 days of training are provided in issues related to specific disabilities or intervention techniques, resulting in a total of 18–20 days of training each year.

Certain characteristics have been the foundation for the Coimbra Project's training program (see Table 11.1). For example, during typical 2- to 3-day workshops, functioning teams as well as administrators participate together. Questioning one's own perceptions, roles, values, behaviors, practices, feelings, and interactions with families are instructional strategies used for self-examination and reflection. Through experience and sharing of self-assessment information, participants learn and practice new ways of interacting with each other, developing new norms for team goals and practices that will be applied to real-life situations. Strategies creating opportunities for active reflection, decision making, and problem solving are provided so that participants become active in their own learning processes as professionals and as teams. The ultimate goal of the workshops is usually a team plan for developing particular skills, such as working with families, being more family centered, or even having a more transdisciplinary approach (McCollum & Catlett, 1997).

Collaboration with experts from the United States was absolutely critical in areas such as family involvement, working with families,

Table 11.1. Key characteristics for development and implementation of the Coimbra Project's training program

Provide team-based training.

Include program values and philosophy in addition to bodies of knowledge and skills.

Develop an interdisciplinary or cross-disciplinary program.

Provide a common core of content across disciplines.

Provide a shared vision and a common philosophy about service delivery.

Involve family members in the delivery of training.

Produce meaningful and enduring change in professional skills and attitudes.

Be responsive to team decisions and identified needs.

Provide opportunities for practice and reflection within the context of training.

Involve participants as active learners.

Be relevant to everyday practice.

Provide opportunities for direct observation of eligible children and families.

Provide ongoing support through appropriate individualized supervision.

Sources: Bailey, McWilliam, & Winton (1995); Gallacher (1997); Malone, Straka, & Logan (2000); McCollum & Catlett (1997); Stayton & Bruder (1999); Winton & McCollum (1997).

development of the PIAF, family-centered services, transdisciplinary teamwork, and supervision. European experts have also participated in training activities in Coimbra but on a smaller scale. Such collaboration, together with all of the experience gathered in the provision of services, has been important for the development of the Coimbra Project's training team. As a result, most of the in-service training curriculum of professionals working in the Coimbra Project is now planned and provided by its own professionals. In addition, the Project is frequently called to train other professionals in Portugal.

The collaboration and interaction with programs and professionals from abroad, especially from the United States, continues to be regarded as a crucial aspect of the Coimbra Project's training program. However, these interactions are likely to be more episodic and selective in nature, as dependence on outside experts has decreased. International collaboration is facilitated by the fact that two of the Coimbra Project's professionals represent Portugal in Eurlyaid.

Supervision

One of the major goals of the personnel training process was the development of a common conceptual and philosophical framework among professionals. Effective supervision is an ongoing process that goes beyond training opportunities. It can facilitate the integration of knowledge, skills, and attitudes gained from training into daily work with children and families. It is also an important way to achieve the complex task of supporting professional change and the new roles and visions of service delivery (Bertacchi, 1991; Copa, Lucinski, Olsen, & Wollenburg, 1999b; Gallacher, 1997; Shanok, 1991). In the Coimbra Project's particular structure, supervision is an intermediate level between the coordinating team and local teams. It incorporates guiding and support functions as well as, to a lesser extent, performance evaluation and administrative functions.

Initially, supervision was basically quality control of home visitors' use of the Portage curriculum. This kind of supervision, still very influenced by the concept of "early stimulation," was performed by supervisors from Lisbon who had specific training in using this curriculum. Gradually, supervision has changed according to the Project's conceptual framework. It has evolved from a process that guides professionals in the use of a specific stimulation curriculum into a process of supervision that supports the development of a common philosophy, language, and a shared vision of teamwork among professionals. Its main goal is to approach professional practice from what is considered best practice. It also establishes a link between interventionists and the coordinating team.

Due to the structure of the Coimbra Project, evaluating the functioning of its supervision has been very limited. Professionals come from different agencies, each of which has its own hierarchy, making difficult the provision of consequences for poor performances. As such, the supervisor is not involved in making decisions about the promotion or exclusion of a professional. This scenario might change with the implementation of the new legislation and the resulting adaptations required of different agencies.

Much of the time, it is difficult to clearly separate the quality control role from the role of promoting personnel development. Supervision is essentially the process of guiding professionals to accomplish goals, always remembering the quality of services provided to families and children. It helps professionals build and refine their early intervention skills, encouraging their development through ongoing reflection. It is intended to improve their technical competencies in a family-centered and strengths-based approach by taking an ecological perspective and promoting a transdisciplinary teamwork and using the different tools and methods adopted by the Coimbra Project. Supervision in the program also helps to integrate new professionals by building a supportive and trustful climate that empowers all professionals.

Supervisors are selected from professionals with recognized knowledge and experience in providing direct services to children and families. Like any other Coimbra Project professional, they come from different agencies; some work on a part-time basis. In addition to being supervisors, they all perform other tasks to support the Coimbra Project's development. The supervisory team is made of five professionals. Each supervisor is assigned a certain number of local teams and meets regularly with them, usually every other week. These meetings can take place more frequently based on the specific needs of teams—for example, assisting a team with new complex cases or helping a team absorb new and inexperienced professionals.

The supervisory team itself meets every month to share some of the most difficult cases, to organize work, and to reflect on and discuss their tasks as supervisors and their responsibilities to their teams. Supervisors attend all training programs, along with direct service providers when the training sessions are conducted by visiting trainers. All supervisors are also part of the Coimbra Project training team. They are responsible for the initial training provided to the new professionals every year.

With the implementation of the new curriculum Growing: Birth to Three, a new challenge has emerged in the Coimbra Project's supervision. This new curriculum helped the professionals focus not only on strengthening the parent–child relationship, but also on the parallel processes of professional–parent interactions and professional–professional interactions (Oser & Ayankoya, 2000). Believing that learning occurs in a relationship context (Fenichel, 1991; Shanok, 1991), the Coimbra Project is beginning to understand and highlight supervision as a privileged place to build relationships and, therefore, to promote learning.

Program Effectiveness

Transforming human services and practices is always a slow task. One of the biggest challenges has been the turnover rate of professionals. Nevertheless, changes in the language, skills, and attitudes of professionals in the Coimbra Project are clear, based on the authors' observations of and experience in implementing in-service training efforts since the 1990s. Although not always easy, it is clearly best practice to be family centered, work according to a transdisciplinary team process, address family as well as child needs, and coordinate services.

The effectiveness of the Coimbra Project's efforts to train primary health providers is demonstrated by a decrease between 1991 and 1996 in the average age of referral from 16 to 10 months, combined with the increasing role of the local health centers in this process. In fact, only 19% of the children were referred to the Coimbra Project by community health centers in 1991 as compared with 46% in 1996. This clearly shows the growing importance of primary health care and the change in medical attitudes toward early intervention (Boavida et al., 2000).

In addition, the previously described survey of families and professionals indicated that 91% of the professionals thought they had benefited from their participation in the Coimbra Project. They attributed the benefits to the interdisciplinary team-based training, teamwork, and the resulting changes in their professional attitudes (Boavida et al., 2000). Finally, the constitution of the Coimbra Project's supervision and training teams, the increasing recognition among early intervention professionals all over Portugal of the Coimbra Project's quality, and increasing requests for training by its trainers contribute to perceived effectiveness.

Future Directions and Considerations

Since the Coimbra Project began, the evolution of both the perception and practices of early intervention services has been significant. The passage of Portuguese legislation in 1999 created additional challenges for planners and policy makers at a national level. Developing and maintaining a skilled and competent work force must be a priority. Given the personnel shortage, the high attrition rates in early intervention, the lack of preservice training provided by higher education institutions, and the need to define a set of competency-based standards of practice, the task will not be easy. The involvement of family members in the preservice and in-service training programs, not a practice widely used until the end of the 20th century, must be regarded as a way of effectively modeling parent–professional relationships (Sandall, 1997; Stayton & Bruder, 1999). Portugal has valuable national resources that were not available when the Coimbra Project began in the late 1980s. The general picture of early intervention in Portugal in the beginning of the new millennium is totally different, and the Coimbra Project has certainly played a key part.

RECOMMENDATIONS FOR PROFESSIONALS IN OTHER COUNTRIES

The development of an early intervention program and the provision of personnel preparation has been a challenging and rewarding experience. Portugal, like any other country with limited resources, has to make creative and wise decisions on how to use those resources. Building on existing human and material resources, articulating relationships between agencies and professionals, and using whatever is available in the community is the most realistic way to provide early intervention services.

Training certainly is the answer to a great number of difficulties that arise from implementing an interdisciplinary and interagency program. Specific features related to the success of the Coimbra Project's training program could be used by similar countries (Boavida & Borges, 1994; Boavida et al., 2000). One feature is the provision of specific training to primary care physicians and nurses to increase their awareness and skills to early referral, as well as their participation in early intervention teams. Another is the definition of a common core of early intervention content. Accepting a common conceptual and philosophical framework also is recommended for professionals seeking to develop early intervention programs in other countries. Team-based training should be provided as well. Furthermore, it is recommended that other programs develop their own training teams, with the help of outside collaborators. A final recommended feature is the development of supervision and ongoing support.

CONCLUSION

The 1990s were the most productive years in Portugal for the field of early intervention. In a little more than a decade, early intervention evolved from an emerging service, provided with a child-centered perspective in ways similar to special education with older children, to a rapidly growing field with a totally different conceptual framework. This evolution was partially triggered by the implementation of a community-based program of early intervention in Coimbra, located in the central region of the country. The Coimbra Project developed a system to provide individualized comprehensive services to children and families by using formal and informal resources already available in the community and by creating a collaborative effort involving health, education, and social service. Because the problems confronting the children and families were so diverse, an array of service providers that cut across different disciplines, agencies, and theoretical orientations was needed. Teamwork skills and collaborative approaches had to be developed. Training played an essential role in the Coimbra Project's development and without a doubt was the single most important factor associated with the program's effectiveness.

In a country with no early intervention preservice training offered by higher education institutions and with no regulations for the provision of services, providing in-service training to professionals with no experience in the field was an extremely difficult task. Some of the strategies developed to address this challenge were using imagination and creativity; consulting with experts from the United States and, to a lesser extent, Europe; and organizing conferences, workshops, interactions with international programs, and coursework.

Early intervention in Portugal at the beginning of the new millennium differs greatly from the scenario in the late 1980s. Professionals, agencies, and policy makers are fully aware of the significant paradigm shift that occurred in the 1990s. A family-centered, inclusive, ecological, and comprehensive early intervention approach is widely accepted throughout the country. In Coimbra, as in some other regions of the country, in-service training and teams of trainers are active components of the approach. In addition, since the passage of legislation (Despacho Conjunto 891/99), early intervention has acquired a growing audience and a promise of increased funding and attention from governmental departments.

With these numerous societal and legislative changes, early intervention trainers and planners will face new challenges. The Coimbra Project's priorities up to 2010 are to 1) develop a common core of content across disciplines that reflects recent changes in service delivery, 2) increase the involvement of family members in training programs, 3) develop and implement preservice personnel development at the university level, and 4) redefine in-service training according to desired outcomes. With so many challenges on the horizon and so many committed professionals, the field of early intervention will continue to be exciting in Portugal and around the world.

REFERENCES

Almeida, I.C. (2000). A importância da intervenção precoce no actual contexto sócio-educativo [The importance of early intervention in the current socioeconomic context]. *Cadernos CEACF, 15–16,* 55–74.

Bailey, D.B., McWilliam, P.J., & Winton, P.J. (1995). Building family-centered practices in early intervention: A team-based model for change. In J.A. Blackman (Eds.), *Working with families in early intervention* (pp. 82–91). Gaithersburg, MD: Aspen Publishers.

Barreto, A. (2000). *A situação social em Portugal, 1960–1999: Indicadores sociais em Portugal e na União Europeia.* Lisboa, Portugal: Imprensa de Ciências Sociais.

Bennett, F.C., & Guralnick, M.J. (1991). Effectiveness of developmental intervention in the first five years of life. *Pediatric Clinics of North America, 38,* 1513–1528.

Bertacchi, J. (1991). A seminar for supervisors in infant/family programs: Growing versus paying more for staying the same. *Zero to Three, 12*(2), 34–39.

Boavida, J. (1992, November). *Community involvement in an early intervention project in the Coimbra region.* Paper presented at the fourth International Portage Conference, Ocho Rios, Jamaica.

Boavida, J. (1993, October). *Early intervention in Coimbra: An interagency project.* Paper presented at the third European Symposium: Early Intervention in the European Community, Butgenbach, Belgium.

Boavida, J., & Borges, L. (1990). Intervenção precoce: Um projecto para o distrito de Coimbra. *Saúde Infantil, 12,* 205–210.

Boavida, J., & Borges, L. (1994). Community involvement in early intervention: A Portuguese perspective. *Infants and Young Children, 7*(1), 42–50.

Boavida, J., Carvalho, L., & Carvalho, C. (1998, May). *Consulta de Desenvolvimento na Comunidade.* Paper presented at the fifth Encontro Nacional de Intervenção Precoce, Coimbra, Portugal.

Boavida, J., Espe-Sherwindt, M., & Borges, L. (2000). Community-based early intervention: The Coimbra Project (Portugal). *Child: Care, Health and Development, 26*(5), 343–354.

Boavida, J., & Violante, A. (1993, April). *The use of the Portage model in a community-based early intervention project in Portugal.* Paper presented at the North European Portage Conference, Birkelid, Norway.

Bronfenbrenner, U. (1977). Toward an experimental ecology of human development. *American Psychologist, 32,* 513–531.

Bronfenbrenner, U. (1979). *The ecology of human development.* Cambridge, MA: Harvard University Press. (ERIC Document Reproduction Service No. ED128387).

Bronfenbrenner, U. (1990). *The ecology of human development: Experiments by nature and design.* Cambridge, MA: Harvard University Press.

Bryant, D., & Maxwell, K. (1997). The effectiveness of early intervention for disadvantaged children. In M.J. Guralnick (Ed.), *The effectiveness of early intervention* (pp. 23–46). Baltimore: Paul H. Brookes Publishing Co.

Carvalho, C., Fidalgo, I., & Carvalho, L. (2000, April). The Coimbra Early Intervention Project. *International Portage Association News, 1.*

Copa, A., Lucinski, B.A., Olsen, E., & Wollenburg, K. (1999a). *Growing: Birth to three* (Rev. ed.). Portage, WI: Cooperative Educational Service Agency.

Copa, A., Lucinski, B.A., Olsen, E., & Wollenburg, K. (1999b). Promoting professional and organizational development: A reflexive practice model. *Zero to Three, 20*(1), 3.

Cruz, A.I., & Fontes, F. (2002, June). *Parent's satisfaction evaluation in the Coimbra Project.* Paper presented at the first ANIP Early Intervention Congress, Coimbra, Portugal.

Despacho Conjunto 891/99. (1999). Ministério da Educação, da Saúde e da Solidariedade Social. Diário da República Portuguesa-II Série. 15566-15568.

Doan-Sampon, M.A., Wollenburg, K., & Campbell, A. (1993). Piecing it all together. In *Growing: Birth to three.* Portage, WI: Cooperative Educational Service Agency.

Dunst, C.J., & Trivette, C.M. (1987). Enabling and empowering families: Conceptual and intervention issues. *Sociological Psychological Review, 16,* 443–456.

Dunst, C.J., Trivette, C.M., & Deal, A. (1988). *Enabling and empowering families: Principles and guidelines for practice.* Cambridge, MA: Brookline Books.

Espe-Sherwindt, M., & Boavida, J. (1995, August). *Translating educational models across cultures.* Paper presented at the fourth biennial International

Conference of the International Association of Special Education, Brighton, England.

Espe-Sherwindt, M., & Boavida, J., (1996, December). *How do we say empowerment in Portuguese?* Paper presented at the International Early Childhood Conference on Children with Special Needs, Phoenix, AZ.

Espe-Sherwindt, M., & Boavida, J. (1997, November). *Taking another look at the IFSP: International perspective.* Paper presented at the International Early Childhood Conference on Children with Special Needs, New Orleans.

Espe-Sherwindt, M., & Kerlin, S.A. (1995). Early intervention with parents with mental retardation: Do we empower or impair? In J.A. Blackman (Ed.), *Working with families in early intervention* (pp. 166–175). Gaithersburg, MD: Aspen Publishers.

Eurlyaid. (1997). *European Parent Satisfaction Scale about Early Intervention, Second Version.* Unpublished scale, Alefpa/Europe, St Vith, Belgium.

Fenichel, E. (1991). Learning through supervision and mentorship to support the development of infants, toddlers, and their families. *Zero to Three, 12*(2), 1–8.

Gallacher, K.K. (1997). Supervision, mentoring and coaching: Methods for supporting personnel development. In P.J. Winton, J.A. McCollum, & C. Catlett (Eds.), *Reforming personnel preparation in early intervention: Issues, models, and practical strategies* (pp. 191–214). Baltimore: Paul H. Brookes Publishing Co.

Instituto Nacional de Estatística. (2000). *Statistical yearbook of Portugal 1999.* Lisboa, Portugal: Author.

Instituto Nacional de Estatística. (2002). *Estimativas da População Residente.* Lisboa, Portugal: Author.

Klein, N.K., & Campbell, P. (1990). Preparing personnel to serve at-risk and disabled infants, toddlers, and preschoolers. In S.J. Meisels & J.P. Shonkoff (Eds.), *Handbook of early childhood intervention* (pp. 428–444). New York: Cambridge University Press.

Lanners, R., & Mombaerts, D. (2000). Evaluation of parents' satisfaction with early intervention services within and among European countries: Construction and application of a new parent satisfaction scale. *Infants and Young Children, 12*(3), 61–70.

Malone, M., Straka, E., & Logan, K.R. (2000). Professional development in early intervention: Creating effective in-service training opportunities. *Infants and Young Children, 12*(4), 53–62.

McCollum, J.A., & Catlett, C. (1997). Designing effective personnel preparation for early intervention: Theoretical frameworks. In P.J. Winton, J.A. McCollum, & C. Catlett (Eds.), *Reforming personnel preparation in early intervention: Issues, models, and practical strategies* (pp. 105–125). Baltimore: Paul H. Brookes Publishing Co.

McGonigel, M.J., Kaufmann, R.K., & Johnson, B.H. (1991). *Guidelines and recommended practices for the individualized family service plan.* Bethesda, MD: Association for the Care of Children's Health.

McGonigel, M.J., Woodruff, G., & Roszmann-Millican, M. (1994). The transdisciplinary team: A model for family-centered early intervention. In L.J.

Johnson, R.J. Gallagher, M.J. LaMontagne, J.B. Jordan, J.J. Gallagher, P.L. Hutinger, & M.B. Karnes (Eds.), *Meeting early intervention challenges: Issues from birth to three* (2nd ed., pp. 95–131). Baltimore: Paul H. Brookes Publishing Co.

Meisels, J.F., & Fenichel, E. (Eds.). (1996). *New visions for the developmental assessment of infants and young children.* Washington, DC: ZERO TO THREE: National Center for Infants, Toddlers, and Families.

Ministry of Education, Department of Basic Education. (2000). *Early childhood education and care policy in Portugal.* Lisboa, Portugal: Author.

Moor, M.H., Van Waesberghe, B.T.M., Hosman, B.L., Jaeken, D., & Miedema, S. (1993). Early intervention for children with developmental disabilities: Manifesto of the Eurlyaid working party. *International Journal of Rehabilitation Research, 16,* 23–31.

Oser, C., & Ayankoya, B. (2000). The early interventionist. *Zero to Three, 21*(2), 24–31.

Roberts, R.N., Rule, S., & Innocenti, M.S. (1998). *Strengthening the family–professional partnerships in services for young children.* Baltimore: Paul H. Brookes Publishing Co.

Sameroff, A.J., & Chandler, M J. (1975). Reproductive risk and the continuum of caretaking casualty. In F.D. Horowitz, M. Hetherington, S. Scarr-Salapatek, & G. Siegel (Eds.), *Review of child development research* (Vol. 4, pp. 187–244). Chicago: University Chicago Press.

Sameroff, A.J., & Fiese, B. (1990). Transactional regulations and early intervention. In S.J. Meisels & J.P. Shonkoff (Eds.), *Handbook of early childhood intervention* (pp. 428–444). New York: Cambridge University Press.

Sameroff, A.J., & Fiese, B. (2000). Transactional regulation: The developmental ecology of early intervention. In S.J. Meisels & J.P. Shonkoff (Eds.), *Handbook of early childhood intervention* (2nd ed., pp.135–159). New York: Cambridge University Press.

Sandall, S.R. (1997). The family service team. In A.H. Widerstrom, B.A. Mowder, & S.R. Sandall (Eds.), *Infant development and risk: An introduction* (2nd ed., pp. 155–173). Baltimore: Paul H. Brookes Publishing Co.

Shanok, R.S. (1991). The supervisory relationship: Integrator, resource and guide. *Zero to Three, 12*(2), 16–21.

Shearer, M.S., & Shearer, D.E. (1972). The Portage Project: A model for early childhood education. *Exceptional Children, 39,* 210–217.

Simeonsson, R.J., & Bailey, D.B. (1990). Family dimensions in early intervention. In S.J. Meisels & J.P. Shonkoff (Eds.), *Handbook of early childhood intervention* (pp. 428–444). New York: Cambridge University Press.

Stayton, V., & Bruder, M.B. (1999). Early intervention personnel preparation for the new millennium: Early childhood special education. *Infants and Young Children, 12*(1), 59–69.

Thorp, E.K., & McCollum, J.A. (1994). Defining the infancy specialization in early childhood special education. In L.J. Johnson, R.J. Gallagher, M.J. LaMontagne, J.B. Jordan, J.J. Gallagher, P.L. Hutinger, & M.B. Karnes (Eds.), *Meeting early intervention challenges: Issues from birth to three* (2nd ed., pp. 167–183). Baltimore: Paul H. Brookes Publishing Co.

Winton, P.J. (2000). Early childhood intervention personnel preparation: Backward mapping for future planning. *Topics in Early Childhood Special Education, 20*(2), 87–94.

Winton, P.J., & McCollum, J.A. (1997). Ecological perspectives on personnel preparation: Rationale, framework, and guidelines for change. In P.J. Winton, J.A. McCollum, & C. Catlett (Eds.), *Reforming personnel preparation in early intervention: Issues, models, and practical strategies* (pp. 3–25). Baltimore: Paul H. Brookes Publishing Co.

Organizational Support for Early Intervention

CHAPTER 12

National Legislation for Early Intervention

Marci J. Hanson

UNITED STATES OF AMERICA —

A good beginning makes a good ending.

It is difficult to capture a country's sentiment in a single phrase or to generalize given the diversity of the U.S. population. However, the preceding quote reflects a core value in the United States regarding the importance of prevention and starting early. Other equally telling proverbs are those that express a belief in human equality ("All men are created equal"), the importance of hard work and persistence ("If at first you don't succeed, try, try again"), and the ability to change ("Where there's a will, there's a way").

Dramatic changes have developed in services for young children with disabilities and their families in the United States in recent decades. Major national legislative initiatives have ensured that services are more universally available for children who are eligible. Prior to the passage of these laws, many localities provided early intervention programs, but many others did not. Thus, service availability was uneven and depended on where families lived, their child's disability, and their child's age. Legislation redressed these inequities and created a new system of services.

This chapter focuses on the Individuals with Disabilities Education Act (IDEA), the federal law that established this new system of services. This law has provided the regulatory infrastructure for establishing a system of early intervention services throughout the country. Key elements are that services should be statewide and comprehensive and should represent interdisciplinary and interagency collaborations. Family involvement is a primary focus as well.

As Florian (1995) explained, this law is remarkable because it came about during a political climate characterized by a national retrenchment of social programs. Furthermore, the passage of this landmark legislation demonstrated the power of individuals to effect change in society. As Margaret Mead stated, "Never doubt that a small group of thoughtful committed citizens can change the world; indeed it's the only thing that ever does" (cited in Florian, 1995, p. 247). Key legislators and staff in the U.S. Congress played pivotal roles in designing and ensuring passage of this legislation. Lawmakers were persuaded of the merits of this program by the economic benefits of providing early services to young children to enable them to become more productive members of society. Empowerment issues were cited as well, describing the need for a shift from a disability policy built on charity to one that empowered families and children to make choices and to help themselves. Public support and participation also contributed greatly to the successful outcome. A massive letter campaign directed at the president persuaded him to sign this major piece of legislation.

This law was built on a long history of parent participation and advocacy, community involvement and activism, and active participation of individual citizens in the political process to ensure that young children with disabilities receive early and appropriate services. Although these actions produced a dramatic piece of legislation, the implementation of services is far from a finished product. As in all initiatives, services must be monitored and analyzed, current needs must be identified, local variations must be considered, and challenges must be solved to ensure that the intent of the law is honored. Thus, although this legislation and the infrastructure that it created are a reality in the United States, services are constantly being evaluated and reshaped as needs demand. This chapter outlines the basic tenets of this legislation and also attempts to describe the chief components and implementation challenges.

The following vignette demonstrates the types of services and supports that are provided to young children with disabilities and their families in the United States. Key features are family involvement and support; specialized services provided in typical early childhood environments, such as the child's home and child care or preschool; interdisciplinary services; and a range of health care, social, and educational services available to families from the child's birth.

 TOMMY AND JIMMY'S STORY ——————————

Mornings are hectic for Josie and Gene, the parents of two active little boys, Thomas (Tommy) and James (Jimmy), and an 8-year-old girl, Sarah. The family has breakfast together before rushing off in different directions each day. Gene drops off Sarah at school on his way to his job at a local technology firm, and Josie drives the boys to their preschool near the elementary school where she teaches. Tommy and Jimmy are nearly 4 years old and both have attended "school" since they were 8 months old.

Josie was told by her physicians that she would unlikely conceive again after the difficulties encountered during her pregnancy with Sarah and Sarah's birth. Therefore, Josie and Gene were overjoyed when they learned that they would be the parents of twins!

Tommy and Jimmy were born several months early. At birth, both boys were whisked away to a neonatal intensive care unit in the hospital, where they remained for around-the-clock care until they were stable enough to be moved home. The twins weighed 1,100 and 1,250 grams at birth, and Jimmy was diagnosed with an intraventricular hemorrhage that necessitated major medical support and care. Josie, Gene, and Sarah visited the hospital daily, and Josie was able to pump her breast milk and bring it to the hospital for the boys. The days of waiting and hoping were difficult for the family, but at last Tommy and Jimmy were able to come home. Their care needs necessitated that Josie take a leave of absence from her job, and Gene obtained a more flexible work schedule to participate in the boys' care. He became increasingly stressed, however, as the medical bills mounted. The family looks back on that period as a cloud of never-ending doctor's appointments, evaluations by a range of specialists, interactions with insurance companies, worries over expenses, daily stress over the boys' care, and an overwhelming lack of rest.

The services for the boys were many and varied. The boys made regular visits to their pediatrician following their discharge from the hospital, and they were enrolled in the hospital's high-risk infant follow-up program, through which the boys' development was assessed at regular intervals. When the boys were 6 months old, their pediatrician recommended that they be referred for further testing. Jimmy's development was of particular concern, and he was enrolled in early intervention services. A home visitor with a background in special education visited the home weekly during the first 2 years and showed Josie and Gene activities for play and caregiving routines that would enhance the boys' development. A pediatric physical therapist also visited periodically to work with Jimmy, to make suggestions for home programs, and to assist the home visitor and family in designing strategies for positioning and handling the boys during their daily routines.

At age 2, the boys began attending a nursery school in the mornings and staying at home with a child care provider in the afternoons. The nursery school teacher and child care provider endeavored to implement the home activities as well. At age 3, the boys entered preschool. Both show some delays in speech and language development, and Jimmy also has significant motor delays. Jimmy has had an individualized education program/individualized family service plan (IEP/IFSP) since he was an infant and receives physical therapy. Both boys receive special education services in the form of speech-language therapy. An inclusion specialist from the local school district also works with Jimmy's teachers to assist them in adapting the environment to ensure that Jimmy can move and actively participate and learn. Jimmy's IEP identifies specific strategies, goals, methods for evaluating progress, and the people responsible for implementing these objectives. Although the boys receive services at their local preschool program through a team of professionals, Josie and Gene experience a continual series of appointments each week with professionals such as physicians, physical and occupational therapists, and speech-language pathologists. Despite the professionals' best attempts to collaborate with one another, Josie and Gene still feel that they are their boys' best advocates and teachers. They are constantly vigilant to ensure that the boys' needs and goals are being met.

Josie and Gene know that they have a long road ahead. They are also thankful that their tiny babies received the early intervention services they needed to support their fragile early development. Josie and Gene are confident that both boys will grow up to be good citizens, to attend school, and to live happy and productive lives like their peers.

NATIONAL CONTEXT

The United States is a rich tapestry of cultures, geographic landscapes, faiths, and beliefs. It is the third largest country in the world in terms of population and the fourth largest in area. The land mass, with an area of 9,363,563 square kilometers, stretches across North America from the Atlantic Ocean in the east to the Pacific Ocean in the west, and to Alaska in the far northwest and Hawaii in the mid-Pacific. The nation consists of 50 states as well as the District of Columbia, the land set aside for the location of the federal capital, Washington D.C.

Every decade a national census is conducted. As of 2000 (U.S. Census Bureau, 2000), the population of the United States was more than 285 million people. Approximately 75% of the population was Caucasian, 12.3% African American, 3.6% Asian, and 1% American Indian and Alaskan Native. Hispanics/Latinos made up 12.5% of the population, with the primary countries of Hispanic origin including Mexico, Puerto Rico, and Cuba. Other groups accounted for 5.5% of the population.

The period from 1990 to 2000 represented the largest population growth in American history, with an increase of 32.7 million people. This growth varied significantly by region, with the western United States (19.7% increase) and the South (17.3% increase) experiencing the highest growth rates. Among the states, California had the highest increase, with an additional 4.1 million people. The ten most populated states are California, Texas, New York, Florida, Illinois, Pennsylvania, Ohio, Michigan, New Jersey, and Georgia. These states are distributed throughout the four basic regions of the United States (Northeast, Midwest, South, West). Approximately 80% of Americans live in metropolitan areas, although almost 98% of the land is classified as rural.

People and Culture

In terms of ancestry, the U.S. population is one of the most varied in the world. Although the largest group of individuals descends from Anglo-European ancestry, great migrations from Latin America and Asia also account for a large portion of America's citizenry. Most African Americans trace their roots to Africa, as a large number of Africans were brought to North America during the 1600s, 1700s, and 1800s as slaves. From 1990 to 1999, the Asian and Pacific Islander population was the fastest growing population, with an increase of 43%. The Latino population grew 38.8%, the African American population increased by 13.8%, the American Indian and Alaska Native population grew by 15.5%, and the white population increased by 7.3%.

The primary language spoken in the United States is English. Spanish is the second most common language. In many parts of the country, a large percentage of families speak a language other than English at home. In California, for example, more than 39% of families speak another language. In some localities, 50–60 language groups may be reflected in a single school district.

All of the world's major religious faiths are practiced in the United States. Many immigrants came to this country to practice their faith, having fled religious persecution in their native lands. Approximately 60% of Americans are members of an organized faith. Among that number, approximately 52% are Protestant, 38% Roman Catholic, 4% Jewish, 3% Mormon, and 3% Eastern Orthodox. Smaller numbers of people practice Islam, Buddhism, Hinduism, and other faiths.

For many years, America was called a "melting pot," referring to a place where people from various backgrounds came together to form a new or unified culture. Though Americans hold many elements in common, that view has been replaced by the notion of *cultural pluralism*. The perspective at the beginning of the 21st century is for populations to retain features of their native cultures and to take pride in native origins and traditions. In addition, some U.S. regions or cities are considerably more diverse than others. The terms *minority* and *majority* now hold little meaning in reference to population groups. For instance, in 1989, California became the first state to have a "majority" of "minority" children in its public schools, and several cities have no majority population.

Political Influences

As nations go, the United States is young. It was established in 1776 when the original 13 colonies broke from Great Britain and established a new nation based on freedom and equal opportunity. The nation grew to 50 states, the District of Columbia, and territories bound together by a federal government. The national government is comprised of three branches—executive, legislative, and judicial—each with separate powers. A system of "checks and balances" gives each the power to affect the others. These branches are represented typically by the President, the Congress, and the Supreme Court. A federal system of government is practiced whereby government operates at three levels: national, state, and local. The United States Constitution has established the powers and duties of the federal and state governments.

The Constitution does not stipulate responsibilities for education. However, it does give states any powers that are not granted to the federal government. Therefore, the states automatically have power over education, and each has established a system of public schools. These state systems are aimed at every level of education, from early childhood through higher education. Although the states retain primary powers with respect to education, health, and welfare, the Constitution grants Congress power to provide for the nation's general welfare. Congress has used this power with respect to education, particularly with matters that affect significant populations or portions of the population.

Education Services System

Although the United States has long focused on education, many schools initially were privately owned and operated, chiefly through church sponsorship. In the early 1800s, public education gained support and states and local governments established public school systems. As of 2003, approximately 75% of elementary and high schools and 45% higher education institutions are public. These systems are operated by states and supported primarily through taxation.

KEY FEATURES OF EARLY INTERVENTION

Public support for education is deeply rooted in America's history, tradition, and values. To illustrate, prior to the birth of the nation, a 1647 statute was enacted in one of the original colonies for the provision of basic literacy and the appointment of teachers to instruct children in reading and writing (Safford & Safford, 1996). Instruction in these early schools was intended "to promote the welfare of the state by making citizens capable of self-government" (Tanner & Tanner, 1990, p. 31; cited in Safford & Safford, 1996). Although models of education have undergone many twists and turns since the country's inception, the notion of universal, publicly supported education is fundamental to life in the United States today.

Public education systems have been in place since the revolution that established this country, but not all children have had equal opportunity to participate despite the fundamental assumptions of equal opportunity. Socioeconomic class, gender, race, and disability, for example, have influenced access to these educational opportunities. Over the years, relief for these inequities has been sought through litigation and legislative reforms, and publicly funded educational services are now available to *all* children in the United States.

Early educational options for very young children, although not mandated, also have proliferated. Moreover, these early intervention services have necessitated cross-disciplinary collaboration to meet the complex and varied needs of young children and their families. Services draw from and include the fields of education, health, social services, and related disciplines.

Foundations of Early Intervention

Shonkoff and Meisels (1990) traced the development of early childhood intervention from the primary contributions of four fields: early childhood education, maternal and child health, special education, and child development. Their review in each area is briefly summarized in the following discussion.

Early Childhood Education

The work of European philosophers and writers from the 17th and 18th centuries established the period of childhood as unique. Philosophers, such as Locke and Rousseau, highlighted the influence of early experiences on the development of children. Although Puritan child-rearing notions regarding discipline and spiritual salvation predominated after the founding of the United States, early learning and education philosophies and practices gradually were transported, chiefly from Europe, to the new country. Based largely on the work of Friedrich Froebel in Germany and on the nursery schools developed in England by Rachel and Margaret MacMillan, kindergartens were established in the United States in the late 1800s and early 1900s. At a later point, Maria Montessori's work with poor children in Rome also influenced curricular practices in preschool education. As early education programs flourished and spread, basic concepts regarding early exploration and nurturing, early socialization, parent involvement, and school readiness became firmly entrenched in U.S. early educational practices. Historical forces, such as the Great Depression of the 1930s and World War II, resulted in more children receiving care and educational services outside the home and solidified this focus on early educational services.

Maternal and Health Services

Concern regarding children's health and high infant mortality rates led to the development of a service delivery system consisting of both publicly and privately funded service components. In 1912, Congress established the Children's Bureau as part of the Department of Labor, which instituted federal programs for data collection and research and granted services to the most vulnerable children, such as children with physical and mental illness. Title V of the Social Security Act of 1935 further expanded federal responsibility and support for children's health and well-being. This act authorized Maternal and Child Health Services, Services for Crippled Children, and Child Welfare Services. Provisions under this law were expanded in 1965 to increase access to medical services for children living in poverty. As a component of this program, the Early and Periodic Screening, Diagnosis and Treatment Program (EPSDT) was designed to ensure early screening, diagnosis, and treatment for children who were economically disadvantaged.

Child Development Research

Theoretical approaches and debates, as well as empirical research, have had a great impact on the development of early educational options, particularly for children who are at risk or have disabilities. Chief among these influences is the fundamental debate of nature versus nurture. The early 20th century was characterized by attention to evaluation and chronicling of child development. The controversial debate over the impact of genetic and maturational forces (nature) versus the influence of environmental factors (nurture) on the child's developmental trajectory and outcomes became a central force leading to the creation of early intervention services. Empirical documentation of early environmental effects and the primacy and impact of early caregiving or nurturing relationships on the child's subsequent development highlighted the effects of early experiences. The transactional interplay between environmental and constitutional factors has been a primary research focus and established the importance of supporting families and early socialization experiences.

Special Education

European educational philosophers and practitioners also had great influence on the development of special education services in this country. Jean-Marc Itard's work in the 19th century with the "wildboy of Aveyron," using sensory training and structured behavioral training approaches to socialize and teach a feral child, is credited with great influence in the field. Eduoard Sequin, a student of Itard's, went on to design a method of education for students with disabilities that focused on sensorimotor activities and a structured approach to observation, assessment, and treatment. His work as the Director of the Hospice des Incurables in Paris influenced the development of educational programs for people with mental retardation worldwide. When he migrated to the United States, his techniques were implemented in residential facilities for people with disabilities. The treatment approach offered in these residential facilities has varied at different points in history from an active focus on treatment and remediation to custodial caregiving.

If children with disabilities received services, they were served in residential treatment facilities until after World War II. In 1946, the U.S. Office of Education established a Section for Exceptional Children that became the Bureau of Education for the Handicapped in 1966. Today, it is the Office of Special Education and Rehabilitative Services (established in 1980).

Policies and services for children with disabilities have shifted over the years from segregation in residential or separate schools to placement in general education schools and early education service options that are open to their same-age peers. These service trends are reviewed in more detail in the section "Services for Children with Developmental Disabilities."

Summary

A focus on early intervention has resulted from various influences, including research on early child development and learning, work done abroad (primarily in Europe), and sociocultural issues (race, poverty, women entering the work force during World War II). The shifts in educational service delivery resulting from these factors has greatly expanded the educational system to ensure that public education is available to *all* of America's children and that public education is provided from an early age for children with disabilities.

Services for Children with Developmental Disabilities

Prior to the 1970s, some children in the United States were denied a public school education because of their disabilities. These children were considered unable to learn, and many schools did not have adequate or appropriate programs for children with disabilities, particularly severe disabilities. Family- and advocate-initiated litigation, court decisions, national legislation, research studies, and grass roots advocacy efforts all served to change this perspective dramatically. Invoking the 14th Amendment to the United States Constitution was central to establishing a legal remedy for this inequity. The amendment guarantees equal protection for all citizens under the law, establishing freedom from discrimination for unjustifiable reasons such as race or disability. As parent-initiated movements and significant court cases were heard in the 1950s and 1960s, shifts in policies began to occur.

Access to public education and special education services and supports were realized for school-age children through a piece of landmark legislation, the Education for All Handicapped Children Act of 1975 (PL 94-142). (See Braddock, 1987, and Turnbull, 1986, for reviews of federal policies and the development of this law in the United States.)

This law subsequently was modified to apply to all preschool-age children with disabilities and, later, through state discretionary programs, to children with disabilities from birth through 2 years. This legislation was retitled the Individuals with Disabilities Education Act (IDEA) of 1990 (PL 101-476) and was amended in 1997 as PL 105-17.

Individuals with Disabilities Education Act Amendments of 1997

IDEA and its amendments provide the framework for educational policies and services for children with disabilities and their families. Six principles are core to this framework.

Free Appropriate Public Education (FAPE)   The provision for a free appropriate public education (FAPE) requires special education and related services to be provided to children at public expense and to meet the standards of the state educational agency. Inherent in this law is a policy of "zero reject," which precludes public schools from excluding children with disabilities. Furthermore, services are to be appropriate for the individual needs of each child.

Appropriate Evaluation   The law stipulates many conditions related to evaluation: a "full and individual initial evaluation," the requirement of parental consent for the initial evaluation, evaluation by a team, assessment in the child's native language or mode of communication, the use of multiple measures rather than a single instrument to determine eligibility, and the provision for reevaluations. In addition, evaluation activities are to include data-gathering information pertinent to the child's involvement and progress in the core general education curriculum, and evaluation procedures must be nondiscriminatory.

Development of an Individualized Education Program   IDEA requires an individualized education program (IEP) to be developed for each child with a disability. IEPs must state the child's current level of educational performance, measurable annual goals and short-term objectives, specified special education and related services, and transition services to the next educational environment as well as the dates, frequency, location, and duration of services. The IEP is developed through a team approach that includes the child's parents and professionals, and the child's strengths and the parents' concerns for enhancing the child's education are to be considered. For children from birth through 2 years, the individualized plan is an individualized family service plan (IFSP). These plans are described in greater detail in a subsequent discussion.

Education Provided in the Least Restrictive Environment   To the maximum extent possible, children with disabilities must receive an appropriate education for their individual needs in environments with peers who do not have disabilities. The intention of the law is to maximize the opportunities for children with disabilities to be educated with their peers and in their neighborhood communities. The emphasis is on creating services and supports that allow young children to participate in the general education curriculum.

Parent and Student Participation in Decision Making Parents have the right to review their child's educational records, and parental informed consent is required for children's initial evaluation and placement. Parents can actively participate in all aspects of the evaluation, placement, and education process. They also have the right to challenge or appeal any decision related to the identification, evaluation, or placement of their child.

Procedural Safeguards to Protect the Rights of Parents and Their Child with a Disability IDEA outlines safeguards to ensure that the rights of children with disabilities and their parents are protected. These include parental access to educational records, the right to request a due process hearing, and the right to appeal the hearing decision via civil action. Rights and requirements related to discipline are specified in the law as well.

Americans with Disabilities Act of 1990

Another landmark piece of legislation with crucial implications for access and education for children with disabilities is the Americans with Disabilities Act (ADA; PL 101-336), passed in 1990. The ADA is a federal civil rights law ensuring that people with disabilities have access to all facets of life, including child care. It gives individuals with disabilities civil rights protection such as that provided to people on the basis of race, sex, national origin, and religion. The ADA requires that reasonable accommodations be made for people to allow them the opportunity to participate in offered services and activities.

Summary

The ADA and IDEA have provided far-reaching guarantees and rights for children with disabilities. The legislation charted new policies and services to ensure equal protection under the law and public education for children with disabilities.

National Early Intervention Legislation

IDEA and its amendments include components that essentially establish a national policy on early intervention for children with disabilities from birth through 5 and their families. As such, this legislation has built the infrastructure for a system of service delivery across the United States. Central to this service system is the recognition of the unique role that families play in children's development.

Two primary components or parts of IDEA that pertain to young children are reviewed and described in the following subsections. One component is the Early Intervention Program for Infants and Toddlers with Disabilities (Part C of IDEA), which covers services to children from birth through age 2. The second is the Preschool Grants Program, Section 619 of Part B of IDEA, which covers services to children ages 3–5. National Head Start legislation is also discussed. Following these descriptions, the lessons learned and the challenges that remain in implementing these services are discussed with the hope that other nations may derive support and meaning from U.S. experiences with implementation of this legislation.

Early Intervention Program for Infants and Toddlers with Disabilities

In 1986, Congress established this program in recognition of "an urgent and substantial need" to enhance the development of infants and toddlers with disabilities, to reduce educational costs by minimizing the need for special education through early intervention, to minimize the likelihood of institutionalization of individuals with disabilities and maximize independent living, and to enhance the capacity of families to meet their children's needs.

The Program for Infants and Toddlers with Disabilities (Part C of IDEA's 1997 amendments) is a federal discretionary grant program that assists states in planning, developing, and implementing a statewide system of early intervention services for children with disabilities birth through age 2 years and their families. The statute and regulations for Part C contain many requirements states have to meet to implement this comprehensive, coordinated, multidisciplinary, and interagency service delivery program. For states to participate in the program, they must ensure that early intervention is available to every eligible child. The law defines an eligible infant or toddler with a disability as

> An individual under 3 years of age who needs early intervention services because the individual (i) is experiencing developmental delays, as measured by appropriate diagnostic instruments and procedures in one or more of the areas of cognitive development, physical development, communication development, social or emotional development and adaptive development; or (ii) has a diagnosed physical or mental condition which has a high probability of resulting in developmental delay. (20 U.S.C. §1432[5][A])

At its discretion, a state also may serve children who are at risk—according to that state's definition of "at risk." Approximately 20% of the states have elected to include children who are at risk. Thus, definitions of eligibility vary considerably across states.

In implementing the program, the governor of each state designates a lead state agency to administer the program. A variety of agencies may function as the lead agency including education, health, human services, social services, developmental disabilities, and rehabilitation service agencies. The governor also appoints an Interagency Coordinating Council (ICC), which includes parents of young children with disabilities, to advise and assist the lead agency. As of 2003, all U.S. states and eligible territories participate in the Part C program. Annual funding to each is based on census figures of the number of children.

Despite potential state differences with respect to child eligibility criteria and the state's lead agency of administration, several elements must be stipulated in each state's plan. These common elements are the minimum components required of a statewide comprehensive system for early intervention for infants and toddlers with special needs (see Table 12.1).

The range and types of services that are funded through this program are varied and represent services from a many different disciplines. Services may include the following:

> (i) Family training, counseling, and home visits; (ii) special instruction; (iii) speech-language pathology and audiology services; (iv) occupational therapy; (v) physical therapy; (vi) psychological services; (vii) service coordination services; (viii) medical services only for diagnostic or evaluation purposes; (ix) early identification, screening, and assessment services; (x) health services necessary to enable the infant or toddler to benefit from the other early intervention services; (xi) social work services; (xii) vision services; (xiii) assistive technology devices and assistive technology services; and (xiv) transportation and related costs that are necessary to enable an infant or toddler and the infant's or toddler's family to receive another service [from this service list]. (20 U.S.C. §1432 [E])

The law also stipulates the types of personnel that may be considered qualified to provide these services. Again, a range of disciplines are reflected and they may include special educators, speech-language pathologists and audiologists, occupational therapists, physical therapists, social workers, nurses, nutritionists, family therapists, orientation and mobility specialists, and pediatricians and other physicians. These services may be provided in a range of environments that include the child's home and community settings such as a child care or infant/toddler program.

Preschool Grants Program

Services for preschool-age children are administered through state education agencies under this legislative provision. Thus, this section of

Table 12.1. Minimum components required of a statewide comprehensive system for early intervention for infants and toddlers with special needs

Definition of developmental delay

Timetable for ensuring appropriate services to all eligible children

Timely and comprehensive multidisciplinary evaluation of needs of children and family-directed identification of the needs of each family

Individualized family service plan and service coordination

Comprehensive child find and referral system

Public awareness program

Central directory of services, resources, and research and demonstration projects

Comprehensive system of personnel development

Policies and procedures for personnel standards

Single line of authority in a lead agency designated or established by the governor for carrying out 1) general administration and supervision, 2) identification and coordination of all available resources, 3) assignment of financial responsibility to the appropriate agencies, 4) development of procedures to ensure that services are provided in a timely manner pending resolution of any disputes, 5) resolution of intra- and interagency disputes, 6) development of formal interagency agreements

Policy pertaining to contracting or otherwise arranging for services

Procedure for securing timely reimbursement of funds

Procedural safeguards

System for compiling data on the early intervention system

State Interagency Coordinating Council

Policies and procedures to ensure that to the maximum extent appropriate, early intervention services are provided in natural environments.

Adapted from 20 U.S.C. §1435(a).
From National Early Childhood Technical Assistance System. (1998, December). *Part C updates* (p. 1). Chapel Hill, NC: Author; adapted by permission.

the law extends to children 3 to 6 years the provisions of IDEA: due process, nondiscriminatory testing and evaluation, IEP development, and placement in least restrictive environments. Important provisions of the law also acknowledge the role of parent involvement, particularly in programs for young children with disabilities, and highlight strengthening the role of parents and ensuring "meaningful opportunities" for parents to participate in their child's education at school and home.

Eligibility criteria for a child with a disability under Section 619 of Part B of IDEA include the following conditions: mental retardation, hearing impairments, speech or language impairments, visual impairments, serious emotional disturbance, orthopedic impairments, autism, traumatic brain injury, other health impairments, or specific learning disabilities. For children ages 3–9 years, the state and local educational agency may at its discretion also serve children who are "experiencing developmental delays" as defined by that state. This may include delays in the areas of physical, cognitive, communication, social, emotional, or adaptive development. The following cutoff is used by most of the states that apply quantitative criteria to determine eligibility: 2.0 standard deviations (*SD*) below the mean in one developmental area and/or 1.5 *SD* below the mean in 2 or more developmental areas (range of 1.0 *SD* in one area to 3.0 *SD* in one area). In other states, a percentage of delay (i.e., range of 20%–33%) in one or more developmental areas is specified to determine eligibility. In still other states, eligibility is determined through professional team consensus, professional judgment, or informed clinical opinion in lieu of quantitative criteria.

Educational and related services for preschoolers are provided in a range of service environments that is typically more broadly construed than the range for school-age children. Educational environments may include child care and Head Start programs as well as school programs. Educational environments are typically classified as follows:

- Regular or general education classroom: Children receive services in programs designed primarily for children without disabilities.

- Resource room: Children receive services in programs designed for children without disabilities, but children with disabilities are in a separate program 21%–60% of the time.

- Separate classroom: Children receive services in separate programs more than 60% of the time.

- Separate school (public or private): Children receive services in a separate public or private facility for children with disabilities 61%–100% of the time.

- Residential facility: Children receive care 24 hours per day through a public or private residential facility such as a public nursing care facility or a residential school.

- Home/hospital: Children receive services either at home (possibly including services from a regular home visitor) or in a hospital setting.

Since the 1990s, general education classrooms have become the most common service environment for children with disabilities. In 1997–1998, states that reported service settings indicated that more than 92% of preschoolers with disabilities received special education or related services in a general education public school environment (U.S. Department of Education, 2000). The majority of these children (52.5%) were served in classrooms with children without disabilities for at least 80% of the day.

A wide range of services may be considered in special education service delivery systems. These types of services under Part B for children 3–5 years old include assistive technology devices and services, audiology, counseling services, early identification and assessment, medical services of diagnosis or evaluation, occupational therapy, parent counseling and training, physical therapy, psychological services, recreation, rehabilitation counseling services, school health services, social work services in schools, special education, speech-language pathology, and transportation.

Head Start

The Head Start program was established through provisions in the Economic Opportunity Act of 1964 (PL 88-452). A primary focus was to provide early educational and social services for young children from low income families in an effort to provide them with a "head start" and break the cycle of poverty. The Economic Opportunity Act subsequently was amended to require that at least 10% of children enrolled in Head Start have disabilities and that their specialized services be provided in these programs. As such, these Head Start service options have had a major impact in expanding inclusive services. Head Start also has had from its inception a strong family and community focus, and it has emphasized multidisciplinary service provision and coordination. These are important components of services for children with disabilities as well. Early Head Start programs for pregnant mothers, infants, and toddlers have been added. They are included in the range of service options under Part C of IDEA.

Key Service Delivery Concepts and Challenges

IDEA addresses a number of key concepts and components regardless of whether the services are for infants and toddlers or for preschoolers. The primary elements are outlined, and challenges to their implementation are briefly discussed.

Individualized Education
Programs (IEPs) for Young Children

Under the law, all young children with disabilities are required to have IEPs. The requirements differ somewhat on this component for infants and toddlers and preschoolers.

The IEP pertains to preschool-age children with disabilities, whose services are stipulated under Part B Section 619 of the law. Just as with school-age children, these children must receive an IEP. The IEP is a written statement consisting of specific information. The child's present level of educational performance is included. Measurable annual goals and objectives to meet the child's educational needs are also provided. Specifications are included for special education and related services, supplementary aids and services, and program modifications or support needed to enable the child to meet educational goals and participate with other children. In addition, if the child will not be fully included in a general education class, an explanation is given for this decision. Moreover, modifications in test administration are listed to allow the child to participate in state or school district assessments of student achievement. The date for beginning services and the frequency, location, and duration of those services and modifications are provided as well. Finally, the system for measuring the child's progress toward goals is defined. The IEP is developed by a team that includes the child's parents, general education teacher, and special education teacher; a representative of the local educational agency, and other individuals who may have knowledge or expertise regarding the child.

The individualized family service plan (IFSP) is the education program under Part C for infants and toddlers and their families. The IFSP is viewed as being logically connected to the IEP. The IFSP is also a written statement covering specific areas. First, the child's present levels of physical, cognitive, communication, social or emotional, and adaptive development are listed. Also included are the family's resources, priorities, and concerns relating to enhancing the development of their child with a disability. The major outcomes expected to be achieved for the child and the family are provided, as well as the criteria, procedures, and timelines to determine progress and whether modifications or revisions of the outcomes or services are necessary. In addition, the early intervention services necessary to meet the unique needs of the child and family (including the frequency, intensity, and method of delivering services) are specified. Furthermore, the natural environments in which early intervention services will be provided are designated, and a justification is included if services will not be provided in a natural environment. The projected dates for initiation of services and the anticipated duration of services are given as well. Another component is selecting the service coordinator from the field most immediately relevant to the child's or family's needs. This person will be responsible for plan implementation and coordination with other agencies and people. Finally, steps to support the child's transition to preschool or other appropriate services are outlined.

IEPs and IFSPs are fundamental to service delivery for children with disabilities. They are designed to meet each child's unique needs, and systems of accountability are stipulated. Challenges in developing and implementing IEPs and IFSPs have centered around providing appropriate and meaningful assessments, establishing parent–professional partnerships for planning and implementation, ensuring parents' meaningful roles, individualizing plans for each family's cultural and linguistic background and preferences, and exercising professional teamwork in developing and providing services.

Family-Centered Service Delivery Models

The full and active participation of parents and family members is encouraged in early intervention service delivery systems for infants, toddlers, and preschoolers. IDEA and its regulatory procedures formalized "due process" and requirements for involving families in decisions regarding their child's assessment, placement, and education program planning and implementation.

The roles of families and the many ways in which families can be involved in their children's early education programs have taken various forms over the years. At times, emphasis has been placed on notions of parents as teachers, parents as advocates, and parents as classroom assistants. Of course, one size does not fit all. Families differ in terms of makeup or structure, roles, cultural and linguistic backgrounds, faith backgrounds, values and belief systems, resources, and priorities and concerns for their children. So, too, do they differ in their preferred roles and levels of involvement.

The family is generally viewed from a family systems perspective (Turnbull & Turnbull, 1997). Its interaction within a broader ecological system of neighborhoods and communities, service structures and systems, and the culture at large are deemed highly influential on the family and the child's development (Bronfenbrenner, 1979; Odom et al., 1996). Active debate over the meaning, focus, and even the terminology used to characterize services with a family focus, has ensued over the years. Models for actively engaging families in the development or planning, implementation, and evaluation of services for young children with disabilities have been proposed and studied (Bailey et al., 1986). Great attention has been given to the notions of family empowerment and family support (Dunst, Trivette, & Deal, 1988, 1994). *Family-centered* or *family-focused* services refer not only to a philosophy of services, but also to a set of recommended practices in the field of early intervention (Shelton, Jeppson, & Johnson, 1987). These services describe a cluster of practices: providing respectful and culturally sensitive family services, identifying families' concerns and priorities for their children, obtaining families' informed consent and ensuring participation in the decision-making process regarding services for their children, using practices that empower families, and using practices that support and enhance families' development and competencies.

Despite this philosophical shift to a more family-centered approach, challenges remain. In many situations, educational decisions are still primarily professionally driven (see Hanson et al., 2000, 2001). Personnel preparation, staffing patterns in programs, staff supervision and support, program leadership, and policy implementation must continue to address increasingly family-focused approaches (Hanson & Bruder, 2001). Furthermore, these services for families must be delivered in a culturally competent manner that respects families and their variability in terms of culture, linguistic backgrounds, beliefs, and values (Lynch & Hanson, 1998).

Inclusion/Least Restrictive Environment/Natural Environment

With respect to preschoolers, the law specifies that services should be provided to the maximum extent possible in educational environments with children who do not have disabilities. It further stipulates that children should be removed from such an environment only when the nature or severity of the child's disability is such that the education cannot be achieved adequately in that environment with supplemental aids or services. This provision is often referred to as education in the *least restrictive environment*. Different terms, such as *mainstreaming* and *integration*, have been used over the years to describe the participation of children with disabilities in educational environments with their peers who do not have disabilities. *Inclusion* is the current term for this practice.

The intent is similar for infants and toddlers, although the language of the law differs somewhat. The Part C program for infants and toddlers states that services should be provided to the maximum extent appropriate in natural environments. Such environments include the child's home and community settings in which children without disabilities participate.

The provision of the children's individualized and specialized services within their homes and community and school programs requires careful planning, teamwork, administrative support, flexibility, and family involvement. Learning opportunities abound in daily routines and family and community activities. Early interventionists, therefore, are challenged to adapt activities, curricula, and environments and to forge new working relationships to meet the needs of children with disabilities in a range of environments (Bruder & Dunst, 2000; Guralnick, 2001; Odom, 2001).

Transitions

The young child's life is characterized by crucial transitions, particularly for children born at risk. Rice and O'Brien defined these transitions as "points of change in services and personnel who coordinate and provide services" (1990, p. 2). The first transition may occur as the child moves from care in the hospital to the family's home. Subsequent transitions for children with disabilities include the transitions to infant and toddler services, to preschool, and to kindergarten. Transitions can be stressful under the best of circumstances. In many states, early intervention services for infants and toddlers and preschool education services are handled by different agencies. Therefore, these transitions may be particularly challenging. Interagency agreements and transition procedures, support for families from key personnel, preparation of children for the transition, information exchange procedures between the sending and receiving services and personnel, and staff training and preparation for transition are but a few of the areas targeted for careful planning and support to ease transitions for children and their families (Hanson, 1999; Rosenkoetter, Hains, & Fowler, 1994).

Personnel Preparation and Interdisciplinary Team Models

Professional standards and personnel licensure, certification, and credentialing requirements may differ by state and also across professions based on the standards set by each discipline. Thus, considerable variability can be found across states, although all must adhere to provisions for a comprehensive system for professional development as stipulated by law.

Most professional groups have expanded curricula at both the preservice and in-service levels to address competencies related to serving young children and their families. Many have separate certification or add-on training programs in pediatric or early care. Creative and cross-disciplinary approaches are needed, however, for personnel development across health, education, and social service fields in early intervention (Winton, McCollum, & Catlett, 1997).

The range of service needs experienced by young children with disabilities and their families bridge professional disciplines. Only through collaborative team models can these service needs be fully addressed. In early intervention, the transdisciplinary team model is considered optimal for service delivery. It highlights a team approach through which "role release" is practiced. That is, one or a few professionals are the primary individuals responsible for implementing a child's program with assistance, consultation, and continuous skill training and development from the full spectrum of team members representing various disciplines (McGonigel, Woodruff, & Roszmann-Millican, 1994). This team approach requires careful collaboration across professional service providers and requires time and resource allocation for training and planning, as well as commitments and effective working relationships among professionals (Hanson & Bruder, 2001).

Service Coordination and Interagency Collaboration

Service coordination is a mandated service under Part C of IDEA, and it is to be provided at no cost to families. It is "defined as an active, ongoing process that assists and enables families to access services and assures their rights and procedural safeguards" (National Early Childhood Technical Assistance System, 2001). Early intervention team members must jointly provide assessment, intervention, and evaluation activities in partnership with the child's family; they also must help families to gain access to the various services they need (Bruder & Bologna, 1993).

Not only do service systems and patterns differ from state to state, but studies found that even within states the agencies differ fundamentally and qualitatively from one another (Harbin, 1996). Harbin noted that differences were found in administrative structures, target populations, mission statements, philosophies, roles, types of decision making, types of agreements, professional backgrounds, resources, priorities, and specificity of policies. Thus, interagency collaboration and coordination is often difficult to achieve. The most promising practice for addressing this concern is the use of interagency agreements, whereby state agencies enter into formal agreements or partnerships with one another to establish collaborative structures, to share resources, to locate and refer children in need of services, to conduct public awareness campaigns, and to develop and offer training activities. Many state education agencies have one or more agreements with other agencies, and these collaborations include a wide range of partnerships between departments such as education, health, human services, social services, and Head Start.

RECOMMENDATIONS FOR PROFESSIONALS IN OTHER COUNTRIES

In the preceding section, key service components were described and the challenges to their implementation were discussed. Each of these service components has been derived from many years of research and advocacy in the United States. As such, they also represent the recommendations for other countries as they develop and/or expand services for young children with disabilities. *Individualized education programs (IEPs)* are the foundation for all services. These individualized programs are specifically planned and implemented for each child based on that child's strengths and needs and the priorities of the child's family. The provision of services using a *family-centered approach* is recommended to ensure that family members are respected as the primary decision-makers for their children. Family-centered services are by definition culturally respectful and sensitive to the needs and preferences of each family. As much as possible, children's educational services are implemented in *inclusive environments* or *natural environments* in which young children spend their time. Children participate in programs and services with their peers, and the child and family's typical routines are utilized for planning educational and therapeutic interventions. This orientation respects the right of the child and family to participate in their community and incorporates services into the family's typical rituals and routine. It is recommended that *transitions* from one type of service to another be carefully planned and that children and families are supported in this process. In some countries, as in the United States, services may be administered by different agencies with different requirements. *Interagency and interdisciplinary service coordination and collaboration,* thus, are also crucial to prevent additional stress for the family and to ensure that the child receives adequate and comprehensive services. Finally, *personnel preparation* and training of service providers are essential to the provision of optimal services. Service providers must be knowledgeable in their field of expertise as well as current in their knowledge and ability to demonstrate "recommended practices" as they provide intervention support to children and families. These components may be manifest in different types of agencies, with different populations of children and families, and in different geographical locations. Regardless, they form the infrastructure for quality services to young children with disabilities and their families.

CONCLUSION

The IDEA and its provisions for young children from birth through 5 years has provided an unprecedented opportunity in the United States to establish a unified service delivery system to address the complex needs of young children with disabilities and their families. The child's individualized service needs and goals and the active inclusion and participation of the child's family are at the core of policies and procedures. The legislation has provided the necessary infrastructure for developing a system that spans the country and incorporates the full range of agencies, structures, and professional disciplines that deliver early intervention services.

This key legislation for early intervention has helped to establish more universal and comprehensive services for young children with disabilities. It has afforded the means to cross boundaries of agencies and professions to serve the diverse needs of children and their families. By the same token, the comprehensive nature of this legislation also has produced tremendous challenges related to interagency coordination, teaming and collaboration, and the provision of full and meaningful participation options for families in a manner that is congruent with their priorities and needs. No less a service system is needed to address the range of service needs for young children with disabilities and their families in the United States.

REFERENCES

Americans with Disabilities Act (ADA) of 1990, PL 101-336, 42 U.S.C. §§ 12101 *et seq.*

Bailey, D.B., Simeonsson, R.J., Winton, P.J., Huntington, G.S., Comfort, M., Isbell, P., O'Donnell, K.J., & Helm, J.M. (1986). Family-focused intervention: A functional model for planning, implementing, and evaluating individualized family services in early intervention. *Journal of the Division for Early Childhood, 10,* 156–171.

Braddock, D. (1987). *Federal policy toward mental retardation and developmental disabilities.* Baltimore: Paul H. Brookes Publishing Co.

Bronfenbrenner, U. (1979). *The ecology of human development.* Cambridge, MA: Harvard University Press. (ERIC Document Reproduction Service No. ED128387).

Bruder, M.B., & Bologna, T.M. (1993). Collaboration and service coordination for effective early intervention. In W. Brown, S.K. Thurman, & L.F. Pearl (Eds.), *Family-centered early intervention with infants and toddlers: Innovative cross-disciplinary approaches* (pp. 103–127). Baltimore: Paul H. Brookes Publishing Co.

Bruder, M.B., & Dunst, C.J. (2000). Expanding learning opportunities for infants and toddlers in natural environments: A chance to reconceptualize early intervention. *Zero to Three, 20*(3), 34–36.

deFosset, S. (Ed.). (2001). *Section 619 profile* (10th ed.). Chapel Hill, NC: National Early Childhood Technical Assistance System.

Dunst, C.J., Trivette, C.M., & Deal, A.G. (1988). *Enabling and empowering families: Principles and guidelines for practice.* Cambridge, MA: Brookline Books.

Dunst, C.J., Trivette, C.M., & Deal, A.G. (Eds.). (1994). *Supporting and strengthening families: Methods, strategies and practices.* Cambridge, MA: Brookline Books.

Economic Opportunity Act of 1964, PL 88-452, 42 U.S.C. §§ 2701 *et seq.*

Education for All Handicapped Children Act of 1975, PL 94-142, 20 U.S.C. §§ 1400 *et seq.*

Florian, L. (1995). Part H early intervention program: Legislative history and intent of the law. *Topics in Early Childhood Special Education, 15,* 247–262.

Guralnick, M.J. (Ed.). (2001). *Early childhood inclusion: Focus on change.* Baltimore: Paul H. Brookes Publishing Co.

Hanson, M.J. (1999, September). *Early transitions for children and families: Transitions from infant/toddler services to preschool education.* Reston, VA: The ERIC Clearinghouse on Disabilities and Gifted Education. (ERIC Digest No. E581).

Hanson, M.J., Beckman, P.J., Horn, E., Marquart, J., Sandall, S.R., Greig, D., & Brennan, E. (2000). Entering preschool: Family and professional experiences in this transition process. *Journal of Early Intervention, 23,* 279–293.

Hanson, M.J., & Bruder, M.B. (2001). Early intervention: Promises to keep. *Infants and Young Children, 13*(3), 47–58.

Hanson, M.J., Horn, E., Sandall, S., Beckman, P., Morgan, M., Marquart, J., Barnwell, D., & Chou, H. (2001). After preschool inclusion: Children's educational pathways over the early school years. *Exceptional Children, 68*(1), 65–83.

Harbin, G. (1996). The challenge of coordination. *Infants and Young Children, 8*(3), 8–76.

Head Start, Economic Opportunity, and Community Partnership Act of 1974, PL 93-644, 42 U.S.C. §§ 2941 *et seq.*

Individuals with Disabilities Education Act Amendments of 1997, PL 105-17, 20 U.S.C. §§ 1400 *et seq.*

Individuals with Disabilities Education Act (IDEA) of 1990, PL 101-476, 20 U.S.C. §§ 1400 *et seq.*

Lynch, E.W., & Hanson, M.J. (Eds.). (1998). *Developing cross-cultural competence: A guide for working with children and their families* (2nd ed.). Baltimore: Paul H. Brookes Publishing Co.

McGonigel, M.J., Woodruff, G., & Roszmann-Millican, M. (1994). The transdisciplinary team: A model for family-centered early intervention. In L.J. Johnson, R.J. Gallagher, M.J. LaMontagne, J.B. Jordan, J.J. Gallagher, P.L. Hutinger, & M.B. Karnes (Eds.), *Meeting early intervention challenges: Issues form birth to three* (2nd ed., pp. 95–131). Baltimore: Paul H. Brookes Publishing Co.

National Early Childhood Technical Assistance System. (1998, December). *Part C updates.* Chapel Hill, NC: Author.

National Early Childhood Technical Assistance System. (2001, October). *Service coordination under IDEA.* Retrieved October 15, 2002, from http://www.nectac.org/topics/scoord/scoord.asp

Odom, S.L. (Ed.). (2001). *Widening the circle.* New York: Teachers College Press.

Odom, S.L., Peck, C.A., Hanson, M.J., Beckman, P.J., Kaiser, A.P., Lieber, J., Brown, W.H., Horn, E.M., & Schwartz, I.S. (1996). Inclusion at the preschool level: An ecological systems analysis. *Social Policy Report: Society for Research in Child Development, 10*(2,3), 18–30.

Rice, M.L., & O'Brien, M. (1990). Transitions: Time for change and accommodation. *Topics in Early Childhood Special Education, 9*(4), 1–14.

Rosenkoetter, S.E., Hains, A.H., & Fowler, S.A. (1994). *Bridging early services for children with special needs and their families: A practical guide for transition planning.* Baltimore: Paul H. Brookes Publishing Co.

Safford, P.L., & Safford, E.J. (1996). *A history of childhood and disability.* New York: Teachers College Press.

Shelton, T., Jeppson, E., & Johnson, B. (1987). *Family-centered care for children with special health care needs.* Washington, DC: Association for the Care of Children's Health.

Shonkoff, J.P., & Meisels, S.J. (1990). Early childhood intervention: The evolution of a concept. In S.J. Meisels & J.P. Shonkoff (Eds.), *Handbook of early childhood intervention* (pp. 3–31). New York: Cambridge University Press.

Turnbull, A.P., & Turnbull, H.R. (1997). *Families, professionals, and exceptionality: A special partnership* (3rd ed.). Columbus, OH: Charles E. Merrill.

Turnbull, H.R. (1986). *Free appropriate public education: The law and children with disabilities.* Denver, CO: Love Publishing Co.

U.S. Census Bureau. (2000). *United States Census 2000.* Retrieved from http://www.census.gov.

U.S. Department of Education. (2000). *Twenty-second annual report to Congress on the implementation of the Individuals with Disabilities Education Act.* Washington, DC: Author.

Winton, P.J., McCollum, J.A., & Catlett, C. (Eds.). (1997). *Reforming personnel preparation in early intervention: Issues, models, and practical strategies.* Baltimore: Paul H. Brookes Publishing Co.

CHAPTER 13

Formal and
Informal Networks

Christine F. Johnston

AUSTRALIA

The sky's the limit!

Although not a proverb and certainly not peculiar to Australia, "The sky's the limit!" encapsulates the view held by Australian parents and professionals regarding the power and importance of early childhood intervention. The phrase also was adopted as the slogan for the annual "Kites for Kids Day," a national campaign that began in 2000 to raise awareness of early childhood intervention in the community. Particular significance lies both in the slogan and in the fact that the campaign is the work of Early Childhood Intervention Australia (ECIA). ECIA is a national network of parents and professionals involved in early childhood intervention, thus demonstrating that the impetus for increased community commitment is coming from those most concerned with the outcome.

The view expressed in the slogan is not that early childhood intervention provides a cure for disability but simply that one does not know what is possible until one tries. No limits or expectations should be set. It is a view that the father of a young child with a severe disability expressed when talking about family-centered early childhood intervention:

> Well, we'll reach for the stars, and if we only get to the moon, well fine, but we'll get there. We're going to set the highest ideals, but if we don't get there, then it's OK. We'll have tried for him, and he will have tried. (Treloar, 1997, no page number)

In Australia the provision of early childhood intervention services is based on community and agency initiatives rather than on legislation (Campbell, 1997). As a consequence, guidelines may be set by government for recommended practice in the field, but the approach adopted is a matter of choice, not prescription. Although the majority of early childhood intervention services would consider themselves family centered, and therefore following recommended practice, they do so because of perceived effectiveness. Implementation is largely governed and maintained through the existence of formal and informal networks of professionals and families.

These networks serve two main functions. First, they legitimize the application of particular models and approaches by making the latest research available to parents and professionals through conferences, newsletters, and other methods of informal education. Second, they provide the means to coordinate a range of services to be utilized by particular families. When working well, these networks enhance

Thanks to Helen Lunn for commenting on a draft of this chapter; to Lesley Burnett and Early Childhood Intervention Australia (New South Wales Chapter); and to Mr. and Mrs. Payne for permitting the photograph of their children to be included.

the family's experience of early childhood intervention, decrease duplication, and ensure that optimum use is made of the services available.
Being an integral part of such networks, therefore, is essential to effective service provision. This chapter focuses on a discussion of the advantages and disadvantages of such a network system.

 ## BEN'S STORY

Ben's parents migrated from southern Europe to Australia as young
children. Their ethnic heritage is central to their lives. They are bilingual
and want their two children to be as well. Ben's parents are university
educated; his father holds a professional position and his mother cares
for Ben and his older sister full time. They live in an area of Sydney
where there is considerable cultural diversity.

Ben was born 2 months prematurely, and his mother recalls that
she had concerns about his development from the time of his birth.
She believed that Ben was not progressing as quickly as his older sister
had. It was not until he was 6 months old, however, that delays in
Ben's motor development were identified by professionals and he was
referred to a local specialized early childhood intervention service for

physiotherapy. This constituted the intervention that occurred until he was formally diagnosed as having spastic diplegia at 19 months of age. At that time, he was referred to the statewide nonprofit agency specializing in services for those with cerebral palsy. Now 4 years of age, Ben uses a walker and has recently taken his first steps without assistance. He talks constantly but does have some articulation difficulties. He is gregarious and one of the most popular children in his preschool class.

Because of the nature of his disability, Ben has required a full range of therapy services, including physiotherapy, occupational therapy, and speech-language pathology. An early childhood special educator and a psychologist have also been involved in his intervention program. Services have been both home- and center-based. His need for orthoses has also necessitated regular appointments with an orthopedic surgeon. The time commitment that his intervention program demands of his family is considerable. In an attempt to address this, the existing intervention program was reviewed and a new one was developed at Ben's individualized family service plan (IFSP) meetings, which are held approximately every 6 months. The agenda of these meetings is set by Ben's parents, who attend them along with individuals who have been working consistently with Ben and his family. Ben's mother has chosen to chair these meetings but prefers the early childhood special educator to act as service coordinator. Since he commenced preschool, Ben's teacher also now attends these meetings.

The community preschool that Ben attends 3 days per week is close to his home. His mother drops him off in the morning and picks him up in the afternoon, as do all of the other parents. This allows her to have constant contact with Ben's teacher and classroom aides and to meet and talk with other parents. Of the 87 children who attend the preschool during the week, 66% come from backgrounds with primary languages other than English and 14% have been identified as having special needs. With the family's and the preschool's agreement, therapists from the specialized agency visit the preschool at least once per term on a consultative basis. Plans are now being made to choose the school that Ben will attend; this also will be an inclusive program in his neighborhood. These services to which the family has access are generally free of cost.

The story of Ben and his family highlights not only some of the successes achieved by early childhood intervention in Australia, but also some of its continuing challenges. Involvement in early intervention has been a largely positive experience for Ben and his family. After some initial difficulty in having their concerns heard, his parents found their way into the system and have access to needed services near their home. The ease with which they were able to enroll Ben in a community preschool was due to that preschool's policy of active inclusion. In addition, professionals in Ben's early childhood intervention service had an existing professional relationship with the preschool through previous clients and with its director through networking committees. Ben's having an identified disability also meant that there was a clear referral path. That his parents are articulate and able to navigate what is a complex system was also to his and their advantage. This situation may have been otherwise if Ben's family did not speak English or lived in an isolated or remote area. In such regions, ready access to services may be problematic because of long waiting lists or a lack of networks between specialized and generic services (i.e., available to the general community). The difficulty, then, lies in ensuring that the system works for everyone.

NATIONAL CONTEXT

In 2001, Australia celebrated its centenary of federation, when the six states formed the Commonwealth of Australia and ceased to be colonies of Great Britain. It was a federation that occurred without revolution or civil war although also with scant regard for the needs and rights of the indigenous population. In addition, the federation took 11 years to achieve after the basic agreement to unite had been made (the notion had been debated as early as 1842). Central to the delay was the relative powers of the Commonwealth and State Governments. States' rights and responsibilities remain a constant theme in Australian politics.

As a consequence of federation, Australia has three tiers of government: federal, state/territory, and local. Specific powers are vested in the federal government through the Constitution, with the residual powers lying with the states and territories. Although at least partially funded by the federal government, the provision of services such as health and education are primarily the responsibility of the state and territory Governments. As a result, considerable differences exist, due in some measure to the varied geography and population spread with which each state or territory must deal. The role of local government in providing such services also varies, but most have some involvement in child care and early childhood services.

Demographics

Australia is an island continent with a land mass of approximately 7.72 million square kilometers—an area only slightly smaller than that of the United States of America. It comprises six states (Queensland, New South Wales, Victoria, Tasmania, South Australia, and Western Australia) and two territories (the Northern Territory and the Australian Capital Territory). The population in 1999 was approximately 19 million people (Australian Bureau of Statistics, 2001a). Most of Australia's population is concentrated in two coastal regions; one in the southeast and east regions of the continent, the other in the southwest. The reality and implications of this population spread are perhaps best understood by considering the population distribution illustrated in Figure 13.1. As shown in the figure, the population is concentrated in urban centers to the extent that 84% of the population inhabits 1% of the country (Australian Bureau of Statistics, 2001a).

This population distribution has implications for service provision that warrant consideration. For those who live in the major cities, early childhood intervention services may be more accessible. It must be said, however, that urban sprawl can result in lengthy travel times to obtain intervention, whether it is the family or the professional who

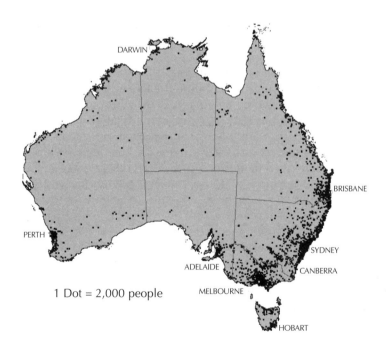

Figure 13.1. Population distribution in Australia. (From Australian Bureau of Statistics. [2001a]. *Australia now—A statistical profile: Population. Population distribution.* Retrieved October 15, 2002, from http://www.abs.gov.au/Ausstats/abs%40.nsf/94713ad445ff1425ca 25682000192af2/fe3fa39a5bf5aa5aca256b350010b3fd!OpenDocument; (ABS data used with permission from the Australian Bureau of Statistics [http://www.abs.gov.au].)

must travel. For those living in the more remote rural areas, what the Australian historian Geoffrey Blainey (1982) has called the "tyranny of distance" becomes critical. The nearest services can be hundreds of kilometers away. As a result, the implementing of intervention programs developed in consultation with specialized early childhood intervention staff largely becomes the responsibility of the family and/or local professionals working in generic services—if they are even available. As technology makes it increasingly possible, services are looking to utilize distance-education models, web-based programs, and teleconferencing as a more affordable means of providing services.

As in many other countries, the nature and composition of families are changing. For example, the percentage of Australian households comprising couples with children has fallen from 60% to 50% since 1980 (Press & Hayes, 2000). An increase both in the number of one-parent families (21.5% in 1998) and couple-only families has accompanied this trend. Australians are delaying having children and are living longer.

Also of importance is the fact that approximately 70% of Australian women have some form of paid employment; in 1997, 49% of women with children younger than 4 years of age worked. However, it appears that women retain primary responsibility for household work (Bittman & Pixley, 1997). Finally, it should also be noted that in 1998 it was estimated that 3% of children birth to 4 years had a disability (Australian Bureau of Statistics, 2001b). Providing appropriate early childhood services within this context is therefore a prime consideration.

People and Culture

Australia's cultural diversity is best illustrated by the fact that in 2000, overseas-born residents totaled 4.5 million or 24% of the population (Australian Bureau of Statistics, 2001d). A further 3.8 million Australians have at least one parent who was born overseas. Moreover, approximately 280 major languages, including 170 Aboriginal and Torres Strait Islander (ATSI) languages, are spoken (Press & Hayes, 2000). There is also considerable religious diversity.

In 1996, the indigenous (ATSI) population was estimated at 386,000 or 2.1% of the total population, with a median age of 20.1 years—some 14 years younger than for the total population (Australian Bureau of Statistics, 2001c). The life expectancy of people of indigenous origin is presently 57 years for males and 62 years for females; this is almost 20 years less than for the rest of the population (Australian Bureau of Statistics, 2001c). Health, education, and employment remain major issues. As these figures demonstrate, a challenge for those working to provide early childhood intervention is to ensure that services are linguistically appropriate and culturally sensitive.

Education Services Systems

Universal schooling is available to all children of compulsory school age. Although there are some variations across the country, schooling generally extends over 7 years of primary school (including kindergarten) and 6 years of secondary school. Children commence school at approximately the age of 5 years (6 years in some states) and are able to leave school from around the age of 15.

For those with disabilities, a range of schooling options are available: inclusion in regular (i.e., general education) classrooms, special units within regular schools, and special schools. Although not mandated, the trend is inclusion wherever possible. Access to the school of choice is not guaranteed, which is a source of contention in many cases and of litigation in some instances.

Schooling is offered through a range of providers. State/territory government schools accounting for 70% of attendance, Catholic system schools account for 20%, and private schools account for 10% (Press & Hayes, 2000). Private schools may be religious or nondenominational. They include schools with unlimited resources and high fees as well as small community schools that meet the particular needs of families with different ethnic or cultural backgrounds or philosophies.

Funding for education comes from all levels of government and from charitable, religious, and other sources. More specifically, the costs of higher education are borne mainly by the Commonwealth and state governments, with students paying a proportion of the costs through various fee systems. Increasingly, there is a move to make undergraduate places in universities available to Australian students willing to pay full fees. Previously, such places had been open only to international students.

Although the Constitution places the responsibility for children's education with the states, the Commonwealth is able to exert influence on areas such as curriculum, literacy levels, and retention rates through targeted funding. That and the relative proportion of money given to the public and private school systems remain a political issue. The cost of early childhood education is carried by all three levels of government, by parents through fees and fundraising, and by charitable organizations. The funding situation for early childhood intervention services is very similar. Thus, the funding arrangements across the education system are complex and subject to variation.

KEY FEATURES OF EARLY INTERVENTION

During the 1970s, community awareness and attitudes regarding individuals with disabilities began to change. Previous practices of institutionalizing young children with disabilities began to be questioned, and the developmental needs of these children considered (McAlpine & Johnston, 1993). Linfoot (1992) noted that in the mid-1970s, Victoria and New South Wales saw the beginning of a rapid expansion of early childhood intervention services. Indeed, in comparing the services offered to children with disabilities in New South Wales born 1970– 1980 to those born between 1981–1988, Foreman (1992) found that there had been almost a 100% increase in recommendations to utilize early intervention services. Coupled with a rise in parent advocacy (noted by Turnbull & Turnbull, 1990, as being a general phenomenon), the impact both on the acceptance of early childhood intervention's importance and on the approach itself has been profound. In 2003, services in Australia have evolved to a family-centered approach.

It also should be noted that there has been a move in Australia to rename the field "early *childhood* intervention." This was done to increase community understanding of its aims and to distinguish it from other forms of early intervention (e.g., for drug and alcohol abuse or mental illness). The term, which was advocated by ECIA, is now gaining acceptance across the country.

Early Childhood Intervention Service System

In attempting to characterize the early childhood intervention system in Australia, differences in defining the group eligible for services are evident among the states and territories. As a consequence, the definition adopted by ECIA is general, stating that early childhood intervention "provides support for infants and young children who have developmental delays or disabilities, their families and communities, in order to promote the child's development and inclusion" (Early Childhood Intervention Australia, 2000). Although sufficient for its purpose to raise awareness and provide a base for lobbying at a federal level, a more specific definition is needed at the service delivery level. For example, the New South Wales government states that the target group is

> Families with children from birth until they enter the school system who:
> Already have a developmental delay or disability; or
> Require specialized services without which it is likely that developmental milestones may not be achieved and/or a handicap may result. (Office on Disability, 1995, p. 4)

Therefore, the provision of early childhood services extends from birth, includes preschool, and generally concludes when the child enters the school system.

Early childhood intervention in Australia is most accurately described as a service system rather than as a collection of discrete services, each with its own agenda and curricula. The system is rather simple in Tasmania, where one government department has responsibility for services and the population is relatively small, if scattered. In states such as New South Wales, where responsibility is spread among four government departments and intervention is offered through more than 500 services, the system becomes more difficult to characterize. In all states and territories, however, the system can be said to comprise in varying proportions and levels of importance specialized early childhood intervention services run by government agencies or nongovernmental organizations (NGOs), generic early childhood education services, and general health services.

The services offered take various forms:

- Home based: primarily for families with children birth through 3 years
- Center based: includes access to therapy, preschool, and inclusion support aides
- Itinerant: when location or need demands only occasional in-person sessions and a consultation model is likely to apply
- Consultative: when occasional assistance is given to professionals in generic services or to another specialized service with respect to a specific disability

The mix of services that families experience is determined by their own needs at any particular time and by the availability of services.

FAMILIES' ROLES

Recommended practice in Australia is the adoption of a family-centered approach. It is at the heart of ECIA's *Code of Ethics,* developed in 2000 for early childhood intervention professionals, and it is the basis for most government policies related to the field (e.g., see Treloar, 1997). When fully implemented, it enables families not only to determine the program to be implemented and their degree of involvement in it but also to influence the conduct of the services themselves through their presence on boards and committees. Although both parents and professionals report satisfaction with and support of the approach, they also acknowledge that improvements in its implementation are still needed (Beamish & Bryer, 1999; Dempsey & Carruthers, 1997).

Theoretical Influences

Australia has a long tradition of providing services to families with young children through "well baby" clinics. Although the exact nature and scope of these services has varied across the states and territories, they have had a number of common functions, such as providing support to new mothers, monitoring children's development, and referring families to additional support services when needed. The development of specialized early childhood intervention services can be seen as simply an extension of this practice.

These specialized services have been greatly influenced by the approaches researched, adopted, and evaluated in the United States. This appears to be so for three main reasons. First, the majority of the early intervention literature comes from the United States and is easily accessible. Second, since 1983, ECIA (encompassing both its state and territory Chapters and, later, its national association) has regularly brought American researchers to its conferences as keynote speakers. Therefore, the opportunity to engage with international experts in the field has been sustained and has served to affect the direction that early childhood intervention has taken in Australia. In this way, the formal parent and professional network has promoted recommended practice to good effect. Third, American research has been influential because of perceived similarities between U.S. and Australian societies. Just how similar they are, however, warrants scrutiny. Indeed, both Ashman (1990) and Beamish and Bryer (1999) argued that the validity of the American data needs to be tested in the Australian context. There is a need, then, for a concerted research effort specific to Australian needs. To date, this has been lacking.

Political Influences

Australia's political system has already been outlined and its impact on the delivery of educational services has been noted. Yet, it should be emphasized that there is support for the provision of early childhood intervention at all levels of government. Difficulties for the system lie in the lack of a legislative base for its provision, which has resulted in funding and policy being subject to the political will of the incumbent government at each level. This is exacerbated by the number of government departments that may be involved. In 2003, four Commonwealth departments have some responsibility for early childhood intervention. At state and territory level, the number varies but may be as many as four. In this respect, the system is complicated, confusing, and piecemeal. Knowing what sources of funding are available and applying and accounting for them becomes a major issue for the service provider. In turn, this can detract significantly from the time available for service delivery. Rationalization of funding and of the procedures attached to it continue to be a concern.

Cultural Influences

The multicultural nature of Australian society places additional demands on early childhood intervention services. A main concern is whether people whose primary language is not English can navigate the system. The use of community languages in materials relating to child health and development has been one approach used to counteract this concern. Services also work to ensure that their practices are culturally sensitive through in-service training for staff, ongoing consultation with community representatives, and the utilization of community liaison workers from relevant ethnic communities. Interpreter services are used when appropriate and possible. A major barrier to services' taking sufficient account of language and other needs remains lack of funding.

Of greatest concern is the low level of involvement of indigenous families in early childhood intervention. Services' lack of connection to and acceptance by indigenous communities has frequently prevented their involvement. When intervention approaches have been successful, they have worked within the established community structures to meet the needs of the individual child and family (Reedman, 2000). It is in this area that the need for research in the Australian context is particularly critical and where the system has failed to be truly family centered.

COORDINATION OF SERVICES

Given that there is no legislative base for the provision of early childhood intervention services, their provision and coordination can only be achieved through the system itself. This occurs through the existence of both formal and informal networks operating at national, state/ territory, and local levels.

At the national level, that network is ECIA, the peak parent and professional body for those involved in the field. As a national group, it is relatively young, having been formally established in 1995. The first state chapters were set up in the 1980s, however, and have had informal ties to each other from that time, thereby forming a loose national grouping. The national organization can be said to serve three main functions:

1. The development of policies for the field (e.g., *Code of Ethics,* Early Childhood Intervention Australia, 2000)

2. The provision of a national voice for lobbying

3. The dissemination of research and knowledge related to practice through conferences and publications

Although there is still much to achieve, ECIA appears to be meeting its goals to provide a focus for both parents and professionals in their attempts to ensure quality early childhood intervention services. A key benefit has been the opportunity for members to meet and talk with others who have experienced similar challenges and to share possible solutions. The value of such informal networking is inestimable.

Networks have also proved beneficial at state and territory level, particularly with respect to the practicalities of service delivery and coordination within community areas. How these function is clearly a product of local factors and conditions. The formal use of networks in New South Wales is examined both because it provides an example of an attempt to deal with a complex and varied service system and because the chapter author has had extensive involvement with it.

Development of the Early Childhood Intervention Coordination Program

In 1991, the New South Wales state government set up what was then called the Early Intervention Coordination Project as a pilot project in three areas (two in metropolitan Sydney and the other in a rural area). The project's purpose was to explore ways to enhance the coordination of early childhood intervention. The original objectives were to

> Identify and assess the planning and delivery patterns of early intervention services and develop strategies to improve planning and delivery of these services to families in need of them, in particular by coordinating service planning and delivery across agencies. (Office on Disability, 1995, p. 1)

The project arose from an awareness of the problems facing families in gaining access to services. Uneven distribution of services across regions and long waiting lists were seen as major problems within the existing system. Its main objective was to develop a consistent response to families with a range of special needs. It was recognized that to achieve this, the participation and ongoing involvement of a number of government departments and NGOs would be required. Furthermore, as the response to families needed to be consistent across the state, a central committee (comprised of representatives from the relevant government departments and the New South Wales chapter of ECIA representing NGOs) worked to establish common goals and systems of accountability. This committee sought to refine the overall philosophy that informed service delivery in the state, establish shared definitions and joint policy, develop a clear understanding of the different responsibilities of the departments involved, and put in place a framework for the development of protocols (Office on Disability, 1995). Most significant, there was a recognition that to understand the system, the local level at which families had their initial and ongoing experiences of early intervention had to be considered. Evaluating the policies, strategies, and guidelines in the pilot areas was an essential part of the process, as was the continuing consultation between local and central levels that ensued (Office on Disability, 1995).

The underlying principles guiding the project were developed at this time, too. They were framed as

- Effective interdepartmental and NGO partnerships
- A family-centered approach to early intervention
- Improved coordination of services, to which families have easy access
- Cost-effective planning and provision of services (Office on Disability, 1995)

The project endeavored from the outset not only to consider procedural issues but also the philosophical framework within which they operated.

External evaluations of the project were conducted in 1994 and 1997. Both were generally positive in their findings. The approach appeared to successfully utilize innovative methods in a time of limited resources. Recommendations were made initially to extend the pilot project across the state and, with the 1997 evaluation, to adopt the project as an ongoing program of the government. These recommendations were accepted. The Early Childhood Intervention Coordination Program (ECICP), as it is now named, extends across the state and was endorsed in 2001 for a second 3-year period.

Early Childhood Intervention Program in Practice

The program is conducted by a designated lead agency—one of the state departments—which provides it with an Early Childhood Intervention Coordinator. As set out in the ECICP Procedures Manual (Ageing and Disability Department, 1999), it has four tiers of committees. The Management Committee comprises senior officers from each of the relevant state departments, officers from the Commonwealth Departments offering major funding to early childhood intervention services, and a representative of the NGOs from the New South Wales Chapter of ECIA. Essentially, this committee is responsible for monitoring policy implementation at a statewide level and dealing with issues of statewide significance. It meets quarterly and provides feedback to the committees below it. The Statewide Committee comprises representatives from each of the Area Committees, representatives of the Management Committee, and the Early Childhood Intervention Coordinator. It meets quarterly with the primary functions of reporting and information exchange. The Area Committees, of which there are 16, consist of representatives of participating government agencies and NGOs and the Local Network Committees. Families also have representation on the Area Committees. The Area Committees' main functions are to promote recommended practice in family-centered intervention, to define and monitor the boundaries and composition of the local networks, and to coordinate training and development activities that support the program's aims. Some funding is available to Area Committees to assist them in meeting these aims. The Local Network Committees consist of representatives of individual service providers, government agencies and NGOs, and families. The Local Network Committees are responsible for developing strategies to support the coordination of services in each local area. In 2002, there were 73 such committees.

The committee structure's hierarchy is designed to ensure consistency and equity in statewide service provision while guaranteeing that local circumstances are taken into account. Thus, although the aim is to provide a family-centered early childhood intervention program to all families, the way in which this might be achieved for a family in a remote, rural area with limited services will differ greatly from that for a family in a metropolitan area. The intention of addressing the situation at a local level is that the outcome will be acceptable to each family's circumstances.

The Area and Local Committees are therefore intended to adopt policies that encourage processes such as using common intake procedures, sharing resources and personnel, exchanging information, and consulting. The objectives are to facilitate the adoption and development of recommended practice at individual service and system levels and to ensure that the needs of individual families are met as far as is possible. In every case, the principles of family-centered intervention apply. Clear guidelines and policy are set regarding confidentiality and family involvement in every phase of their program's development.

This approach also allows and encourages the utilization of informal networks. Committee membership at each of the levels promotes professional relationships among those who attend meetings. There are opportunities to discuss common concerns and to seek advice or possible solutions. These relationships also facilitate referrals. Negotiating shared responsibility or involvement in a child's program also becomes easier if professional relationships already exist.

The potential benefits of such networking are therefore considerable. The system is not without its difficulties, however, and they also need to be considered. Chief among these is the time required for such networking. Meeting attendance, no matter how beneficial, takes away from client time. Thus, meetings need to have clear agendas, definite time frames, and show immediate gains for those who attend.

The success of such formal networks also largely depends on the commitment and goodwill of the participants. If there is no commitment at an individual or systemic level, then the networks will fail. In fact, this is a recurring complaint to the Management Committee from the Area and Local Committees. Constant changes in committee membership block smooth and effective functioning, as do differing levels of participation and commitment from the participants. This has been perceived as particularly so with members from government departments, as they may not be directly involved in service delivery and see involvement in the ECICP as tangential to their core responsibilities. If such networks are to prosper, then involvement must be designated as part of the individual's job description and as a factor in his or her performance appraisal.

The long-term success of the Local and Area Committees may also depend on the extent to which the system can provide job tenure and a career path. Funding insecurity is a very real deterrent and is something that the system must address.

Efficacy of the Networks

The advantages of the approach are perhaps best demonstrated through its achievements. Since its inception, these have included:

- Development of recommended practice standards
- Production of *Partners,* a training package on recommended practices in family-centered early childhood intervention, which has been distributed nationally and internationally

- Implementation of a statewide training program that uses the *Partners* training package and is conducted by professionals and parents for professionals and parents to enhance collaboration and improve the quality of service delivery
- Provision of the Early Childhood Intervention Infoline (run by the New South Wales chapter of ECIA), which is a telephone service for those interested in the location of services throughout the state
- Production of the Procedures Manual, which assists committees in their work through the ECICP

These are the tangible products that have arisen from the project as of 2003. Less easily quantified, but perhaps even more important, are the benefits to families through the improvement in service delivery. Issues for which solutions are still needed include adopting common eligibility criteria, funding requirements, funding cycles, and reporting procedures across the various government funding bodies, as well as addressing the inequity of service provision across regions.

RECOMMENDATIONS FOR
PROFESSIONALS IN OTHER COUNTRIES

Networking is an approach to coordination that has the potential to deliver a consistently high level of service in a timely and cost-effective way. If they are to be successful, however, networks must not be superimposed on the system but, rather, be the framework for it. The difficulties that the ECICP continues to experience result from its dealing with a plethora of funding requirements, different accountability procedures, and inequities in the distribution of services across the state. Linking service accreditation and accountability to the networks would not only ensure their continued relevance but also make them more able to raise the quality of the early childhood intervention services. Networks need more than goodwill to endure and prosper.

CONCLUSION

Early childhood intervention works in Australia largely because of the commitment, dedication, and goodwill of the families and professionals involved. Yet, the professionals are too often confronted with large caseloads, insecure job tenure, and no clear career path. Families can experience difficulties gaining access to and navigating a system whose options can vary greatly both within and between states and territories.

It is doubtful, however, that having a legislative base for the provision of early childhood intervention services would solve all of these difficulties. Rather, what is needed is an acknowledgement of and commitment to the efficacy of early childhood intervention at all levels of government. Furthermore, although additional and adequate funding is critical to the further development of quality services, that will not prove sufficient. The problems that the system is facing are largely due to its complexity and fragmentation. The saying "too many cooks spoil the broth" may aptly describe the system as it currently exists in Australia. The mosaic of services and funding sources that characterize service provision may offer choice and diversity of approaches but can also cause confusion for families, professionals, and governments.

Families consistently state that the most critical issues for them are information and access to and coordination of services. Networks, both formal and informal, provide the most effective means of ensuring that these needs are met. Such networks should also serve to simplify the system, not complicate it. This frees professionals to work with children and their families instead of adding more layers of administrative duties. At their best, networks operate at local levels and not only use community resources but also are part of these resources.

REFERENCES

Ageing and Disability Department. (1999). *Early Childhood Intervention Coordination Program: Procedures manual.* Sydney, Australia: Author.

Ashman, A.F. (1990). Setting a research agenda for the study of intellectual disability in Australia. *Australia and New Zealand Journal of Developmental Disabilities, 16,* 169–172.

Australian Bureau of Statistics. (2001a). *Australia now—A statistical profile: Population: Population distribution.* Retrieved October 2001 from http://www.abs. gov.au/Ausstats/abs%40.nsf/94713ad445ff1425ca25682000192af2/ fe3fa39a5bf5aa5aca256b350010b3fd!OpenDocument

Australian Bureau of Statistics. (2001b). *Australian statistics—Main features: 4120.0 Disability and handicap, Australia.* Retrieved October 2001 from http:// www.abs.gov.au/Ausstats/abs%40.nsf/b06660592430724fca2568b 5007b8619/1618215db8a5c6abca25692d0083019d!OpenDocument

Australian Bureau of Statistics. (2001c). *Australian statistics—Main features: 3230.0 Experimental estimates of the Aboriginal and Torres Strait Islander population, 30 June 1991–30 June 1996.* Retrieved October 2001 from http://www. abs.gov.au/Ausstats/abs%40.nsf/b06660592430724fca2568b5007b8619/ e1b3119470f95e02ca2568a900139384!OpenDocument

Australian Bureau of Statistics. (2001d). *Australian statistics—Main features: 3412.0 Migration, Australia.* Retrieved October 2001 from http://www.abs. gov.au/Ausstats/abs%40.nsf/b06660592430724fca2568b5007b8619/ 2c6d9db6b7ef7c97ca2568a9001393d5!OpenDocument

Beamish, W., & Bryer, F. (1999). Practitioners and parents have their say about best practice: Early intervention in Queensland. *International Journal of Disability, Development and Education, 46*(2), 261–278.

Bittman, M., & Pixley, J. (1997). *The double life of the family: Myth, hope and experience.* St. Leonards, New South Wales: Allen & Unwin.

Blainey, G. (1982). *The tyranny of distance: How distance shaped Australia's history* (Rev. ed.). New York: Macmillan.

Campbell, J. (1997). The next step: Parent perspectives of transition to preschool of children with disabilities. *Australian Journal of Early Childhood, 22*(3), 30–34.

Dempsey, I., & Carruthers, A. (1997). How family-centered are early intervention services? Staff and parent perceptions. *Journal of Australian Research in Early Childhood Education, 1,* 105–110.

Early Childhood Intervention Australia. (2000). *Code of ethics.* Brisbane, Australia: Author.

Foreman, P. (1992). Services to children with intellectual disability in New South Wales government schools: Parental perceptions. *Australasian Journal of Special Education, 16*(2), 3–12.

Linfoot, K. (1992). The delivery of early intervention services for infants and preschool children: A 10 year retrospective. *Australasian Journal of Special Education, 16*(1), 42–47.

McAlpine, E., & Johnston, C. (1993). The role of early intervention. In C. Johnston (Ed.), *Does this child need help? Identification and early intervention* (pp. 43–68). Sydney, Australia: Australian Early Intervention Association (New South Wales Chapter).

Office on Disability. (1995). *Disability direction: Tomorrow's blueprint. Final Report.* Sydney, Australia: Author.

Press, F., & Hayes, A. (2000). *OECD thematic review of early childhood education and care policy: Australian background report.* Canberra: Commonwealth Government of Australia.

Reedman, L. (2000). Beside the Arafura Sea: A case study of supportive early childhood intervention in a remote location in the Northern Territory of Australia. Supporting not controlling: Strategies for the new millennium. In *Proceedings of the 4th Biennial National Conference of Early Childhood Intervention Australia* (pp. 177–183). Brisbane, Queensland: Early Childhood Intervention Australia.

Treloar, R. (Ed.). (1997). *Recommended practices in family-centred early intervention.* Sydney, Australia: Ageing and Disability Department.

Turnbull, A.P., & Turnbull, H.R. (1990). *Families, professionals, and exceptionality: A special partnership* (2nd ed.). Columbus, OH: Charles E. Merrill.

CHAPTER 14

Supporting the Early Intervention Team

Franz Peterander

GERMANY

Zwischen zu früh und zu
spät liegt ein Augenblick.

A moment lies between too early and
too late. (Franz Werfel, 1890–1945)

Early childhood intervention was established in Germany in 1970 and is a well-recognized system of early help for children with disabilities. The concept of the early intervention centers is to offer a wide spectrum of help—based on family-oriented, interdisciplinary, and holistic treatment—for children from birth to school age. The aim is that any actual or potential disability is diagnosed as soon as possible and that individual intervention compensates for or minimizes the disability. In Germany, *early intervention* is a generic term for the diagnosis and treatment of children, for parental counseling, and for cooperation between the different institutions that are involved in a child's therapy. The system of early intervention is primarily concerned with the initial interdisciplinary process and final diagnosis and with educational, psychological, and medical/therapeutic help. It is further concerned with establishing cooperation with the child's family and with others involved in the family's immediate environment with the aim of improving the environment for a child who has a disability or is at risk for developing one. The professions involved work on an interdisciplinary basis and collaborate with additional services and institutions, such as independent physicians and therapists and heilpedagogic centers (centers with highly qualified educational personnel who receive an additional year of special training in pedagogics and medicine at a special academy). The early intervention centers offer outpatient treatment as well as home visits.

The concept of early intervention as a holistic approach cannot possibly be implemented to the required standard by individual specialists. Teamwork is essential as the background against which questions and answers from individual specialists in various fields converge, developing the details into an integrated picture. Each person complements the other, because no individual has a complete overview of an entire case. Such cooperation between experts requires an exchange of views and ideas on the individual case; agreement on conceptual basic issues, values, aims, specialized fields, and organizational issues; and agreement on forms of communication within the team.

The therapeutic benefits of teamwork are evident in the development or implementation of new ideas and stimulation and in the exchange among the relevant experts. Therapists involved also develop an awareness of different approaches. Furthermore, they realize that responsibility is shared and that the quality of their work in early intervention and in parental cooperation will no doubt improve.

This chapter was sponsored by the Bavarian State Ministry of Labor and Social Affairs, Women and Family Affairs, by the Bavarian State Ministry of Education and Cultural Affairs, and the Federal Ministry of Education and Research.

 ## SARAH'S STORY ——————————————————————

Sarah was born premature as a triplet in the 28th week of pregnancy. One of the other infants died in a week. When Sarah and her sister Barbara were 8 months old, they were referred to the early intervention center by the family's pediatrician. They have been receiving treatment at the local early intervention center. For a long time, their treatment focused on swallowing difficulties. For Sarah, intervention also has focused on severe spastic paralysis (tetraparesis), particularly in her legs, and generally delayed development.

Sarah's family lives in its own house in a small town where the early intervention center is located. Her father is a self-employed locksmith; her mother no longer works because she cares for her daughters at home. Sarah's parents wanted children, but her mother was not able to conceive until she received hormone treatments. The death of one of the triplets and of Sarah's maternal grandmother caused the parents considerable emotional strain. This was further aggravated by the infants' severe feeding problems and Sarah's disability.

Certain aspects of intervention specifically focus on Sarah's needs. Since March 1999, Sarah has been receiving physiotherapy in the home for spastic paralysis (60 minutes per session, once per week). In addition, since March 2000, remedial therapy has been given every 2 weeks. These sessions focus on nutrition and social and emotional development. Sarah also attends therapeutic swimming classes once per week.

Other aspects of intervention are geared toward the family. Initially, Sarah's parents were given 6 months of support and assistance by a specially trained social worker from the community's general social services. She spent 5 hours in the home each day. In particular, the social worker helped feed Sarah and Barbara. During the entire course of intervention, Sarah's mother also has received counseling in the family home, which Sarah's father attends sometimes. The aim of this assistance is to help the parents to cope with their child's disability and the resulting intensive care that is needed.

Interdisciplinary cooperation among specialists is a key part of the intervention. At the early intervention center, the physiotherapist, remedial teacher, psychologist, and orthopedist all work closely together. As needs arise, the team meets to discuss them. At least every 4 months, the intervention is evaluated on the basis of progress in Sarah's development. The supply of devices, such as leg splints to help her walk, is secured by specialists from an orthopedic clinic.

For almost 3 years, Sarah received physiotherapy each week at the early intervention center. Now, a year later, intervention also includes remedial heilpedagogic therapy and, occasionally, supervision of the therapists by a psychologist.

Sarah has made obvious developmental progress regarding her spastic paralysis, but further intervention is necessary. Her parents are now in a better position to address Sarah's disability and the family's difficult emotional situations. As a result, interaction and communication between mother and child has improved during feeding.

All intervention and counseling has been provided to the family free of charge. Physiotherapy is classified as medical treatment and is covered by the family's health insurance. Remedial heilpedagogic therapy and supervision by the psychologist are paid for by the family's local social services, as stipulated in the German Federal Social Security Act, articles 39 and 40. Most of the costs for parental counseling are also covered by local social services. The institution responsible for the early intervention center (a nationwide charity run by the Protestant Church) bears all remaining expenses.

NATIONAL CONTEXT

Germany is a federal and democratic social state based on the rule of law, as well as an industrial state taking part in the global economy. With 82 million inhabitants, it is the most populous country in Europe. The constitution ("Basic Law") is the basis of all legislation, hence also for the entire educational and social system. In 1994, the German Basic

Law was changed and extended by the addition of article 3, paragraph 3, sentence 2: "No one may be discriminated against on account of their disability." The federal-level Ministry of Education and Science is the department concerned with education and training for vocational and academic purposes. It also finances projects on a federal level (in the areas of preschool, school, higher education, and inclusion for people with disabilities in the labor market) and represents Germany abroad in the field of educational issues. However, it is not the political agency responsible for schools and preschools in general. The 16 federal states have sole responsibility of this educational sphere.

The right of children with disabilities to receive education and training appropriate to their needs is covered by the state constitutions, and more detailed provisions are set out by the states' educational legislation. To assist the ministries in their work, the states established their own research institutes for school and higher education. The 16 ministries of education have established the Standing Conference of Ministers of Education and Cultural Affairs (Kultusministerkonferenz, or KMK) to coordinate education policies, deal with supraregional cultural policy matters (with the aim of forming a common viewpoint and will), and represent common interests. Resolutions passed by the KMK are considered recommendations until they are enacted as binding legislation by the parliaments of each state. These recommendations are the basis for developments in the different states and influence the inclusion policy, the laws, the curricula, the change of paradigm, and the definition of special educational needs.

People and Culture

Christianity has had a long, formative influence on Germany. The south of the country is mainly Catholic; the north, mainly Protestant. In the east, which formed the German Democratic Republic (DDR) before reunification in 1990, the majority of the 16 million inhabitants are not members of any church. There are also about 8 million immigrants in Germany, making up approximately 30% of the population in the highly urbanized regions and far exceeding this figure in certain neighborhoods. Three million of these people are Muslims, mostly from Turkey, making Islam the third-largest religion in Germany. As in other European countries, there is a great deal of debate regarding the integration of foreign children into kindergarten and school life. The aim is to enable them, through additional language tutoring and education, to take an active part in society.

The federal state of Bavaria, whose system of early childhood intervention is the focus of this chapter, has a population of more than 12 million. It is positioned in the south of Germany, north of the Alps,

and borders Austria, Switzerland, and the Czech Republic. Munich is
the capital city of Bavaria. Since the 1960s, Bavaria has developed from
an agricultural state to an industrialized, modern, high-tech region; it
is one of the most financially powerful states in Germany. Yet, even
in 2003, it is deeply rooted in its traditions.

Educational Services Systems

The school system in Germany is organized both horizontally and verti-
cally. Children start school at the age of 6 years. After 4 years of primary
schooling, the system divides into four types of school: 5 years of general
secondary schooling or 6 years of intermediate schooling; 9 years of
grammar school or a nonselective comprehensive school, which both
lead to university level education. Although details differ, this is the
basic pattern for all 16 states. There also are schools for special education. Special education in the states was developed and organized by
several decisions adopted by the KMK, particularly the March 1972
Recommendations on the Organization of Special Education (Empfeh-
lungen für die Organisation der Sonderpädagogik) and Recommendations for all types of Special Schools (Förderschulen).

The situation as of 2003 results from the decisions made in May
1994. The aim is to create equal opportunities for people with disabilities
by developing a better standard of special educational support in special
schools as well as in general education schools. In the years up to 1999,
the KMK enacted Recommendations for the Emphasis of Individual
Educational Report (Förderschwerpunkte) regarding learning, speech,
socioemotional development, cognitive development, physical development, hearing, vision, autism, and chronic illness. These recommendations can be retrieved (in German) from http://www.KMK.org. As
of 2003, it is agreed that schooling's aim is full social (and later, professional) inclusion for people with disabilities. However, the different
states have different positions as to how these aims are to be reached—
through special education schools or in general education schools with
both children who have disabilities and children who do not have
disabilities.

At the age of 3 years, children are entitled kindergarten placement,
and children born with disabilities have a legal right to immediate early
intervention. The foundation for interdisciplinary early intervention is
principally the guidelines laid down in articles 39 and 40, subsection
1, number 2a of the German Federal Social Security Act and in article
30 of the 9th code of Social Law. This statutory basis is geared toward
helping children with disabilities from birth to school age, regardless
of the type and degree of disability. Article 39, 2 of the Federal Social

Security Act makes provision for intervention for those children who are at risk for developing disabilities—that is, preventive treatment if development is threatened.

KEY FEATURES OF EARLY INTERVENTION

The system of early identification and intervention in Germany comprises various services and institutions. In addition to interdisciplinary early intervention centers and socio-pediatric centers, the system also includes special kindergartens, educational and family counseling centers, heilpedagogic day centers, socio-psychiatric services, and independent physicians and psychotherapists. Early Identification and Early Intervention of Children with Disabilities, a report by educator Otto Speck (1973) that was commissioned by the German Board of Education, gave the impetus for the establishment of a comprehensive system of interdisciplinary early intervention. This report recommended regional, family-oriented, and interdisciplinary early intervention centers. It also formulated the basic principles of interdisciplinary early intervention. This expert report led to the establishment of the first interdisciplinary early intervention centers in Bavaria in October 1974, which were founded with the support of the Bavarian Ministry of Science, Education and Cultural Affairs. Sohns noted, "Since that time, Bavaria has held a leading position in the field of early intervention in Germany" (2000, p. 330).

Organization and the Need for Intervention

More than 1,000 institutions in Germany offer early intervention for children with disabilities. These early intervention centers are mainly run by major national charities such as Caritas, Diakonie, Paritätischer Wohlfahrtsverband, and Lebenshilfe. The systems of early intervention vary from one federal state to another, making it impossible to offer detailed statistical data regarding the need for early intervention and the number of children receiving treatment in Germany. For example, in Bavaria 4% of children up to the age of 3 years need early intervention. In 2002, 123 regional early intervention centers in Bavaria provided a well-established network of early help within easy reach for everybody; no early intervention center is further away than 10 kilometers for any family. This system provides treatment to 25,000 infants and young children, of which 50% are center outpatients and 50% receive early intervention from mobile teams at home.

Children receiving early intervention services have various disabilities: perceptual disorders, partial impairment of certain faculties, behavior problems, speech disorders, severe motor disorders (e.g., cerebral paresis), visual impairments, hearing impairments. One third of the children have severe cognitive or physical disabilities. The average age is 3–4 years, and 60% are boys. Approximately 14% (more than 25% in urban areas) of children receiving services are immigrants (Sohns, 2000). Treatment is given according to the individual need—generally, one or two sessions per week. Children typically receive early intervention for 2 years.

An average of 11 therapists from different fields work together in a team. For instance, a team may consist of educational personnel, a social worker, a special education teacher, a psychologist, an occupational therapist, a physiotherapist, a speech-language therapist, a heilpedagogue, and a pediatrician. The number of people working in one center varies from 5–30; 80% are women. On average, the staff remain in one center for 5.7 years, which means that competent teams can develop in which 20% of staff have worked for longer than 10 years (Peterander & Speck, 1993). This structure ensures to a large extent the continual development of the team's concepts and professional competence.

The centers receive funding for the usual weekly requirement of one or two intervention sessions (either outpatient services or home visits), parental cooperation, interdisciplinary teamwork, and collaboration with partners outside the center (independent therapists, physicians, kindergarten staff). In Bavaria, early intervention is offered free of charge. It is financed by the collaborative work of various bodies, such as municipal authorities; health insurance; the Bavarian Ministry of Science, Education and Cultural Affairs; and the Bavarian Ministry of Social Affairs.

Early intervention is open to anyone. The system attempts to ease parents' apprehensions when they first attend a center, whether they attend because of their own concerns for their child or because of physician referral. The Bavarian system of early intervention is composed of subsystems with a high degree of flexibility, adapting their structure and organization to their environment and the challenges they confront. In the other federal states, the network of interdisciplinary centers is not as well developed. They also have different structures, systems of financing, and facilities.

Diagnosis and Intervention

Diagnosis and intervention are geared solely to the individual needs and the environment of the child. Due to a paradigm shift—from a deficit-oriented and child-oriented approach to holistic, family-oriented early intervention—there is no generally acceptable curriculum. Specialists base their treatment on a combination of the principles and indicators of early intervention that have proven successful, as well as on theoretical and conceptional ideas. For Spodek and Brown (1993) and others, *curriculum* has this wider meaning. Each therapist must work in cooperation with the parents and the interdisciplinary team to develop a course of intervention designed to meet the needs of the child. Standardized programs of early intervention are not used; however, this does not mean that elements of such programs cannot be integrated into an individual course of intervention. Considering this situation, all parties concerned must be highly flexible in their professional work as part of the transdisciplinary teams and be willing to bear a great deal of responsibility.

Diagnosis

Because disabilities or developmental delays often result from complex interactions between biological and psychosocial factors, diagnosis in the field of early intervention is an extremely exacting and complex process. For instance, a problematic family environment can lead to a number of functional deficits that do not appear to be connected in any way with the initial problem. Diagnosis must therefore consider the various paths of development that a disability may take and a multidimensional view of diagnosis and intervention (Peterander, 2003). Standardized systems of classification only take superficial syndromes into consideration and offer little help for the planning of a course of intervention.

Generally, parents are offered the opportunity to speak to counselors before a diagnosis is made. Diagnosis is divided into initial, process, and final stages, covering all dimensions of a child's personality and development. Diagnosis is based on an action and an everyday-life approach, aiming at participation in natural surroundings. Individuals making diagnoses use norm-oriented methods such as standardized screenings, specialized diagnoses, and clinical-psychological development tests to establish the individual problems in a child's development. They use therapeutic-diagnostic methods, including free and hypotheses-based observation of the spontaneous and reactive behavior of the child. Those making diagnoses also integrate single diagnostic findings into a systematic overview that in the last analysis serves as a basis for planning a course of intervention.

The different phases of diagnosis can be broken down into 1) first contact, 2) initial consultation and anamnesis (exploration of the child's history), 3) diagnosis, 4) explanation and counseling diagnostic information, and 5) recommendation for treatment and course of therapy

(Thurmair & Naggl, 2000). It is important to distinguish among types of diagnoses. A *medical diagnosis* is often carried out by independent pediatricians who do not work in the early intervention center. Among other things, the components of medical diagnosis are developmental neurological, general pediatric initial, and accompanying diagnosis; establishment of the indications for medical treatment, with accompanying counseling; and anamnestic discussion with parents or caregiver. A *medical therapeutic diagnosis* comprises physical-therapeutic, occupational-therapeutic, and speech-therapeutic initial and accompanying diagnoses. Also included are an analysis of the child's environment regarding stimulation of physical movement, the child's communicative opportunities and everyday activities, and the child's actual opportunities to act. The *psychological diagnosis* includes recording the child's special developmental problems. Noted in particular are psychological development, diagnosis of early childhood, a neuro-psychological diagnosis, a clinical-psychological diagnosis of atypical development and behavior disorders, and specific indicators of resilience. The *heilpedagogic diagnosis* focuses especially on targeted analysis of the child's environment. The purpose is to determine whether circumstances are conducive to development and to evaluate the child's developmental strengths. Diagnosis is conducted throughout the entire period of early intervention (Pretis, 2001). Since 1994, computer-aided analysis and evaluation programs have been developed for early intervention diagnosis. These ease the specialists' workload and open up new possibilities for diagnosis, diagnostic reports, and expert opinions (Peterander, 2000b). Sharing with parents the diagnosis and intervention recommendations is a particularly sensitive and delicate process, calling for kindness and consideration on the part of the specialist, as the results so often conflict with the parents' hopes and expectations.

Furthering and Therapy

Furthering (i.e., "to rear" or "to educate") and therapy for children are complex interventions. Like diagnosis, they include heilpedagogic, psychological, physician, and medical-therapeutic treatment. Multicausal explanations in early intervention result in multimodal approaches in early intervention. This reflects the necessity of developing interventions based on the individual, as well as varied forms of cooperation with parents and others in the child's environment. "Playful learning," or learning by playing, is given very high priority in this context (Oerter, 1996). Peterander's (2002) analysis of the conditions conducive to effective intervention had the following findings:

- Orient intervention to a child's actions.
- Promote the child's self-initiative and independence.

- Promote the child's well-being.
- Promote the child's attention and motivation.
- Initiate and encourage actions by the child that are rich in meaning.
- Strengthen the child's self-confidence.
- View functional therapy as a way to help develop the child's personality.

Since the 1980s, many concepts and methods for furthering children have been developed (see Shonkoff & Meisels, 2000).

Families' Roles

Early intervention offers parents a variety of opportunities for cooperation. An essential feature of quality early intervention is the conceptual link between the therapeutic services available to the child and the counseling services and the opportunities for cooperation with the parents. In Germany, family-oriented services encompass many areas; for example, initial consultation, discussion with parents, and an explanation of the diagnosis. Discussion and counseling may also be provided regarding the child's developmental process and the process of early intervention. Information is also given regarding the family's general social benefits and financial questions. Instruction for following the intervention in everyday situations is provided as well. If the family faces crises and conflicts, services may include family therapy. Finally, service providers can help the family find additional resources such as self-help groups.

The model of cooperation in partnership that is commonly found in many other European countries is characterized by an interactive reciprocal process of understanding between parents and specialists (Björck-Åkesson & Granlund, 1997; Helios II, 1996). The interventionist's and the parents' knowledge complement each other, resulting in a holistic understanding of the situation and task ahead. Contributions from both sides are equally important for intervention success. This cooperative partnership makes it necessary to consider parents experts, too, and to consider their ideas and expectations. One aim of this approach is to improve the collaborative process. Another aim is to find a basis, underpinned by empirical knowledge, for furthering cooperation. The reciprocal process of the well-being of the child and the parents underlines the importance of cooperation between parents and experts for successful early intervention. An analysis of the relevant literature found various components to be indicators of successful cooperation between experts and parents, including strengthened parental competence and an established dialogue between parents and professionals about the child's intervention (Peterander, 2000a).

Theoretical Influences

Since the 1970s, Germany has seen an essential change in the theoretical and conceptional principles of early intervention (Schlack, 1989; Speck & Warnke, 1983). Initially, Germany followed the directive uniform concept (behaviorist learning theories, development therapy, dominance of experts, directive behavioral model of change). Then, it progressed toward interactive concepts (partnership with parents, a true-to-life approach, an emphasis on the child's autonomy) (Speck, 1995). Bronfenbrenner's (1979) systemic-ecological approach greatly influenced these developments in the 1970s and still influences early intervention in Germany today. Bronfenbrenner contended that a person's individual genetic potential can only develop in an environment that is conducive to the individual's development. This assumption led to a paradigm shift regarding the significance of parents in early intervention. They were no longer seen as laymen or used as co-therapists; instead, they were increasingly viewed as partners with the early intervention team.

A systemic-oriented theory of development assumes a dynamic interaction of different factors on various system levels (Guralnick, 2001; Sameroff & Fiese, 2000; Simeonsson, 2000). According to this thinking, a child's development does not take the course of a continual process (Largo, 1993). Rather, sudden spurts in a child's development occur that can be categorized as processes of self-organization. Biopsychosocial models are becoming increasingly important (Ramey & Landesman Ramey, 1998). It has been found that the developmental stage in which synapses are formed is a critical period. In this time, the fetus reacts with neural plasticity in response to certain environmental influences (Nelson, 2000). Critical periods, which can vary in duration from one area of the brain to another, can be seen as a biological presetting to learn from certain experiences. Thus, there are developmental stages in which specific experiences are of particular relevance for the formation of neuronal structures; these, in turn, form the basis for learning (Farran, 2001). Contrary to earlier assumptions on rigid critical phases, the biopsychosocial models stress the significance of dynamic interchange between the individual and the environment. Concepts based on the results of long-term studies on risk and protection factors, vulnerability, and resilience play a vital role in explaining the developmental processes in childhood (Clarke & Clarke, 2000; Werner & Smith, 1992).

Principles

The change in the theoretical concepts is also reflected in the principles that underlie the practice of early childhood intervention in Germany.

The Holistic Approach   Intervention for a child with disabilities cannot simply start at the child's "deficits" but must include the child's whole personality with all of its strengths and weaknesses. This means that in addition to functional aspects (motor, sensory, cognitive, emotional, speech-language), the interactions among various aspects (medical, psychological, heilpedagogic, social) must be considered for each child and family.

Family Orientation   Germany's systemic-ecological orientation of early intervention makes it necessary to include the family in early intervention. Parents are seen as the most important partners in this process. The professionals with their expert knowledge and the parents with their varied experiences in daily life with their child, as well as the expectations they place in the experts, determine the quality of cooperation and the success of intervention (Peterander, 2000a).

Regional and Mobile Early Intervention   Early intervention close to home cuts hours of traveling and makes it easier to further a child's development in a natural environment. As a rule, 50% of early intervention is covered by interventionists visiting families. According to a comprehensive study, nearly 70% of early intervention staff consider mobile treatment the most important part of Germany's early intervention system (Peterander & Speck, 1993). Parents see mobile therapy in the same positive light (Peterander, 2000a).

Interdisciplinary Teamwork   The individuality of children and the complexity of their disabilities or delays require intensive interdisciplinary cooperation. Various professionals are involved in making a diagnosis, establishing the plan for furthering, and fostering intervention progress. Regional early intervention centers have multidisciplinary staff and work together on an inter- and transdisciplinary basis. This system facilitates the exchange of information among team members and makes feedback and mutual supervision possible. Thus, team meetings become forms of internal in-service training.

Networks   Prior to, during, and after treatment, early intervention centers collaborate with a number of institutions and private practices that are also involved with the child. Information is gained to make recommendations concerning further assistance, such as helping the family choose a suitable school for the child.

Social Inclusion   Early intervention should ease children's inclusion in their families and the social surroundings in which they live, play, and learn. As a preventive system, early intervention has to promote childhood skills so that the children with disabilities can be fully included in general education schools. An additional essential goal is the intensive public relations work of the early intervention field to create positive social environments for children with disabilities. Aside from its importance in Germany, this topic is being discussed in depth on a European level (Helios II, 1996; Soriano, 1998).

Political Influences

Since 1999, early intervention in Germany has faced numerous challenges because of new legislation regarding quality assurance in social institutions (Federal Social Security Act, article 93). To qualify for funding, each center must present a comprehensive account that gives quality assurance. Documentation and the evaluation of social work have been increasingly discussed since the introduction of this new legislation. Funding for social issues is becoming more stringent; therefore, innovation is a must in early intervention. What interventionists need is new answers to old questions, such as "How can we develop the quality and competence of social services?" Since the late 1990s, Germany's early intervention field has seen the publication of numerous manuals on quality management, which are intended to support a long-standing process of quality development in the institutions. An example is Arbeitsstelle Frühförderung Bayern (1999), a unit created especially for the promotion of early intervention in Bavaria. For the first time, concepts and methods for quality assurance and management in early intervention have been taken from business administration (see Donabedian, 1982).

Cultural Influences

Social reality governs to a large extent the developments in social welfare. This was applied when early intervention was initiated in the 1970s, when supporting children with disabilities became a priority. A general atmosphere of optimism prevailed. At the time, three things facilitated the establishment of a comprehensive early intervention system in Germany. First was the discussion about equal opportunities in the educational system. Then, the new behavior modification approach took it for granted that human behavior could be changed swiftly (Eysenck & Rachman, 1972). Finally, recognizing the significance of the ecological context for a child's development served as a theoretical basis for numerous practical innovations (Bronfenbrenner, 1979). The fact that financial resources were available in Germany in the mid-1970s made it possible to develop the present-day system of early intervention.

Since the 1990s, the social context in Germany has changed significantly. The atmosphere of optimism is largely a thing of the past. The belief that it is possible to effect changes in behavior quickly has dwindled to insignificance. The financial clout of the government has been replaced by a severe lack of funds, especially since the German reunification of 1990. To add to this, society's split into the "haves" and the "have-nots" has—for whatever reason—progressed dramatically. In 2003, Germans find themselves in a painful process of social change. Therefore, it is hardly surprising that for many children, growing up has become more of a risk. An increasing number of German and (at a disproportionate rate) foreign families depend on social security and/ or live in poverty with all the accompanying risks to childhood development (Klocke & Hurrelmann, 1995). At the beginning of the 21st century, there is much talk of a new poverty in Germany. Early intervention, also intended as a preventive measure to help children at risk, is more critical than ever.

SUPPORTING THE EARLY INTERVENTION TEAM

Work in the team is one of the most important aspects in early intervention. This leads to the question of under what circumstances people can work to their utmost and still be content. Certain criteria must be met for top performance and contentment in the team: pursuit of joint and clearly defined targets, a common understanding of the targets, positive working relationships and intense team spirit, exchange of positive feelings, and the ability to express negative feelings and to cope with them (Block, 2000). There is no doubt that the constructive use of an interdisciplinary team's resources contributes significantly to the quality and effectiveness of treatment at the early intervention centers (Guralnick, 1997). Early intervention teamwork aims can take many forms:

- Establishing the team setting (e.g., place and time of meetings)
- Determining which forms of team work to use—subject-related work groups (questions on diagnosis, therapy, evaluation, and documentation) or workshops (further development of the working concepts, the organization, and the team)
- Taking action to qualify team members (e.g., through in-service training)
- Developing a team culture (e.g., mutual appreciation)

Quality of Teamwork in Bavaria

The importance of teamwork in early intervention, and its effects on the work of team members, was analyzed in a study covering more than 90 centers in Bavaria (Peterander & Speck, 1993). The purpose of the study was to highlight conditions that impair or enhance teamwork. It was intended to establish an empirical basis for the further development of teamwork (Peterander, 1996). After discussing some of the study's results, this chapter discusses how each team member's expertise and team cooperation can be enhanced—particularly how all of this is implemented in Bavaria's early intervention system.

Aspects of a Positive Team Climate

Overall, professionals in Bavaria view the team climate in their centers positively (this is more likely the case in centers that are predominantly staffed by women). They feel recognized by their colleagues and see evidence of interdisciplinary cooperation in the team. The professionals surveyed said that their teams largely agree on early intervention concepts but that different opinions are accepted. Criticism can be voiced openly. In addition, the whole team plans and allocates the work, with work being distributed equally and carried out faithfully. They also encourage each other in difficult work situations. Even members' private problems can be addressed within the team.

Positive team climate is often conditioned by other organizational and personnel variables. First, a positive team atmosphere reflects the good professional and emotional relationships among the team members. In the same manner, a positive climate in the team is conducive to the emotional well-being of the staff. Good leadership is important—survey respondents cited the team leader's skills as something particularly positive. Individual team members also believe that they can influence conceptual and personnel decisions, yet seldom find themselves under pressure to succeed.

The professional competence of all team members is especially respected and appreciated, and the team's overall work is considered high quality. The study found that in a positive team climate, weekly team sessions planned in a way that allows team members to receive internal in-service training and/or advice for specific cases. In addition, the team members can draw expertise and strength from other team members in carrying out particular intervention aspects. Furthermore, a high standard of teamwork in early intervention is indicated by members being convinced of their position, being established in their profession, being guided by a clear idea of their work, and having many years of experience.

Aspects of a Negative Team Climate

Negative conditions are not per se the opposite of a positive climate in a team. The team climate is seen as negative if the experts have too little time for team sessions and if there are too few discussions of individual cases. As a result, there is a lack of communication about diagnostic intervention topics. Further reasons for a negative team climate in a team are vague definitions of responsibility, team conflicts that are ignored, poor management in early intervention centers, fruit-less team discussions, lack of team support for individual members when professional problems arise, tension among various professions in the team, the dominant position of certain members, and an excessive workload.

A negative climate in a team is also the result of organizational and personnel variables. There is a significant correlation with poor team leadership and a lack of individual team member independence in certain decisions. If members leave an institution, the reasons are more likely due to a negative climate. This can include dissatisfaction with the center's public relations work, unsatisfactory team sessions, and the lack of frequent in-service training. Survey respondents also considered several team sessions per week negative, as well as large teams (20–30 members). Professionals in negative team climates often found themselves under too much pressure to succeed and having problems meeting their professional commitments. This affects emotional well-being, which can in some cases lead to depression.

Content and Quality of Team Sessions

Team sessions are central to inter- and transdisciplinary cooperation in the centers. In addition to their informative function, they are particularly relevant for the professional relationships between the team members. In no other work situation do the professionals communicate with each other so intensely as in such a structured situation. In no other situation do they receive so much information about colleagues' competence and expectations and methods for a particular child's intervention. Dynamic interactive processes dominate each member's daily experience and have a bearing on his or her professional actions. The success of team sessions also depends on where and when they are held. Generally, there is a weekly 2-hour team session. On average, 11 members from different professions attend the weekly session.

There is a marked discrepancy between subjects that team members consider important and how frequently this topic is actually addressed in the session. Fortunately, the most common topic (the systematic presentation and discussion of individual cases) is also what team members consider the most important topic. Yet, other topics team members consider very important are dealt with less frequently. For instance, there is very little mutual supervision in the team sessions, whereas a majority of team members said that they would welcome this. Contrary to the wishes of the members, there are few discussions about research findings on particular disabilities, and only rarely do members demonstrate diagnostic therapeutic methods in sessions.

Team Leaders

Team leaders not only influence the content of the work, but also to a large extent they bear the responsibility for intervention organization and motivation. The characteristics of positive leadership are numerous. Systematic coordination and organization of the work, recognition of team members' achievements, and joint decision making in important cases are all important. Survey respondents also said that members can rely on a good leader in difficult situations and look to the leader as an example who is always ready to motivate his or her colleagues. Good team leaders also make clear decision and contribute new ideas.

Positive leadership greatly influences the quality and the form of cooperation among the team members. It has a positive impact on the development of high-quality organizational structures, public relations work, in-service training, the form and content of team sessions, and on the general well-being of the team members. Clear leadership in early intervention centers also has a positive influence on interdisciplinary dialogue and group dynamics. It enhances the competence and professionalism of individual colleagues, as well as the team's levels of openness and energy. Finally, it improves the flow of information that is so important to the centers' networking. Thus, in the future, there is a particular need to train leaders for their specific responsibilities as head of a center. This requirement must be given priority in modern curricula for preservice and in-service training in the social professions, as has long been done in preparation for those in the organizational psychology and business administration fields (Rosenstiel, Regnet, & Domsch, 1999).

Approaches to Team Development

Despite the unquestioned importance of teamwork for early intervention, the courses of study at German colleges and universities do not provide any special training for teamwork competence. Seldom is there an opportunity to bring students of various disciplines together so they can learn and test teamwork skills. Steps in this direction have been taken in the United States (Winton, 1991). Certain U.S. colleges and universities offer an additional course in which students from different fields are taught by an interdisciplinary team of lecturers from various faculties. In this way, students can begin preparation for their future roles and tasks in interdisciplinary teams (Bailey, 1996).

The common ground regarding creative and productive teamwork should be that the members of the team have at least some knowledge about different teamwork models; factors influencing teamwork; and strategies in decision making, problem solving, and conflict management. Team members must be willing and able to take an active part in shaping the dynamic process of teamwork. Garland and Frank (1997) gave a detailed survey of the development of effective strategies of teamwork in U.S. early intervention. They concluded, "Building skills in teamwork at both the preservice and the in-service levels is the prerequisite for the changes in early intervention service delivery that will result in coordinated, collaborative, family-centered teams" (p. 378).

Discussions in the United States make it clear that the extent of teamwork structure and content depends on the legal, cultural, and social framework on which an early intervention system is based. Looking at early intervention in Bavaria raises some teamwork questions that point in a different direction. Due to structural conditions, teamwork in early intervention centers has been given priority from the start. That is, the 123 independent early intervention centers in themselves form 123 multidisciplinary "teams" in which, based on the holistic approach of furthering, experts often work together in the same environment and with the same colleagues for years. The members of one center form a multidisciplinary group, which also is led by an early intervention specialist. Such a group alone is not an actual team. What needs to be added is a structure that to a large extent is nonhierarchical and that encourages common aims, intensive interactive relationships, and team spirit. Yet, this is already present in early intervention in Bavaria. In addition, the previously mentioned working principles make it necessary for each center to want to reflect and systemically develop the process of team development.

However, team development is a demanding business. It concerns all individuals working in the field of early intervention, regarding their competence and intentions, and it has far-reaching consequences for the organization of and concepts in early intervention centers. If a center decides to develop a team, then it must also decide to develop personnel and organization. When some aims of a team's further development are achieved, intervention quality and cooperation with parents will improve, as will the situation among team members. To a growing extent, they can identify with their actions and are proud of what they have achieved. They have cut out a field for themselves in which joint learning and acting both within the center and outside the center is possible and visible.

In addition to the initiative and efforts of the individual team members and leaders, teams also need continual support from outside. The legal framework in Germany guarantees the centers the independence that they require. The teams are also given support at various levels. There is a federal association of interdisciplinary early intervention with a branch in each state. This association organizes a conference every 2 years, whereas the state associations offer additional seminars. Since 1982, the quarterly journal *Frühförderung interdisziplinär* has been available, which focuses on current issues in early intervention from a scientific and practically oriented view.

In Bavaria, team members can also turn to the Bavarian Support Center for Early Intervention (Arbeitsstelle Frühförderung) for additional help and consulting on specific issues. Bavaria was the first state to establish such an Arbeitsstelle in 1975, which acts as a model for the other states. It comprises a pedagogic and medical department, each with staff members from various professions working in close cooperation. The common aims are to expand on the knowledge of early intervention, to help develop practical work, to promote exchange and discussion between the various early intervention centers, and to improve the quality of work and interdisciplinary exchanges. With this in view, the Arbeitsstelle offers a wide and varied selection of in-service training, as well as individual consultancy services for the Bavarian early intervention centers.

Learning in the Team

Teamwork depends on the ability to work in collaboration and the ability to learn in and with the team. Each member benefits regarding his or her own professional, methodological, and social competence. The team must be able to learn from teamwork. *Learning* is generally understood to mean the acquisition of expertise to improve future professional actions. Early intervention professionals gain new knowledge during their everyday work, which makes them experts in their field. Without teamwork, colleagues would not have this essential knowledge at their disposal. As team members tend to have different goals, it must be possible to fine-tune the various contributions and to revise one's own original position. It is important that contradictory information and deviating views are accepted and discussed. This is a vital step toward learning through organization. Organizational learning is one of the most important aims of knowledge management; this is also becoming increasingly important in social institutions (Reinmann-Rothmeier & Mandl, 2000). Only after as much knowledge has been compiled as possible through communication can new common approaches and perspectives be developed.

Basic Course for Early Interventionists

The Arbeitsstelle in Munich offers basic courses for the introduction and the training of therapists who are new in the field. They last 1 year and include 13 days of in-service training, to be conducted by the experts from the Arbeitsstelle and by guest speakers. The courses cover the whole process of early intervention from the initial contact with parents and child to the completion of intervention. The course focuses on

- Help for the child (diagnosis, individual intervention needs, toys and equipment, medical-therapeutic and pedagogic-psychological aspects)
- Cooperation with the parents (professional counseling, additional advice through discussion, organization of the intervention process)
- Cooperation among the experts (consultation with colleagues, inter-disciplinary exchanges)

Internal Continuing Professional Development

In more than half the early intervention centers in Bavaria, ongoing internal training is particularly significant for the quality of teamwork. These events are often organized in the form of workshops on particular subjects, which are given by the center, by guest speakers, and, to a limited extent, by the head of the center. It is a sign of the center's quality if the weekly team sessions also serve as internal in-service training; the same applies to the frequency of such sessions. The results of the study in Bavaria show, for instance, that the members of these centers have more influence on personnel and conceptional decisions, are able to read specialized literature during working hours, and focus on public relations and contacts with other social institutions in the region. Again, this positive atmosphere directly affects the personal situation of the staff—namely, they are more likely to have a clear standpoint regarding their professional identity and are strongly committed to their work.

Quality Circles

Quality circles can also serve as a framework for the further development of teamwork. This is a way to use the knowledge and expertise of those who are directly involved in the process of early intervention to solve problems and find ways of achieving intervention goals. Working in a quality circle means not only solving problems, giving answers, and acquiring expert knowledge, but also developing methodological and social competence. A quality circle is a group of 4–8 specialists who do similar work in the centers. They meet at regular intervals, such as 2–3 hours every week. A moderator is elected within the group to chair the discussions, or a moderator is invited from outside. The purpose is to work on a problem defined by the group; to analyze mistakes and problems; to develop, record, and implement solutions; and to evaluate the extent to which aims and solutions have been realized. Research has shown that this procedure not only results in improved methods or the answers, but also improves communication, motivation, and satisfaction among staff.

In addition, the quality circle enhances the professional and social qualifications of participants and promotes successful work, which then boosts team culture. Bungard (1999) gave the following sample procedures for a quality circle:

1. Define the topic.
2. Analyze the status quo.
3. Define goals and problems.
4. Set goals and requirements.
5. Discuss expectations.
6. Work out solutions gradually.
7. Give everybody an opportunity to contribute.
8. Implement solutions and evaluate outcomes.

Consulting Sessions for Colleagues

Consultation for colleagues in early intervention—especially in the form of team discussion regarding particular children's situations—is seen as a generally recognized and highly valued part of team development. Teams may need outside support, as the implementation of these complex tasks is not easy. Problems lie in the structure of this process and in negative experiences from previous discussions with colleagues. This situation is being addressed with a mobile, 1-day, in-service training session to be held at each early intervention center in Bavaria. On the one hand, this approach offers the opportunity to talk about individual situations—that is, learning by doing. On the other hand, it allows staff to learn a simple process for use in everyday work. The case-oriented consulting sessions are open to all topics that arise in the course of an intervention process (e.g., ways of facilitating an intervention, ways to promote cooperation with the family).

Leadership Guidance

The demands placed on anyone responsible for management and leadership of an early intervention center have become increasingly complex and challenging. The purpose of offering guidance is to enable the team leader to see management and leadership as an opportunity to shape and develop the team. Leadership is seen as a service to the team members as individuals and to the team as a whole. This guidance provides the basis for developing various models and viewpoints of leadership. It also offers ways of solving problems, shaping team interactions, and further developing early intervention concepts. Various topics could be at the center of leadership guidance, such as levels of leadership, quality management, and cooperation among the team. These guidance sessions are offered by the Arbeitsstelle on an individual or group (3–6 participants) basis.

Concepts Guidance

The wide variety of services offered by the early intervention centers, as well as the individual needs of children and families, require well–thought out concepts and clear goal setting. The further development of early intervention concepts has increasingly become a challenge for early interventionists as new standards and conditions emerge. The validity of old concepts has to be checked regularly; new developments and changes in target groups, the regulatory framework, and basic conditions are to be considered. An important step toward reviewing concepts is an assessment of previous work and an evaluation of past cases. Conceptual development enhances the interventionists' motivation to further develop their competence and to secure a modern standard. Most Bavarian early intervention centers conduct yearly concept seminars. All team members attend the 2- to 3-day seminars, which are often held at a venue other than the center.

Mobile Day Seminars

The Arbeitsstelle offers its training seminars on fixed dates, but individual centers also have the opportunity to arrange flexible sessions. Many topics were offered in this format during the first 6 months of 2002. Examples include support for premature infants and their parents, poverty as a developmental risk, and ways to initiate and support parent self-help groups and quality development at the early intervention center (quality of structure, process, and results).

Working Groups

Various regional working groups offer support for the team in each of the seven districts in Bavaria. In turn, these groups are given organizational support by the Arbeitsstelle. The purpose is to provide 1-day meetings, during which staff receive help specific to their profession.

Twice per year, "Round-Table Talks" are held. Attendees include representatives from the bodies that run the early intervention centers (charitable organizations), those responsible for funding, representatives of the state association for early intervention in Bavaria, and those in charge of the Arbeitsstelle. During these talks, financing, further development of early intervention, and all current issues relating to the organization are addressed. The purpose is to clarify any possible problems through constructive dialogue. Round-Table Talks are also held on a regional basis. These are attended by the individual early intervention centers and institutions that network with them, the local authorities, and interested parents.

Self-Evaluation

One way to improve the quality of early intervention is self-evaluation of specific interventions. Self-evaluation covers and describes the whole process of early intervention and help for the families. It also systematically examines the effects and results of treatment. For this reason, it must be designed in a multidimensional manner. Considering the improved quality of intervention and counseling, self-evaluation offers a good starting point for joint reflection on objective data and has increasingly become a hallmark of modern early intervention in Germany (Weiss, 1999).

The high quality of available information and communication technologies provide a multitude of new possibilities. In the course of research and development in Bavaria, technical terms have been clearly defined and operationalized and diagnosis and analysis programs have been developed that are customized to early intervention centers (Peterander, 2000b). Based on the Münchner Analyse und Lernsystem (MAL) program, this computer-aided self-evaluation system for early intervention has many purposes. For example, it presents and highlights expert knowledge to develop instruments for the self-evaluation of intervention and team processes. In addition, it provides scientific assessment of data with a view of recording and describing the factors that make early intervention effective and successful. It offers analysis of long-term processes as well. Furthermore, the system establishes data pools, specific to early intervention, about individual intervention processes and about the quality of the teams' work. This information can be used as a starting point for Internet-based quality and knowledge management. In the future, these data pools will supply the individual centers, as well as the entire early intervention system in Bavaria, with information for the further development of their concepts and methods.

Making Expert Knowledge Transparent

The system of early intervention has well-trained staff. A great majority of them have many years of experience working with children and parents and have expanded their professional knowledge as well as their practical skills through additional qualifications. These therapists have become experts in their specialized fields. When they leave a system, so does their specific knowledge and experience. No system can afford this or should let it happen. On the one hand, many interventionists do not have access to conventional further training courses. On the other hand, in social institutions, there is an increasing need for new forms of knowledge transfer and utilization of expert knowledge. In industry, this aspect already plays a central role in connection with knowledge management. For this reason, the centers in Bavaria have garnered the specific knowledge of individual "experts" in small groups and made this transparent for team members by integrating it into computer-aided analysis and counseling programs (Peterander, 1996). This process contributes to the professional and conceptional development of teams and the early intervention system.

The Benefits of Teamwork

The numerous advantages of first-class teamwork can be found in various areas of early intervention work. It promotes and stimulates the standard of professional work, team satisfaction, and the personal well-being of the team members, as well as increases parents' degree of satisfaction with early intervention (Garland & Frank, 1997; Peterander & Speck, 1993; Sexton, Snyder, Lobman, Kimbrough, & Matthews, 1997). It is clear that individual intervention benefits accordingly. It is regrettable that this particular, important reciprocal process has not been researched in depth.

The available studies (e.g., Peterander, 2000a) provide evidence of some effects of good interdisciplinary or transdisciplinary teams in early intervention. What is special about these teams is the wide range of their professional thinking and the individual members' professional competence that extends into other fields. In some cases, fewer therapists are needed for a child's intervention or for parental cooperation because individuals are so competent. Their decisions in team sessions, as well as their actions, are well-founded and are readily accepted. Teamwork promotes a new understanding of conflicting opinions among experts, which often occur. In an ideal situation, the team members begin to trust each other more, which, in turn, benefits the early intervention process. Also, communication within the team improves and, consequently, its members observe and register their colleagues' work without passing judgment. Moreover, if the professional opinion of a colleague is assessed, then open communication ensures that the colleagues' values, opinions, and preferences will become transparent. Teamwork also helps members to discuss sensitive issues in a creative, productive, and supportive manner and to find practical solutions. Individual members are then more likely to support such solutions. Parents who work with members of interdisciplinary teams display a high degree of confidence in the intervention. They consider the experts competent and extremely knowledgeable. They also see discussions with these interventionists in a positive light and believe that their child and family benefit from the early intervention work.

RECOMMENDATIONS FOR PROFESSIONALS IN OTHER COUNTRIES

Interdisciplinary teamwork is closely linked with the theoretical foundations, principles, and organizational circumstances of early intervention. If the teamwork and team development described in this chapter are to be transferred to other countries, several structures should be borne in mind.

An ideal starting point to acquire general team-related skills is to expand project-oriented teaching at school. This would give children an opportunity early in life to grasp the basic skills required for successful teamwork. They would also gain experience in this form of learning and solving problems together.

To underpin the acquisition of professional competence for teamwork, multidisciplinary groups should be formed during the early stages of university studies. In Bavaria, students from various fields of study who plan to enter the early intervention field learn together with other faculties. They develop an awareness for differences and an appreciation of an approach that is used in other fields of study. Teaching staff from different faculties must develop an interdisciplinary curriculum and offer such courses in seminars through several university semesters. Such a structure allows an intensive transfer of knowledge between the students of the various faculties and, through project-related and problem-related learning, makes it possible to practice interactions and communication that benefit teamwork.

A learning process focused on teamwork should be backed up on various levels of working life. External courses, covering a longer period of time, must be made available to new early interventionists to underpin the initial experiences of teamwork in the relevant institution. For both new staff and lecturers, these courses should be of a multidisciplinary nature.

A method should be developed for weekly team sessions also to serve as internal further training sessions for interventionists. Important

areas to include are systematic case discussion, a focus on the initial
phase of intervention, diagnosis, therapy, cooperation with parents,
completion of intervention, and evaluation. Applying such discussions
to individual children and families could take the form of a case supervision. Other components might be brief reports from team members
about in-service training and further training courses that they have
attended, as well as about new theoretical and conceptional developments in their relevant fields.

In-service and further training must be available to optimize interdisciplinary teamwork in the field of early intervention. These courses
should be held regularly to broaden specific early intervention knowledge and skills, bearing in mind an individual's own experiences in an
interdisciplinary team.

Conducting day courses is recommended for further training for
all team members. These courses should cover the development of
concepts and their team's organization. It may be advantageous to
engage speakers or moderators from the outside and choose venues
other than the relevant institution. These steps have proved worthwhile
in ensuring a neutral setting that is more conducive to concentrated
work.

Due to the fact that the leadership and management of a team is
a decisive variable in effective interdisciplinary teamwork, the qualifications required by a team leader are accordingly demanding. A prospective team leader must therefore have organizational talents and distinct
communication skills, both within the team and beyond it. A candidate
for such a position must serve as a role model for team members and
must have the unmistakable personal and professional competence to
motivate, lead, and develop an interdisciplinary team. He or she must
be able to stimulate new early intervention ideas and methods as well.
Important developments to promote leadership and team quality
include the following:

- Compile a requirements profile for positions of leadership in
  early intervention.
- Select team leaders with the help of job-oriented assessment.
- Establish further training courses for those in positions of leadership
  and management in early intervention. Such courses must focus
  on communication and interaction skills both inside the center and
  outside. They also must emphasize concepts and strategies aimed
  at successful teamwork, knowledge of modern developmental theories, intervention methods, and competence in institutional networks.

Regular team meetings are needed for self-assessment and reflection. Use of an outside moderator is advantageous. An ideal choice would be someone who is an expert in the field of early intervention as well as in team development.

Networking should be established. Cooperation between various teams in early intervention boosts the work in individual teams and improves the transfer of knowledge. This is a good opportunity to see curricula and intervention in action in other teams, as well as to promote understanding of complexity and nuances used across early intervention teams. Internet communication groups can be established as a networking option. These could act as a forum for early interventionists to provide information on curricula, share intervention results, discuss experiences, and exchange ideas.

Another suggestion is producing videotapes of "good" teams. These can demonstrate different forms of successful teamwork and positive team development. The aim here is to provide team members with a basis for reflecting on their teamwork and finding ways to improve and develop it.

Future research of teamwork must be founded on more of an empirical basis. The subtly differentiated indicators of a high standard of interdisciplinary teamwork need to be highlighted. In addition, the complex interactions among the quality of teamwork, the competence of individual interventionists, and the effectiveness of intervention must be demonstrated. Furthermore, the effects of teamwork on the family must be examined—namely the impact of teamwork through a specific interventionist's work with a particular child's family. The information gained would allow conclusions to be drawn about the significance of a particular family-oriented concept.

Early intervention programs should publicly present their aims and working methods and the results of early intervention, specifically noting the significance of teamwork. This would increase awareness about early intervention achievements among the general public, politicians, and those responsible for funding such treatment. All of these groups influence political decisions in favor of establishing and extending this system of early help.

CONCLUSION

A team needs a vision. This is what differentiates good teams from others. They can develop effective solutions for many areas. Early intervention has been recognized as successful and must be developed particularly in the areas of interdisciplinary cooperation in research and practice. This will ensure that the quality of teamwork will promote the continued efficiency and success of early intervention. In this context, one paramount issue is interdisciplinary and empirical action research toward an extension and consolidation of the theoretical and conceptional foundations of early intervention for the further development of diagnosis and therapy. Also paramount is the improvement of cooperation with the families. Intensive use of the new information and communication technologies offers innovative potential for training, research, and daily practice. These items open new dimensions for documentation and evaluation of child development processes, as well as for institutions' self-evaluation and long-term studies in collaboration with early intervention centers (Peterander, 2000b).

In the future, it will be necessary to prove effectiveness of early intervention in individual cases to fulfill new funding requirements. This can be achieved by conducting analysis of early intervention processes. A prerequisite of such studies will be to highlight the reciprocal interaction between the situation of the family and child on the one hand, and the quality of the transdisciplinary team's work on the other hand. Finally, a comprehensive curriculum of early intervention must be developed. Bruder quoted a widely-recognized definition of an early intervention curriculum:

> A curriculum is an organized framework that delineates the content that children are to learn, the processes through which children achieve curricular goals, what teachers do to help children achieve these goals, and the context in which teaching and learning occur. (1997, p. 523)

In an extended curriculum, in view of the vital significance of good teamwork for the success of early intervention, the "team factor" must be given more prominence than has so far been the case.

REFERENCES

Arbeitsstelle Frühförderung Bayern. (1999). *Organisationshandbuch zur Qualitätsentwicklung an interdisziplinären Frühförderstellen in Bayern* [Handbook of organization for the development of quality in interdisciplinary early intervention centers in Bavaria]. Munich, Germany: Author.

Bailey, D.B. (1996). Preparing early intervention professionals for the 21st century. In M. Brambring, H. Rauh, & A. Beelmann (Eds.), *Early childhood intervention: Theory, evaluation, and practice* (pp. 488–503). Hawthorne, NY: Walter de Gruyter.

Björck-Åkesson, E., & Granlund, M. (1997). Changing perspectives in early intervention for children with disabilities in Sweden. *Infants and Young Children, 9,* 56–68.

Block, C.H. (2000). *Von der Gruppe zum Team* [From groups to teams]. Munich, Germany: Beck.

Bronfenbrenner, U. (1979). *The ecology of human development. Experiments by nature and design.* Cambridge, MA: Harvard University Press. (ERIC Document Reproduction Service No. ED128387).

Bruder, M.B. (1997). The effectiveness of specific educational/developmental curricula for children with established disabilities. In M.J. Guralnick (Ed.), *The effectiveness of early intervention* (pp. 523–548). Baltimore: Paul H. Brookes Publishing Co.

Bungard, W. (1999). Qualitäts-Zirkel und neue Organisationsstrategien [Quality circles and new strategies for organizations]. In L.v. Rosenstiel, E. Regnet, & M.E. Domsch (Eds.), *Führung von Mitarbeitern* [Leadership and staff] (pp. 681–694). Stuttgart, Germany: Schäffer-Poeschel.

Clarke, A., & Clarke, A. (2000). *Early experience and the life path.* London: Jessica Kingsley Publishers.

Donabedian, A. (1982). An exploration of structure, process and outcome as approaches to quality assessment. In H.K. Selbmann & K.K. Überla (Eds.), *Quality assessment of medical care* (pp. 69–92). Gerlingen, Germany: Brinkmann.

Eysenck, H.J., & Rachman, S. (1972). *Neurosen: Ursachen und Heilmethoden* [Neurosis: Causes and methods of therapy]. Berlin: VEB German Publishing Company of Science.

Farran, D.C. (2001). Critical periods and early intervention. In D.B. Bailey, J.T. Bruer, F.J. Symons, & J.W. Lichtman (Eds.), *Critical thinking about critical periods* (pp. 233–266). Baltimore: Paul H. Brookes Publishing Co.

Federal Ministry of Labour Affaires. (2000). *German Federal Social Security Act* (and revisions).

Garland, C.W., & Frank, A. (1997). Building effective early intervention teamwork. In P.J. Winton, J.A. McCollum, & C. Catlett (Eds.), *Reforming personnel preparation in early intervention: Issues, models, and practical strategies* (pp. 363–391). Baltimore: Paul H. Brookes Publishing Co.

Guralnick, M.J. (Ed.). (1997). *The effectiveness of early intervention.* Baltimore: Paul H. Brookes Publishing Co.

Guralnick, M.J. (2001). A developmental systems model for early intervention. *Infants and Young Children, 14,* 1–18.

Helios II. (1996). *Final report: Early intervention.* Brussels, Belgium: European Commission.

Klocke, A., & Hurrelmann, K. (1995). Armut und Gesundheit. Inwieweit sind Kinder und Jugendliche betroffen? [Poverty and health: To what extent are children and youth affected?] *Zeitschrift für Gesundheitswissenschaften [Journal of Health Science], 2,* 138–151.

Largo, R. (1993). *Babyjahre* [Infants]. Hamburg, Germany: Carlsen.

Nelson, C.A. (2000). The neurobiological basis of early intervention. In J.P. Shonkoff & S.J. Meisels (Eds.), *Handbook of early childhood intervention* (2nd ed., pp. 204–227). New York: Cambridge University Press.

Oerter, R. (1996). *Fördert Spiel Entwicklung?* [Does play further development?] In G. Opp & F. Peterander (Eds.), *Focus Heilpädagogik* [Focus heilpedagogics] (pp. 260–271). Munich/Basel, Germany: Ernst Reinhardt.

Peterander, F. (1996). Frühförderung im gesellschaftlichen Umbruch: Entwicklungspotentiale [Early intervention in social upheaval: Perspectives for developments]. In G. Opp & F. Peterander (Eds.), *Focus Heilpädagogik* [Focus heilpedagogics] (pp. 311–324). Munich/Basel, Germany: Ernst Reinhardt.

Peterander, F. (2000a). The best quality cooperation between parents and experts in early intervention. *Infants and Young Children, 12,* 32–45.

Peterander, F. (2000b). Vom Beobachten zum Wissen: Computerbasierte Analyseprogramme zur Unterstützung einer praxisnahen Frühförderung [From observation to knowledge: Computer-based analysis-programs supporting early intervention]. In C. Leyendecker & T. Horstmann (Eds.), *Große Pläne für kleine Leute: Grundlagen, Konzepte und Praxis der Frühförderung* [Great plans for little people: Basis, concepts and practice of early intervention] (pp. 337–341). Munich/Basel, Germany: Ernst Reinhardt.

Peterander, F. (2002). Qualität und Wirksamkeit der Frühförderung [Quality and effectiveness in early intervention]. *Frühförderung interdisziplinär [Journal of Interdisciplinary Early Intervention], 21,* 96–106.

Peterander, F. (2003). Multivariate Diagnostik in der Frühförderung [Multivariate diagnosis in early intervention]. *Kindheit und Entwicklung [Journal of Childhood and Development], 12,* 24–34.

Peterander, F., & Speck, O. (1993). *Strukturelle und inhaltliche Bedingungen der Frühförderung* [Structure and content of early intervention]. Munich, Germany: Ludwig-Maximilians University.

Pretis, M. (2001). *Frühförderung planen, durchführen, evaluieren* [Planning, conveying, evaluating early intervention]. Munich/Basel, Germany: Ernst Reinhardt.

Ramey, C.T., & Landesman Ramey, S. (1998). Early intervention and early experience. *American Psychologist, 53,* 109–120.

Reinmann-Rothmeier, G., & Mandl, H. (2000). *Individuelles Wissensmanagement* [Individual knowledge-management]. Bern, Switzerland: Hans Huber.

Rosenstiel, L.v., Regnet, E., & Domsch, M.E. (1999). *Führung von Mitarbeitern* [Leadership and staff]. Stuttgart, Germany: Schäffer-Poeschel.

Sameroff, A.J., & Fiese, B.H. (2000). Transactional regulation: The development ecology of early intervention. In J.P. Shonkoff & S.J. Meisels (Eds.), *Handbook of early childhood intervention* (2nd ed., pp. 135–159). New York: Cambridge University Press.

Schlack, H.G. (1989). Paradigmenwechsel in der Frühförderung [Paradigm-shift in early intervention]. *Frühförderung interdisziplinär [Journal of Interdisciplinary Early Intervention], 8,* 13–18.

Sexton, D., Snyder, P., Lobman, M.S., Kimbrough, P.M., & Matthews, K. (1997). A team-based model to improve early intervention programs: Linking preservice and inservice. In P.J. Winton, J.A. McCollum, & C. Catlett (Eds.), *Reforming personnel preparation in early intervention: Issues, models, and practical strategies* (pp. 495–526). Baltimore: Paul H. Brookes Publishing Co.

Shonkoff, J.P., & Meisels, S.J. (Eds.). (2000). *Handbook of early childhood intervention* (2nd ed.). New York: Cambridge University Press.

Simeonsson, R.J. (2000). Early childhood intervention: Toward a universal manifesto. *Infants and Young Children, 12,* 4–9.

Sohns, A. (2000). *Frühförderung entwicklungsauffälliger Kinder in Deutschland* [Early intervention of developmentally delayed children in Germany]. Weinheim, Germany: Beltz.

Soriano, V. (1998). *Early intervention in Europe: Trends in 17 European countries.* Middelfart, Denmark: European Agency for Development in Special Education.

Speck, O. (1973). Früherkennung und Frühförderung behinderter Kinder [Early identification and early intervention of children with disabilities]. In J. Muth (Ed.), *Deutscher Bildungsrat, Behindertenstatistik, Früherkennung, Frühförderung* [German Board of Education, statistics of disabilities, early screening, early intervention]. Stuttgart, Germany: Klett.

Speck, O. (1995). Wandel der Konzepte in der Frühförderung [Changes of concepts in early intervention]. *Frühförderung interdisziplinär [Journal of Interdisciplinary Early Intervention], 14,* 116–130.

Speck, O., & Warnke, A. (Eds.). (1983). *Frühförderung mit den Eltern* [Early intervention with parents]. Munich/Basel, Germany: Ernst Reinhardt.

Spodek, B., & Brown, P.C. (1993). Curriculum alternatives in early childhood education: A historical perspective. In B. Spodek (Ed.), *Curriculum alternatives in early childhood education: A historical perspective* (pp. 91–104). New York: Macmillan.

Thurmair, M., & Naggl, M. (2000). *Praxis der Frühförderung* [Practice of early intervention]. Munich/Basel, Germany: Ernst Reinhardt.

Weiss, H. (1999). Evaluation in der Frühförderung unter dem Aspekt der fachlichen Qualität [Evaluation of early intervention and the quality of treatment]. In F. Peterander & O. Speck (Eds.), *Qualitätsmanagement in sozialen Einrichtungen* [Quality-management in social institutions] (pp. 199–213). Munich/Basel, Germany: Ernst Reinhardt.

Werner, E.E., & Smith, R.S. (1992). *Overcoming the odds: High risk children from birth to adulthood.* Ithaca, NY: Cornell University Press.

Winton, P.J. (1991). *Working with families in early intervention: Interdisciplinary perspectives.* Chapel Hill: Frank Porter Graham Child Development Center, University of North Carolina at Chapel Hill.

CHAPTER 15

Early Intervention Themes and Variations from Around the World

Samuel L. Odom and Sudha Kaul

A knowledge of one other culture should sharpen our ability to scrutinize more steadily, to appreciate more lovingly, our own. (Mead, 1928)

As noted throughout this book, the spirit of early intervention speaks through the metaphors and proverbs of many cultures and many different languages:

- *Tian sheng wo cai bi you yong.* [Heaven gives me my talent necessarily for some use.] (People's Republic of China)
- *Cho-cho-ik-son.* [The earlier, the better.] (South Korea)
- *Each child should be taught in his own way.* . . . (Israel)
- *Zaf beljenet yetarekal.* [It is easy to straighten a tree during its nursery stage.] (Ethiopia)
- *Shubhasya Sheegram.* [Good work should begin as early as possible.] (India)
- *Learning when young is like carving in stone.* (Egypt)
- *Lekarna, ja hur de fyllde våra dagar! Vad skulle min barndom ha varit utan dem!* [Play, how it fills our days! What would childhood be without it!] (Sweden)
- *Weh no dead, nu dash wey.* [A child who looks dead, you don't give up; it may turn around.] (Jamaica)
- *A good beginning makes a good ending.* (United States of America)
- *The sky's the limit!* (Australia)
- *Zwischen zu früh und zu spät liegt en Augenblick.* [A moment lies between too early and too late.] (Germany)

These proverbs and metaphors convey a belief that providing early support to children and their families has positive ramifications that extend well into later development and well outside of the school and family contexts. This fundamental belief propels the intervention efforts of families, service providers, and governments to provide early and necessary care. These proverbs, as well as an additional one in Chapter 13 ("Too many cooks spoil the broth"), also convey the challenges of providing effective early intervention services.

In this book, authors from around the world describe the early intervention practices in their countries. In these descriptions, and in the broader literature, a number of commonalities or themes exist, with variations across cultures. The variations—that is, the activities that constitute early intervention—are staggering in their breadth and inspiring in their intentions. They span the range of human activity. In Ethiopia, for example, mothers from a village meet for a coffee ceremony in a family's home to drink coffee and discuss the village happenings. When the mothers meet in the home of a family that has a child with a disability, a home visitor from the community rehabilitation agency joins the group to share information about the care of the child with a disability, thereby raising awareness and acceptance in the community (Chapter 5). In Germany, a team of early intervention professionals use computerized expert systems technology and artificial intelligence to plan programs for infants and young children and their families. Through multidisciplinary collaboration, team members share this information with families in the home and community to enhance the care of infants and young children with disabilities (Chapter 14). The two countries differ in resources, training for professionals, and cultures. Yet, early intervention workers share the same ultimate goal of improving the care and development of children with disabilities and have shaped their practices to fit the cultural context.

This chapter examines common themes among the early intervention programs and countries described in this book. These themes include the following:

- Conceptual/theoretical basis of early intervention
- Cultural and ecological niches that shape early intervention activity
- Child participants
- Family-centered nature of early intervention
- Inclusion and natural environments
- Necessity and nature of training
- National support for early intervention
- International collaboration

CONCEPTUAL/THEORETICAL BASIS OF EARLY INTERVENTION

Human actions are based on beliefs about the way the world works. At a professional level, these beliefs are formalized as theories of child development or theories of practice (Odom & Wolery, in press). In Chapter 1, Blackman provides a comprehensive description of the theoretical basis for early intervention, which was based primarily on Western psychological and sociological research. Descriptions of programs from nearly all countries represented in this book acknowledge the theories and research of Piaget, Vygotsky, Sameroff, Skinner, Bronfenbrenner, and others as foundations for their practices. For example, in Chapter 5, Klein describes a program in Israel, based on the theories of Feuerstein and Vygotsky, which teaches parents to mediate learning experiences for their infants and young children. She replicated and documented the effects of this intervention approach in Israel, Europe,

Africa, and the United States (Klein, 1996). In Chapter 2, Hsia, McCabe, and Li describe the use of applied behavior analysis approaches for children with autism in the People's Republic of China (PRC). Teferra (Chapter 5) and Björck-Åkesson and Granlund (Chapter 9) acknowledge the importance of the transactional conceptualization of development (Sameroff & Fiese, 2000) for early intervention in Ethiopia and Sweden respectively. In addition to developmental and behavioral theory, however, all countries draw on the basic medical and public health research described by Blackman in Chapter 1, conducted by researchers from around the world, and fostered by the World Health Organization (WHO).

Although early intervention practices are based on scientific knowledge and beliefs, they sometimes compete with traditional knowledge and beliefs from the culture of the community or country. Traditional knowledge or beliefs may attribute the cause of a child's disability to parental actions or circumstances, possession of the child by an evil spirit, or other supernatural factors. Klein notes in Chapter 4 that practitioners should not compliment Ethiopian children because of their parents fear that it will elicit "the evil eye." Similarly, parents in some countries may seek treatment for disabilities through traditional medicine prescribed by a healer or shaman. Some traditional treatments or practices have positive effects for infants, such as the *wegehas* practice (physiotherapy) in Ethiopia and the infant handling routine that comes after bathing in Jamaica. Unfortunately, traditional beliefs, knowledge, and/or practices that are not effective delay or prevent access to early intervention when it is available.

The divergent views of scientific and traditional knowledge and practices may conflict. Fadiman (1997) eloquently described the clash of beliefs, values, and understanding between a Hmong family whose daughter had severe disabilities and the scientific medical community. This ongoing conflict eventually resulted in tragic consequences for the child. It is important to note that such traditional knowledge and beliefs are not unique to developing countries; many exist in the United States and in industrialized Western European countries. For example, according to fundamentalist Christian beliefs in some American communities, a child's disability is a family burden from God, which may lead families to attempt to provide for all of their children's needs and not seek early intervention. Also, one must recognize that scientific knowledge may not always provide the ultimate or even correct answers. For instance, Western science once held that autism was caused by a cold emotional climate created by the mother. As a result, in the 1960s, a "scientifically based" treatment for young children with autism was to remove them from their families.

CULTURAL AND ECOLOGICAL
NICHES THAT SHAPE EARLY INTERVENTION

Bronfenbrenner's ecological systems theory reminds us that all human activity, and most intermediary influences on human activity, are seated within a cultural context, termed the *macrosystem* (1979; Bronfenbrenner & Morris, 1998). Across countries, cultural views of childhood are quite different. Kaul, Mukherjee, Ghosh, Chattopadhyay, and Sil (Chapter 6) report that young children are considered small adults in India; childhood is a time of inculcating proper habits, and playfulness is not seen as a means of learning. Björck-Åkesson and Granlund (Chapter 9) report that in Sweden, childhood is valued for its own sake and not seen as a time of preparation. In China, the relationship between a young child and parent is one of the six relationships upon which all social interactions are based, and *xiao* is the value that children owe unquestioning respect and obedience to their parents (Chapter 2). In countries with much diversity, such as the United States and Israel, a range of cultural values underlies relationships that exist between children and parents. The challenge is to design programs that are culturally sensitive in a pluralistic society.

This book's chapters provide rich and important examples of how early intervention activities with the same overall goals are shaped to fit the ecological niches in which families and children live:

- In India, community visitors use indigenous objects and materials in the home and within family routines (sometimes under the circumstances of poverty) to promote the motor development and participation of young children with cerebral palsy (Chapter 6).

- Community rehabilitation workers in Ethiopia raise awareness and acceptance of individual children's disabilities by talking to mothers during a community coffee ceremony (Chapter 5).

- In the PRC, two teachers jointly conduct home visits. This allows one teacher to play with the child with disabilities and his or her siblings while the other works with the parents. Because teachers are highly respected in this culture, they make direct recommendations to parents based on observations of the child and the home (Chapter 2).

- In Jamaica, a special handling routine, which may have originated in West Africa, is used after an infant's bath. It consists of the mother or grandmother using "stretching, tossing, molding, range-of-motion exercises, and propping [the baby] in the sitting position" (p. 200). This practice may be of therapeutic value for infants with disabilities (Chapter 10).

- In Germany, members of different interdisciplinary early intervention teams meet in "quality circles" to solve a common problem or address a common issue that exists for infants, young children, and their families (Chapter 15).

Although not described in this book, the developers of New Zealand's national early childhood curriculum, *Te Whariki* (New Zealand Ministry of Education, 1996), had a clear intent of representing both the Maori culture and mainstream New Zealand cultures. This bilingual curriculum specifically addresses the goals of children with special needs and children enrolled in the Maori cultural emersion program (New Zealand Ministry of Education, 1998).

In most countries, disability results in a low or reduced social status for the child and perhaps the family. Across cultures, the birth of an infant with a disability is greatly distressing for parents and family members. The degree of shame may be intensified in countries and communities that traditionally have not accepted individuals with disabilities. For some parents, the shame of having a child with a disability has led them to seclude or hide their child and/or not to seek services. An extreme example of such seclusion is that parents in some countries do not register their child's birth with local authorities. Without certification of birth and proper registration, young children do not have official identifies in their countries. Internationally, a public health effort has been directed toward making sure that infants with disabilities—and, more generally, female infants—are registered at birth (G. Habibi, personal communication, April 5, 2002). A common goal across many of the programs described in this book has been to promote community awareness of, positive attitudes toward, and acceptance of infants and young children with disabilities and their families.

CHILD PARTICIPANTS

In her review of international inclusive early childhood care and development programs, Evans (1998) described three levels of developmental risk, which are similar to Blackman's (Chapter 1) description of levels of prevention. Evans identified the most severe level as *established risk*; children in this level are often identified as "differently abled" and begin life with a clearly identifiable condition, such as cerebral palsy, a sensory impairment, and/or mental retardation requiring high levels of support. Teferra (Chapter 5) calls these children "the poorest of the poor." Evans acknowledged few special education services are available in many developing countries, a fact supported by a number of chapters in this book. Even in the United States, which is relatively rich in resources, not all children who are eligible for early intervention services receive or participate in them (Chapter 12). A subsequent section discusses the trend for countries to pass laws that support the provision of early intervention services for all eligible children.

Children at *biological risk* represent a second group in Evans's (1998) classification of development risk. These children have medical problems that may be remediated with proper care. Authors of chapters in this book describe infants who were born prematurely, had low birth weights, and required specialized care. For many of these infants, the prospect of typical development, given proper health care and early intervention services, is bright.

A third group of children may live in circumstances that create what Evans (1998) called *environmental risk,* with poverty being the greatest environmental risk in most countries. Also, children may belong to ethnic minority groups that do not receive services that others in the country receive, or they may live in countries with war or political turmoil. For example, in his book *The Twelve Who Survive*, Myers (1995) described the devastating poverty in São Paulo, Brazil, which led to child abandonment and infant mortality. He chronicled programs in developing countries that have addressed the problems of environmental risk posed by poverty.

FAMILY-CENTERED NATURE OF EARLY INTERVENTION

One central, unifying theme in this book is the preeminence of the family as the center of care for infants and young children with disabilities. During the 1990s, early intervention evolved into a family-centered approach. For example, Boavida and Carvalho (Chapter 11) describe how early intervention in the Coimbra region of Portugal began as a clinic-based medical model and over the years moved to a community-based, family-centered approach. In Egypt, the Seti Center, Caritas–Egypt (Chapter 8) works in partnership with families, educating parents on carrying out intervention activities in the home, providing information about the child's disability, and supporting the parents in overcoming shame and embarrassment of their child's disability. In Israel, Klein's (Chapter 4) Mediational Intervention for Sensitizing Caregivers (MISC) program assists parents in understanding and enjoying their infants as a foundation for providing a responsive style of interaction that may support development. In Korea, parents of children with disabilities are shown ways to work with their child

(Chapter 3), and in the Xiang Yang Child Development Center in the PRC, home visitors work with parents to include the child in daily family activities as well as to respond to family-identified needs (Chapter 2). In Jamaica, parent education is the center of the early intervention program; family members are also trained to be community rehabilitation workers and to work with other parents (Chapter 10). The family-centered approach is at the heart of the code of ethics adopted in 2000 by Early Childhood Intervention Australia (Chapter 13). Home visitors from the Indian Institute of Cerebral Palsy work with mothers and caregivers to plan learning activities that can occur in regular daily routines and help the child to be an active family participant (Chapter 6). These and other examples throughout the book illustrate the emphasis on and centrality of families in early intervention. Klein represents this value well by stating that professionals can assume "that there are certain universal conceptions, feelings, and attitudes in the caregiver–child relationship that are crucial for optimal child development in any culture" (p. 84).

INCLUSION AND NATURAL ENVIRONMENTS

In many countries, early intervention services have gone through a transition from a clinical model, often focusing primarily on health care, to a community-based model in which infants and young children with disabilities are included in natural environments such as the home and family and the community. Evans (1998) pointed out that this shift is in part a recognition of children's rights. In 1989, the United Nations convened the Convention on the Rights of the Child, which proposed rights of all children. Article 23 of this convention declared that it is the right of a child with a disability to "enjoy a full and decent life, in conditions which ensure dignity, promote self-reliance and facilitate the child's active participation in the community." Further, the convention stated that educational, health, and medical service should be designed "in a manner conducive to the child's achieving the fullest possible social integration and individual development, including his or her cultural and spiritual development."

International support for inclusion was extended in the World Conference on Special Needs Education: Access and Quality (United Nations Education, Scientific and Cultural Organization [UNESCO], 1994). Article 53 from that conference specified that

> The success of inclusive schools depends considerably on early identification, assessment and stimulation of the very young child with special educational needs. . . . Programmes at this level should

recognize the principle of inclusion and be developed in a comprehensive way by combining pre-school activities with early childhood health care.

The movement toward inclusion is clear in the descriptions of many early intervention systems in this book. Lee (Chapter 3) describes changes in South Korea's legislation that provide financial support for placing preschool children with disabilities in children's houses and providing special education personnel. Hanson, in Chapter 12, and Bruder (1997) have noted the movement in the United States to provide early intervention services in natural environments for infants and toddlers with disabilities and in the least restrictive environment for preschool children. Lumpkin and Aranha (Chapter 7) describe a pilot program in Brazil in which young children with disabilities are included in child care centers or crèches. In this program, 5% of the child care slots are designated for children with disabilities, which is similar to the policy in the U.S. Head Start Program, in which 10% of the enrollment consists of children with disabilities. A further illustration of the international effort toward inclusion in natural environments was presented by UNESCO in *First Steps: Stories on Inclusion in Early Childhood Education* (Dust, 1997). This book chronicles inclusive programs in Australia, Chile, Denmark, France, Greece, Guyana, India, Laos, Lebanon, Mauritius, Portugal, and South Africa.

In nearly all countries, barriers to inclusion clearly exist, and they seem to be consistent across countries. Examples are

- Quality of child care or available early childhood education services (Bailey, McWilliam, Buysse, & Wesley, 1998; Chapter 3)
- Access to trained teachers (Chapters 3 and 7)
- The belief that inclusion must be postponed until child is "ready" (Evans, 1998; Odom, Schwartz, & ECRII Investigators, 2001)
- A negative perception of children with disabilities in the community, which may lead to seclusion within the home (Chapters 2 and 5)
- The belief that only specialized staff can provide effective services to children (Evans, 1998)

All of these issues represent significant obstacles to inclusion, yet inclusion efforts continue to emerge around the world.

NECESSITY AND NATURE OF TRAINING

Models for providing early intervention services in different countries are influenced and even dictated by the resources available. In more industrialized, relatively well-resourced countries, professionals from multiple agencies may provide health and developmental services to children and families. In countries with fewer economic resources, individuals from the community who are trained as paraprofessionals provide services. Both face challenges, and the chapter authors describe models for training and team collaboration in both contexts.

In less affluent countries, the challenge has been to locate and provide trained personnel. In Jamaica, Thorburn (Chapter 10) and colleagues developed an innovative approach in which they train paraprofessionals from the communities served to provide screening and home support for families and children. This program, now into its third decade, has provided valuable service in a context where resources are few. In Ethiopia (Chapter 5), community-based rehabilitation centers (CBRs) train paraprofessionals working with families and community members in the countryside to create a positive attitude toward children with disabilities as well as to promote basic skills (e.g., feeding) for individual children. In Brazil (Chapter 7), there is a multiagency effort to provide public awareness and capacity building related to children's rights and inclusion of children with disabilities. Two features of Brazil's project are 1) a "Kids on the Block" model (i.e., puppets representing children with disabilities) in a national media campaign to foster positive attitudes in the community and 2) training guides related to inclusion for teachers enrolled in the national distance education teacher training program.

In countries with greater resources, early intervention services may be available but professional development may not adequately prepare individuals to work with children with disabilities, or the formation of interdisciplinary teams and collaboration may be an issue. Björck-Åkesson and Granlund (Chapter 9) describe an interdisciplinary training program in Sweden, delivered partially through distance education and in-service training, which focuses on team building and the provision of service within a holistic family context. Johnston (Chapter 13) notes that an issue in Australia is "too many cooks spoiling the broth," a condition that almost anyone involved in interdisciplinary work has experienced. To avoid this dilemma, Peterander (Chapter 14) and colleagues describe a model of professional development in Germany for supporting collaboration and team building for early intervention teams. Their ongoing efforts to support early intervention team development include initial preparation of new professionals, internal training within the team, quality circles, case-oriented consultation among team members, mobile day seminars, computerized expert knowledge, and self-evaluation. Boavida and Carvalho (Chapter 11) report on Portugal's 10-year evolution of early intervention from a clinical-based, medically oriented model to an interdisciplinary, team-based model. As in Germany, this model also involves intensive team-based training.

NATIONAL SUPPORT FOR EARLY INTERVENTION

Bonfenbrenner's ecological systems model also stated that environments in which children participate (e.g., early intervention programs) are influenced by factors in addition to culture outside the child/family context. He suggested *exosystem* as a term for these collective influences; for instance, the sociopolitical factors that underlie early intervention efforts are an exosystem influence. Many chapter authors identify changes in national or state/provincial laws that have begun providing support for services to infants and young children with disabilities and their families. For example, South Korea's Promotion Law for Special Education provides support (Chapter 3); Egypt's National Strategy to Combat Handicaps has begun to raise awareness and garner support (Chapter 8); and Sweden's legislation has established the national social insurance system and the Child Health Services, with Child Rehabilitation Centers being part of the foundation for early intervention (Chapter 9). In the United States, federal law mandates that children ages 3–5 years with disabilities have access to early intervention services, and it provides financial support to the states for services for infants, toddlers, and their families (Chapter 12). The importance of such legislation and social policy at the national level cannot be understated.

In other countries, such as Germany (Chapter 14), states or provinces are responsible for services. Johnston (Chapter 13) notes how the absence of national legislation has been problematic in Australia and describes how grass roots movements involving families and a national professional organization (Early Childhood Intervention Australia) fill the void of support at the national level. In other counties, nongovernmental organizations (NGOs) initiate and provide early intervention services. These organizations often are funded from national and international sources and are discussed in the next section of this chapter.

INTERNATIONAL COLLABORATION

The theme of international collaboration and support surfaces in many of this book's chapters. International support is sometimes provided through NGOs. For example, Khouzam, Chenouda, and Naguib (Chapter 8) note that their early intervention program in Egypt is part of an NGO associated with Caritas Internationalis. In Jamaica, the community-based program that Thorburn (Chapter 10) describes is supported through an NGO. Lumpkin and Aranha (Chapter 7) describe early intervention services in Brazil as often being a "package" of services involving NGOs, municipal and national governmental agencies, and the Catholic church.

CBR programs constitute a particular form of support sponsored by NGOs in several countries (e.g., Ethiopia, Portugal). These programs tend to base their services within the contexts in which children live and have different goals, such as raising awareness (Ethiopia; Chapter 5), training community workers (Jamaica; Chapter 10), and training families to carry out intervention in the home (Egypt; Chapter 8). In a case study of the Hopeful Steps program in the Rupununi region of Guyana, O'Toole and Stout (1998) provided an excellent example of the work of a CBR program. In this impoverished region, the goal of the CBR program was to establish a firm base of family and community support for individuals with disabilities in a wider context of poverty, malnutrition, superstition, and armed conflict. This CBR established a system of health education and literacy training through a process of cultural affirmation that involved the use of local materials and cultural practices. This CBR program and others described in this book embody the movement away from traditional clinic-based rehabilitation approaches and toward the development of programs built on features and values of the local community. As O'Toole and Stout (1998) noted, the goal of their project was to reinforce, nurture, and empower local individuals to take responsibility for services and the quality of life of children with disabilities in their community.

In this book, NGOs and CBRs are mentioned most often by authors from countries in which resources are limited. However, before special education laws were established in the United States, NGOs like the National Association for Retarded Citizens (now The Arc of the United States), the United Cerebral Palsy association, and the March of Dimes provided services for young children with disabilities and their families. These and other NGOs in the United States continue to provide valuable services to families and young children with disabilities.

Chapters in this book also illustrate how international collaboration and support is also provided through the sharing and adoption of practices and model programs from other countries. The efforts to promote inclusion in South Korea (Chapter 3) appear to parallel similar efforts occurring in the Unites States. Boavida and Carvalho (Chapter 11) and Thorburn (Chapter 10) mention the adoption of the Portage model, a form of early intervention originating in the United States, early in their program development efforts. Klein (Chapter 4) describes the replication of the MISC model developed in Ethiopia, Europe, and the United States. Hsia, McCabe, and Li (Chapter 2) note the influence of a model early intervention program from Taiwan on the development of the program in the Xiang Yang Child Development Center. It is important to note that these authors raise concerns about the direct replication of models of early intervention originating in a different country and/or culture. In most cases, the early intervention models described had evolved into service practices that fit the cultural, demographic, and socioeconomic contexts of the country.

CONCLUSION

Early intervention for infants and young children with disabilities is an emerging and growing worldwide effort. In developing countries with limited economic resources, early intervention originated and still exists within a medical model, with health concerns taking precedence. In other countries with greater economic resources, where medical concerns presumably have been addressed, early intervention approaches have at times followed a more educational, developmental, and/or social services model. Across countries, there is general acknowledgement that interdisciplinary approaches are essential. In addition, there is almost unanimous agreement that early intervention must involve the family as the center, and perhaps the mediator, of services for infants and young children. The early intervention efforts also are shaped to fit the cultural, demographic, and political context of the countries and local communities. In this way, early intervention is creating its niche in world society. By learning about these niches and the ways they differ across countries and culture, we hope readers obtain ideas that may be applicable in their own country and, as Mead suggested, may have a greater appreciation for their own practice.

REFERENCES

Bailey, D.B., McWilliam, R.A., Buysse, V., & Wesley, P.W. (1998). Inclusion in the context of competing values in early childhood education. *Early Childhood Research Quarterly, 13*, 27–48.

Bronfenbrenner, U. (1979). *The ecology of human development: Experiments by nature and design.* Cambridge, MA: Harvard University Press.

Bronfenbrenner, U., & Morris, P.A. (1998). The ecology of developmental process. In R. Lerner (Ed.), *Handbook of child psychology: Vol. 1. Theoretical models of human development* (5th ed., pp. 993–1028). New York: John Wiley & Sons.

Bruder, M.B. (1997). Inclusion for pre-school age children: A collaborative services model. In K. Dust (Ed.), *First steps: Stories on inclusion in early childhood education* (pp. 111–122). Paris, France: UNESCO.

Dust, K. (Ed.). (1997). *First steps: Stories on inclusion in early childhood education.* Paris, France: UNESCO.

Evans, J.L. (1998). Inclusive EECD: A fair start for all children. *Coordinators' Notebooks: An International Resource for Early Childhood Development, 22,* 1–23.

Fadiman, A. (1997). *The spirit catches you and you fall down.* New York: Farrar, Straus & Giroux.

Klein, P.S. (1996). *Early intervention: Cross-cultural experiences with a mediational approach.* New York: Garland Publishing.

Mead, M. (1928). *Coming of age in Samoa.* New York: William Morrow.

Myers, R. (1995). *The twelve who survive: Strengthening programmes of early childhood development in the Third World.* Ypsilanti, MI: High/Scope Press.

New Zealand Ministry of Education. (1996). *Te whariki* [Early childhood curriculum]. Wellington, New Zealand: Author.

New Zealand Ministry of Education. (1998). *Quality in action, Te mahi whai hua: Implementing the revised statement of desirable objectives and practices in New Zealand early childhood services.* Wellington, New Zealand: Author.

Odom, S.L., Schwartz, I.S., & ECRII Investigators. (2001). So what do we know from all this? Synthesis points of research on preschool inclusion. In S. Odom (Ed.), *Widening the circle: Including children with disabilities in preschool programs.* New York: Teachers College Press.

Odom, S.L., & Wolery, M. (in press). A unified theory of practice in Early Intervention/Early Childhood Special Education: Evidence-based practice. *Journal of Special Education.*

O'Toole, B., & Stout, S. (1998). Hopeful steps in the Rupununi: One response to meeting the challenges of special needs in the interior of Guyana. *Coordinators' Notebooks: An International Resource for Early Childhood Development, 22,* 28–35.

Sameroff, A.F., & Fiese, B.H. (2000). Transactional regulation: The developmental ecology of early intervention. In J. Shonkoff & S. Meisels (Eds.), *Handbook of early intervention* (2nd ed., pp. 135–159). New York: Cambridge University Press.

UNESCO. (1994, June.) *World Conference on Special Needs Education: Access and Quality.* Salamanca, Spain.

United Nations. (1989). *Convention on the Rights of the Child.* Retrieved November 12, 2002, from http://www.unicef.org/crc/fulltext.htm

Index

Page numbers followed by *f* indicate figures; those followed by *t* indicate tables.